Recommended by Teachers
Trusted by Toppers

AF814326

All in One®

Artificial Intelligence

Code-417

CBSE Class 10

Focused Theory | Practice Exercise | Sample Papers & Board Papers

Author
Lalita Kaler *(MCA)*

arihant
SUCCESS AND NOTHING LESS

arihant
SUCCESS AND NOTHING LESS

ARIHANT PRAKASHAN
(School Division Series)

卐 ADMINISTRATIVE & PRODUCTION OFFICES

Regd. Office

'Ramchhaya' 4577/15, Agarwal Road, Darya Ganj, New Delhi -110002
Tele: 011- 47630600, 43518550; Fax: 011- 23280316

卐 *Head Office*

Kalindi, TP Nagar, Meerut (UP) - 250002, Tel: 0121-7156203, 7156204

卐 SALES & SUPPORT OFFICES

Agra, Ahmedabad, Bengaluru, Bareilly, Chennai, Delhi, Guwahati, Hyderabad, Jaipur, Jhansi, Kolkata, Lucknow, Nagpur & Pune.

PO No : TXT-XX-XXXXXXX-X-XX

Published By Arihant Publications (India) Ltd.

For further information about the books published by Arihant, log on to www.arihantbooks.com or e-mail at info@arihantbooks.com

Follow us on

卐 PRICE ₹250.00

PRODUCTION TEAM

Publishing Managers
Mahendra Singh Rawat & Keshav Mohan

Cover Designer
Rakesh Rawat

Inner Designer
Ankit Tyagi

Project Head
Shruti Aggarwal

Page Layouting
Ravinder Kumar

Index *cum* Study Planner

PART A: Employability Skills

PART B: Subject Specific Skills		Studied	Revised	Exam ready

One Book- Endless Features
to Help you Succeed

Chapter Intro

A quick information about the coverage of the chapter to explain students about what they are going to study.

CHAPTER **01**

Revisiting AI Project Cycle & Ethical Frameworks for AI

This chapter will guide you through the fundamental stages of the AI project cycle, including problem identification, data acquisition, model development, evaluation, and deployment. Additionally, it will explore prominent ethical frameworks that help mitigate risks associated with AI systems.

1.1 AI Project Cycle

It is a step-by-step process that a person should follow to develop an AI Project to solve a problem. AI Project Cycle provides us with an appropriate framework which can lead us to achieve our goal.

The AI project cycle is a structured roadmap for developing and deploying artificial intelligence projects to solve real-world problems.

This systematic approach helps define objectives, collect relevant data, uncover hidden insights, create models for AI systems, and assess their performance.

Different Stages of AI Cycle

The AI project cycle mainly has 5 stages

(i) **Problem Scoping** understanding the problem
(ii) **Data Acquisition** collecting accurate and reliable data
(iii) **Data Exploration** arranging the data uniformly
(iv) **Modelling** creating models from the data
(v) **Evaluation** evaluating the project

Illustrative Figures

To make the concepts completely visible, illustrative diagrams have been given at various place.

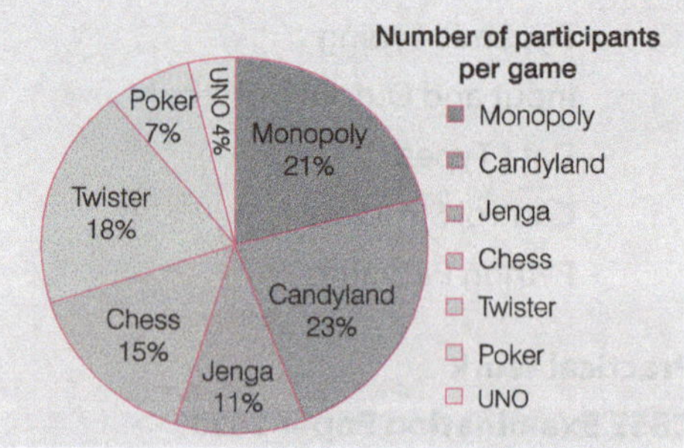

Simplified Theory

Each chapter has Complete, Easy to Understand and Simplified theory covering latest syllabus and rationalized NCERT Textbook. Theory is developed in such a way that it perfectly rectifies the complexity of NCERT Text making it suitable for all types of learners.

Try These 1.1

1. Name the five stages of AI project cycle.
2. Explain a project life cycle with the help of an example.
3. The sustainable development goals aim is to achieve by the end of year
   (a) 2025 (b) 2030
   (c) 2035 (d) 2040
4. What should be the characteristics of a good problem statement template?

Try These

A set of 3-5 Questions given in between the text, helps students to remain connected with the text while studying. They can instantly assess themselves for their understanding.

One Book- Endless Features

to Help you Succeed

33. Which form of learning-based approach does the following diagram indicate? **2025**

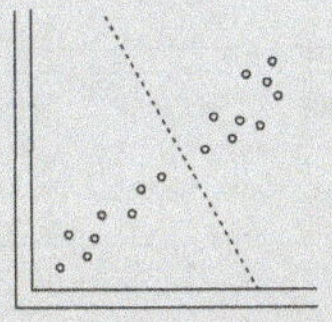

(a) Clustering (b) Classification
(c) Regression (d) Dimensionally Reduction

Board Exams' Questions

Solving Board Exams' Questions while studying the chapters, always prove to be confidence booster. For this purpose, each chapter has selected Questions from last 6 years Board Exams upto 2025.

NCERT Folder

Complete explanations of all the questions of NCERT Exercises.

NCERT FOLDER

Complete Explanations of all NCERT's Questions

A. Multiple Choice Questions

1. **What is the purpose of defining the problem statement during the Problem Scoping stage in an AI project cycle?**
(a) To collect data
(b) To understand the aim and objective of the project
(c) To train the model
(d) To process data
2. **In what ways can AI models be categorized based on the type of data fed into them?**
(a) Two domains
(b) Four domains
(c) Three domains
(d) Five domains
3. **In Statistical Data, what is the primary function of the system in relation to data?**
(a) Generating large datasets
(b) Analyzing data to extract insights
(c) Converting data into images
(d) Distributing data across networks
4. **What is the main goal of Computer Vision projects?**
(a) Translating audio data into visual descriptions
(b) Converting digital data into analogue signals
(c) Teaching machines to understand textual information
(d) Converting digital visual data into computer-readable language
8. **What is the central focus of virtue-based value-based frameworks?**
(a) Maximizing utility
(b) Protecting human rights
(c) Aligning actions with ethical principles and beliefs
(d) Ensuring compliance with legal regulations
9. **Which of the following best describes rights-based value-based frameworks?**
(a) Prioritizing human rights and dignity, valuing human life over other considerations
(b) Evaluating actions based on maximizing overall good and minimizing harm
(c) Centering on the character of the decision-maker and the alignment of actions with personal or societal virtues
(d) Focusing on achieving outcomes that offer the greatest benefit
10. **What is the primary domain of application for Bioethics?**
(a) Agriculture
(b) Healthcare and life sciences
(c) Information technology
(d) Environmental conservation
11. **Assertion (A)** Ethics provide guidance in distinguishing right from wrong.
Reason (R) Ethics consist of a set of values and morals that aid individuals in making moral judgments

EXAM PATTERN EXERCISE

Including Competency Based Questions

Part I

Multiple Choice Questions

1. **Choose the five stages of AI project cycle in correct order** **2024**
(a) Evaluation → Problem Scoping → Data Exploration → Data Acquisition → Modelling
(b) Problem Scoping → Data Exploration → Data Acquisition → Evaluation → Modelling
(c) Data Acquisition → Problem Scoping → Data Exploration → Modelling → Evaluation
(d) Problem Scoping → Data Acquisition → Data Exploration → Modelling → Evaluation
2. **________ helps us to summarise all the key points into one single outline so that in future, whenever there is need to look back at the basis of the problem, we can take a look at it and understand the key elements of it.**
(a) 4Ws Problem canvas (b) Problem Statement Template
(c) Data Acquisition (d) Algorithm
3. **The ________ canvas helps you in identifying the key elements related to the problem.**
(a) Problem scoping (b) 4Ws Problem
(c) Project cycle (d) Algorithm
4. **Name any two methods of collecting data.**
(a) Surveys and Interviews
(b) Rumors and Myths
(c) AI models and applications
(d) Imagination and thoughts
5. **Give two examples of Supervised Learning models.**
(a) Classification and Regression
(b) Clustering and Dimensionality Reduction
(c) Rule Based and Learning Based
(d) Classification and Clustering

Exam Pattern Exercise

Chapter exercise having all types of questions; MCQs, Statement Based, Assertion-Reason, VSA, SA & LA.

Sample Question Papers

To make students practice of examination in real sense, there are 3 Sample Question Papers at the end. All these Sample Questions Papers are exactly prepared on the latest syllabus & pattern of examination.

Sample Question Paper 1

Artificial Intelligence

Time : 2 hrs M.M. : 50

1. Please read the instructions carefully.
2. This Question Paper consists of **21 questions** in two sections: Section A & Section B.
3. Section A has Objective type questions whereas Section B contains Subjective type questions.
4. **Out of the given (5 + 16 =) 21 questions, a candidate has to answer (5 + 10 =) 15 questions in the allotted (maximum) time of 2 hours.**
5. All questions of a particular section must be attempted in the correct order.
6. **SECTION A - OBJECTIVE TYPE QUESTIONS (24 MARKS):**
i. This section has 05 questions.
ii. Marks allotted are mentioned against each question/part.
iii. There is no negative marking.
iv. Do as per the instructions given.
7. **SECTION B – SUBJECTIVE TYPE QUESTIONS (26 MARKS):**
i. This section has 16 questions.
ii. A candidate has to do 10 questions.
iii. Do as per the instructions given.
iv. Marks allotted are mentioned against each question/part.

Section A : Objective Type Questions

1. **Answer any 4 out of the given 6 questions on Employability Skills** ($1 \times 4 = 4$ Marks)
(i) **Physical exercise is used as a stress management technique because**
(a) it improves blood circulation
(b) improves self-image
(c) makes us feel better
(d) All of the above
(iv) **It provides scheduling to each process to be run on.**
(a) Time sharing OS (b) Distributed OS
(c) Real-time OS (d) Single-user OS
(v) **Visual communication among the people are dependent on ....**
(a) Signs, symbols and pictures
(b) Text messages

Latest Course *Structure*

	UNITS	No. of Hours for Theory and Practical		Max. Marks for Theory and Practical
Part A	**Employability Skills**			
	Unit 1: Communication Skills - II	10		2
	Unit 2: Self-Management Skills - II	10		2
	Unit 3: ICT Skills-II	10		2
	Unit 4: Entrepreneurial Skills-II	10		2
	Unit 5: Green Skills-II	10		2
	Total	**50**		**10**
Part B	**Subject Specific Skills**	**Theory**	**Practical**	**Marks**
	Unit 1: Revisiting AI Project Cycle & Ethical Frameworks for AI	11	4	7
	Unit 2: Advanced Concepts of Modeling in AI	18	7	11
	Unit 3: Evaluating Models	21	4	10
	Unit 4: Statistical Data	-	28	-
	Unit 5: Computer Vision	10	20	4
	Unit 6: Natural Language Processing	20	7	8
	Unit 7: Advance Python		10	-
	Total	**160**		**40**
Part C	**Practical & Project Work :**			**Marks**
	Practical File with minimum 15 Programs			15
	Practical Examination • Unit 4: Statistical Data • Unit 5: Computer Vision • Unit 6: Natural Language Processing • Unit 7: Advance Python			15
	Viva Voce			5
	Project Work / Field Visit / Student Portfolio (Any one to be done)			10
	Viva Voce (related to project work)			5
	Total			**15**
	GRAND TOTAL	**210**		**100**

UNIT 1 : Revisiting AI Project Cycle & Ethical Frameworks for AI

SUB-UNIT	LEARNING OUTCOMES	ACTIVITY/ PRACTICAL
AI Project Cycle	Understand the stages of the AI Project Cycle.	**Session:** Revisiting AI Project Cycle
Introduction to AI Domains	Understand the concept of Artificial Intelligence (AI) domains and the illustrations of practical applications within each AI domain.	**Session:** The three domains of AI and their applications.
Ethical Frameworks of AI	Learn about the ethical framework for AI and its category. Explore Bioethics, a popular framework that is used in the healthcare industry.	**Session:** Frameworks, Ethical Framework and need of Ethical Frameworks for AI. Activity: My Goodness https://www.my-goodness.net/ **Session:** Types of Ethical Frameworks.
		Session: Bioethics and a case study in bioethics.

UNIT 2 : Advance Concepts of Modeling in AI

SUB-UNIT	LEARNING OUTCOMES	SESSION/ ACTIVITY/ PRACTICAL
Revisiting AI, ML, DL	Understand AI, ML and DL	**Session:** Differentiate between AI, ML, and DL
		Session: Common terminologies used with data
Modeling	• Familiarise with supervised, unsupervised and reinforcement learning based approach • Understand subcategories of Supervised, Unsupervised and deep learning models	**Session:** Types of AI Models: Rule Based Approach, Learning Based Approach **Session:** Categories of Machine learning based models: Supervised Learning (https://teachablemachine.withgoogle.com/), Unsupervised Learning (https://experiments.withgoogle.com/ai/drum- machine/view/), Reinforcement Learning **Session:** Subcategories of Supervised Learning Model: Classification Model, Regression Model **Session:** Subcategories of Unsupervised Learning Model: Clustering, Association **Session:** Subcategories of Deep Learning: Artificial Neural Network (ANN), Convolutional Neural Network (CNN)
Artificial Neural Networks	• Understand Neural Networks • Understand how AI makes a decision	**Session:** What is Neural Network? **Session:** How does AI make a Decision? **Activity:** Human Neural Network – The Game **Suggested Neural Network Activity:** https://playground.tensorflow.org/

UNIT 3 : Evaluating Models

SUB-UNIT	LEARNING OUTCOMES	SESSION/ ACTIVITY/ PRACTICAL
Importance of Model Evaluation	Understand the role of evaluation in the development and implementation of AI systems.	**Session:** What is evaluation? **Session:** Need of model evaluation
Splitting the training set data for Evaluation	Understand Train-test split method for evaluating the performance of a machine learning algorithm	**Session:** Train-test split
Accuracy and Error	Understand Accuracy and Error for effectively evaluating and improving AI models	**Session:** Accuracy **Session:** Error **Activity:** Find the accuracy of the AI model
Evaluation metrics for classification	Learn about the different types of evaluation techniques in AI, such as Accuracy, Precision, Recall and F1 Score and their significance.	**Session:** What is Classification? **Session:** Classification metrics **Activity:** Build the confusion matrix from scratch **Activity:** Calculate the accuracy of the classifier model **Activity:** Decide the appropriate metric to evaluate the AI model
Ethical concerns around model evaluation	Understand ethical concerns around model evaluation	**Session:** Bias, Transparency, Accuracy

UNIT 4 : Statistical Data (To be assessed through practicals)

SUB-UNIT	LEARNING OUTCOMES	SESSION/ ACTIVITY/ PRACTICAL
Introduction & No code AI tool	Define the concept of Statistical Data and understand its applications in various fields. Define No-Code and Low- Code AI. Identify the differences between Code and No-Code AI concerning Statistical Data.	**Session: No code AI tool** • Introduction to Data Science & its applications • Meaning of No-Code AI • No-Code and Low-Code. • Some no-code tools **Orange Data Mining Tool:** https://orangedatamining.com/download/
Statistical Data: Use Case Walk through	Relate AI project stages to the stages of No-Code AI projects Able to use no-code tool Orange Data mining. To perform data exploration, modeling and evaluation with Orange data mining.	**Session** • Important concepts in Statistics. • Orange data mining • AI project cycle in Orange data mining (Palmer penguins case study) **Activity:** MS Excel for Statistical Analysis. Link: https://docs.google.com/spreadsheets/d/1f5 G-JXyP7EV2fy1hax47YVaH5gyq8KZy/edit?usp=dri ve_link&ouid=109928090180926267402&rtpof=tr ue&sd=true Case study using Orange data mining (Palmer Penguins). Link: https://drive.google.com/drive/u/0/folders/1fmcRVb-ilTyUhmUv4DWT1BFsaCoQ2BmF

UNIT 5 : Computer Vision (To be assessed through Theory)

SUB-UNIT	LEARNING OUTCOMES	SESSION/ ACTIVITY/ PRACTICAL
Introduction	Define the concept of Computer Vision and understand its applications in various fields.	**Session:** Introduction to Computer Vision **Session:** Applications of CV
Concepts of Computer Vision	Understand the basic concepts of image representation, feature extraction, object detection and segmentation.	**Session:** Understanding CV Concepts ● Computer Vision Tasks ● Basics of Images-Pixel, Resolution, Pixel value ● Grayscale and RGB images **Activities:** ● Game- Emoji Scavenger Hunt https://emojiscavengerhunt.withgoogle.com/ ● RGB Calculator: https://www.w3schools.com/colors/colors_r gb.asp ● Create your own pixel art: www.piskelapp.com ● Create your own convolutions: http://setosa.io/ev/image-kernels/
No-Code AI Tools	To demonstrate proficiency in using no-code AI tools for computer vision projects. To deploy models, fine-tune parameters and interpret results. Skills acquired include data preprocessing, model selection and project deployment.	**Introduction to Lobe:** https://www.lobe.ai/ **Teachable Machine:** https://teachablemachine.withgoogle.com/ ● Activity: Build a Smart Sorter **Orange Data Mining Tool:** https://orangedatamining.com/download/ ● Activity: Build a real-world Classification Model: Coral Bleaching (Use Case Walkthrough) ● Link to the steps involved in project development and dataset: https://drive.google.com/drive/folders/1ppJ 4d-8yOFJ2G22rHHpjNrK0ejdlAe5Q?usp=shar ing
Image Features & Convolution Operator	Apply the convolution operator to process images and extract useful features.	**Session:** Understanding Convolution operator **Activity:** Convolution Operator
Convolution Neural Network	Understand the basic architecture of a CNN and its applications in computer vision and image recognition.	**Session:** Introduction to CNN **Session:** Understanding CNN ● Kernel ● Layers of CNN **Activity:** Testing CNN

UNIT 6 : Natural Language Processing (To be assessed through Theory)

SUB-UNIT	LEARNING OUTCOMES	SESSION/ ACTIVITY/ PRACTICAL
Introduction	Comprehend the complexities of natural languages. and elaborate on the need for NLP techniques for machines to understand various natural languages effectively.	**Session:** Features of natural languages. **Session:** Introduction to Natural Language Processing
Applications of Natural Language Processing	Explore the various applications of NLP in everyday life, such as, voice assistants, auto generated captions, language translation, sentiment analysis, text classification and keyword extraction.	**Session:** Various real-life applications of NLP **Activity:** Keyword Extraction https://cloud.google.com/natural-language
Stages of Natural Language Processing (NLP)	Understand the concepts like lexicon, syntax, semantics and logical analysis of input text.	**Session:** Explore the various stages of NLP that involve in understanding and processing human language.
Chatbots	Understand the concept of chatbot and the differences between smartbots and script bots.	**Activity:** Play with chatbots Elizabot - https://www.masswerk.at/elizabot/ Mitsuki - https://www.kuki.ai/ Cleverbot - https://www.cleverbot.com/ Singtel - https://www.singtel.com/personal/support **Session:** Script Bot V/s Smart Bot
Concepts of Natural Language Processing: Text Processing	Learn about the Text Normalisation technique used in NLP and the popular NLP model - Bag-of-Words	**Session: Text Processing** ● Text Normalisation ● Bag of Words **Hands-on:** Text processing ● Data Processing ● Bag of Words ● TFIDF
Natural Language Processing: Use Case Walkthrough	Explore the sentiment analysis process using real-life datasets with the Orange Data Mining tool.	**Session:** Examples of Code and No-code NLP Tools **Session:** Applications of NLP- Introduction to Sentiment Analysis **Hands-on:** Case Walkthrough – Steps involved in project development Link to steps and dataset: https://drive.google.com/drive/u/2/folders/1geFLXxV5890kfcakMfEg_KsH1LPcS_Iz

UNIT 7 : ADVANCE PYTHON (To be assessed through Practicals)

SUB-UNIT	LEARNING OUTCOMES	SESSION/ ACTIVITY/ PRACTICAL
Recap	Understand to work with Jupyter Notebook, creating virtual environments, installing Python Packages.	**Session:** Jupyter Notebook
	Able to write basic Python programs using fundamental concepts such as variables, data types, operators, and control structures.	**Session:** Introduction to Python
	Able to use Python built-in functions and libraries.	**Session:** Python Basics

PART-C : PRACTICAL & PROJECT WORK

Practical Work :	
Suggested Programs List	• Write a program to add the elements of the two lists. • Write a program to calculate mean, median and mode using Numpy • Write a program to display line chart from (2,5) to (9,10). • Write a program to display a scatter chart for the following points (2,5), (9,10),(8,3),(5,7),(6,18). • Read the csv file saved in your system and display 10 rows. • Read csv file saved in your system and display its information • Write a program to read an image and display using Python • Write a program to read an image and identify its shape using Python
Important Links	Link to AI Activities & steps to AI project development considering real life problem statement along with the required dataset https://docs.google.com/spreadsheets/d/1ZQCTT8RM-l7QfeTzH0n-5wJLBAoiXu7TFM0Pcp31cX0/edit?usp=sharing

Project Work / Field Visit / Student Portfolio
*** relate it to Sustainable Development Goals**
Suggested Projects/ Field Visit / Portfolio (any one activity to be one)

Sample Projects	AI Project Development Using 1. Statistical Data for AI: Prediction of palmer penguin species 2. Computer Vision: Early detection of coral bleaching 3. Natural Language Processing: Sentiment Analysis
Field Work	Students' participation in the following- • AI for Youth Bootcamp • AI Fests/ Exhibition • Participation in any AI training sessions • Virtual tours of companies using AI to get acquainted with real-life usage
Student Portfolio (to be continued from class IX)	• Maintaining a record of all AI activities • Hackathons • Competitions (CBSE/Inter School) Note: Portfolio should contain minimum 5 activities

PART A
Employability Skills

CHAPTER 01

Communication Skills-II

In the present time, a thorough knowledge of language with communication skills is very important in any occupation or business. Communication skills are important to everyone to communicate effectively i.e. to give and receive information and convey our ideas and opinions to those around us.

The word communication comes from the Latin word **communicare** meaning **to share**. Being able to communicate effectively is one of the most important life skills.

Communication is defined as a process of exchange of information between two or more people by speaking, writing signaling or using any other effective medium.

Clear and concise communication is an important factor for meaningful interpretation of information. There are three important parts of communication.

- **Transmission** The sender transmits the message to the receiver through a medium.
- **Receiver** The receiver gets the message and interprets it into meaningful information.
- **Feedback** The feedback of this meaningful information is conveyed back to the sender to complete the communication cycle.

For example, during a personal interview, employers are impressed by a job candidate who answers questions with more than one-word answers, demonstrates that he is listening, and shares information and ideas by asking questions for clarification and follow-up.

1.1 Methods of Communication

The methods or types of communication are described below:

Verbal Communication

Verbal communication means communication through spoken oral and written words. It implies use of words which make up a language. It is the ability to communicate using words in understandable language i.e. English, Hindi, French, Urdu etc. Language plays a significant role in verbal communication. The effectiveness of the verbal communication depends on the tone of the speaker, clarity of speech, volume, speed, body language and the quality of words used in conversation.

Verbal communication are of various types. These are

1. **Oral communication** Oral communication is the exchange of information and ideas through spoken word. Two individuals conversing with each other, either face-to-face or through the telephone is an example of oral communication. Interviews, speeches, presentations, conferences, workshops and group discussions are also forms of oral communication.
2. **Written communication** This is a medium of communication that entails the written word. Letters, e-mails, websites, memorandums, reports, notices, manuals, quotations, newsletters, newspapers etc., are forms of written communication.

Intrapersonal Communication

Interpersonal Communication

Public Communication

Methods of verbal communication can be classified into different categories

- Intrapersonal communication
- Interpersonal communication
- Small group communication
- Public communication
- Mass communication

Advantages of Verbal Communication

- It is quick in obtaining feedback once delivered.
- It saves time in communication.
- It is more reliable method of communication.
- It is cheaper way of communication and hence saves money.
- It provides complete understanding of communication delivered and there is chance to make it more clear in case of doubts in interpretation of words or ideas.

Disadvantages of Verbal Communication

- It has no legal validity and hence will lead to problems in certain situations. Emotions are visible and hence leads to trouble in certain cases.
- It has issues when communicating with distant people.
- It does not provide permanent record unless it is recorded with modern means of storage.
- This form of communication is not suitable for lengthy message.

Non-Verbal Communication

Non-verbal communication is the expression or exchange of information or messages without using any spoken or written word. It relies on various non-verbal cues such as physical movements, colors, signs, symbols, body language etc., to express feelings, attitudes or information. Although no word is used in non-verbal communication, this form of communication can effectively communicate many human feelings more accurately than verbal methods of communication.

Facial Expression & Silence, Olfactics (smell), Chronemics (time), Vocal Intonations, Body Gestures, Haptics (touch)

Various forms of non-verbal communication are

- Eye contact
- Facial expressions
- Gestures
- Body language
- Proximity
- Touch
- Personal appearance
- Para-linguistic (tone/ pitch/ inflection)
- Posture and body orientation
- Space and Distance
- Humour
- Silences

Info Wall

Prof. Albert Mehrabian in 1970s proved that in personal communication, non-verbal communication is very important as it conveys 93% while verbal communication conveys only 7%. The exact breakup percentage he came up with is:

7% words } **Verbal communication**

38% tone of voice
55% body language } **Non-verbal communication**

Advantages of Non-Verbal Communication

- It conveys clear and precise meaning to the receiver.
- It is presentable through visuals, audio-visual and silent means.
- This type of communication serves as substitute for verbal communication.
- It provides clarity in conversation, especially with those who do not speak the some language.
- It is can be more inpactful and real than verbal communication because people pay more attention to non-verbal communication like facial expression, voice of tone, body language etc.
- Non-verbal messages reaches faster than verbal and written communication, so it reduces the wastage of time.

Disadvantages of Non-Verbal Communication

- In the absence of language, this type of communication do not convey actual meaning of the message. This makes communication imprecise.
- It can be confusing as no clear message is conveyed.
- Long conversation are not possible in non-verbal communication.
- It can be costly as Neon signs, PowerPoint presentation movies involve huge cost.

Visual Communication

Visual communication is the process of conveying meaning—be it ideas, instructions, data, or other kinds of information—through graphics rather than text or audio. This is a efficient and accessible way of sharing knowledge and adding context.

Visual communication can be achieved in a variety of different ways.

Examples of visual communication include:

- Videos and photos
- Graphs, charts, infographics, and other types of data visualisation
- Typography
- Maps (such as mind maps and content maps)
- Illustrations and graphic design
- Slide decks and presentations
- GIFs

These types of visual assets are commonly used in social media and content marketing, to communicate ideas and information, where more text-heavy formats fail to make an impact.

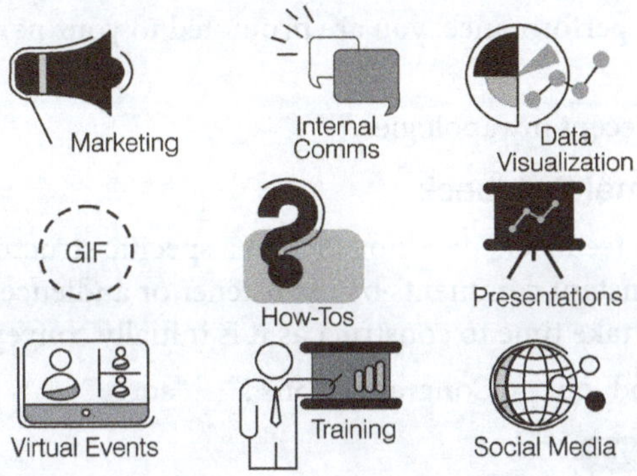

Advantages of Visual Communication

- It is more interactive.
- It brings clarity to oral communication.
- Good for the uneducated receiver.
- Can be used for presentations and sharing complex ideas.

Disadvantages of Visual Communication

- It cannot be used for detailed information.
- Some information cannot be communicated visually, such as policy, rules etc.
- Information could be misinterpreted.
- It could be costly to prepare graphs, charts, cartoons etc.

Try These 1.1

1. **Name the form of oral communication.**
2. **Name the form of written communication.**
3. **Verbal communication consists of .... communication and .... communication.**
4. **During a personal interview, employers are impressed by a job candidate who answers questions with .... answers.**
5. **What visual communication is used to indicate an area which is dangerous to human life?**

1.2 Communication Cycle

In the communication process, one person is a sender who conveys a message to another person (or a group of persons) known as the receiver.

When the receiver gets the message, he acknowledges it and sends back a response. This leads to a cyclic process known as a Communication Cycle.

The cycle describes how an idea, impression or feeling is made known to others. A communication cycle includes resources such as e-mail threads, social media outlets, VoIP message outlets, etc.

The effectiveness of a communication cycle depends on how long it takes for the feedback to be received by the initial sender. The quicker the response, the more effective is the cycle.

These steps are shown and explained below

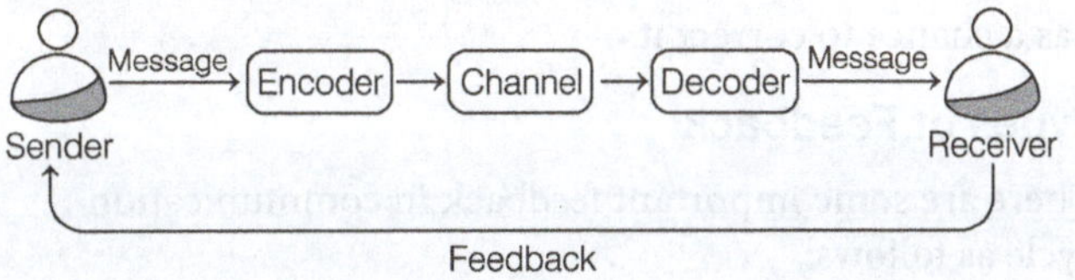

- The **Communicator** or **Sender** is the person or organisation originating the communication. It decides what the message is, how it will be expressed and sent, and who it is to be sent to.
- **Encoding** means to change the message into a form suitable for sending. The factors which must be considered when a encoding messages are language, cultural differences etc.
- The **Message** is the actual information that the sender wishes to convey to the receiver.
- The **Medium** or **Channel** is the means by which the message is sent. Some messages are more effective in written form, others may be more effective on the telephone (e.g. urgent messages), while others may be more effective if sent *via* electronic means such as e-mail.
- The **Receiver** is the person or organisation to whom the message is sent.
- **Decoding** is the process in which the receiver interprets and understands the message. Sometimes errors in decoding occur if the receiver isn't sure it understands the message but doesn't make the effort to ask for a clarification.
- **Feedback** is the receiver's response to the message. Requesting clarification is part of a good feedback phase of a communication cycle. Without feedback, the communication cycle remains incomplete.

Meaning and Importance of Feedback

Feedback is the final step in the communication cycle. It is the receiver's response to the message, which enables the sender to evaluate the effectiveness of the message sent.

Thus, feedback plays a very important role in communication cycle. If there is absence of feedback then it will lead to a communication barrier.

For example, if the receiver doesn't understand the meaning of the message, the sender can know this by the feedback received and can improve the message accordingly. Thus, the sender must create an environment that encourages feedback.

For the feedback to be effective, it must be clear, well in time, specific, having the right attitude, true and honest, impersonal and informative. It is important because proper feedback helps avoid **misunderstandings**. Thus, if the receiver has interpreted the message incorrectly, the sender has a chance to correct it.

Types of Feedback

There are some important feedback in communication cycle as follows:

1. Descriptive Feedback

A descriptive feedback, provides meaningful information in a detailed, expensive manner that also contains some analysis or suggestion etc.
This form of feedback is most suited to teacher-student interactions when the students are attending a course taught by the teacher. In such a case, it has the specific purpose of helping students improve while they are still gaining knowledge and practising their skills in the subject.

2. Non-descriptive Feedback

A non descriptive feedback provides some specific information but does not give details descriptions.

e.g., "I like your only second paragraph. Others needs improvement."

Each of the above discussed types of feedback can be either a positive feedback (i.e. it indicates that the sender can continue his communication in the same manner as before) or a negative feedback (i.e. it indicates a need for a change in the manner of communication).

3. Specific Feedback

The specific feedback talks about a thing or particularly without talking about a general overview.

e.g., I like the way you described your grandfather's character. It makes me feel like I know him too.

4. Non-Specific Feedback

The non-specific feedback, talks about the entire think while giving a general overview. It does not particularly pinpoint is specific think/feature.

e.g., I like your story. It is good.

5. Formal Feedback

A formal feedback follows a present format or structure using which the receiver sends feedback. Formal feedback covers many predefined points and has a specific blueprint. The receiver sends the feedback as per this blueprint. Formal feedback takes time to construct and hence, is not instant.

e.g., "Congratulation on scoring with A Grade in your final test performance. you are promoted to your next class."

"please accept my apologies."

6. Informal Feedback

Informal feedback, does not stick to a specific structure such as instant comments by the listener or audience. It does not take time to construct as it is initially conveyed.

e.g., "good job! Congratulations !" "sorry"

Try These 1.2

1. **Name any two step in the communication cycle.**
2. **Without feedback, the communication cycle remains ....**
3. **How do errors in decoding occur in a communication cycle?**
4. **The .... form of feedback is most suited to teacher-student interactions.**

1.3 Effective Communication

It is the process of exchanging ideas, thoughts, opinions, knowledge and data so that the message is received and understood with clarity and purpose. When we communicate effectively, both the sender and receiver feel satisfied.

Barriers to Effective Communication

Anything that prevents or disturbs the sending or receiving of a communication or message is considered as a barrier to communication. Such as barriers can retard or distort the message or intention of the message being conveyed. It may result in failure of the communication process or cause an effect that is undesirable.

The types of barriers to effective communication include

Physical Barriers

Physical barrier is the environmental and natural condition that act as a barrier in communication in sending message from sender to receiver. Not being able to see gestures, posture and general body language can make communication less effective.

Interpersonal Barriers

They arise from the judgements, emotions and social values of people. They cause a psychological distance between people similar to the physical distance. Thus, sometimes the message may not be understood at all.

Our emotions also affect nearly all our communications. For example, if we are feeling angry, we may say something which we would say differently if we were not angry. In such situation, we are communicating what we are feeling is correct.

Semantic Barriers

These refer to symbols or visuals used in the message. The barrier may arise due to the symbol we use, as it may mean different things to different people. For example, the 'thumbs up' gesture is recognised as a sign of approval or agreement in European countries, but it may be interpreted as an indecent gesture in rural areas of India.

Symbols are of the following three types:

1. **Linguistic or Related to Language** Language, whether spoken or written, is the most used method of communication. However, a major difficulty with language is that nearly every common word has several meanings, depending on the context in which it is used. In fact, the Oxford Dictionary records an average of 28 separate meanings for each of the 500 most used words in the English language.
2. **Pictures** Organisations make extensive use of pictures such as blueprints, charts, maps, films, three-dimensional models and other similar devices for communication in their normal work, which would otherwise require many words for describing each visual.
3. **Action** A person communicates his intentions and meaning of his communication through his actions.

Intra-Personal Barriers

It refers to the elements within the individuals personality which acts as a barrier in receiving, analysing and interpreting the information that is available. There are different types of intra-personal barriers in an individuals's personality like selective perception, individual differences in communication skills, emotions, preconceived ideas etc.

Organisational Barriers

Organisational barriers are those barriers that are caused due to the structure, rules and regulations present in the organisation. The various types of barriers that can be encountered due to superior subordinate relationships, where the free flow of communication is not possible.

Sometimes the complexity of organisational structure and multiple managers make it difficult to convey information properly, and the information gets distorted leading to miscommunication.

Cultural barriers

Cultural barriers are those that arise due to lack of similarities among the different cultures across the world. A term that can be harmless in one culture can be regarded as a slang in another culture. Moreover, various beliefs can differ from one culture to another.

Measures to Overcome Barriers

To ensure that barriers to communication do not arise or can be overcome, we can take some steps related to the factors causing the barriers. The steps to be taken for overcoming some of these factors are:

- **Be Prepared before Communicating** Often we are not properly prepared for communicating a message because we do not have enough information or knowledge of what we want to communicate. At other times, we are not the behaviour expected of the receiver of the communication. Either of these creates a barrier between sender and the receiver.
- **Give Sufficient Time** The message should not be communicated too fast; this is particularly true for oral messages. If it is not done at a suitable speed the receiver may miss its important points or may not understand it at all. Thus, oral communication in a group, such as a speech, debate or group discussion, must be done at a measured rate so that the entire audience is able to grasp what is being said.
- **Simplify the Language** Both the sender and receiver of the communication must have sufficient knowledge of the language in which they are communicating. If this is not confirmed, it is better to use simplified language with easily understood words and simple ideas.
- **Don't Assume Anything** Without appropriate feedback, the sender of the message should not assume that his message has been understood. He should only

rely on suitable feedback about the understanding of the message.

- **Avoid Overconfidence** Have a humble attitude when communicating a message. Similarly, the receiver should not be egocentric, otherwise he may fail to understand some important points of the message he has received.
- **Preconceived Notions/Expectations, Perceptions and Assumptions** When the receiver has a different perception from that of the sender, communication is affected. This can be overcome by thinking from the speaker's point of view. In addition, if the communication is not clear, the receiver must ask for clarifications instead of assuming anything.
- **Avoid Making Judgements** Communication can fail if the message communicated passes some judgement against the receiver, as then the content of the message is not understood in its real sense. It makes the receiver defensive, thus creating a barrier. So, this kind of situation should be avoided.
- **Information Overload/ Attention Span** Overload of information or giving too many details reduces the receiver's ability to concentrate on the important parts of the message. It also reduces his attention span. So, the sender must try to eliminate unnecessary information and stick to important information only.

1.4 Principles of a Effective Communication

The most basic principle for a communication to be effective is that the intended message of the sender and the interpreted message of the receiver are one and the same. Although this should be the goal in any communication, it is not always achieved. Thus, a set of principles needs to be followed to ensure it. The most popular name of these basic principles is known as 7C's of Effective Communication.

The 7C's of Effective Communication

We communicate at home, at work, with our neighbour etc. We communicate in written or oral, audio or visual, so it is important that we follow the 7C's of effective communication.

These principles of effective communication are:

1. **Completeness** The message must be complete, meaning that it should convey all the information required by the receiver. Nothing which may be required by the receiver should be left out of the message. The sender of the message must take into consideration the requirements of the receiver while making the message. For example, if there is a query by a customer, he must be provided complete information about his query in a short span of time. Your prompt and complete reply will enable you to maintain a good business relation with the customer. One way to make your message complete is to answer the five W's: 'Who?', 'What?', 'When?', 'Where?' and 'Why'? The five question method is useful when you write requests, announcements or other informative messages.
2. **Conciseness** It means communicating what you want to convey in the least possible words so that there are no unnecessary bits of information in it. A concise communication is both time-saving as well as cost-saving. It highlights the main message, thus making it more appealing and comprehensible to the audience. For example, Instead of saying 'at this time', we can use the single word 'now'.
3. **Coherent** For good communication, a message should follow a logical structure. All of your ideas should be well connected and relevant to the critical point. This is known as coherence. Organising your message logically from introductory statements to the conclusion will ensure that the message is coherent. When the ideas in your message flow neatly from one end to another in a proper sequence, the overall message becomes easier to follow and recall.
4. **Concreteness** It implies being objective and clear, rather than vague, confused or obscure. A concrete message will have specific facts and figures. For example, if you are a salesperson talking to your client, always use facts and figures instead of generic or irrelevant information. Concrete information makes use of words that are clear. It will build up the reputation of the sender as one who knows what he wants to say. Further, concrete messages are not misinterpreted.
5. **Clarity** It implies emphasising a specific message in a communication instead of trying to cover too many items in one communication. It makes understanding of the message easier by the receiver. Complete clarity of thoughts and ideas enhances the meaning of the message. For achieving complete understanding, the message must make use of exact, appropriate and precise words which are familiar and easy to understand.
6. **Courtesy** A courteous message is politely worded. It implies that the message should use words which show the sender's respect for the receiver. Thus, the

sender of the message should be sincerely polite and well-mannered.

Knowing the person who you are sending the communication to allow you to use appropriate statements of courtesy. Using socially accepted manners is a form of courtesy. It is politeness that grows out of respect and concern for others. Courtesy implies taking into consideration both the viewpoints as well as the feelings of the receiver.

7. **Correctness** It implies that there are no grammatical, spelling or punctuation errors in the communication being sent. Further, use the level of language appropriate to the status of the receiver. The three levels of language are formal (e.g. Respected Sir), informal (e.g. Hi there!) and sub-standard, avoid substandard language. Using incorrect words (e.g. 'ain't' for 'isn't'), incorrect grammar, faulty pronunciation etc., all suggest as inability to use good English.

The message should also be sent at the correct time, i.e. it is correctly timed. A correct message has a greater impact on the receiver if the facts and figures mentioned in the communication are also accurate and true.

Try These 1.3

1 Symbols may be related to which type of communication?
2 Name two factors causing barrier to communication.
3 A .... communication is both time-saving as well as cost-saving.
4 Courtesy implies taking into consideration both the viewpoints as well as the feelings of the ....
5 What is the most basic principle for a communication to be effective?

1.5 Basic Writing Skills

Writing skills are important part of communication. Good writing skills allow you to communicate your message clearly and easily to a large audience. You may be asked to write a report, plan or strategy at work; write an application for granting something; or a press release; or a well written CV or résumé; all with no spelling, punctuation or grammatical mistakes. In any of these, poor writing skills create poor first impression and many readers will have an immediate negative reaction if they spot a spelling or grammatical mistake in what you have written.

So, to ensure that we write correctly, we should understand some basic parts of a document such as **kinds of sentences, phrases, parts of a sentence, parts of speech** and **construction of a paragraph**.

The Sentence

A sentence is a set of words that is complete in itself and which contains a subject and a predicate part. It conveys a statement, question, exclamation or command. It consists of a main clause and sometimes one or more subordinate clauses.

Examples of sentences are:

- Lions roar.
- The house behind my home is the one where you have to go, isn't it?
- What a lovely shot that was!
- Go to the end of the road and turn right.

Kinds of Sentence

There are four types of English sentence, classified by their purpose:

- **Declarative sentence** (statement)
- **Interrogative sentence** (question)
- **Imperative sentence** (command)
- **Exclamative sentence** (exclamation)

form	function	example sentence (clause)	final punctuation
1. Declarative	**statement** It tells us something	John likes Mary.	.
2. Interrogative	**question** It asks us something	Does Mary like John?	?
3. Imperative	**command** It tells us to do something	Stop! Close the door.	! or .
4. Exclamative	**exclamation** It expresses surprise	What a funny story he told us!	!

Phrases

Phrases are a group of words that work together in a sentence but does not contain a subject or a verb. Often phrases are used for descriptions of people, things or events.

Examples,

Filled with joy, the girl jumped up and down. The man **with the red jacket** is my father.

Parts of a Sentence

A sentence consists of two parts, a **subject part** and a **predicate part**. Each part of a sentence has a particular function, though sometimes both parts may not be written for it to be complete.

The subject refers to that part of the sentence which tells who or what the sentence is about. The subject is a noun, pronoun or noun phrase. Instances of typical sentences with such subjects are:

- Kailash ran across the road. ('Kailash' is a noun)
- They went to the market. ('They' is a pronoun)
- The brown dog is sleeping. ('The brown dog' is a noun phrase)

The predicate part of a sentence includes the verb and the words that relate to it. It tells what the subject does with an action verb or describes the subject.

Predicates can contain much information and may be quite long. Predicates often have several parts in addition to the verb, including objects and complements. Instances of predicates are underlined in the sentences given below:

- The letter contained exciting news.
- The army officers are experienced persons who acquired their experience in the Kargil War.
- I am going to outside and may take some time to return.

Parts of Speech

According to their function in a sentence, words in the English language are classified as different parts of speech.

These are discussed below:

- **Noun** It is a word for a person, place, thing or idea. Nouns are sometimes used with an article (the, a, an). Proper nouns always start with a capital letter; common nouns do not. Nouns can be singular or plural, concrete or abstract. Example of nouns are underlined in the sentences given below:
    - The young boy brought me a very long letter from the teacher.
    - He went to Rashid and told him the secret of his happiness.
- **Pronoun** It is a word used in place of a noun. A pronoun is usually substituted for a specific noun, which is called its antecedent. The types of pronouns are personal, possessive, reflexive, relative and demonstrative.

  Examples of pronouns are underlined in the sentences given below:
    - Jagdish was in a hurry, so he washed the car himself.
    - He went to Rashid and told him the secret of his happiness.
- **Verb** In a sentence, the verb expresses an action or the state of the subject in the sentence. There is a main verb and sometimes one or more helping verbs in a sentence. Verbs also take different forms to express tense.

  Instances of verbs are underlined in the sentences given below:
    - Jagdish was in a hurry, so he washed the car himself.
    - He went to Rashid and told him the secret of his happiness.
- **Adjective** It is a word used to modify or describe a noun or a pronoun. It usually answers the question of which one, what kind, or how many. Examples of adjectives are underlined in the sentences given below:
    - The young boy brought me a very long letter from the class teacher.
    - I have two large brown dogs in my spacious home.
- **Adverb** It describes or modifies a verb, an adjective, or another adverb, but never a noun. It usually answers the questions of when, where, how, why, under what conditions, or to what degree. Examples of adverbs are underlined in the sentences given below:
    - She laughed loudly.
    - Harish forgot to bring his lunch yesterday and again today.
    - I started running so that I wouldn't be late.
- **Preposition** It is a word placed before a noun or pronoun to link it to another word in the sentence. Examples of prepositions are underlined in the sentences given below:
    - The mouse jumped off the table onto the floor of the room.
    - The members of the environment club were standing around the tree in a circle.
- **Conjunction** It joins words, phrases, or clauses and indicates the relationship between them. Examples of conjunctions are underlined in the sentences given below:
    - You can have either chocolate or vanilla ice-cream.
    - He not only plays the guitar but also the drums.
    - Such was his strength that he was able to break the chains on his arms.
- **Interjection** It is a word used to express emotion. It is often followed by an exclamation mark. Examples of interjections are underlined in the sentences given below:
    - Oh God! I don't know what to do about this mess.
    - Congratulations! So, you have finally got your master's degree.

Articles

An article is a kind of adjective which is always used with a noun and gives some information about it.

The words 'a' (used before a word beginning with a consonant sound while speaking) and 'an' (used before a word beginning with a vowel sound while speaking) are called indefinite articles because the noun they go with is indefinite or general. Instances of indefinite articles used in sentences are:

- I will reach home within an hour.
- It is difficult to find a one-rupee currency note in the present day.

The word "the" is known as a definite article because it refers to a specific noun. The difference between the sentences, "I sat on a chair." and "I sat on the chair." is that the second sentence refers to a particular, specific chair, not just any chair.

Whenever we see an article, we will find a noun after it. The noun may be the next word as in "the man" or there may be adjectives and perhaps adverbs between the article and the noun as in "the very angry, young man".

Construction of a Paragraph

A paragraph is a group of sentences dealing with a particular topic. Paragraphs can be of any length and can vary from only one sentence to even more than ten sentences. However, for maintaining clarity, paragraphs should be as short as possible.

For examples, the paragraph you are reading has only four sentences. The first sentence of a paragraph is usually the topic sentence, as it states the main point to be developed or explained in the paragraph. Each sentence following it should be relevant to that topic, giving the paragraph a look of unity. Each sentence in a paragraph should also be connected to the sentence that comes before it. This can be done by:

- Inserting transition words and phrases such as 'In addition', 'Further', 'Next', 'Finally' etc.
- Repeating key words or their synonyms, such as 'rewriting' may change to 'revising' in the next sentence, 'writer' may change to 'he' in the next sentence, and so on.

An instance of a typical paragraph with comments added in brackets is given below:

Good writing comes from hard work (*topic sentence*). But (*transition word*) hard work (*repeating a key word*) has never scared me.

In fact (*transition word*), I relish the challenge of creating something new, no matter how difficult (*key word synonym*) or time consuming. I have spent weeks on a few pages, months on an essay, and years on a book (*parallel structure for similar items*).

Try These 1.4

1. **The sentence "A paragraph has many sentences which are about a single, clearly-defined topic." is a .... sentence.**
2. **In the sentence "He ate the <u>chocolate</u> cake greedily.", the underlined word is a/ an ....**
3. **A .... expresses an action or the state of the subject in the sentence.**
4. **The first sentence of a paragraph is usually the ....**
5. **What does the subject in a sentence refer to?**

Glossary

Feedback is the receiver's acknowledgement and response to the message.

Non-verbal communication is the expression or exchange of information or messages without using any spoken or written word.

Part of speech indicates how a particular word functions in meaning as well as grammatically within the sentence.

Noun is a word (naming word) that refer to a person, place, thing or idea.

Preposition connects one word with another to usually answer the questions 'where', 'when' and 'how'.

ACTIVITY Time

ACTIVITY 1

Group Practice Role play on communication and identify elements of the communication cycle

Material required

Paper and pencil

Procedure

- Form groups with four students in each group.
- The situation is that a student is Sales Executive at a toy store and he or she is supposed to communicate to customers about the various types of toys available with the store for different age group.
- The other students will reach the Sales Executive one by one and ask different types of questions related to toys.
- Develop a script for the role play and act on the same.
- Each student will draw a communication cycle.
- Discuss what you all learned from this activity and entire class will then discuss how each element affected communication.

ACTIVITY 2

Group-Practice Role Play of a Telephonic Conversation

Material required

Notebook, pen

Procedure

- Form groups with three students in each group.
- Write a phone conversation based on a given scenario of a student calling a university academic coordinator to know about study courses and admission procedure.
- One student acts as caller and the other as receiver.
- Read out the conversation by enacting the roles.
- The third student gives feedback based on the 7Cs of communication (clear, concise, concrete, correct, coherent, complete and courteous).

ACTIVITY 3

Group-Practice on Public Speaking

Material required

Notebook, pen

Procedure

- Form groups with three students in each group.
- Within the group, choose a topic for a short speech.
- For example, Importance of Punctuality, Healthy Food Habits, etc.
- Each person should make a speech to the others in the group; who then give feedback based on whether the person was able to communicate properly.
- One student from the group volunteers to give the same speech in front of the class.

ACTIVITY 4

Group-Practice Role-play on Non-verbal Communication

Material required

Notebook, pen

Procedure

- Form groups with three students in each group.
- Prepare the script for the role play, based on the given scenario. For example, a hearing impaired salesperson is attending a female customer at an apparel store.
- Act it out in front of your group.
- One group volunteers to act before your whole class. Discuss how students used non-verbal communication. Was this communication effective?

ACTIVITY 5

Group-Practice How to Avoid Body Language Mistakes

Material required

Notebook, pen

Procedure

- In the same group of three students as above, discuss what are the Dos and Don'ts of avoiding miscommunication because of body language.
- Each student should write down a list of these Dos and Don'ts. (Prepare the lists as homework, if there is less time left to complete the task in class).

ACTIVITY 6

Individual-Practice Comparing Methods of Communication

Material required

Notebook, pen

Procedure

- Discuss the three methods of communication (Verbal, Non-verbal and Visual).
- Ask each student to write a list of the advantages and disadvantages of each method.
- Practice: In all your conversations at home and school, pay attention to the non-verbal signs others are using. Practice using the non-verbal methods you learnt here in the right manner.

ACTIVITY 7

Role Play on Providing Feedback

Material required

Notebook, pen

Procedure

- Form groups with five students in each group.
- Two volunteers in the group should act out a role play of a hotel staff. For example, Volunteer A can act as a front desk executive and Volunteer B as a guest enquiring availability of rooms.
- After the role play, remaining members of group will give constructive feedback to both the volunteers.

ACTIVITY 8

Group-Practice on Constructive Feedback

Material required

Notebook, pen

Procedure

- Form groups with five students in each group.
- Each member in the group should write down three sentences showing how feedback should NOT be given.
- Then, each group forms a circle. One person in the circle starts by saying a sentence or feedback. The next person in the circle tries to make the feedback more constructive.
- Keep repeating until all written feedback have constructive alternatives.

ACTIVITY 9

Role Play on Barriers to Effective Communication.

Material required

Notebook, pen

Procedure

- Form groups with five students in each group.
- Two volunteers from the group should act out a role play of a salesperson in a shopping mall. For example, Volunteer A can act as a sales executive, and Volunteer B as a customer enquiring about a television set. The customer is from a foreign country.
- Enact the communication barriers or challenges the customer or salesperson may face while interacting with each other.

ACTIVITY 10

Group practice: Overcoming Barriers

Material required

Notebook, pen

Procedure

- Form groups with five students in each group.
- Each member in a group should write down three ways to overcome barriers to effective communication. The group members will then stand in a circle. Each student should say aloud one point each; till all the ways have been discussed.

ACTIVITY 11

Identifying Parts of Speech

Material required

Notebook, pen

Procedure

- Form groups with five students in each group.
- In the paragraph given below (taken from 'La Bamba'—a short story; Gary Soto pp. 115), identify the different parts of speech and write them down accordingly.
  "Manuel walked on stage and the song started immediately glassy-eyed from the shock of being in front of so many people manuel moved his lips and swayed in a made-up dance step he couldn't see his parents but he could see his brother mario who was a year younger thumb-wrestling with a friend mario was wearing manuel's favourite shirt he would deal with Mario later. He saw some other kids get up and head for the drinking fountain and a baby sitting in the middle of an aisle sucking her thumb and watching him intently."
- This paragraph contains examples of the parts of speech you learnt about in this lesson.
- Identify as many of these parts of speech as you can and mark them. Discuss what was difficult in this activity.
- Write the paragraph with correct capitalisation and punctuation. One of the groups will volunteer and present to the class what they have marked. They write out the paragraph on the board with proper punctuation. The other students will share if it is correct.

ACTIVITY 12

Pair Activity: Sentence Construction

Material required

Notebook, pen

Procedure

- Form pairs of students.
- List out nine parts of speech that you learnt in the lesson. Select any three of them and create five simple sentences which use these parts of speech.
- For each part of speech, a volunteer reads out their sentences. The other students share if it is correct.

ACTIVITY 13

Group Practice: Identify Name, Place, Animal, Thing

Material required

Notepad and pens

Procedure

- Number yourselves from 1 to 5.
- One set of 1–5 is in one group and so on.
- Each member of a group has to say a word that is either a name, place, animal, thing or feeling; the fifth member has to perform any kind of action.
- Each group gets 30 seconds to think what they are going to say and do.

NCERT FOLDER

Complete Explanations of all NCERT's Questions

A. Multiple Choice Questions

Q.1 Which of the following is not an element of communication within the communication process cycle?

(a) Channel (b) Receiver
(c) Sender (d) Time

Q.2 You need to apply leave at work? Which method of communication will you use?

(a) e-mail (b) Poster
(c) Newsletter (d) Blog

Q.3 By which action can senders send their messages?

(a) Gestures (b) Speaking
(c) Reading (d) Writing

Q.4 Which of the following is an example of oral communication?

(a) Newspapers (b) Letters
(c) Phone call (d) e-mail

Q.5 What are the types of words we should use for verbal communication?

(a) Acronyms (b) Simple
(c) Technical (d) Jargons

Q.6 Why do we use e-mails?

(a) To communicate with many people at the same time.
(b) To share documents and files.
(c) To talk to each other in real-time.
(d) To keep a record of communication.

Q.7 Which of these is a positive (good) facial expression?

(a) Frowning while concentrating
(b) Maintaining eye contact
(c) Smiling continuously
(d) Rolling up your eyes

Q.8 What does an upright (straight) body posture convey or show?

(a) Pride (b) Professionalism
(c) Confidence (d) Humility

Q.9 Which of these is NOT an appropriate non-verbal communication at work?

(a) Keeping hands in pockets while talking
(b) Talking at moderate speed
(c) Sitting straight
(d) Tilting head a bit to listen

Q.10 Which of the following statement is true about communication?

(a) 50% of our communication is non-verbal
(b) 20% communication is done using body movements, face, arms, etc.
(c) 5% communication is done using voice, tone, pauses, etc.
(d) 7% communication is done using words

Q.11 Which of these are examples of positive feedback?

(a) Excellent, your work has improved.
(b) I noticed your dedication towards the project.
(c) You are always doing it the wrong way.
(d) All of the above

Q.12 Which of these are examples of negative feedback?

(a) I hate to tell you this but your drawing skills are poor.

(b) You can surely improve your drawing.

(c) This is a good drawing but you can do better.

(d) None of the above

Q.13 Which of the following are effective components of a good feedback?

(a) Detailed and time consuming

(b) Direct and honest

(c) Specific

(d) Opinion-based

Q.14 Which of these is not a common communication barrier?

(a) Linguistic barrier (b) Interpersonal barrier

(c) Financial barrier (d) Organisational barrier

Q.15 Which of these are ways to overcome communication barriers?

(a) Respecting each other's differences

(b) Using a translator

(c) Not communicating at all

(d) Using your own language for comfort

Q.16 In which of the following, the underlined word is an adjective?

(a) Radha has a red dress.

(b) I can speak French.

(c) The Girl on the Train is a best-seller.

(d) Abdul can swim fast.

Q.17 Which of these sentences is capitalised correctly?

(a) Ravi and i are going to the movies.

(b) Salim is visiting India in july.

(c) The Tiger is a strong animal.

(d) She is arriving on Monday.

Q.18 Which of these sentences are punctuated correctly?

(a) When is the party.

(b) I had bread omelette and a Banana for breakfast.

(c) I am so excited about my first foreign trip!

(d) This is Abdul's notebook.

Q.19 In which of these sentences can you find an adverb?

(a) Divya drinks milk every day.

(b) Sanjay gifted me a new pen.

(c) I opened the door lock.

(d) Sita is 5-feet tall.

Answers

1. (d)	2. (a)	3. (d)	4. (c)	5. (b)
6. (a,b)	7. (b)	8. (c)	9. (a)	10. (d)
11. (a,b)	12. (a)	13. (b,c)	14. (c)	15. (a,b)
16. (a)	17. (c)	18. (c,d)	19. (a)	

B. Subjective Questions

Q.1 Put a X mark against the actions below which are examples of bad non-verbal communication.

- Laughing during formal communication
- Scratching head
- Smiling when speaking to a friend
- Nodding when you agree with something
- Standing straight
- Yawning while listening
- Sitting straight
- Maintaining eye contact while speaking
- Biting nails
- Firm Handshake
- Clenching jaws
- Looking away when someone is speaking to you
- Intense stare

Ans.

Laughing during formal communication	✕
Scratching head	✕
Smiling when speaking to a friend	✓
Nodding when you agree with something	✓
Standing straight	✓
Yawning while listening	✕
Sitting straight	✓
Maintaining eye contact while speaking	✓
Biting nails	✕
Firm Handshake	✓
Clenching jaws	✕
Looking away when someone is speaking to you	✕
Intense stare	✕

Q.2 List the different types of verbal communication. Include examples for each verbal communication type.

Ans. (i) **Face-to-Face Communication:** Direct communication between individuals who are physically present in the same location.

Example: Conversations between friends at a coffee shop.

(ii) **Telephone Communication:** Communication conducted over the phone, allowing for real-time conversation between individuals who may be geographically distant.

Example: Calling a family member to catch up on news.

(iii) **Video Communication**: Communication using video technology, enabling individuals to see and hear each other in real-time.
Example: Participating in a video conference call with colleagues from different offices.

Q.3 Draw any five common signs used for Visual Communication. Explain what each conveys and where did you see it?

Ans.

Stop Sign

The stop sign is a red octagonal sign with white letters spelling "STOP." It conveys the message for vehicles to come to a complete halt at the designated location.

Stop signs are commonly seen at intersections on roads and highways to regulate traffic flow and ensure safety.

No Smoking Sign:

The no smoking sign features a graphic symbol of a cigarette with a red circle and diagonal line across it, indicating that smoking is prohibited in the designated area.

No smoking signs are commonly posted in indoor and outdoor public spaces, such as restaurants, airports, parks, and public transportation vehicles, to enforce smoking regulations and promote a smoke-free environment.

Fire Exit Sign:

The fire exit sign features the word "EXIT" in white letters on a green background. It indicates the location of emergency exits or escape routes in buildings.

Fire exit signs are prominently displayed in public buildings, such as offices, schools, theaters, and hotels, to guide people to safety in the event of a fire or emergency evacuation.

Speed Limit Sign:

The speed limit sign features a numerical value indicating the maximum allow able speed for vehicles in a specific area or on a particular road.

Speed limit signs are commonly posted along roads and highways to regulate vehicle speed and ensure safe driving conditions.

Danger Sign:

The danger sign features the word "DANGER" in bold, capitalized letters and often includes a graphic symbol or pictogram to convey a specific hazard or risk.

Danger signs are commonly used in industrial facilities, construction sites, laboratories, and other hazardous environments to warn people of potential dangers and promote safety awareness.

Q.4 Write down the common communication barriers you may come across when you move to a new city or country.

Ans. (i) **Language Barrier**: If the primary language spoken in the new city or country is different from your native language, you may encounter difficulties in understanding and expressing yourself effectively.

(ii) **Cultural Differences**: Differences in cultural norms, customs, gestures, and communication styles can lead to misunderstandings and misinterpretations during interactions with locals.

(iii) **Accent and Dialect**: Even if you speak the same language as the locals, differences in accent, dialect, slang, and pronunciation may pose challenges in understanding and being understood.

(iv) **Non-Verbal Communication**: Non-verbal cues such as body language, facial expressions, gestures, and eye contact may vary across cultures, leading to misunderstandings or misinterpretations of intentions and emotions.

(v) **Social Etiquette**: Unfamiliarity with social norms, etiquettes, and taboos in the new environment can result in unintentional breaches of etiquette and social faux pas during interactions with others.

Q.5 Identify the conjunctions and prepositions from the list below and write these in the correct box.

Over, Because, Under, And, Since, In, At, Although, Or, Up, On, Beside

Ans. **Conjunctions** And, Although, Or, Because, Since
Prepositions Over, Under, In, At, Up, On, Beside

Q.6 Write two sentences of each type of sentence-statement, question, exclamatory and order.

Ans. Refer from text on page No. 9 (Kinds of Sentence).

EXAM PATTERN EXERCISE

Including Competency Based Questions

Part I

Multiple Choice Questions

1 Oral communication is based on ....

(a) Facial expressions (b) Listening and Hearing
(c) Body language (d) Language and tone of voice

2 Visual communication among the people are dependent on ....

(a) Signs, symbols and pictures
(b) Text messages
(c) Posture
(d) Body language

3 .... feedback is specific information, in the form of written comments or verbal conversations that help the learner understand what she or he needs to do in order to improve.

(a) Descriptive (b) Specific
(c) General (d) Sign

4 .... communication is the use of body language, gestures and facial expressions to convey information to others.

(a) Verbal (b) Written
(c) Non-verbal (d) Visual

5 There are many reasons why interpersonal communications may fail. While communicating, the message may not be received exactly the way, the sender intended and therefore it is important that the communicator seeks .... to check that their message is clearly understood.

(a) description (b) feedback
(c) channel (d) sign

6 Which one of the following is not a barrier to effective communication?

(a) Physical barrier (b) Linguistic barrier
(c) Interpersonal barrier (d) Subjective barrier

7 It is a word used in place of noun that is ....

(a) Adverb (b) Verb
(c) Pronoun (d) Preposition

8 A word used to express emotion and is often followed by an exclaimation mark is called ....

(a) Preposition (b) Conjunction
(c) Interjection (d) Adverb

9 .... is an instance of non-verbal communication.

(a) A speech (b) Proximity
(c) A notice (d) An e-mail

10 Which of the following is the process in which the receiver interprets and understands the message?

(a) Decoding (b) Encoding
(c) Feedback (d) None of these

11 Speaking louder to drown out the noise is a .... barrier to communication.

(a) type of (b) factor causing a
(c) measure to overcome a (d) None of these

12 If we take into consideration both the viewpoints as well as the feelings of the receiver of a communication, which of the 7 C's are we fulfilling?

(a) Clarity (b) Consideration
(c) Courtesy (d) Correctness

13 Remya travelled to Sweden from India to pursue her higher education. But she doesn't know how to speak Swedish (language of Sweden). Because of this, she was unable to find a part time job. This is an example of .... Competency Based Qus.

(a) Interpersonal barrier (b) Physical barrier
(c) Organisational barrier (d) Linguistic barrier

14 Some American and Israeli managers were on a conference call. The topic of the call was transitioning from an on-premise product to a cloud-native product. In the middle of the discussion, one Israeli manager said that the R&D staff in Israel 'don't care' about some of the changes. An American manager, although usually polite, couldn't restrain himself when he heard that statement. "What's that supposed to mean, they DON'T CARE??" he thundered. Competency Based Qus.

This is an example of

(a) Organisational Barrier (b) Interpersonal Barrier
(c) Linguistic Barrier (d) Cultural Barrier

15 Identify the object, verb and subject in the sentence, 'The car crashed into a tree.'

(a) Object: a tree; Verb: crashed; Subject: the car
(b) Object: The car; Verb: crashed; Subject: a tree
(c) Object: crashed; Verb: the tree; Subject: the car
(d) Object: crashed; Verb: the car; Subject: the tree

16 Which of the following types of communication takes place when the number of people is small enough to communicate with each other effectively? 2025

(a) Interpersonal communication
(b) Public communication
(c) Intrapersonal communication
(d) Small group communication

Answers

1. (b) 2. (a) 3. (a) 4. (c) 5. (b)
6. (d) 7. (c) 8. (c) 9. (b) 10. (a)
11. (c) 12. (c) 13. (d) 14. (c) 15. (a)
16. (d)

Statement Based Questions

1 Statement 1 Sender is the person beginning the communication.

Statement 2 Feedback is the means by which the information is sent.

(a) Both Statement 1 and Statement 2 are correct
(b) Both Statement 1 and Statement 2 are incorrect
(c) Statement 1 is correct but Statement 2 is incorrect
(d) Statement 2 is correct but Statement 1 is incorrect

2 Statement 1 Verbal communication includes sounds, words, language, and speech.

Statement 2 By improving your verbal communication skills you will build rapport, and have a better connect.

(a) Both Statement 1 and Statement 2 are correct
(b) Both Statement 1 and Statement 2 are incorrect
(c) Statement 1 is correct but Statement 2 is incorrect
(d) Statement 2 is correct but Statement 1 is incorrect

3 Statement 1 Non-verbal communication is the expression or exchange of information or messages without using any spoken or written word.

Statement 2 38% communication is done using voice, tone, pauses, etc.

(a) Both Statement 1 and Statement 2 are correct
(b) Both Statement 1 and Statement 2 are incorrect
(c) Statement 1 is correct but Statement 2 is incorrect
(d) Statement 2 is correct but Statement 1 is incorrect

4 Statement 1 Words used in place of a noun are adverbs.

Statement 2 Words that show action are nouns.

(a) Both Statement 1 and Statement 2 are correct
(b) Both Statement 1 and Statement 2 are incorrect
(c) Statement 1 is correct but Statement 2 is incorrect
(d) Statement 2 is correct but Statement 1 is incorrect

Answers

1. (c) 2. (a) 3. (a) 4. (b)

Assertion & Reason Based Questions

1 Assertion (A) The initial messages to students in the classroom by a teacher need not be critical to establish interactions later.

Reason (R) More control over the communication process means more control over what the students are learning.

(a) Both(A) and (R) are correct and (R) is correct explanation of (A)
(b) Both (A) and (R) are correct. But (R) is not correct explanation of (A)
(c) (A) is correct but (R) is incorrect
(d) (A) is incorrect but (R) is correct

2 Assertion (A) Verbal communication takes place in real time.

Reason (R) Written communication is synchronous in character as it appears at different level.

(a) Both(A) and (R) are correct and (R) is correct explanation of (A)
(b) Both (A) and (R) are correct. But (R) is not correct explanation of (A)
(c) (A) is correct but (R) is incorrect
(d) (A) is incorrect but (R) is correct

3 Assertion (A) To communicate well in the classroom is a natural ability.

Reason (R) Effective teaching in the classroom demands knowledge of the communication process.

(a) Both(A) and (R) are correct and (R) is correct explanation of (A)
(b) Both (A) and (R) are correct. But (R) is not correct explanation of (A)
(c) (A) is correct but (R) is incorrect
(d) (A) is incorrect but (R) is correct

4 Assertion (A) Communication does not include all human behaviour for the exchange of information.

Reason (R) Communication involves use of all five senses.

(a) Both(A) and (R) are correct and (R) is correct explanation of (A)
(b) Both (A) and (R) are correct. But (R) is not correct explanation of (A)
(c) (A) is correct but (R) is incorrect
(d) (A) is incorrect but (R) is correct

5 Assertion (A) Non-verbal communication is related to expression of feelings and emotions.

Reason (R) Body language is a kind of verbal communication.

(a) Both(A) and (R) are correct and (R) is correct explanation of (A)
(b) Both (A) and (R) are correct. But (R) is not correct explanation of (A).
(c) (A) is correct but (R) is incorrect
(d) (A) is incorrect but (R) is correct

Answers

1. (d) 2. (c) 3. (d) 4. (c) 5. (c)

Part II

Very Short Answer Type Questions

1 Karan lives at a Hostel in Shimla. He calls his mother who lives in Delhi, to get her approval for the robotics class which is going to start in his school next week onwards. However, due to disruption in the phone line, his mother could not understand and reply to him. He got very upset. Which another medium can he use to get immediate approval of his mother? **Competency Based Qus.**

Ans. E-mail

2 Nisha works in ABC organisation. Recently she got a very good job offer from XYZ Ltd. By what means of communication do she submit her resignation?

Ans. Email

3 An organisation wants to inform all its employees about the shifting of office location. What means would be the best to do it?

Ans. notices/posters

4. Mr Anmol is working with a presentation, where he is trying to give one for using exact words and facts. Which word is best fit for the same? **Competency Based Qus.**

Ans. Concrete

5. Ms. Mohini is presenting a persentation for a new launch of product. She is delivering her lecture but due to lack of confidence. She could not deliver in the way it should be. Which type of barrier it is? **Competency Based Qus.**

Ans. Interpersonal

6. Mr. Rakesh is working in an IT company. He wanted to implement a new strategy for his new project but his team leader couldn't find time to discuss with him and company policy won't allow Mr. Rakesh to call him without appoinment which type of barrier it is? **Competency Based Qus.**

Ans. Organizational

7. Mr. C.A yyappan is trying to convey his message to his colleagues. But his tone of speaking is different as most of his colleagues are from North India and he is from South India. This type of barrier is known as? **Competency Based Qus.**

Ans. Cultural

8 Name the four main categories of communication styles.

Ans. Verbal, Non-Verbal, Written and Visual

9 Define verbal communication.

Ans. Verbal communication means communication through spoken and written words. It implies use of words which make up a language.

10 What do you understand by feedback?

Ans. It is the receiver's response to the message, which enables the sender to evaluate the effectiveness of the message sent.

Short Answer Type Questions

1 Describe the term descriptive feedback.

Ans. Descriptive feedback can be written, oral or may even be the response of students to a question while they are working. It is relevant to the task students are performing, and allows them to re-focus and improve their mastery of the subject. This form of feedback is most suited to teacher-student interactions when the students are attending a course taught by the teacher.

2 Which measures must be adopted to overcome the factors causing communication barriers? **Competency Based Qus.**

Ans. Some measures must be adopted to overcome the factors causing communication barriers and these include:

(i) Be prepared before communicating the message to the receiver.

(ii) The message should not be communicated fast so sufficient time must be taken to communicate the message correctly to the receiver.

(iii) It is better to use simplified language with easily understood words and simple ideas.

(iv) There should be mutual respect for each other by the sender and the receiver for a message to be successfully communicated.

3 Explain the principle of conciseness and correctness in detail.

Ans.
- **Conciseness** It means communicating what you want to convey in the least possible words so that there are no unnecessary bits of information in it. A concise communication is both time-saving as well as cost-saving. It highlights the main message, thus making it more appealing and comprehensible to the audience.
- **Correctness** It implies that there are no grammatical, spelling or punctuation errors in the communication being sent. The message should also be sent at the correct time. A correct message has a greater impact on the receiver if the facts and figures mentioned in the communication are also accurate and true.

4 What are the various methods of communication? Describe them in one sentence each with examples.

Ans. The various methods of communication are:

(i) **Verbal** This is communication through spoken and written words such as making sounds, using language and changing tone of voice etc.

(ii) **Non-verbal** It consists various non-verbal cues such as physical movements, gestures, colours, signs, symbols, body language etc., to express feelings, attitudes or information.

(iii) **Visual** It conveys ideas and information in forms that can be seen, such as facial expressions, personal appearance, gesture, posture, printed picture, sign, signal, symbol, map, poster etc.

5 In a communication cycle, explain the term 'medium'. What problems may the medium create and how? **Competency Based Qus.**

Ans. In a communication cycle, the term 'medium' means the channel through which the message is sent.

Some messages are more effective if sent through the medium of being in written form, others may be more effective if given verbally on the telephone, while some others may be more effective if sent *via* the electronic media such as e-mail. The medium may create a problem such as noise, which may interfere with the communication.

The noise introduced may cause misunderstanding of the message or even disrupt the message completely so that it is not even received.

6 Describe the three types of barriers to communication in one sentence each with examples.

Ans. The three types of barriers to communication are:

(i) **Physical** These are environmental factors which prevent or reduce the sending and receiving of communications, such as physical distance, distracting noises and similar interferences.

(ii) **Personal** These cause a psychological distance between people similar to the physical distance, as they include judgements, emotions and social values of people, which change or distort the communication.

(iii) **Semantic** These barriers refer to symbols or visuals used in the message, such as those related to languages, pictures and actions.

7 Which principle of effective communication is covered by the five question method? List three aspects of this principle which need to be covered by these questions. **Competency Based Qus.**

Ans. The communication principle of 'Completeness' is covered by the five question method. Three aspects of this principle which need to be covered by these questions are:

(i) The message should convey all the information required by the receiver.

(ii) Nothing which may be required by the receiver should be left out of the message.

(iii) The sender of the message must take into consideration the requirements of the receiver while making the message.

8 Describe, by giving some examples of each, the following three parts of speech: pronoun, adverb and conjunction.

Ans. The three parts of speech are described below:

(i) **Pronoun** It is usually substituted for a specific noun, which is called its antecedent, such as he, yourself, we, my etc. The types of pronouns are personal, possessive, reflexive, relative and demonstrative.

(ii) **Adverb** It describes or modifies a verb, an adjective, or another adverb, but never a noun. Instances of adverbs are loudly, yesterday, fast, slowly etc. It usually answers the questions of when, where, how, why, under what conditions, or to what degree.

(iii) **Conjunction** It joins words, phrases, or clauses and indicates the relationship between them. Instances of conjunctions are and, but, or etc.

9 List two best practices for effective communication. **SQP 2023-24, SQP 2024-25**

Ans.
1. Use simple language
2. Be respectful of others' opinions
3. Do not form assumptions on culture, religion or geography
4. Try to communicate in person as much as possible
5. Use visuals
6. Take help of a translator to overcome differences in language.

10. If you are a team leader of a team of 20 people in an organization, mention any two methods that you will use for effective communication with your team members. **2025**

Ans. Effective Communication Methods for a Team Leader (20 people):

- **Regular Team Meetings** Provide a platform for open discussion, updates, and addressing concerns.
- **One-on-One Check-ins** Allow for personalized communication, feedback, and addressing individual needs.

SELF ASSESSMENT

Multiple Choice Questions

1. .... is an instance of visual communication.
   (a) An e-mail (b) A speech
   (c) Eye contact (d) Bar chart
2. Which of the following is not a factor causing a barrier in oral communication?
   (a) Preconceived notions (b) Physical hearing problem
   (c) Emotions (d) Semantics
3. Which of the following skills are essential for working in an organisation?
   (a) Stress (b) Communication
   (c) Good communication (d) None of these
4. Which of the following is an important step that helps in collection of information from the receiver?
   (a) Information (b) Message
   (c) Feedback (d) Data
5. A .... feedback follows a preset format or structure using which the receiver frames and sends it.
   (a) Formal (b) Informal
   (c) Descriptive (d) Non-descriptive
6. A .... feedback is spontaneously framed and does not have a specific structure.
   (a) Formal (b) Informal
   (c) Descriptive (d) Non-descriptive

Very Short Answer Type Questions

7. What is a semantic barrier to communication?
8. What is the function of an adjective in a sentence?

Short Answer Type Questions

9. Differentiate between negative and positive feedback.
10. Explain the difference between specific feedback and non-specific feedback by giving examples of each.
11. Write a typical paragraph containing five sentences on the topic 'The power of money' which fulfils all the requirements of a good paragraph.
12. Explain the types of barriers to effective communication in detail.

Self Management Skills-II

CHAPTER 02

Self-management is our ability to regulate emotions and control actions and behaviours. Strong self-management skills prevent us from missing deadlines and help us navigate workplace conflicts. Simply put, self-management is about preparing for the future, not just acting in the present.

Self-management, also referred to as **self-control**, is the ability to control one's emotions, thoughts and behaviour effectively in different situations. This also includes motivating oneself, and setting goals.

To perform well at work and life in general, you must be able to manage and improve yourself in various skills including discipline and timeliness, goal-setting, problem solving, teamwork, professionalism, etc.

2.1 Stress

Stress is identified as a condition in which a person is tensed and worried. It can affect both our body and mind. People having large amounts of stress can become tired, sick and unable to concentrate or think clearly. Sometimes they even suffer mental breakdown or what is called **burn out**.

Stress is our body's way of responding to any kind of demand. Stress can cause symptoms such as cold hands or feet, increased sweating, a nervous stomach, a dry mouth etc. These are all short-term symptoms of stress. It can be caused by both good and bad experiences.

When people feel stressed by something going on around them, their bodies react by releasing chemicals into the blood. These chemicals give more energy and strength, which can be a good thing if their stress is caused by physical danger but it can also be a bad thing, if the stress is in response to something emotional and there is no outlet for this extra energy and strength. The good stress is called **Eustress**, whereas the bad stress is termed as **Distress**.

2.2 Stress Management

Stress management refers to focusing human efforts for maintaining a healthy body and mind capable of better with standing stressful situations. Stress refers to a physical, mental or emotional strain or tension. Small amount of stress have a positive effect and they help us stretch ourselves to a new level.

Always keep in mind the ABC of stress management

A: Adversity or the stressful event

B: Beliefs or the way you respond to the event

C: Consequences or actions and outcomes of the event

Steps to Manage Stress are

Step 1: Be aware that you are stressed

Step 2: Identify what is causing you stress

Step 3: Apply stress management methods

Importance of Stress Management

Stress management is critical for dealing with challenges and setbacks. It helps people bounce back from failure and forge ahead.

- **For a better life** Learning stress management skills and applying them to everyday life helps a person take control of his or her life. Handling stress effectively builds a positive outlook. A solution oriented approach helps in overcoming problems and living a better life.
- **To improve health** Constantly being under stress affects your health. It makes you prone to various diseases and accelerates your aging process.

Research shows that stressed individuals age faster than those who are stress free. Stress also causes weight gain and obesity. It is important to identify and treat stress at an early stage in order to lead a healthy life.

- **To enhance performance** Stress at work has become common in today's fast paced world. Workplace stress hampers one's ability to perform well and succeed.

  Workplace stress may lead to emotional burnout, low self-esteem or a feeling of worthlessness. It can also impact your career growth. Hence, believe in the importance of stress management in an organisation and take necessary steps to reduce stress. Don't be stressed about things that are beyond your control.

- **To improve communication** Once you start handling stress, everything falls in place. Stress management starts untangling your problems. Your communication process improves. You open up more and try to express your feelings. Misunderstanding are cleared.

Stress Management Techniques

They are shown in the diagram below:

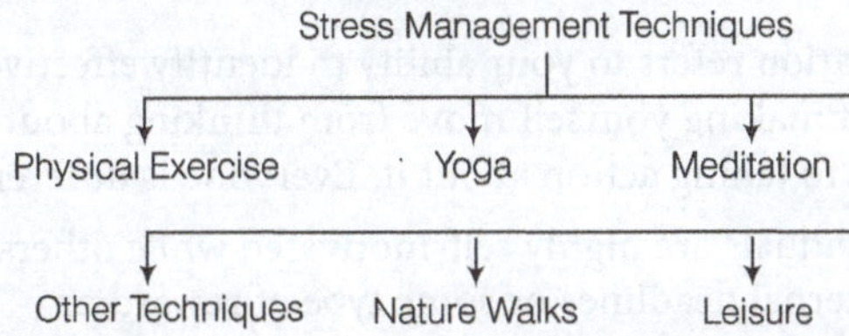

- **Physical Exercise** It is an activity done to achieve physical fitness and overall health. It improves blood circulation, lowers blood pressure, clears the mind of worrying thoughts, improves our self-image, makes us feel better about ourselves and increases social contact. It also has some direct stress-busting benefits which pumps up endorphins-chemicals in the brain that act as a natural pain killers. It also improves the ability to sleep which in turn reduces stress.
- **Yoga** Yoga is a mind-body practice that combines physical poses, controlled breathing and meditation or relaxation. It will help in stress management by relaxing the body and mind, develop a connection between the mind and the body, releasing emotional energy and helping to breathe more effectively.
- **Meditation** In meditation, we change from our normal activities to silence. We go beyond the noisy thoughts in the mind and enter a state of restful alertness. During meditation, although we are in a state of deep rest, our mind is fully alert and awake.

  At this time, the body experiences many healing effects which are the reverse of the 'fight-or-flight' response, such as decreased heart rate, normalisation of blood pressure, deeper breathing, reduced production of stress hormones, higher immunity, more efficient use of oxygen by the body and reduced inflammation.
- **Leisure** This means spending holidays with your family and friends, travelling to other areas in the country or outside and any other similar activities. Leisure gives you the benefits of enabling you to indulge in your interests or hobbies, gives you a 'break' from stress, provides an outlet for relief and also provides social contact.
- **Nature Walks** It means walking in the local park or similar such activity. These walks may be done more than once a day for short periods of time during which we indulge in 'thought-stopping', i.e. not to think about our day-to-day activities. Such an activity will help us to avoid 'burn out', promote adequate sleep, ease muscle tension and decrease mental worries.
- **Other Techniques** These include getting adequate sleep, which is a good stress reducer. When we wake refreshed after a night's sleep, we have adequate day time energy.

  Progressive relaxation and contraction of the body parts will effectively reduce tension, lower the blood pressure, combat fatigue, promote sleep, reduce pain, ease muscle tension, decrease mental worries and also increase productivity, concentration and clear thinking.

Try These 2.1

1. **Worrying about matters, we can do nothing about or worrying for no reason at all is a sign of ....**
2. **Spending holidays with our family and friends to manage stress may be called as what?**
3. **Stress can be caused by both .... and .... experiences.**
4. **Too much sweating, shivering, biting your nails etc., are signs of what?**

2.3 Ability to Work Independently

One of the abilities that we require to develop in us is that of working independently. For doing this, we have to become a self-aware, self-motivated and self-regulating independent person.

A good way to start becoming independent is by carefully thinking about our own learning style. We should find out whether

- We prefer working independently or we need a more structured environment to work efficiently.
- We are self-motivated or we need regular feedback in order to make progress in our work.
- We work best at our own pace or we need to be prodded by others to work faster.
- We know what it means to be independent.

Necessary Skills for Independent Working

From the above, we can understand that some skills are required for developing an independent working style. These are:

- Becoming self-aware, self-monitoring and self-correcting.
- Knowing what we need to do.
- Taking the initiative rather than waiting to be told what to do.
- Doing what is asked to the best of our ability, without the need for external prodding and working until the job is completed.
- Learning to work at a pace that we can sustain for a long time.
- Taking ownership of our mistakes without looking for excuses.
- Refusing to let self-doubt or negative emotions due to negative past experiences take us away from the task.

Thus, the key to being independent is our self-awareness, self-motivation and self-regulation.

2.4 Self-awareness

Self-awareness refers to our knowledge and understanding of ourselves. It includes our emotions, beliefs, assumptions, biases, knowledge base, abilities, motivations, interests etc., So, we should make a conscious effort to learn about ourselves, i.e. our abilities, beliefs, likes and dislikes. The feeling of self-awareness enhances our self-confidence.

Types of Self-awareness

There are two types of self-awareness as follows

1. Internal Self-awareness

Internal self-awareness is about focusing on your inner values. The emotions, values, goals, aspirations, everything which we possess in our inner feelings. Behaviours, thoughts, our weaknesses and strength which help us present our views and feel in a certain way. These things come under the category of internal self-awareness.

2. External Self-awareness

External self-awareness deals with our feelings and behaviour with others. It is the ability to look at others. This awareness helps you decide what others think about you. If you can judge whether a person is happy with you or not, then you have better external self-awareness. It certainly makes a person more effective in paying attention to others.

Developing Self-awareness

There are four areas of self-awareness that you should continously develop

1. **About Your Strengths** To find out your strengths, find out what you like to do, what you are enthusiastic about doing and what work done by you is given good comments by others.
2. **About Your Weaknesses** If you know what you find difficult to do or cannot do, you can ask other people to help you in that task. Otherwise you can remove this weakness by learning that particular task.
3. **About Your Flaws** You should not hide your flaws but take other people's help in overcoming them.
4. **About Your Emotional Problems** A typical emotional problem is getting angry on small matters. Such emotional problems in your character should be kept under control when some incident triggers them.

2.5 Self-motivation

Self-motivation refers to your ability to identify effective methods of making yourself move from thinking about something to taking action about it. Everyone is different.

Some individuals are highly self-motivated while others require external deadlines or some type of reward or penalty in order to move from thought to action. Identifying your specific needs in this area is the first step.

A common barrier to action is often the perception that a task is too large or too complex to accomplish. If that is an issue for you, then a useful practice is to break down the job into several smaller and easier tasks, each of which can be accomplished in a set time period.

Types of Motivation

1. **Internal Motivation** Internal motivation refers to the drive that comes from within an individual. It is based on personal desires, interests, values, and goals.

   Examples pursuing activities because they are inherently enjoyable or fulfilling, striving for personal growth and self-improvement, and engaging in tasks that align with one's passions and aspirations.
2. **External Motivation** External motivation refers to the drive that arises from outside sources such as rewards, recognition, or pressure from others.

   Examples working towards a promotion or salary increase, seeking approval or praise from others, or avoiding punishment or negative consequences.

Developing Self-motivation

There are four steps for building self-motivation, which are as given below.

1. **Find out your strengths** Identify your strength to about your likes or dislikes and what makes you happy and sad.
2. **Set and focus on your goals** Define the goals that you want to achieve and focus all your energy to achieve your goal.
3. **Develop a plan to achieve your goals** Develop a plan and set timelines to achieve your goals and plan a list of activities that you will do to achieve each goal.
4. **Stay loyal to your goals** For achieving your goals stay loyal to work, even when you are facing difficult time.

2.6 Self-regulation

Self-regulation focuses on your ability to influence personal and professional improvement based on your self-awareness and motivation. Useful questions you should ask yourself in an effort to self-regulate yourself are:

- Who will directly supervise or guide in my project? With what frequency (daily, weekly etc.)?
- What are the deadlines, if any, relevant to my project?
- What are the requirements, if any, for my project? These might include progress reports, oral presentations, a final written report or any other documents?
- What are the outcomes that I desire from my participation in this project? What, if anything, do I need to do in order to achieve these outcomes?

Goal Setting

It is all about finding and listing your goals and then planning on how to achieve them. Goals allow you to separate out what's important. It helps you to focus on the end result instead of less important work. This will make you successful in your career and personal life.

We can use SMART method to set goals. SMART stands for:

- **Specific:** Well defined, clear, and unambiguous
- **Measurable:** With specific criteria that measure your progress toward the accomplishment of the goal
- **Achievable:** Attainable and not impossible to achieve
- **Realistic:** Within reach, realistic, and relevant to your life purpose
- **Timely:** With a clearly defined timeline, including a starting date and a target date. The purpose is to create urgency.

Time Management

Time management is the ability to plan and control how you spend the hours of your day well and do all that you want to do.

Steps for Effective Time Management are

1. **Organize** Plan your day-to-day activities and make a timetable that you follow.
2. **Priorities** You make a to-do list that has all your activities and you rank them in the order of importance. It helps you to get the most important task done first and also to track what is pending.
3. **Control** You have a control over your activities and time.
4. **Track** You identify and note where you have spent your time. This will help you analyse if you have used your time effectively or not. It also helps you to identify time-wasting activities

Try These 2.2

1 **What is a necessary skill for independent working?**

2 **Name a kind of self-awareness.**

3 **We should not hide our .... but take other people's .... in overcoming them.**

4 **What is the key to be able to work independently?**

Glossary

Stress is our body's way of responding to any kind of demand and can be caused by both good and bad experiences.

Self-awareness means our knowledge and understanding of our strengths, weaknesses, flaws and emotions.

Self-motivation is our ability to identify effective methods of making ourselves move from thinking about something to taking action about it.

Self-regulation is our ability to influence personal and professional improvement based on our self-awareness and motivation.

ACTIVITY Time

ACTIVITY 1

Role Play on Avoiding Stressful Situation

Material required

Pen, notepad or sheets of paper

Procedure

- Form groups of three.
- Choose any one situation from below.
- Prepare a skit (role play) and perform within your groups.
- Two members will perform the skit and one member will observe and share feedback.

Situation 1

You have missed your school bus and you are getting late. What will you do? Will you panic or call for help or try to find a way?

Situation 2

You have to perform your best in the next cricket or badminton match so you get a chance to play for your school at the national level cricket or badminton tournament. You have been anxious (worried or stressed). Will you lose your sleep worrying about it or will you go to the field and practice?

ACTIVITY 2

Self-reflection

Material required

Pen or pencil

Procedure

- Complete the below table by listing the situation(s) that can cause stress and what will you do to avoid stress in such situations.
- Use the stress management techniques shared in the lesson to complete the exercise.

Stress Causing Situation(s)	Stress Management Techniques

ACTIVITY 3

Benefits of taking a holiday

Material required

Pen or pencil

Procedure

- Write an essay to describe the place and your experience during a holiday trip or summer camp.
- Highlight how the trip helped you de-stress.

ACTIVITY 4

Pair Activity: Aim in Life

Material required

Pen, notepad or sheets of paper

Procedure

- Form pairs of students.
- Each student will make a list of things that they can do well based on the given format.
- Share your notes with your partner.
- One volunteer from the pair comes and reads, in front of the class.

Here is the format for you to fill in

I am ______________________

I can (abilities) ______________________

I will (plan) ______________________

My aim is ______________________

ACTIVITY 5

Individual Activity: Interests and Abilities Worksheet

Material required

Student textbooks, pen

Procedure

- Each student has to complete the given worksheet, containing a list of statements and questions.

- Each student has to be real and honest when filling the worksheet as it is for their own understanding of themselves.
- If they are not real and honest, they will get incorrect results about their own interests and abilities.

Worksheet - My Interests and Abilities

I am happiest when
My idea of a perfect day
Five things I really enjoy doing
Three things I like to do every day
I am most passionate about
Ideas or issues I care deeply about
If I had the talent or ability, I would
If I could choose any job, it would be
The three activities that I love to do?
How often do I do them?

ACTIVITY 6

Staying Motivated (Group Discussion)

Material required

Pen, notepad or sheets of paper, chart paper

Procedure

- Form groups of three.
- Choose any one of the following situation and write down the steps you would take to motivate yourself.
- Your teacher gives you feedback on the essay you had written. There are a lot negative remarks. What will you do to motivate yourself to improve the essay?
- Your father has given you the responsibility of arranging for a birthday party for your little sister who is turning 3 years old. You do not want to do this task. How will you motivate yourself to do the work?

ACTIVITY 7

SMART Goal or Not (Group Work)

Materials required

Pen, notepad or sheets of paper

Procedure

- Indicate whether the below mentioned goals are SMART or not. If they are SMART goals then tick mark against each aspect of SMART.

Goals	Specific (Yes or No)	Measurable (Yes or No)	Achievable (Yes or No)	Realistic (Yes or No)	Time bound (Yes or No)
I want to earn INR 1 crore in my first job.					
I want to become a teacher after my post-graduation.					
I want to travel to many places.					

ACTIVITY 8

Long-term Goals and Short-term Goals (Peer Feedback)

Material required

Pen, notepad or sheets of paper

Procedure

- Form groups of four. Work individually in your group and complete the below table. Once completed, share with your group and seek feedback on your goals. Share your feedback when other members of the groups are presenting their goals.

Short-term Goals (What are your goals in the next 6 months to 2 years?)	Long-term Goals (What are your goals in the next 5 years?)
1.	1.
2.	2.
3.	3.

ACTIVITY 9

Self Reflection

Material required

Pen or pencil

Procedure

- Complete the table below by writing how you will make sure that the goals you set for yourself are SMART. Use the tips shared in the lesson for doing this.

SMART Goals	How will make sure the goals are SMART
Specific	
Measurable	
Achievable	
Realistic	
Time-bound	

ACTIVITY 10

Pair Work: Making a List of Activities

Material required

Pen, notepad or sheets of paper

Procedure

- Form groups of two. Complete the below table with a list of activities that you do on a daily basis. Remember to include in the list, every small activity that you do.
- The next step would be to group them into three types 'Must Do', 'Should Do' and 'Nice to Do'.
- Use a tick mark to indicate the group. An example is given below.
- Once completed share with your partner and discuss each other's table.

List of Activities	Must Do (Urgent and Important tasks)	Should Do (Important Tasks)	Nice to Do (Not Urgent and Not Important)
Complete Homework	✓		
Chat with friends		✓	
Book movie tickets for tomorrow			✓

ACTIVITY 11

Managing your time to reach school on time

Material required

Pen

Procedure

- List out the to-do plan with timing to make sure you reach school on time.

To-do List
1.
2.
3.
4.

NCERT FOLDER

Complete Explanations of all NCERT's Questions

A. Multiple Choice Questions

Q.1 What makes you complete work or studies without others cheering you?

(a) Self-confidence (b) Communication
(c) Self-motivation (d) Self-esteem

Q.2 Which of the following are types of motivation?

(a) Internal (b) Intermediate
(c) External (d) Extensive

Q.3 Ravi works hard to get the best student award at the end of year. What type of motivation is this?

(a) Internal
(b) External
(c) Both internal and external
(d) Not any specific type of motivation

Answers

1. (c) 2. (a,c) 3. (c)

B. Subjective Questions

Q.1 Describe stress and stress management in your own words.

Ans. Stress can be defined as our emotional, mental, physical and social reaction to any perceived demands or threats. Stress management offers a range of ways to help you better deal with stress and difficulty, also called adversity, in your life.

Q.2 List your favorite stress management technique and elaborate why you find it the most effective.

Ans. Some stress management techniques are

- Physical Exercise
- Yoga
- Meditation
- Leisure
- Nature Walks

They are about observing your thoughts, feeling, bodily sensation, and the surrounding environment calmly and without reacting.

Q.3 What is Goal Setting?

Ans. Goal setting is all about finding and listing your goals and then planning on how to achieve them.

Q.4 In SMART goals, what does 'S' stand for? Explain.

Ans. In SMART goals, S refers for Specific, it refers to being as specific as possible with the desired goal.

Q.5 What is time management and how can you manage your time?

Ans. Time management is the ability to plan and control how you spend the hours of your day well and do all that you want to do.

You can manage your time simply by knowing the things that you are going to do from there you will know what time or what are your plans on doing it.

Q.6 How can tracking your time help you?

Ans. Time tracking helps you gain a better insight into how you spend your time, so you can prioritize better.

EXAM PATTERN EXERCISE

Including Competency Based Questions

Part I

Multiple Choice Questions

1 Stress is identified as a condition in which a person is ....

(a) tensed (b) worried
(c) relaxed (d) Both (a) and (b)

2 Physical exercise is used as a stress management technique because

(a) it improves blood circulation
(b) improves self-image
(c) makes us feel better
(d) All of the above

3 Self-awareness refers to

(a) our knowledge and understanding of ourselves
(b) systematic efforts to direct thoughts and actions
(c) ability to identify effective methods to move from thought to action.
(d) None of the above

4 Sonika gets up at 6 am and goes for her hobby classes. Then, she comes back home and finishes her homework before going to school. She does all work by herself. No one tells her to do so. This is called .... Competency Based Que.

(a) self-awareness (b) self-motivation
(c) self-regulation (d) discipline

5 To perform well at work and life in general, you must be able to manage and improve yourself in various skills. Which of the following skills helps you to prioritise the things you have to do remove waste and redundancy from work? Competency Based Que.

(a) Responsibility (b) Time management
(c) Self-awareness (d) Adaptability

6 Which of the following does not help in stress management? 2025

(a) Healthy food (b) Sound sleep
(c) Yoga asanas (d) Negative thoughts

7 We have the ability to work independently, if we ....

(a) need regular feedback to make progress in our work
(b) work best at our own pace
(c) need a structured environment to work efficiently
(d) need to be prodded to work faster

8 High expectations from self can leave one with chronic anxiety and stress, thus leading to .... stress.

(a) physical (b) emotional
(c) mental (d) financial

9 ________ the work is all about identifying and noting how we spent our time, and analysing how to spend our time effectively. SQP 2023-24, SQP 2024-25

(a) Organising (b) Prioritising
(c) Controlling (d) Tracking

10 Which of the following can cause stress? SQP 2022-23

(a) Yoga and meditation
(b) Driving during rush hour
(c) Organised academic life
(d) Enjoying holidays with family

11 ______________ refers to focusing human efforts for maintaining a healthy body and mind capable of better withstanding stressful situations

(a) Mental Health (b) Emotional Health
(c) Self-Management (d) Stress Management

12 **Which of the following is not a step to build self – motivation?** **2025**
(a) Focusing on your goal
(b) Planning to achieve your goal
(c) Being indisciplined
(d) Finding out your strength

13 **SMART method can be used to set goals to make you successful in your career and personal life. What does 'A' in SMART stand for?** **2024**
(a) Abrupt (b) Accountable
(c) Achievable (d) Admirable

14 **Which of the following is not a key element of self-management skills?** **2024**
(a) Prioritizing your work (b) Not taking feedback.
(c) Goal setting
(d) Staying updated about new practices

15 **Stress management is vital because it leads to following benefits:** **2023**
(a) Improves mood (b) Promotes longevity
(c) Boosts immune system (d) All of these

16 **Which of the following is an inner urge to do something, achieve their goals without any external pressure I lure for award or appreciation?** **2023**
(a) Self-awareness (b) Self-motivation
(c) Self-regulation (d) Self-control

Answers

1. (d) 2. (d) 3. (a) 4. (b) 5. (b)
6. (d) 7. (b) 8. (c) 9. (d) 10. (b)
11. (d) 12. (c) 13. (c) 14. (b) 15. (d)
16. (b)

Statement Based Questions

1 **Statement 1: A realistic goal is one that has no timeline or plans for execution.**
Statement 2: Breaking down big goals into smaller parts will make the goal achievable.
(a) Both Statement 1 and Statement 2 are correct
(b) Both Statement 1 and Statement 2 are incorrect
(c) Statement 1 is correct but Statement 2 is incorrect
(d) Statement 1 is incorrect but Statement 2 is correct

2 **Statement 1: Stress can be defined as our emotional, mental, physical and social reaction to any perceived demands or threats.**
Statement 2: Managing stress is about making a plan to be able to cope effectively with daily pressures.
(a) Both Statement 1 and Statement 2 are correct
(b) Both Statement 1 and Statement 2 are incorrect
(c) Statement 1 is correct but Statement 2 is incorrect
(d) Statement 1 is incorrect but Statement 2 is correct

3 **Statement 1: Self-motivation is what pushes us to achieve our goals, feel happy and improve our quality of life.**
Statement 2: We do things because they give us respect, recognition and appreciation are internal motivations.
(a) Both Statement 1 and Statement 2 are correct
(b) Both Statement 1 and Statement 2 are incorrect
(c) Statement 1 is correct but Statement 2 is incorrect
(d) Statement 1 is incorrect but Statement 2 is correct

4 **Statement 1: Goals allow you to separate out what's important.**
Statement 2: Goal setting is all about finding and listing your goals and then planning on how to achieve them.
(a) Both Statement 1 and Statement 2 are correct
(b) Both Statement 1 and Statement 2 are incorrect
(c) Statement 1 is correct but Statement 2 is incorrect
(d) Statement 1 is incorrect but Statement 2 is correct

Answers

1. (d) 2. (a) 3. (c) 4. (a)

Assertion & Reason Based Questions

1 **Assertion (A) A specific goal is one that has no timeline or plans for execution.**
Reason (R) Breaking down big goals into smaller parts will make the goal achievable.
(a) Both A and R are correct and R is the correct explanation of A.
(b) Both A and R are correct and R is not the correct explanation of A.
(c) A is correct but R is incorrect.
(d) A is incorrect but R is correct.

2 **Assertion (A) Stress is a symptom, not a disease.**
Reason (R) The immediate outcome of harmful external provocations leads to state of stress causing various diseases.
(a) Both A and R are correct and R is the correct explanation of A.
(b) Both A and R are correct and R is not the correct explanation of A.
(c) A is correct but R is incorrect.
(d) A is incorrect but R is correct.

3 **Assertion (A) Stress is usually thought of as a negative experience, but it can be a positive one.**
Reason (R) Motivation is what pushes us to achieve our goals, feel more fulfilled and improve the overall quality of our life.
(a) Both A and R are correct and R is the correct explanation of A.
(b) Both A and R are correct and R is not the correct explanation of A.
(c) A is correct but R is incorrect.
(d) A is incorrect but R is correct.

Answers

1. (a) 2. (a) 3. (b)

Part II

Very Short Answer Type Questions

1 "M D Gulati started with a small shop with his focus, dedication and clear ideas, MDH became one of the most popular brands in India besides having a good reputation all over the world". Which self-management skill is clearly visible in the given statement? SQP 2024-25, Competency Based Ques.

Ans. Self-Motivation

2 Pranjali gets up at 5 am and goes to her badminton classes. Then, she comes home and finishes her homework before going to school. She does this all by herself. No one tells her to do it. What is this an example of? Competency Based Ques.

Ans. Self-motivation

3 There was a young boy who was fond of playing football and wanted to become a football player. He joined a football academy and came regularly to practice but never made it to the team. For four days, the boy didn't show up for practice. The matches had begun and his team was playing the finals. He showed up for the finals. He went up to the coach and pleaded him to let him play for the match. The coach had never seen the boy plead like this before. The Game started and the boy played like a ball on fire. Every time he got the ball, he shot a goal. Needless to say, he was the star of the game and his team won. What type of motivation did the boy demonstrate? Competency Based Ques.

Ans. Internal

4 What happens when people have large amounts of stress?

Ans. People having large amounts of stress can become tired, sick and unable to concentrate clearly. Sometimes they even suffer from mental breakdown.

5 What are the symptoms of stress?

Ans. Stress can cause symptoms such as cold hands or feet, tenseness, increased sweating, day mouth etc. These are all short-term symptoms of stress.

6 How leisure activities benefits in stress management?

Ans. Leisure gives the benefits by enabling a person to indulge in his/her interests, hobbies, gives them a break and provides an outlet for relief.

7 How can a person manage stress?

Ans. With proper planning and use of the right techniques, stress can be reduced or managed to remain within tolerable limits.

8 What should we do when we become aware of our flaws?

Ans. When we become aware of our flaws, we should not hide them, but take other people's help in overcoming them.

9 What are the personal signs of stress?

Ans. We must understand our own personal signs of stress and some signs may be too much sweating, shivering, biting nails, lack of concentration, poor judgement, constant worrying etc.

10 How can we become self-aware about our strengths?

Ans. We can become self-aware about our strengths by finding out what we like to do, what we are enthusiastic about doing and what work done by us is given good comments by others.

Short Answer Type Questions

1 Why is self-regulation important in life?

Ans. Self-regulation is important in life due to following reasons:

(i) Self-regulation allows you to keep a tab on your own emotions.

(ii) Self-regulation enables to develop the idea about 'what is appropriate behaviour' and 'what is inappropriate behaviour' in a given social condition.

(iii) It helps in controlling negative impulses and reciprocate emotions for actualising set goals.

2 How can we self-motivate ourselves for completing a task which appears to be too large or too complex to be done by us? Competency Based Ques.

Ans. For completing a task which appears to be too large or too complex to be done by us, we can break down the job into several smaller and easier tasks, each of which can be accomplished in a set time period.

This is possible only through self-motivating ourselves to find a workable solution to the task, as self-motivation is our ability to identify effective methods of thinking about something to taking action about it.

Breaking down the job into smaller tasks comprises the thinking part, whereas accomplishing each small part of the task comprises the 'taking action' part.

3 What is the importance of setting goals in life? SQP 2023-24, SQP 2024-25

Ans.
1. The process of goal setting in your life helps you decide on how to live your life, where you want to be, and how you want to be in the future.
2. It helps you to focus on the end result instead of less important work.
3. This will make you successful in your career and personal life.

4 In SMART goals, what does 'A' stand for? Explain. SQP 2022-23

Ans. In SMART goals, A refers for Achievable, it means breaking down big goals into smaller parts will make the goal achievable.

For example, Bigger Goal: "I want to become a teacher in my school."
Breaking it into smaller goals:
Complete higher secondary
Complete Graduation
Complete B.Ed.
Apply for jobs in the teaching field

5 Sameera is always punctual at school. She has a regular schedule that she follows every day. She plans for study and play time in advance. Enlist the four steps, Sameera must have followed for effective time management. Competency Based Ques.

Ans. The four steps of effective time management which Sameera must have followed are: (i) Organise (ii) Prioritise (iii) Control (iv) Track

6 What is the importance of time management in effectively dealing with stress? Provide any one strategy for improving time management skills to reduce stress. 2024

Ans. Good time management skills increase your productivity and help you get more done. Time management skills help you reduce stress and prioritise your time. Effective time management clarifies your goals and prioritises your most important tasks.

Prioritizing tasks: By identifying the most important tasks and focusing on them first, you can avoid feeling overwhelmed by a long to-do list.

7 How does mediation help in Managing Stress? Discuss briefly. 2023

Ans. In meditation, we change from our normal activities to silence. We go beyond the noisy thoughts in the mind and enter a state of restful alertness. During meditation, although we are in a state of deep rest, our mind is fully alert and awake.

At this time, the body experiences many healing effects which are the reverse of the 'fight-or-flight' response, such as decreased heart rate, normalisation of blood pressure, deeper breathing, reduced production of stress hormones, higher immunity, more efficient use of oxygen by the body and reduced inflammation.

8 Mention any two benefits of working independently. 2023

Ans. **Flexibility and autonomy** Independent work allows individuals to set their own schedules and work on their own terms.

Creativity and innovation Working independently fosters an environment where individuals can explore new ideas and solutions without the constraints of traditional structures.

9 What are the techniques that are used to manage stress?

Ans. Following are the techniques that are used to manage stress and they are as follows :

(i) **Physical Exercise** It improves blood circulation, lowers the blood pressure, clears the mind of worrying thoughts, improves our self-image and makes us feel better about ourselves.

(ii) **Yoga** It helps in relaxing mind and body by developing a connection between the mind and body, releasing emotional energy and helping to breathe more effectively.

(iii) **Meditation** At this time, body experiences many healing effects which are reverse of 'fight or flight' response, such as decreased heart rate, reduced production of stress hormones, higher immunity and reduced inflammation.

(iv) **Leisure** Leisure gives you benefits of enabling you to indulge in your interests or hobbies, gives you a break from stress, provides an outlet for relief and also provides social contact.

(v) **Nature Walks** It promotes adequate sleep, ease muscle tension and decrease mental worries.

10. Explain the importance of following a healthy lifestyle in effectively dealing with stress .Write any one common factor that causes stress among the children now-a-days . 2025

Ans. Importance of a Healthy Lifestyle in Dealing with Stress:

- **Physical Health** Exercise releases endorphins, improving mood and reducing stress hormones.
- **Mental Clarity** Proper nutrition and sleep enhance cognitive function, making it easier to manage stressors.
- **Resilience** A healthy lifestyle builds resilience, making you better equipped to handle challenges.

Common Stress Factor Among Children Now-a-days

- **Academic Pressure** High expectations and competition in school create significant stress.

SELF ASSESSMENT

Multiple Choice Questions

1. Which one of the following is not a leisure activity?
   (a) Getting adequate sleep.
   (b) Spending holidays with family and friends.
   (c) Travelling to other areas.
   (d) Indulging in your interests or hobbies.
2. Which of the following skills are not required for developing an independent working style?
   (a) Taking ownership of our mistakes.
   (b) Waiting to be told what to do.
   (c) Knowing what we need to do.
   (d) Learning to work at a sustainable pace.
3. What are the six W's of a SMART goal?
   (a) Who, what, when, why, will, where
   (b) Who, what, when, where, will, why
   (c) Who, what, when, where, why, which
   (d) Who, what, we, where, which, why
4. What is the purpose of a SMART Goal?
   (a) To have fun
   (b) To know exactly what you are working toward
   (c) To waste time
   (d) To keep you out of trouble

Very Short Answer Type Questions

5. What is self management? How is it different from management?
6. What changes in the body does progressive relaxation and contraction of the body parts bring?
7. What is the first step in getting self-motivated?
8. Why is self-motivation important?

Short Answer Type Questions

9. How is internal motivation different from external motivation? Explain two such differences.
10. What are the questions we should ask ourselves, if we want to self-regulate ourselves? List three such questions.
11. What are the necessary skills required for independent working?
12. How can we identify stress? Explain.

CHAPTER 03

ICT Skills-II

ICT skills help us to communicate, run our business and stay connected with our family and friends. Hence, every person needs to acquire ICT skills and build them to stay updated with the latest softwares and applications.

The basic ICT skills that you need are knowing how to

- operate computers.
- browse the Internet for collecting, storing and disseminating information.

3.1 Introduction to Operating System

Operating System (OS) is the system software that performs all the basic tasks of a computer system. It works like an interface between the user and the computer hardware resources. It actually controls the execution of all the tasks that are performed in a computer.

Some examples of operating systems are Unix, MS-DOS, Windows 98/2000/XP etc. It enables a user to utilise hardware resources very efficiently. So, operating system makes it easy for a user to use computer system.

"An operating system is a collection of programs that controls and coordinates all the tasks and functions in a computer system. It mediates between application programs and hardware components."

Types of Operating System

Types	Features
Time Sharing Operating System	• In this OS, a small amount of time is allocated for the processing simultaneously. • It provides scheduling to each process to be run on. e.g. Mac OS
Real-Time Operating System	• It was designed to respond to an event within a predetermined time. • It aims to execute real time applications such as auto pilot mechanism used in aircrafts. • It has very little user-interface capability and no end-user utilities. e.g. Windows CE, QNX, RTLINUX, Vx Works, Free RTOS, etc.
Single-User Operating System	• It is designed for one user to effectively use a computer at a time. e.g. Windows 95/NT/2000, DOS, etc.
Multi-User Operating System	• It allows many users to take advantage of the computer's resources simultaneously. • It ensures that problem with one user doesn't affect the entire community of users. e.g. Unix, VMS, Linux, Windows 2000, etc.
Single-Tasking Operating System	• It allows only a single program to run at a time. e.g. Palm OS, etc.
Multi-Programming Operating System	• It allows to run several programs at a time using time sharing. • This operating system keeps several jobs in memory at a time. e.g. Linux, Unix, etc.
Multi-Tasking Operating System	• This operating system is the logical extension of multi-programming operating system. • In this OS, more than one processes can be executed concurrently. • It reduces CPU idle time. e.g. Microsoft's Windows and Apple's Mac OS.

Types	Features
Distributed Operating System	• It uses multiple central processors to serve multiple real time applications. • It manages a group of independent computers and makes them appear to a single computer. • Data processing jobs are distributed among the processors according to their efficiency. e.g. LOCUS etc.
Batch-Processing Operating System	• Similar types of jobs are grouped under batch and these batches are executed without user's interruption. • Jobs are processed in the order of submission, i.e. on First Come First Serve (FCFS) basis. e.g. DOS, IBM OS/2, etc.
Multi-Processing Operating System	• Use of two or more CPUs within a single computer system. • Simultaneous processing of two or more programs by multiple processors. e.g. Linux, Unix, Windows 2000, etc.

Operating Systems for Desktop and Laptop

Some commonly used operating systems for desktop and laptop are as follows :

UNIX

It is an operating system which was first developed in the 1969s. UNIX systems have a Graphical User Interface (GUI) similar to different Microsoft Windows which provides an easy way to use platform. It supports fully multi-tasking with protected memory which means multiple users can run multiple programs at the same time without interfering with each other or crashing the system.

UNIX was one of the first operating system to be written in a high level programming language, namely C. This meant that it could be installed on virtually any computer for which a C compiler existed.

Linux

It is an open source operating system designed primarily for the PCs and laptops. Linux was designed considering Unix compatibility. Its functionality list is quite similar to that of Unix. One of the most valued advantage of Linux over the other platforms lies with the high security levels. It is a virus free operating system.

Mac OS (Apple Macintosh)

It is an operating system which was introduced on March 24, 2001 by Apple Inc and was initially named as system software, which was later renamed as Mac OS.
One drawback of this system is that it can only be run on Apple produced products.

MS-Windows

It is a series of Graphical User Interface (GUI) operating systems developed, marketed and sold by Microsoft. Microsoft introduced an operating environment named Windows on November 20, 1985 as an add-on to MS-DOS in response to the growing interest in Graphical User Interfaces.

The most popular versions of Windows for personal computers, mobile devices and server computers are as follows :

(a) **Windows NT** (New Technology) The first version of Windows NT was Windows NT 3.1 released on July 27, 1993 by Microsoft. It is a processor independent, multi-processing and multi-user operating system.

(b) **Windows 95** It was developed in August, 1995 by Microsoft. It is an operating system based on consumer oriented application. Although, it can run older Windows and DOS applications. It has essentially removed DOS as a underlying platform.

(c) **Windows 98** It was released in 1998 by Microsoft. It was produced in two main versions, i.e. the first version was plagued with programming errors but the second edition (which came out later) was much better with many errors resolved.

(d) **Windows 2000** It was released in February, 2000 by Microsoft. A better version of the Windows NT OS, that works well both at home and as a workstation in a business.

(e) **Windows ME** (Millennium Edition) It was released in September, 2000 by Microsoft. An upgraded version of Windows 98 but it has been historically plagued with programming errors, which may be frustrating for home users. It includes Internet Explorer 5.5, Windows Media Player 7.

(f) **Windows XP** (eXPerience) It was released on October 25, 2001 by Microsoft. It is an OS produced for personal computers. Two versions of Windows XP are Windows XP Home Edition and Windows XP Professional Edition.

(g) **Windows Vista** It was released on January, 2007 by Microsoft. It offers an advancement in reliability , security, ease of deployment, performance and manageability over Windows XP.

(h) **Windows 7** It was released on July 22, 2009 by Microsoft. It is an upgrade of Windows XP and Vista. It does not include some standard applications like Windows Movie Maker, Windows Mail, etc. Now-a-days, it is the most commonly used operating system.

(i) **Windows 8** It was released on August 1, 2012 by Microsoft. It introduced major changes to the operating system's platform and user interface to improve its user experience on tablets, where Windows was now competing with Mobile OS, including Android and iOS.

(j) **Windows 10** It was released to manufacturing in July, 2015 by Microsoft. It is a personal computer operating system as a part of the Windows NT family of operating systems.

Solaris

It is a free operating system originally developed by Sun Microsystems in 1992. Oracle Solaris, as it is now known and owned by Oracle Corporation since Oracle's acquisitions of Sun in January 2010.

Solaris is known for its scalability, reduced cost, protected investments in applications. It is a standard operating system with excellent performance, system management and network functions.

MS-DOS (Microsoft-Disk Operating System)

It is an operating system that runs on PC and developed by IBM corporation in 1981. It was the most commonly used member of the DOS family of operating system.

Initially, MS-DOS was targeted at Intel 8086 processors running on computer hardware using floppy disks to store and access not only the operating system, but application software and user data as well.

Operating Systems for Mobile Phone and Tablets

It is an OS that operates on smartphones, tablets and digital mobile devices. A mobile OS controls a mobile device and its design supports wireless communication and different types of mobile applications. It has built-in support for mobile multimedia formats. The most common operating systems for mobile phone and tablets are as follows :

Android

It is the most popular Linux based open source software developed by Google in September, 2008. It is basically designed for touch screen mobile devices like tablets, smartphones, etc. Now-a-days, it is most common OS used in mobile phones.

iOS

It is the popular mobile operating system developed by Apple Incorporation. iOS was introduced on June 29, 2007 when the first iPhone was developed. This operating system is commonly used in Apple iPhone, iPod Touch, iPad, Second Generation Apple TV, etc.

BlackBerry

This is the most secure operating system used in leading smartphones developed by BlackBerry company. BlackBerry was introduced on January 19, 1999. It also supports WAP 1.2.

Symbian

Symbian is an open source mobile OS. It was developed on 5th June, 1997 and sold by Symbian Ltd. It is a mobile OS targeted at mobile phones that offer a high level of integration with communication and Personal Information Management (PIM) functionality. It has been used by many major handset manufacturers including Motorola, Nokia, Samsung, Sony, etc.

3.2 User Interface

The user interface is one of the most important parts of any operating system because it allows users to easily access the applications and the hardware. It is set of commands or menus. The user can interact with the computer by using mainly two kinds of interfaces:

1. **Character User Interface (CUI)** This is a mechanism of interacting with a computer system or software by typing commands to perform specific tasks. Programs with Character User Interface are generally easier to automate via scripting. CUI only uses text types one after another. It is also known as Command Line Interface (CLI).
2. **Graphical User Interface (GUI)** It is used as an interface between program and user. This is a computer program that enables a user to communicate with a computer through the use of symbols, visual metaphors and pointing devices. The first graphical user interface was designed by Xerox Corporation in 1970s. GUIs can be found in hand-held devices such as MP3 players, portable media players, gaming devices, etc.

Try These 3.1

1 **When was Windows 10 operating system released?**
2 **Name any two mobile operating systems.**
3 **What is the full name of GUI?**
4 **iOS is a mobile operating system developed by ....**

3.3 Menu, Icons and Taskbar on the Desktop

Let's discuss about Windows 10 operating system.

Windows 10

Windows 10 is a personal computer operating system developed and released by Microsoft in 2015. It is easy to use social media sites like Facebook and Twitter. Windows 10 will also include a 'game DVR' mode to allow recordings of the last 30 seconds of play, all better for the social gaming. Windows 10 interface is adapted by hardware, it is running on.

Desktop

Desktop is the main screen of the Windows 10 operating system. The background image of desktop is called **wallpaper**. A small arrow or blinking symbol, moving on the desktop is called **cursor**. There are three components as Icons, taskbar and desktop background.

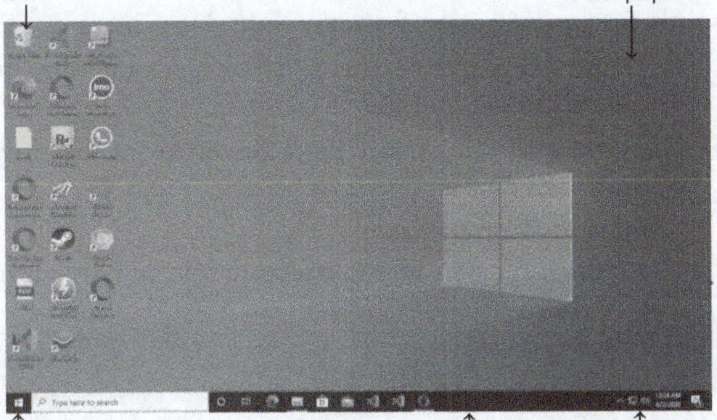

Icons An icon is a picture or graphic representation of an application or a file. If you want to open or access an icon, double click on it.

Taskbar It is present at the bottom of the screen. Its parts are

1. Start menu 2. Opened program 3. Notification area

- **Start Menu** To search for an application, you can also open the Start menu. An alphabetical list of all the applications installed on the computer appears. To open the Start menu, click on Start button. The Windows 10 Start menu has two panes. The left pane displays a list of programs. A **program** is also called an application in Windows 10. The right pane features tiles. A **tile** is an application icon.
- **Notification Area** It is located at the right side of the taskbar. It shows different types of notifications for your computer such as, your Internet connection or the volume level. By default, the notification area shows only a few icons but you can click the upward arrow on its left side to see the other options.

File Concept, File Operations, File Organisation, Directory Structures and File System Structures

Everything you store on your computer is stored in the form of a **file**. File system is a way in which you give name to a file, store it and retrieve it. There are specific naming conventions for naming files or folders, like characters that can be used, maximum number of characters etc.

Files can be separately placed into groups, called folders/directories. Each directory/folder can contain related files and/or sub-folders. A **sub-folder** may contain one or more files and sub-folders within. This allows easy accessibility of files. Files are managed in a hierarchy. This allows you to view the files in the current directory and then move to sub-directories.

3.4 Creating and Managing Files and Folders

Creating a Folder

The steps to create a new folder are as follows

1. Double click on This PC.
2. Select the drive in which you want to create a new folder.
3. Window will open up showing files and folders in Local Disk.
4. Click New Folder on the toolbar.

Or Right click anywhere in the blank area.

A drop-down menu will appear. Select New → Folder.

5. A new folder is created with name New Folder highlighted.
6. Type a name for the folder.

Creating a File

To create a new file, steps are as follows:

1. Right-click anywhere in the blank area.
2. A drop down menu will appear. In the drop down menu, click New and select the type of the file you want to create.

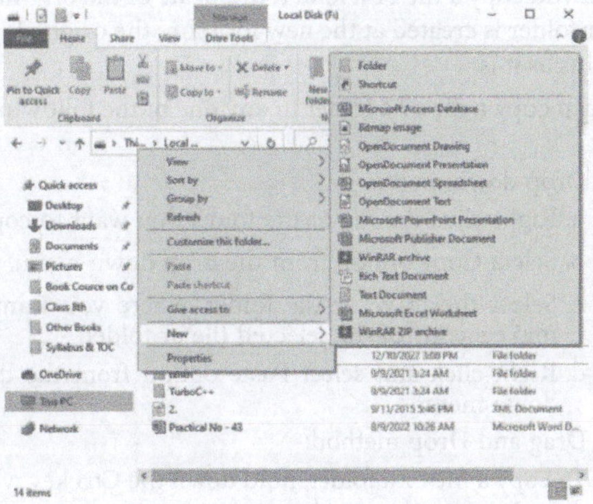

Renaming Folders and Files

To rename a file or a folder, the steps are as follows:

1. Right-click the file or the folder.
2. From the drop down menu, select Rename option.

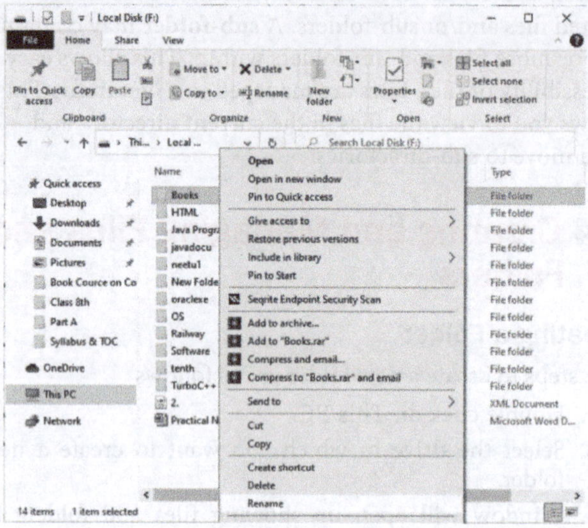

3. Type the new name or edit the existing name and press the Enter key.

Or

Just select the file/folder and press Function key F2.

Deleting Files or Folders

To delete a file or a folder, steps are as follows:

1. Click the file or the folder.
2. Press the Delete key.

Or Right-click and select Delete option from the drop down menu.

Copying Files and Folders

When you copy a file or a folder, duplicate of the original file or folder is created at the new location, the original remains as it is.

You can copy a file or a folder in any one of the following ways:

1. Drop down menu:
   a. Right-click the file or the folder you want to copy.
   b. Select Copy option from the drop down menu.
   c. Select the drive or the folder, where you want to make a copy of the selected file or folder.
   d. Right-click and select Paste option from the drop down menu.
2. Drag and Drop method:

   To copy a file or a folder, hold down the Ctrl key while dragging it to the new location.
3. Using Keyboard:
   a. Select the file or the folder.
   b. Press Ctrl + C to copy the file or the folder.
   c. Open the destination folder.
   d. Press Ctrl + V to paste the copied file.

Moving Files and Folders

When you move a file or a folder, the original file or folder is moved to the new location. You can move a file or a folder in any one of the following ways:

1. Drop down menu:
   a. Right-click the file or the folder you want to move.
   b. Select Cut option from the drop down menu.
   c. Select the drive or the folder where you want to move the selected file or folder.
   d. Right-click and select Paste option from the drop down menu.
2. Drag and Drop method:

   To move a file or a folder, select the file and drag it to a new location.
3. Using Keyboard:
   a. Select the file or the folder.
   b. Press Ctrl + X to cut the file or the folder.
   c. Open the destination folder.
   d. Press Ctrl + V to paste the cutted file.

Permanently Delete Files

You can permanently delete the contents of the Recycle Bin in any one of the following ways:

Right-click the Recycle Bin icon and then click Empty Recycle Bin.

Or

1. Double-click the Recycle Bin icon.
2. The Recycle Bin window will appear.
3. Click Empty the Recycle Bin.

Restore Files/Folder from Recycle Bin Window

To recover a file from the Recycle Bin, right-click the file, and then click Restore.

Or

Select the file and click Restore this item option from the toolbar.

Try These 3.2

1 **What is icon?**
2 **What is sub folder?**
3 **Mention any one way in which you can create a new folder.**
4 **How can you empty the Recycle Bin?**

3.5 Apply Basic Skills for Care and Maintenance of Computer

Importance and Need of Care and Maintenance of Computer

Computer systems require maintenance, so that the system works efficiently. Poor maintenance may lead to system failure. Regular care and maintenance may help you detect any issues at an early stage and keep it functioning well.

Since, a lot of important data is stored in the computer, it is necessary to have regular maintenance of the computer to be done.

Computer virus, malware, and other harmful software can cause damage to the working of the computer.

A large number of files are stored on the computer. These files can be disorganised and fragmented and may result in slowing down of the computer.

Regular maintenance of the system includes installing updates, security, taking backups, scans, etc.

Both internal and external parts of the computer system should be taken care of

1. Keep the computer dust free.
2. Do not eat or drink while working on the computer.
3. To keep the keyboard clean, make sure your hands are clean before using it.
4. CDs and DVDs should be handled carefully, so that it does not get any scratches.
5. Keep keyboard covered when not in use.

Cleaning the Computer Components

Computer components need proper care to last longer. Preventive maintenance increases the life of the components.

For example, a cable is damaged, but still working. It should be replaced or repaired immediately to prevent any other damage.

General precautions to be taken while cleaning the computer components are:

- Always Power Off the computer system before cleaning.
- Never spray cleaning fluid directly on the components of the computer. First spray the liquid on the cloth and then wipe the component.
- Do not allow the cleaning liquid to drip near the circuit board.
- Preferably use anti-static wrist band which helps to prevent building up of static electricity near electronic device.

Let's discuss how to clean common peripheral devices of computer

Computer Monitor

To clean the computer monitor, you can use a soft lint-free cloth, like cotton and water or special cleaning liquid. You should not spray water or cleaning liquid directly on the computer monitor as it may run through the seams. Spray water or cleaning liquid on the cloth and gently wipe the computer monitor.

Keyboard

Dirt and dust can cause damage to the keyboard. Keys of the keyboard may not function properly, if dirt enters the keys. You should always clean the keyboard periodically by holding upside down and shaking it.

You can also clean it by blowing it with compressed air. After this, use a damp lint-free cloth to clean top of the keys. You should never spray any liquid cleaner or water directly on the keys of the keyboard.

Optical Mouse

You can clean the bottom of the optical mouse with a clean lint-free cloth. Lens area can be cleaned by blowing air or cotton swab.

Digital Camera

Never touch the lens of the camera. To remove the dust, you can use soft lens brush or wipe with a soft dry cloth. For stubborn dust, you can use special fluid for lens cleaning which should be first pot on the tissue and then wipe the lens. Never put the fluid directly on the lens.

CDs and DVDs

Keep CD/DVD in proper case to prevent damage. If there is some dirt on the CD or DVD, it may not work at all. Finger prints and dirt can be removed by lightly rubbing with a clean lint-free cotton cloth. If the dirt is hard to remove, you can use special cleaning fluid. Put the drop of fluid on a swab of cotton and gently rub on the media.

Preparing a Maintenance Schedule

Some of the maintenance activities are:

- keep the components of the computer, like keyboard, mouse, monitor, etc. clean
- replace hardware that is not functioning properly
- keep food items away from the computer
- cables and chords should not be messed up
- removing unauthorized software from the computer
- take regular backups of the data

- ensure backups are working properly by periodically restoring or checking of data. You should use external hard drive for backup of data on your computer.
- run anti-virus periodically
- keep anti-virus software up to date
- do not overcharge the batteries
- do not block the vents
- always shut down the computer properly

A regular disk defragmentation should be done to remove all unnecessary information that slows down the computer. Disk defragmentation done at regular intervals helps the disc space to be used at an optimal level.

Take regular backup of the data on your computer. In case the data is lost due to any reason, system failure, virus attack, etc. , you can easily retrieve your data using backup files till your last update.

Try These 3.3

1. **Why keyboard should be covered, if not in use?**
2. **What is the use of fan in the CPU?**
3. **Name two activities that included by regular maintenance of system.**

Protecting Computer Against Viruses

A computer virus is a software program that attaches itself to other programs and alters their behavior. A virus may or may not be destructive. Some viruses erase data or corrupt programs on the computer. VIRUS is an acronym for **Vital Information Resources Under Seize.**

When a virus enters a computer system, it makes copies of itself and carries out the harmful tasks that it is programmed for. Some viruses get activated at a certain date and time. Viruses also attach to the files stored on the computer or the storage media and harm these files.

A computer virus can infect only the software and not the hardware, but computer may stop working.

A computer can get infected with virus in any of the following ways:

- infected files
- infected pen drives
- infected CD-ROMs/DVD-ROMs
- through infected file attachment of e-mails

A computer virus cannot do the following:

- it cannot infect files on CD or DVD, if they are closed for writing.
- it cannot infect computer hardware like, keyboard, mouse, etc.

Some of the common signs of a virus attack are:

- computer runs very slow
- there is change in the file size
- computer often stops responding
- there is an increase in number of files (unusual)
- unusual error message appears on the screen
- computer restarts on its own

Scanning and Cleaning Viruses and Removing Spam Files, Temporary Files and folders

The following points should be kept in mind to prevent virus infection:

- install and use anti-virus software
- keep anti-virus software updated
- scan all the files that you download from the Internet
- do not open e-mails of an unknown person/sender
- don't allow any untrustworthy person to use your system
- never use unknown pen drive/CD on your computer
- never click on the window that pop-up when you are surfing the Internet

Preparing Computer Against Virus

To prevent our computer from being infected with virus, we should install anti-virus software, run it periodically and keep it updated, so that it can scan and remove new viruses.

Anti-virus software is a program designed to detect and remove malicious programs from the computer.

Some examples of anti-virus software are McAfee Virus Scan, Norton Anti-virus, Microsoft Security Essentials, and Quick Heal.

For an anti-virus program to be effective:

- it needs to run in the background at all times.
- keep the anti-virus software updated, so that it can recognize new viruses.
- run full disk scans periodically.

Scanning and Cleaning Virus

Let us discuss how to use Quick Heal Total Security to scan the computer system.

1. Click Start → All Programs → Quick Heal → Total Security Quick Heal

Or Double-click the Quick Heal Anti-virus icon on the desktop.

2. The main window of Quick heal Total Security will open up.

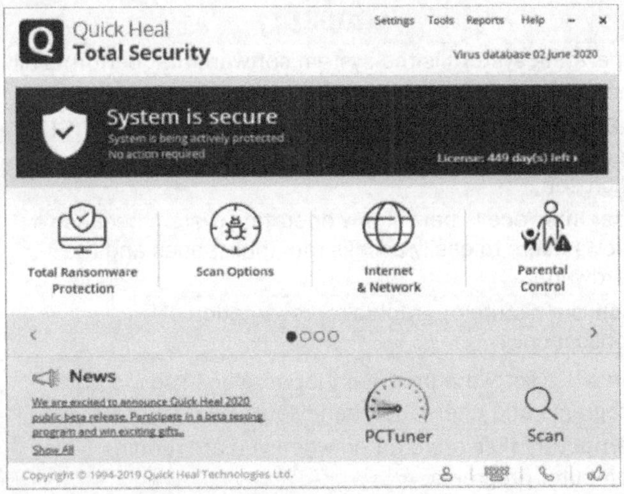

To perform full system scan,

1. Click Scan → Full System Scan.
2. The scan process will begin.
3. On completion of the scan, the scan statistics and reports are provided.
4. Click Close.

   Other anti-viruses, like, Norton Anti-virus, McAfee, etc. have almost the same method to scan full computer system for viruses and remove them.

Removing SPAM from your Computer

Spam emails are unwanted, unsolicited email messages sent in bulk. But they're not just annoying; spam emails can also contain dangerous links or lead to other malicious threats.

By following these steps, you can effectively remove spam from your computer

- **Enable Spam Filters** Activate built-in spam filters in your email settings.
- **Delete Unwanted Emails** Regularly delete suspicious emails or those from unknown senders.
- **Unsubscribe** Opt-out from unwanted mailing lists.
- **Block Senders** Block known spammers or persistent unwanted senders.
- **Use Security Software** Install and regularly update antivirus and anti-malware software.
- **Avoid Clicking Suspicious Links** Refrain from clicking on links in suspicious emails.
- **Clear Browser Data** Periodically clear browser cache and cookies to remove tracking data.

Removing Temporary Files

Temporary files are created when you are running computer programs. Microsoft Windows and Windows programs often create a .TMP file as a temporary file. Temporary files are also created by web browsers to store your web browser history. These temp files take up a large amount of disk space, so it should be removed to clear space.

The steps to remove temporary files are as follows:

1. Double-click This PC on the desktop.
2. This PC window will open.
3. Right-click Local Disk C: and select Properties option from the drop down menu.
4. The Properties window will appear. Click on Disk Cleanup.
5. The Disk Cleanup for C: window will appear.

6. Click the Check box next to Temporary Files, Temporary Internet files, etc. that you want to delete.
7. Click OK. A confirmation message will appear.

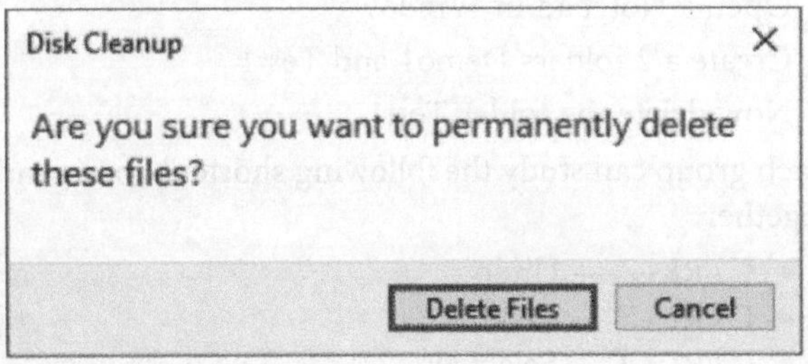

8. Click on Delete Files.
9. Windows will delete all the temporary files from the computer.

Removing Files of Temporary Folder

The steps to remove files of temporary folder are as follows:

1. Press Windows button + R on the keyboard.
2. The Run dialog box will appear.

3. Type %temp% and click on OK.
4. The Temp folder will open.
5. Click Ctrl + A to select all the files in the folder. Press Delete key.
6. A message box will appear. Click Yes to confirm.
7. All the files in the Temp folder will be deleted. Some files which are related to current open files may not get deleted. You can ignore those files and close the pop-up window.

Try These 3.4

1. **Mention one way in which a computer gets infected with virus.**
2. **How can you select all the files in a folder using the keyboard?**
3. **What command will you write in the Open text box to open the Temp folder?**

Glossary

Operating system is the system software that performs all the basic tasks of a computer system.

MS-Windows is a series of Graphical User Interface (GUI) operating system developed, marketed and sold by Microsoft.

User interface is part of any operating system because it allows users to easily access the applications and the hardware.

Icon is a picture or graphic representation of an application.

Virus is a software program that attaches itself to other programs and alters their behaviour.

Temporary files are created when you are running computer programs.

ACTIVITY Time

Activity 1

Creating a folder

Material required

Pen, notebook, computer

Procedure

- Form groups depending on the number of computers available. Each member of the group creates a new folder. Others can watch and give feedback on what was done correctly and what can be improved.
- Open a Notepad in Windows
- Create a 2 folders Demo1 and Test1
- Now delete the folder Test1

Each group can study the following shortcut commands together.

- CTRL+Z — Undo
- CTRL+Y — Redo
- CTRL+A — Select all
- CTRL+X — Cut
- CTRL+C — Copy
- CTRL+V — Paste
- CTRL+P — Print
- CTRL+S — Save

- The first group asks the other groups a question (e.g. what does CRTL + Z do? (Answer is Undo) or what is the shortcut for Copy (CTRL+C). Whichever group answers correctly gets one point otherwise the next group answers and so on. Whichever group gets most points, wins.

Activity 2

Making a Chart

Material required

Pen, notebook, chart paper, pictures.

Procedure

- Form groups and make a chart to list down all the ways in which a device can be damaged and how it can be prevented.
- Make sure all students in the group get a chance to participate.

Activity 3

Group Chart Making

Material required

Pen, notebook, computer, Chart paper, colours

Procedure

- Form groups depending on the number of students available. Make a chart to show all the different threats faced by a computer and how you can protect a computer from such treats.

NCERT FOLDER

Complete Explanations of all NCERT's Questions

A. Multiple Choice Questions

Q.1 Which one of the following shortcut keys is used to paste a file?

(a) Ctrl + C
(b) Ctrl + P
(c) Ctrl + V
(d) Ctrl + X

Q.2 Which of the following is a valid file extension for Notepad file?

(a) .jpg
(b) .doc
(c) .text
(d) .txt

Q.3 What keys do you use to copy something?

(a) Ctrl+X
(b) Ctrl+C
(c) Ctrl+Z
(d) Ctrl+Y

Q.4 What happens if you leave a device plugged in even after it is charged 100%?

(a) It can break.
(b) It can stop functioning.
(c) It can over-heat.
(d) Data can get corrupt.

Q.5 How can an anti-virus protect your device?

(a) It can protect it from over-heating.
(b) It can increase its performance.
(c) It can prevent data from getting corrupt.
(d) It can backup data.

Q.6 Which option is not required to keep a device cool?

(a) Keep the device unplugged when in use.
(b) Do not cover a laptop with a blanket.
(c) Make sure computer's CPU fan is working.
(d) Avoid leaving the device in the sun.

Q.7 Which of the following is essential for maintaining keyboard?

(a) Turn the keyboard upside down and shake it to remove foreign material.
(b) Blow dust and other particles with help of a blower.
(c) Use a very dilute combination of soap and water applied with a non-abrasive cloth to remove stains from the keycaps.
(d) All of the above

Q.8 What should you do to ensure secure online transactions?

(a) Lock your computer
(b) Give credit card or bank details only on safe websites
(c) Use anti-virus
(d) Do not use pirated software

Q.9 Which of the following trap small children into inappropriate relations?

(a) Online predators
(b) Worms
(c) Trojan Horse
(d) Anti-Virus

Q.10 What should a strong password consist of?

(a) Only letters
(b) Numbers and special characters
(c) Name of a person
(d) Letters, numbers and special characters

Answers

1. (c)	**2.** (d)	**3.** (b)	**4.** (c)	**5.** (c)
6. (a)	**7.** (d)	**8.** (b)	**9.** (a)	**10.** (d)

B. Subjective questions

Q.1 How is a computer file system similar to our physical file system in a school?

Ans. Both computer file systems and physical file systems in schools organize and store information:

Organization: They both use a hierarchical structure to organize files or documents into folders or categories.

Storage: Both systems allocate space to store data efficiently, whether it's on a computer's storage drive or in physical filing cabinets.

Access: Users can retrieve and modify files or documents stored in both systems as needed.

Navigation: They both allow users to navigate through the system to locate specific files or documents quickly.

Q.2 Explain how to clean a computer on a daily basis.

Ans. (a) **Dust Removal:** Use a soft, dry microfiber cloth or compressed air to gently remove dust from the exterior surfaces.

(b) **Keyboard and Mouse:** Use compressed air to blow out dust and debris from between the keys and mouse crevices.

(c) **Monitor:** Clean the monitor screen with a lightly dampened microfiber cloth.

(d) **Cable Management:** Organize and untangle cables to prevent hazards and improve airflow.

(e) **Ventilation:** Ensure vents and air intake/exhaust ports are clear of dust using compressed air.

(f) **Desktop Organization:** Remove clutter from the desktop and organize files.

Q.3 How can you increase the performance of a computer?

Ans. Here are some ways to increase the performance of a computer in short:

(a) **Upgrade Hardware**: Increase RAM, upgrade to a solid-state drive (SSD), or install a faster processor.

(b) **Optimize Software**: Remove unnecessary startup programs, update drivers, and keep the operating system and software up to date.

(c) **Manage Storage**: Free up disk space by deleting unnecessary files and programs, and defragment the hard drive (if not using an SSD).

(d) **Adjust Power Settings**: Optimize power settings to balance performance and energy efficiency.

(e) **Cooling System**: Ensure proper ventilation and cooling to prevent overheating, which can degrade performance.

(f) **Use Antivirus Software**: Keep the system protected from malware and viruses that can slow down performance.

Q.4 Explain how Trojan Horse virus works.

Ans. A Trojan Horse virus disguises itself as legitimate software or files to trick users into downloading and executing it. Once activated, the Trojan Horse can perform various malicious actions, such as stealing sensitive information, damaging files, or giving hackers remote access to the infected computer. Unlike other types of malware, Trojans do not self-replicate but rely on social engineering tactics to infiltrate systems and carry out their malicious activities.

Q.5 List the various ways you can use to protect your data.

Ans. Here are various ways to protect your data in short:

(a) **Regular Backups**: Backup important data regularly to an external hard drive or cloud storage.

(b) **Strong Passwords**: Use complex passwords and consider using a password manager.

(c) **Encryption**: Encrypt sensitive data, especially when transmitting it over the internet or storing it on portable devices.

(d) **Update Software**: Keep your operating system, antivirus, and other software updated to patch security vulnerabilities.

(e) **Firewalls**: Use firewalls to monitor and control incoming and outgoing network traffic.

(f) **Secure Wi-Fi**: Secure your Wi-Fi network with a strong password and encryption to prevent unauthorized access.

(g) **Awareness Training**: Educate yourself and others about common cybersecurity threats and best practices.

(h) **Two-Factor Authentication**: Enable two-factor authentication for added security when accessing accounts.

EXAM PATTERN EXERCISE

Including Competency Based Questions

Part I

Multiple Choice Questions

1 **The primary purpose of the operating system is**
(a) to make the most efficient use of the computer hardware
(b) to allow people to use the computer
(c) to keep systems programmer's employed
(d) to make computers easier to use

2 **........ is responsible for creation and deletion of files and directories.**
(a) Operating system (b) Application software
(c) Programs (d) Peripherals

3 **It provides scheduling to each process to be run on.**
(a) Time sharing OS
(b) Distributed OS
(c) Real-time OS
(d) Single-user OS

4 **........... provides process and memory management services that allow two or more tasks, jobs or programs to run simultaneously.**
(a) Multi-tasking
(b) Multi-threading
(c) Multi-processing
(d) Multi-computing

5 **........... is an operating system which was first developed in 1969.**
(a) Windows (b)Mac OS
(c) Linux (d) Unix

6 **Which software is a series of graphical user interface operating systems developed by Microsoft?**
(a) Mac OS (b) MS-Windows
(c) Linux (d) Solaris

7 **Which operating system is developed by Apple Incorporation?**
(a) iOS (b) BlackBerry
(c) Android (d) Symbian

8 **GUI stands for** 2023
(a) Graphical User Interface
(b) Graphical Used Interface
(c) Great User Interface
(d) None of the above

9 **GUI is used as an interface between**
(a) hardware and software (b) man and machine
(c) program and user (d) None of these

10 **It uses pictures (called icons) and menus displayed on the screen to send commands to the computer system.**
(a) Command-based user interface
(b) GUI
(c) System Utility
(d) API

11 **The 'desktop' of a computer refers to**
(a) the visible screen
(b) the area around the monitor
(c) the top of the mouse pad
(d) the inside of a folder

12 **A blinking indicator that shows you where your next action will happen, is**
(a) CPU (b) cursor
(c) toolbar (d) boot

13 **The long horizontal bar at the bottom of desktop is known as**
(a) Status bar (b) Task bar
(c) Menu bar (d) Title bar

14 **A .... is a collection of information saved as a unit.**
(a) Folder (b) File
(c) Path (d) File extension

15 **Files are organised after storing in**
(a) archives (b) folders
(c) indices (d) lists

16 **File extensions are used in order to**
(a) name the file
(b) ensure the file name is not lost
(c) identify the file
(d) identify the file type

17 **A named area on a disk that is used to store related sub folders and files is called as a ....**
(a) desktop (b) folder
(c) menu (d) window

18 **...... may be included in other folder while making hierarchical folder structure.**
(a) Mini folder (b) Tiered folder
(c) Sub folder (d) Object

19 **Spam refers to** 2025
(a) Unnecessary images (b) Temporary files
(c) Junk mails (d) Music files

20 To search for an application, you can also open the
(a) title bar (b) file menu
(c) start menu (d) task bar

21 Right clicking on File or Folder opens ______ **2023**
(a) Main Menu (b) Shortcut Menu
(c) Back Menu (d) Front Menu

22 When you bring the mouse over a file in File Explorer, it will show the details of that file. This is known as **SQP 2023-24, SQP 2024-25**
(a) Drag and drop (b) Double click
(c) Hover (d) Single click

23 What is the term used when you quickly click the left mouse button twice? **SQP 2022-23**
(a) Hover (b) Drag and drop
(c) Double clicking (d) Moving

24. Ravi learnt that if a laptop gets overheated, the internal parts get damaged. What happens if he leaves his device plugged in even after it is charged 100%? **SQP 2022-23**
(a) It can break (b) It can stop functioning
(c) It can overheat (d) Data can get corrupt

25 Which one of the following is an example of Operating System?
(a) Microsoft Word (b) Microsoft Windows
(c) Microsoft Excel (d) Microsoft Access

26. A ______________ is a software program that attaches itself to other programs and alters their behavior.
(a) Operating system (b) Firewall
(c) Antivirus (d) Computer Virus

27. The most important software in any computer is the This is the software that starts working as soon as we switch on a computer. **2024**
(a) Web Browsers (b)Operating System
(c) Office Software (d) Designing Software

Answers

1. (d)	2. (a)	3. (a)	4. (a)	5. (d)
6. (b)	7. (a)	8. (a)	9. (c)	10. (b)
11. (a)	12. (b)	13. (b)	14. (b)	15. (b)
16. (d)	17. (b)	18. (c)	19. (c)	20. (c)
21. (b)	22. (c)	23. (c)	24. (c)	25. (b)
26. (d)	27. (b)			

Statement Based Questions

1. Statement 1 All information stored in a computer is kept in files.
Statement 2 Different types of files store different types of information.
(a) Both Statement 1 and Statement 2 are correct
(b) Both Statement 1 and Statement 2 are incorrect
(c) Statement 1 is correct but Statement 2 is incorrect
(d) Statement 2 is correct but Statement 1 is incorrect

2. Statement 1: We should not eat anything over a keyboard.
Statement 2: If a computer, laptop or mobile device gets overheated, the external parts can be damaged.
(a) Both Statement 1 and Statement 2 are correct
(b) Both Statement 1 and Statement 2 are incorrect
(c) Statement 1 is correct but Statement 2 is incorrect
(d) Statement 2 is correct but Statement 1 is incorrect

3. Statement 1: You can wipe the screen with a soft cloth to remove any finger marks.
Statement 2: Avoid leaving a device in the sun or in a closed car.
(a) Both Statement 1 and Statement 2 are correct
(b) Both Statement 1 and Statement 2 are incorrect
(c) Statement 1 is correct but Statement 2 is incorrect
(d) Statement 2 is correct but Statement 1 is incorrect

4. Statement 1: Spam email is unsolicited and unwanted junk email sent out in bulk to an indiscriminate recipient list.
Statement 2: Typically, spam is sent for commercial purposes.
(a) Both Statement 1 and Statement 2 are correct
(b) Both Statement 1 and Statement 2 are incorrect
(c) Statement 1 is correct but Statement 2 is incorrect
(d) Statement 2 is correct but Statement 1 is incorrect

Answers

1. (a) 2. (c) 3. (a) 4. (a)

Assertion & Reason Based Questions

1 Assertion (A) Operating system is a software program that enables the computer hardware to communicate and operate with the computer software.
Reason (R) Windows is an open source operating system.
(a) Both A and R are correct and R is correct explanation of A.
(b) Both A and R are correct and R is not the correct explanation of A.
(c) A is True but R is False.
(d) A is False but R is True.

2 Assertion (A) Directory is a container that is used to contain folders and file.
Reason (R) File system provides a way of organising a drive.
(a) Both A and R are correct and R is correct explanation of A.
(b) Both A and R are correct and R is not the correct explanation of A.
(c) A is True but R is False.
(d) A is False but R is True.

3 **Assertion (A) In Windows, you can create user accounts.**

Reason (R) You can only have one user account on a Windows computer.

(a) Both A and R are correct and R is correct explanation of A.
(b) Both A and R are correct and R is not the correct explanation of A.
(c) A is True but R is False.
(d) A is False but R is True.

4. **Assertion (A) Recycle Bin is a reserved space where files and folders you no longer want can be disposed off.**

Reason (R) When you move a file to the Recycle Bin, it will be immediately deleted from your drive.

(a) Both A and R are correct and R is correct explanation of A.
(b) Both A and R are correct and R is not the correct explanation of A.
(c) A is True but R is False.
(d) A is False but R is True.

Answers

1. (c) **2.** (a) **3.** (c) **4.** (a)

Part II

Very Short Answer Type Questions

1. **Sneha created a file in Notepad and saved the file by name "hello" so what will be the complete name of file?**

Ans. hello.txt

2 **Name any three operating systems.**

Ans. Linux, Unix, Windows 10

3 **Name the button to the left of the taskbar.**

Ans. Start button

4 **Name two special icons on the desktop.**

Ans. Recycle Bin, This PC

5 **How can you delete a folder?**

Ans. (i) Click the folder (ii) Press the Delete Key

6 **Name the set of commands to move a folder from one location to another.**

Ans. Cut, Paste

7 **Why we should remove temporary files from the computer?**

Ans. Temporary files take up a large amount of disk space, so it should be removed to clear space.

8 **Identify which is a temporary file from Project.docx and Mathsite.tmp?**

Ans. Mathsite.tmp is a temporary file because it has .tmp extension.

9 **What is the possible cause of slowing down of computer?**

Ans. A large number of files are stored on the computer. These files can be disorganised and fragmented and may result in slowing down of the computer.

10 **Can computer virus infect hardware?**

Ans. No, computer virus cannot infect hardware.

11 **Which key combination will you press to get the Run dialog box?**

Ans. Windows key + R

12 **How can you prevent your computer from virus infection?**

Ans. Install anti-virus

Short Answer Type Questions

1 **What is an operating system?**

Ans. Operating system is the system software that performs all the basic tasks of a computer system. It works like an interface between the user and the computer hardware resources. An operating system is a collection of programs that controls and coordinates all the tasks and functions in a computer system. It mainly provides an environment to run the software and serves services to the computer hardware.

2 **Difference between file and folder.**

Ans. Differences between file and folder are as follows

File	Folder
Files may or may not have extensions.	Folders do not have extensions.
A file cannot contain another file/folder.	A folder can contain any number of file/folders.
A file has certain size and memory consumption.	A folder has no size of its own. It derives the size from the files it contains.
Files cannot be shared on network on their own.	Folders can be shared on network.

3 **What is the difference between moving and copying a folder?**

Ans. Differences between moving and copying a folder are as follows

Copying a Folder	Moving a Folder
Copying a folder means to make a duplicate copy of a folder.	Moving a folder means to transfer a folder from one location to another.
It uses Copy and Paste option.	It uses Cut and Paste option.
The original folder remains at the source locations.	The original folder is moved to the destination location.

4 What are the common signs of a virus attack?

Ans. Some of the common signs of a virus attack are

- computer runs very slow
- there is change in the file size
- computer often stops responding
- there is an increase in number of files
- unusual error message appears on the screen
- computer restarts on its own

5 What are antivirus? Name any two antivirus.

Ans. Anti-virus software is a program designed to detect and remove malicious programs from the computer. Two commonly used anti-virus softwares are McAfee and Norton.

6 Why regular disk defragmentation should be done? **Competency Based Ques.**

Ans. A regular disk defragmentation should be done to remove all unnecessary information that slows down the computer. Disk defragmentation done at regular intervals helps the disc space to be used at an optimal level.

7 What general precautions should you take while cleaning the computer/components?

Ans. (i) Always Power off the computer system before cleaning.

(ii) Never spray cleaning fluid directly on the component of the computer. First spray the liquid on the cloth and then wipe the component.

(iii) Do not allow the cleaning liquid to drip near the circuit board.

(iv) Preferably use anti-static wrist band which helps to prevent building up of static electricity near electronic device.

8 "The Trojan Horse was a wooden horse said to have been used by the Greeks during the Trojan War to enter the city of Troy and win the war". What does Trojan horse mean in computer terminology? **SQP 2023-24, SQP 2024-25**

Ans. A Trojan Horse is a type of malware which disguises itself i.e., it appears to be a useful software program but once it reaches a computer it starts behaving like a virus and destroys data.

9 Enlist any two methods to protect our data on the computer. **SQP 2022-23**

Ans Two methods to protect our data on the computer:

1. Use passwords to login to your computer.
2. Install Anti-virus and Firewall

10 Gurmeet has just bought a new computer for his office. Suggest him any two points which he should keep in mind to prevent his computer from virus infection. **2023**

Ans. (i) Gurmeet should install a reliable antivirus software and ensure that it is always updated to the latest version.

(ii) He should be wary of opening email attachments or downloading files from unknown sources.

11. Enlist any two measures that an individual should follow to take care of his/her digital devices. **2025**

Ans. Measures to Take Care of Digital Devices:

- **Regular Software Updates** Protect against security vulnerabilities and improve performance.
- **Physical Cleaning** Remove dust and debris to maintain functionality and prevent damage.

SELF ASSESSMENT

Multiple Choice Questions

1. The example(s) of operating system is/are
   (a) Windows (b) Linux
   (c) Unix (d) All of these
2. It is used as an interface between program and user.
   (a) GUI (b) CUI
   (c) CLI (d) None of these
3. Linux is which type of operating system?
   (a) Open source (b) Microsoft
   (c) Windows (d) Mac
4. Which one of the following is an example of Operating System?
   (a) Microsoft Word (b) Microsoft Windows
   (c) Microsoft Excel (d) Microsoft Access
5. ………… is the area of the desktop that contains apps and buttons for all open programs.
   (a) Desktop (b) Taskbar
   (c) Recycle bin (d) Start menu

Very Short Answer Type Questions

6. What is spam?
7. Who developed the Android operating system?
8. Write two ways computer get infected with virus.
9. Write steps to restore a deleted file.

Short Answer Type Questions

10. How to clean digital camera?
11. What is the use of operating system?
12. What is user interface? Also, explain the types of user interface.
13. How to clean the computer components?

Entrepreneurial Skills-II

CHAPTER 04

Entrepreneurship is an individual's ability to turn ideas into action. It includes creativity, innovation and risk taking, as well as the ability to plan and manage projects in order to achieve objectives. Entrepreneurs are driven by a desire to make a difference and create something new. They are often resourceful and have a strong work ethic. In addition, successful entrepreneurs are adaptable and can pivot their businesses when needed.

The word 'entrepreneur' is derived from the French word 'entreprendre' which means "to do something" or "to undertake". An entrepreneur is an individual who creates a new business, bearing most of the risks and enjoying most of the rewards. According to **Howard W. Johnson**, "Entrepreneur is composite of these basic elements i.e. invention, innovation and adaptation".

The term **entrepreneurship** refers to the functions performed by an entrepreneur. It is the process involving various actions to be undertaken by the entrepreneur in establishing a new enterprise.

4.1 Entrepreneurship and Society

While the concept of entrepreneurship has a wide meaning, it describes as starting a business using the resources available to a person. Society is provided with goods and services. In turn, society provides market for products and services provided by the entrepreneur.

Entrepreneurship has some positive impact on society such as

- Accentuates economic growth
- Fosters creativity
- Stimulates innovation and efficiency
- Creates jobs and employment opportunities
- Solves the problems of the society
- Encourages welfare of the society

Society plays a role in boosting entrepreneurship by

- Creates needs and demands
- Provides raw materials
- Enables financial support
- Creates a need for education
- Catalyses policy formation and reform
- Facilitates networking
- Supports infrastructure development

However, entrepreneurship also creates some adverse impact on society sometimes. This happens in the form of environmental degradation, trade imbalance, labour exploitation etc.

Types of Entrepreneurship Activities

Some common entrepreneurship activities related to society include:

1. Social Entrepreneurship

Social entrepreneurship can be understood as creation of sustainable solutions for social problems that leads to social change by employing entrepreneurial mindset, processes and operations.

In social entrepreneurship, research is conducted to completely define a specific and core social problem. Many social problems are tackled by social entrepreneurs such as low reach of quality education, health and sanitation, unemployment, child labour etc.

2. Agricultural Entrepreneurship

Agricultural Entrepreneurship can be defined as being primarily related to the marketing and production of inputs and products used in agricultural activities. Farmers have benefited the most with rise in agricultural entrepreneurship as it has led to low-cost innovations in farming processes.

3. Women Entrepreneurship

Women entrepreneurship is referred to the entrepreneurial activity led by women, where women undertake risks, create enterprises, organise factors of production, innovate with products/services and generate employment opportunities. Government of India has defined women entrepreneurship as "an enterprise owned and controlled by a woman having a minimum financial interest of 51 per cent of the capital and giving at least 51 per cent of the employment generated in the enterprise to women."

4. Small Scale Entrepreneurship

Small scale entrepreneurship refers to starting industries in which manufacturing, trading, providing services, productions are done on a small scale or micro scale. These businesses serve as the backbone of many developing countries.

Characteristics/Qualities of Entrepreneur

For the successful enterprise, it is important to understand the characteristics/qualities of successful entrepreneurs and it is described below :

- **Leadership** An entrepreneur must possess the characteristics of leadership and must lead a team for achievement of goals. The leader is able to clearly articulate their ideas and has a clear vision. An entrepreneurial leader realises the importance of initiative and reactiveness and they go out of their way to provide a support to the team.
- **Risk Taking** An entrepreneur with rational planning and firm decisions bear the risks. They have differentiated approach towards risks. Good entrepreneurs are always ready to invest their time and money but they always have a back up for every risk they take.
- **Innovativeness** With the changing needs and requirements of customers production should meet requirements with the help of innovative ideas. An entrepreneurial venture does not have to restrict itself to just one innovation or even one type of innovation.
- **Goal-oriented** Goal-oriented entrepreneurs achieve the maximum results from their efforts in business due to the fact they work towards clear and measurable targets.
- **Decision-Maker** An entrepreneur has to take many decisions to put his business idea into reality. He chooses the best suitable and profitable alternative.
- **Highly Optimistic** A successful entrepreneur is always optimistic and the present problems does not matter to them. He is always hopeful that the situation will became favourable for business in future.
- **Motivator** An entrepreneur has to create a spirit of team work and motivate them. So that he gets full cooperation from the employees.
- **Self-confident** An entrepreneur should have confidence to achieve his goals otherwise he won't be able to convince his team to achieve his goals.
- **Action-oriented** An entrepreneur should have an action oriented vision and ideology to plan things well.
- **Dynamic Agent** An entrepreneur creates new needs and new means to satisfy them. He has the ability to visualise new ventures and new plans.
- **High Achiever** Entrepreneurs are high achievers as they have a strong urge to achieve. The most important characteristic is his achievement motivation.
- **Trust in Self** An entrepreneur believes on their own decisions and actions as he has trust in his perseverance and creations. He does not believe in luck.

Functions of an Entrepreneur

The various functions of an entrepreneur are as follows :

- **Innovation** It includes introducing new products, opening new markets, new sources of raw material and new organisation structure.
- **Decision-Making** It includes stabilising organisation's aims and objectives and changing them according to changing conditions, taking decisions on effective techniques, utilisation of financial resources etc.
- **Organisation and Management** An entrepreneur organise and manage various economic and human factors through planning, coordination, control, supervision and direction.
- **Size and Scale of Business Unit** An entrepreneur has to decide about the size of business unit as he wants to establish one production unit or more dependent upon the demand of the product. Similarly, he has to decide about scale of production i.e. small scale, middle scale or large scale.
- **Appointment of Managerial and Other Work Force** It is the entrepreneur who appoints the management staff as well as other work force as per the requirement and needs of the enterprise.

- **Factors of Production** The factors of production i.e. land, labour, capital etc., should be in appropriate proportion and to maximise output of these factors is the responsibility of the entrepreneur.
- **Control and Direction** He must exercise control over all departments and direct them on a timely basis.
- **Finding Suitable Market** A proper research must be done to find a suitable market for selling the products. Other functions like advertisement and publicity, appointment of selling agents, providing incentives to various selling intermediaries to promote sales should be given priority.
- **New Inventions and Innovations** New inventions and innovations must be encouraged and introduced in production, sales, marketing, advertisement etc.
- **Establishing Relations with Government** An entrepreneur must establish good relations with government and its functionaries. His functions are to obtain licences, payment of taxes, selling the product to government, provision for export-import etc.
- **Establishing Contacts with Competitors** An entrepreneur must form contacts with the competitors to analyse the market. He must be in a position to make opportunities out of the given situation.

Role and Significance of Entrepreneurs

The role and significance of entrepreneurs are as follows :

- **Organiser of Society's Productive Resources** An entrepreneur is the organiser of society's productive resources. He is the person who assembles the unused natural, physical and human resources of the society, combines them as properly, establishes effective coordination between them and makes the economic activities dynamic.
- **Helpful in Capital Formation** An entrepreneur is helpful in capital formation as we know that increase in the rate of capital formation is quite essential for the economic development of any country. Those nations which are not able to increase the rate of capital formation or does it nominally remain backward from industrial development's point of view.
- **Increase in Employment Opportunities** An entrepreneur creates maximum employment opportunities in the society by way of establishing new industries, developing and expanding the existing industries and by undertaking innovative activities.
- **Development of New Production Techniques** An entrepreneur does not feel contended only with the existing techniques of production. Hence, he carries out various experiments for saving time, labour and capital in the production, as also to improve the variety and quality of the product and service.
- **Visionary Leader** An entrepreneur has a good vision towards the achievement of his goals. He is able to recognise profitable opportunities and conceptualise strategies.
- **Contribution of the Execution of Government Policies** An entrepreneur provides an important contribution in implementing government policies and achieving the national goals. An entrepreneur cooperate with the government for implementations of development plans of the country.
- **Higher Productivity** Entrepreneurs have the ability to produce more goods and services with less inputs. They play an important role in raising productivity.
- **Initiator** An entrepreneur is the one who initiates the process of creating an enterprise by coming up with the idea for the business and planning out how to turn that idea into reality.
- **Risk Taker** In an enterprise, an entrepreneur, being the owner, is the biggest risk taker. He is the one who finds the capital to back up his idea and also the person who is accountable in the face of the failure of that particular idea.
- **Backbone of Capitalist System** Capitalist economy is one in which there is a freedom to save and invest to compete and operate any business. An entrepreneur plays a vital and prominent role in the enterprise because he controls market by assuming the role of a competitor and a leader.
- **Ingredient of Modern Production System** An entrepreneur has become the 'balancing wheel' of modern global economy. They seek the unique product, change the technical frontiers and reshape public desires. Today, entrepreneurs act as an ingredient of modern production system as they create wealth and employment.

Try These 4.1

1. **An entrepreneur should have an .... vision.**
2. **How much percentage of the employment is generated in the entreprise to women?**
3. **Name any two functions of entrepreneur.**
4. **What is risk taker?**

4.2 Importance of Entrepreneurs

The importance of entrepreneurs are as follows

- **Free Market Evolution** In a free market, entrepreneurs are able to respond to changing customer preferences, prices, shifts in demand etc. Entrepreneurs bring change in technology, trends and markets.

- **Efficiency Improvements** Entrepreneurs tend to adapt in an established business and increase their own efficiency. They innovate with current systems and introduce new technologies which can significantly create advancement in an industry. Hence, during any major changes in the economy, entrepreneurs adapt and do not have to go out of business.
- **New Markets** Entrepreneurs can often 'redefine the rules' of an established industry. They do this by creating new markets for existing products and slightly innovating in small ways to suit the needs of a new target market.
- **New Values** Sometimes, entrepreneurs choose ethics over profit and offer a more ethical product to the world and are transparent about it.

Myths/Misconception about Entrepreneurship

Entrepreneurship is a set of activities performed by the entrepreneur. It is the process of identifying opportunities in the market place. It is the attempt to create value. Many entrepreneurs believe a set of myths about entrepreneurship and the most common are as follows :

- **Starting a Business is Easy** In reality, it is a very difficult and challenging process to start a successful business. The rate of failure of new ventures is very high but small entrepreneurships are comparatively easier to start.
- **Lot of Money to Finance New Business** Successful entrepreneurs design their business with little cash also.
- **Start up's cannot be Financed** Under the schemes like MUDRA, entrepreneurs can raise loans from banks.
- **Talent is More Important than Industry** This is not true as the nature of industry an entrepreneur chooses greatly effects the success and growth of the business.
- **Most Start up's are Successful** Mostly in the developing countries start up's fail as they could not manage to earn high profits.

4.3 Advantages of Entrepreneurship

The main advantages of entrepreneurship are discussed below :

- **Independence** An entrepreneur is himself a boss or owner and he can take all the decisions independently.
- **Exciting** Entrepreneurship can be very exciting with many entrepreneurs considering their ventures highly enjoyable. Everyday will be filled with new opportunities to challenge your determination, skills and abilities.
- **Wealth Creation** The principal focus of entrepreneurship is wealth creation and improved livelihood by means of making available goods and services. Entrepreneurial venture generates new wealth, new and improved products, services or technology form entrepreneurs, enable new markets to be developed and new wealth to be created.
- **Flexibility** As an entrepreneur you can schedule your work hours around other commitments, including quality time you would spend with your family.
- **Status** Success in entrepreneurship beings a considerable fame and prestige within the society.
- **Ambition-fulfilment** Through entrepreneurship one can fulfil his ambitions into original products or services.

4.4 Disadvantages of Entrepreneurship

Some of the disadvantages of entrepreneurship are as follows :

- **Huge Amount of Time** You have to dedicate a huge amount of time to your own business. Entrepreneurship is not easy and for it to be successful, you have to take a level of time commitment.
- **Risk** An entrepreneurship involves high risk of loss. If the business fails then it will wipe away all the personal savings.
- **Hard Work** An entrepreneur has to work very hard to make the new business very successful.
- **Uncertain Income** There is no regular or fixed income available to an entrepreneur. So, there is uncertain kind of income received by an entrepreneur.
- **Incompetent Staff** A new entrepreneur may not be able to hire qualified and experienced staff so there are chances of incompetency by the staff due to lack of experience and knowledge.

4.5 Entrepreneurship as a Career Option

There is nothing wrong with working for any organisation, it is basic for youngsters to be educated that they have two options-they can be job creators or job seekers. Once the awareness of the two career choices comes in, it is important to understand how taking the route of entrepreneurship benefits an individual.

Let's us see real-life few examples of entrepreneurship

- **Uber** started as an idea to revolutionize the taxi industry and after attracting investments, the company exploded and grabbed massive market share in a very short time.
- **Tesla** is known for its electric cars. Although the Tesla customers are limited, the enterprise enjoys a large market share and high profit margins.

There are various example of entrepreneurship around us

1. Nurtures Development of Entrepreneurial Skills and Capabilities

Entrepreneurship cultivates unique skills and encourages outside the box thinking. It instils confidence, creates opportunity, offers solutions and stimulates the economy. Entrepreneurship education provides with the skills and knowledge to come up with business ideas and develop ventures. It is broadly about learning to practice core business areas such as marketing, sales, finance, accounting, management etc., and developing skills such as effective communication, creative problem solving, adaptability etc.

2. Enables Application of an Entrepreneurial Mindset

Entrepreneurial mindset and skills are not necessarily only relevant to becoming an entrepreneur, but also in any field. Even the top employability skills of today are basically entrepreneurial skills. In fact, having an entrepreneurial mindset and wide range of business-relevant skills acquired through studying entrepreneurship would make one an ideal candidate in most fields.

3. Develops the Ability to Handle Failure and Ambiguity

In the Indian culture, since childhood failure is looked upon as something intolerably bad. However, a critical part of learning in the entrepreneurial process is to learn from failure. Hence, going through this process helps to learn from mistakes, take failure positively and stay motivated to work towards achieving the goal. Similarly, just like life is uncertain, business is full of ambiguity. While actually finding solutions to deal with ambiguity, one develops certain traits such as risk management, perseverance and persistence.

4. Enhances Critical Thinking and Problem-Solving Ability

The ability to think critically and solve problems is essential to succeed in the world of business. The focus of learning is not on these aspects during our school years. Learning entrepreneurship exposes one to numerous opportunities that force one to think critically, analyze all alternatives and consider possible solutions.

5. Provides Early Exposure to the Real World

Ultimately, working professionally in the real world requires one to collaborate, think creatively and demonstrate proficiency. In most cases, real life exposure during educational years remains limited.

Entrepreneurship practice at an early stage in one's career encourages activities such as going out and interacting with customers, creating tangible concepts and ideas, preparing detailed documents, working with investors etc., which gives great exposure and knowledge about the trends and needs of the real world.

6. Inspires to Think about One's Career Differently

Many students do not even consider that they can try to work on business ideas, take up entrepreneurial projects, take the initiative to impact society etc. Thus, they tend to develop a certain trail of thought about their career-from graduating high school to college to looking for a job.

If entrepreneurship exposure is given at the first point when one starts thinking towards building a career, it can help them to think of different career options and exploring what they are actually passionate about.

7. Leads to Creating Difference in Society

Entrepreneurs not only economically impact society but they also work on identifying the real needs and problems of people and solving them. Learning entrepreneurship encourages one to find problems that need to be solved, invent a solution for them, and ultimately, make the world a better place.

Try These 4.2

1. **......... is a set of activities performed by the entrepreneur.**
2. **Name the scheme, with the help entrepreneurs can raise loans from banks.**
3. **There is no .... income available to an entrepreneur.**
4. **For the educated youngsters have two career options. Name them.**

Glossary

Entrepreneurs are innovators who use the process of entrepreneurship to shatter the status quo of the existing products and services, to set new products, new services.

Entrepreneurship is non-beneficial also due to huge amount of time, risk, hardwork, uncertain income and incompetent staff.

Society A community, nation or broad grouping of people having common traditions, institutions and collective activities and interest.

Myth A widely held but false belief or idea, often based on tradition or misinformation.

ACTIVITY Time

ACTIVITY 1

Entrepreneurs I know: Individual Practice

Procedure

In this activity, we will think of the entrepreneurs we know.

Instructions

1. Think of 4 entrepreneurs whom you know or have seen.
2. Draw circles and in each circle write the name of that entrepreneur, what business they run, and one thing that you really like about their business.
3. After writing, share the details of the entrepreneurs with your class.

ACTIVITY 2

Field Work: Let's be an Entrepreneur

Procedure

- In this activity, students will find problems on their school campus that can be turned into business opportunities.

Instructions

1. Form groups of 3 each.
2. Take 30 minutes to go around your school.
3. Note down 2–3 problems you see on your school campus.
4. Write down some business ideas to solve these problems in the table given below.
5. Also think about how your business ideas will help the school. One example has been written for you.

Problem	Business ideas	How will this help the school?
For example, plastic cola bottles from the canteen are harming the environment	1. Make plant pots out of bottles and sell to students and parents. 2. Sell cola in glass bottles.	1. The school will look green and beautiful. The air will be fresh. 2. The canteen owner will spend less money on buying glass bottles because they can be used again.

ACTIVITY 3

Let us Solve a Problem!

Procedure

In this activity, students will try and solve a problem in their vicinity.

Instructions

1. Similar to Activity 1.2, select a problem in the area near your home. This could be a problem that really bothers you.
2. Make a 5-step plan for how you will solve the problem.
3. Implement step 1 of your solution!
4. After that, try implementing all the steps. Try your solution for a week.

ACTIVITY 4

Interview an entrepreneur

Procedure

In this activity, students will observe entrepreneurs at work, and speak to them and their employees about their work.

Instructions

1. Identify an entrepreneur in your area that you like or know.
2. On a weekend, spend some time in their shop and note everything that they do.
3. After that, speak to the entrepreneur and ask them in detail what activities they do in a day.
4. Also speak to somebody who works for them. Ask them what activities they see the entrepreneur do in a day. Write all your notes in figure.

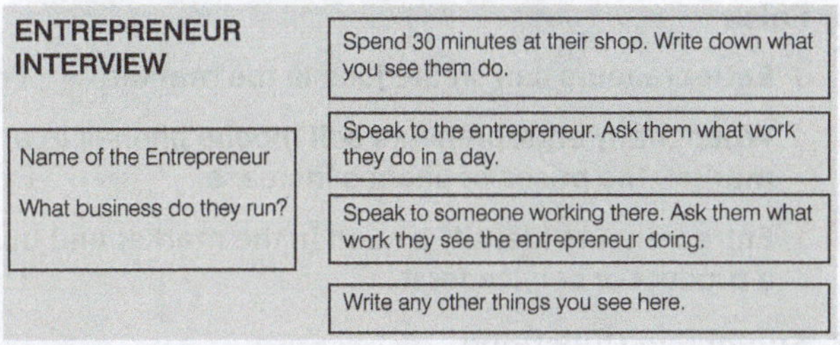

5. After you are back in class, make a list of all the actions you listed with your teacher. Compare your list with the list of your friends. Notice how many actions get repeated.

ACTIVITY 5

Identifying Everyday Heroes

Procedure

In this activity, the teacher will make chits about different professions and the students will act them out. There will be a discussion after that. The professions are

1. a vegetable seller not using plastic bags
2. a businesswoman running a delivery system
3. a chai wala selling fruit flavoured tea
4. a gold seller selling gold teeth

Instructions

1. There will be professions of different people written on each chit of paper. The student reads the profession and acts it out for the class.
2. Identify what each person is doing differently in their business.

ACTIVITY 6

Make and sell

Procedure

In this activity, students make an item in class and step out to sell it to someone.

Instructions

1. Form groups of 5 people each. The group should have a mix of boys and girls.
2. Look into your bags and desks and find any three items. Put them on your desk.
3. With the materials you've collected, make an object. Take 15 minutes to do this.
4. Now, take 30 minutes to sell it for money, to someone in school.

ACTIVITY 7

Presenting about the Power of Entrepreneurship

Procedure

In this activity, students shall prepare and present why they think entrepreneurship is a good life option for a person and for the society

Instructions

1. Get into groups of 5 each.
2. Imagine you believe that people should become entrepreneurs. You are speaking at your school assembly. You have to talk to the audience about the power of entrepreneurship. Prepare a presentation for the same.
3. You can use any way to present - talk, draw, act, sing, or dance.
4. You have 15 minutes to prepare. You will have 5 minutes to present.

NCERT FOLDER

Complete Explanations of all NCERT's Questions

A. State whether the following statements are True or False

Q.1 **Entrepreneurs can create jobs in the market.** True

Q.2 **When many entrepreneurs sell mobile phones in a market, the prices of phones increase.** False

Q.3 **Entrepreneurs identify a need in the market and build a product or service for it.** True

B. Subjective Questions

Q.1 **List the ways in which an entrepreneur affects a society.**

Ans. Here are various ways in which an entrepreneur affects society in short

(a) **Job Creation** Entrepreneurs create job opportunities, reducing unemployment and stimulating economic growth.

(b) **Innovation** Entrepreneurs drive innovation by developing new products, services, and technologies that improve quality of life.

(c) **Wealth Creation** Entrepreneurs generate wealth through business ventures, contributing to economic prosperity.

(d) **Social Impact** Entrepreneurs address societal challenges by offering solutions to pressing issues and promoting social change.

(e) **Community Development** Entrepreneurs invest in local communities, supporting infrastructure, education, and public services.

(f) **Inspiration** Entrepreneurs inspire others to pursue their dreams, fostering a culture of ambition and creativity.

Q.2 What is the difference between a misconception and reality? Give an example.

Ans. A misconception is a belief or idea that is incorrect or based on false information, while reality refers to the actual state of things as they exist.

For example:

Misconception "Cracking your knuckles causes arthritis."

Reality Scientific research has shown that cracking knuckles does not increase the risk of arthritis.

EXAM PATTERN EXERCISE

Including Competency Based Questions

Part I

Multiple Choice Questions

1 Innovation of an entrepreneur includes

(a) division of work
(b) opening new markets
(c) introducing new products
(d) Both (b) and (c)

2 To find a suitable market an entrepreneur performs the functions of

(a) advertisement and publicity
(b) appointment of selling agents
(c) new organisation structure
(d) Both (a) and (b)

3 Incompetent staff means

(a) experienced staff
(b) qualified staff
(c) not experienced and qualified
(d) None of the above

4 Reema has started her own restaurant. She keeps on trying new ideas to make different dishes for her customers. As an entrepreneur, Reema is: 2025

(a) Impatient (b) Creative
(c) Under-confident (d) Lazy

5 In which situation an entrepreneur will not be able to convince his fellow beings to achieve his goals?

(a) Low self-confidence (b) Innovativeness
(c) Risk-taking (d) None of these

6 How can entrepreneur can get the work done from his/her team?

(a) By creating a spirit of teamwork
(b) By motivation
(c) Using harsh words and actions
(d) Both (a) and (b)

7 Srishti is a young woman who makes earrings. She buys jute from a farmer and makes earrings from that. She sees that most women in her village do not work. So, she hires two women to help her. As her orders increase, she hires three more women to work for her. How was she helping her village grow? Competency Based Ques.

(a) By selling earrings to women without a job
(b) By purchasing earrings from the local market
(c) By buying jute from the local farmer and by providing jobs to local women
(d) By attracting the women in her village with her creative earrings

8 Mary has two people who work for her. Every day, she spends one hour with them to learn about what they've done that day. Competency Based Ques.

(a) Creates a new product
(b) Divides income
(c) Manages the business
(d) Takes risks

9 .... refers to recruitment, employment, selection, training, development and compensation of the employees with an organization.

(a) Entrepreneurs
(b) Management
(c) Human Resource Management
(d) Employer

10 Which of the following is a quality of successful entrepreneurs? 2024

(a) Hard working (b) Resistance to change
(c) Lazy (d) Less-confident

11 **Which of the following is not a task of an entrepreneur?** 2023

(a) Sharing of wealth
(b) Preferably using foreign materials
(c) Fulfilling customer needs
(d) Helping society

12 **Which of the following is a function of an entrepreneur?** 2023

(a) Following the traditional method of business
(b) Innovation
(c) Keeping all the profit to himself/herself
(d) Avoid taking decisions

Answers

1. (d) **2.** (d) **3.** (c) **4.** (b) **5.** (a)
6. (d) **7.** (c) **8.** (c) **9.** (c) **10.** (a)
11. (b) **12.** (b)

Statement Based Questions

1 **Statement 1** **Self-employed people are those who start businesses to satisfy the needs of people.**
Statement 2 **Wage employed people are people who work for a person or an organization and get paid for that work.**

(a) Both Statement 1 and Statement 2 are correct
(b) Both Statement 1 and Statement 2 are incorrect
(c) Statement 1 is correct but Statement 2 is incorrect
(d) Statement 2 is correct but Statement 1 is incorrect

2 **Statement 1** **A Myth is a false belief or opinion about something.**
Statement 2 **Some people think being an entrepreneur is easy, and some people think it is difficult.**

(a) Both Statement 1 and Statement 2 are correct
(b) Both Statement 1 and Statement 2 are incorrect
(c) Statement 1 is correct but Statement 2 is incorrect
(d) Statement 2 is correct but Statement 1 is incorrect

3 **Statement 1** **There is only one entrepreneur in the market.**
Statement 2 **The entrepreneur has to remain in a competitive market.**

(a) Both Statement 1 and Statement 2 are correct
(b) Both Statement 1 and Statement 2 are incorrect
(c) Statement 1 is correct but Statement 2 is incorrect
(d) Statement 2 is correct but Statement 1 is incorrect

4 **Statement 1** **Entrepreneurs have a positive relationship with society.**
Statement 2 **They make profits through activities that benefit society.**

(a) Both Statement 1 and Statement 2 are correct
(b) Both Statement 1 and Statement 2 are incorrect
(c) Statement 1 is correct but Statement 2 is incorrect
(d) Statement 2 is correct but Statement 1 is incorrect

Answers

1. (a) **2.** (c) **3.** (d) **4.** (a)

Assertion & Reason Based Questions

1 **Assertion (A)** **A doctor works for a renowned hospital.** SQP 2023-24, SQP 2024-25

Reason (R) **The statement given above is an example of wage employment.**

(a) Both A and R are correct and R is the correct explanation of A
(b) Both A and R are correct but R is not the correct explanation of A
(c) A is correct but R is not correct
(d) A is not correct but R is correct

2 **Assertion (A)** **Entrepreneurs keep trying new ideas in their business.**
Reason (R) **Entrepreneurs are creative and think differently about business ideas.**

(a) Both A and R are correct and R is the correct explanation of A
(b) Both A and R are correct but R is not the correct explanation of A
(c) A is correct but R is not correct
(d) A is not correct but R is correct

3 **Assertion (A)** **Entrepreneurs run their businesses in a market.**
Reason (R) **The market has people who buy products and services and people who sell them also.**

(a) Both A and R are correct and R is the correct explanation of A
(b) Both A and R are correct but R is not the correct explanation of A
(c) A is correct but R is not correct
(d) A is not correct but R is correct

4 **Assertion (A)** **With the growth of a business, entrepreneurs look for more people to help them.**
Reason (R) **They buy more material, and also hire more people to work for them.**

(a) Both A and R are correct and R is the correct explanation of A
(b) Both A and R are correct but R is not the correct explanation of A
(c) A is correct but R is not correct
(d) A is not correct but R is correct

Answers

1. (a) **2.** (a) **3.** (a) **4.** (a)

Part II

Very Short Answer Type Questions

1 Define an entrepreneur.

Ans. An entrepreneur is someone who perceives opportunity, organises resources needed for exploiting that opportunity and exploits it.

2 Give any one quality of a successful entrepreneur.

Ans. Leadership is one quality of an entrepreneur. An entrepreneur is essentially a leader. They have to lead a team for achievement of goals.

3 Name the term used for a false belief or opinion about something.

Ans. Myth is the term used for a false belief or opinion about something.

4 How decision-making is an important function of an entrepreneur?

Ans. Decision-making is an important function because it includes stabilising organisation's aims and objectives and changes them according to the changing conditions.

5 How an entrepreneur acts as a visionary leader? **Competency Based Ques.**

Ans. Entrepreneur acts as a visionary leader as he is able to recognise profitable opportunities and successfully conceptualise strategies according to it.

6 What is the contribution of the entrepreneurs in the execution of Government policies? **Competency Based Ques.**

Ans. The entrepreneurs provide an important contribution in implementing government policies and achieving the national goals.

7 Write any two qualities for being a good entrepreneur.

Ans.
- They are confident. They believe in themselves and their abilities.
- They keep trying new ideas in their business.

8 Entrepreneurship has a positive impact on society. Write down any two.

Ans.
1. Some of them work towards saving the environment.
2. Some of them give money to build schools and hospitals.

9 "To get success, every business idea needs to be unique or special".
Is the above statement a myth or fact? **2022**

Ans. Myth

Short Answer Type Questions

1 How is society helping entrepreneurs in their business? **SQP 2023-24, SQP 2024-25**

Ans. Society is helping entrepreneurs by
(i) Creating needs (ii) Providing raw material
(iii) Buying/selling of items (iv) Making money

2 What do entrepreneurs do when they run their business? Mention any two points. **SQP 2022-23**

Ans. Entrepreneurs perform a variety of tasks to run their business. Two key activities include:

(i) **Strategic Planning and Decision-Making** Entrepreneurs set goals, define business strategies, and make crucial decisions that affect the direction and success of the business. This includes market research, financial planning, and risk assessment.

(ii) **Operational Management** Entrepreneurs oversee daily operations, ensuring that the business runs smoothly. This involves managing employees, handling supply chain logistics and maintaining product or service quality.

3 Raj has a small convenience store in his locality. There are many other convenience stores in the area. Yet, Raj's store survives the competition and does well. Which stage of an entrepreneur's career process can you relate this to? Explain. **Competency Based Ques.**

Ans. This stage is the Survive stage of an entrepreneur's career process. In this stage, even if there are many entrepreneurs in the market, the new entrepreneur has to remain in a competitive market.

4 Write any two tasks that entrepreneurs do when they run their business. **2025**

Ans. Two Tasks Entrepreneurs Do:
- **Market Research** Understanding customer needs and market trends to inform business decisions.
- **Financial Management** Handling budgets, investments, and ensuring the business's financial health.

5 List any two common misconceptions about entrepreneurship. **2024**

Ans. Refer to text on page No. 53 (Myths/Misconception about Entrepreneurship).

6 Give any two key roles performed by an entrepreneur. **2023**

Ans. Refer to text on page No. 52 (Role and Significance of Entrepreneurs).

7 Define the term agricultural entrepreneurship. How are farmers benefitted from it? **2023**

Ans. Agricultural entrepreneurship involves applying innovative approaches to farming and related activities to create value and generate income. Farmers benefit from it through increased profitability, diversification of income, access to new markets, adoption of technology, and empowerment for rural development.

SELF ASSESSMENT

Multiple Choice Questions

1. Decision-making function of entrepreneur includes
(a) Hard work (b) Risk bearing
(c) Utilisation of financial resources (d) All of these

2. Which system is being promoted by Entrepreneurs indirectly?
(a) Capitalist (b) Socialist
(c) Both (a) and (b) (d) None of these

3. Which of the following is/are function(s) of an entrepreneur?
(a) Innovation (b) Decision making
(c) Factors of Production (d) All of these

4. How does agricultural entrepreneurship help farmers?
(a) Finding low-cost innovations in farming processes
(b) Giving loans to farmers
(c) Giving jobs to the family members of farmers
(d) All of the above

5. Ravi's customer comes to his store and starts shouting at him. He does not get angry. He listens to what his customer is saying. He is ……… .
(a) hardworking (b) confident
(c) patient (d) prying new ideas

Very Short Answer Type Questions

6. Describe the risk taking factor of an entrepreneurs.

7. Do you think an entrepreneur is innovative by nature. Explain?

8. Write four misconceptions about entrepreneurship.

Short Answer Type Questions

9. Explain the wealth creation factor of entrepreneurship.

10. Explain the risk taking quality of an entrepreneur.

11. Write a note on qualities of an entrepreneur.

CHAPTER 05

Green Skills-II

Green skills are the knowledge, abilities, values and attitudes needed to live in, develop and support a sustainable and resource-effecient society. These skills are becoming increasingly important as the world transitions towards a more sustainable future.

5.1 Meaning and Definition of Sustainable Development

Sustainable development is the development that satisfies the needs of the present without compromising the capacity of future generations, guaranteeing the balance between economic growth, care for the environment and social well-being.

The important principles of sustainable development are:

- To carefully utilise all resources.
- To conserve resources so that they meet the demands and requirements of the future generations.
- To minimise the depletion of natural resources.

Sustainable development is the organising principle for meeting human development goals. It has its roots in ideas about sustainable forest management which were developed in Europe during the 17th and 18th centuries. The idea of sustainable development gained wide acceptance due to environmental concerns in the 20th century.

The concept of sustainable development was popularised in 1987 by the United Nations World Commission on Environment and Development. In its **Our Common Future Report** or **Brundtland Report** it defined the idea as "Development that meets the needs of the present, without compromising the ability of future generations to meet their needs."

Importance of Sustainable Development

Sustainable development is necessary for the maintenance of the environment. The importance of sustainable development are as follows:

- **Proper Use of Means and Resources** Sustainable development teaches people to make use of means and resources for the maximum benefit without wastage. It helps to conserve and promote the environment.
- **Development of Positive Attitude** Sustainable development brings about changes in people's knowledge, attitude and skills. It awares the people the responsibility to use and preserve natural resources. It creates the feeling that natural resources are the common property of all and nobody can use the property according to his personal will. It helps to conserve natural and social environment.
- **Development Based on People's Participation** People's participation is to be given priority in development work in order to achieve the aim of sustainable development. It creates the interest of local people in development work and environment conservation with the feeling of ownership.
- **Limitation of Development** Limited but effective use of means and resources are enough for the people to satisfy their basic needs. Limited and non-renewable means and resources go on decreasing in globally due to over-use. Development works should be conducted as per carrying capacity.

- **Long Lasting Development** Sustainable development aims at achieving the goal of economic and social development without destroying the Earth's means and resources. It attempts to create the concept of maintaining the present work for the future and conserving the natural resources for future generation.

So, due to the realisation of importance of sustainable development, now there is a transcending concern for survival of the people and planet. We need to take a holistic view of the very basis of our existence. It is important to reconcile ambitious economic development and preserving the natural resources and ecosystem.

Try These 5.1

1. **What is the principle of sustainable development?**
2. **Sustainable development is necessary for the .... of the environment.**
3. **The idea of sustainable development gained wide acceptance due to environmental concerns in the ....**
4. **Define sustainability.**

5.2 Problems Related to Sustainable Development

- Poor management of natural resources combined with growing economic activities will continue to pose serious challenges to environment.
- The most significant environmental problems are associated with resources that are renewable such as air and water. They have finite capacity to assimilate emissions and wastes but if pollution exceeds this capacity ecosystem can deteriorate rapidly.
- To assess the regenerative capacity of natural resources is difficult to determine. In the cases of soil erosion, atmospheric pollution etc., there is substantial uncertainity about the extent and outcomes of environmental degradation.
- The overall effects of economic activities on the environment are continuously changing.
- Due to rise in income, the demands for improvement in environmental quality will increase as well as the resources available for investment but it is not mandatory in some cases as problems are observed to get worse as income rise.
- Rise in population is another problem that would further lead to severe environmental degradation in the future.
- Another challenge is rise in demand for energy as it is estimated that the total manufacturing outputs in developing countries will increase to about six times the current levels by 2030.
- An environment friendly way for production of power is using solar energy from the sun which is unlimited. One major example of large scale production of solar power is seen in Charanka-Gujarat Solar Park. This has reduced the dependence on non-renewable fossil fuels in Gujarat.
- Another challenge is rise in demand of food crops with the growth of population. To protect fragile soils and natural habitats, this will have to be achieved by raising yields on existing crop land.

5.3 Solutions for Sustainable Development

- Inspite of difficult circumstances sustainable development is achievable however, it would require a lots of concentrated and coordinated effort. The achievement of sustainable development requires the integration of economic, environmental and social components at all levels.
- The main principles of sustainable development are:
  - Respect and care for all forms of life.
  - People should learn to conserve the natural resoures in order to protect the living beings.
  - Conserving the Earth's vitality and diversity.
  - Improving the quality of human life.
  - Changing personal attitude and practices towards the environment.

Short-Term Solutions

- Illegal deforestation and smuggling of forest resources should be stopped.
- Proper balance ought to be maintained between deforestation and afforestation.
- Planning and building of industrial zones to manage and process are types of wastes.
- Proper treatment system, recycling of waste and their proper disposal should be undertaken.
- Adoption of Rainwater Harvesting Techniques, drip/Sprinkler irrigation and use of alternative sources of energy. Less chemical fertilizers should be used along with environment-friendly pesticides and weedicides.
- Polluting industries should be relocated outside the cities, far away from the populated areas.

Long-Term Solutions

- Government should make policies against illegal activities.
- Awareness campaigns should be launched for farmers and industrialists.

- Ecology must be protected through imposition of taxes and fines.
- Practice of sustainable agriculture must be promoted such as permaculture, agroforestry, mixed farming, multiple cropping and crop rotation.

United Nations Sustainable Development Summit (2015) sets global development goals. These goals are termed as Agenda 2030. The goals are:

1. End poverty in all forms everywhere.
2. End hunger, achieve food security and improved nutrition and promote sustainable agriculture.
3. Ensure healthy lives and well-being for all.
4. Ensure inclusive and quality education for all and promote lifelong learning.
5. Achieve gender equality and empower all women and girls.
6. Ensure access to water and sanitation for all.
7. Ensure access to affordable, reliable, sustainable and modern energy for all.
8. Promote inclusive and sustainable economic growth, employment and decent work for all.
9. Build resilient infrastructure, promote sustainable industrialisation and foster innovation.
10. Reduce inequality within and among countries.
11. Make cities inclusive, safe, resilient and production.
12. Ensure sustainable consumption and production.
13. Take urgent action to combat climate change and its impacts.
14. Conserve and sustainably use oceans, seas and marine resources.
15. Sustainably manage forests, halt and reverse land degradation, halt biodiversity loss.
16. Promote peaceful and inclusive societies.
17. Revitalise the global partnership for sustainable development.

Try These 5.2

1. **What is the most significant environmental problems are associated with resources?**
2. **Awareness campaigns should be launched for what?**
3. **United Nations Sustainable Development Summit goals are termed as ....**
4. **The achievement of sustainable development requires the integration of economic, ... and .... components at all levels.**
5. **Write any one short-term solution related to sustainable development.**

Glossary

Sustainable development refers to the process of economic development where resources are used judiciously to satisfy needs of not only present generation but also to conserve them for the use of future generations.

Sustainable development takes place without depleting the present natural resources. It is the organising principle for meeting human development goals.

Sustainable development is necessary for proper use of means and resources, development of positive attitude, development based on people's participation, limitation of development and long lasting development.

There are several problem related to sustainable development like poor management of resources, rise in population, rise in demand for energy etc.

We can use short-term as well as long-term solutions to achieve the target of sustainable development through planning and coordinated effort.

United Nations Sustainable Development Summit (2015) sets global development goals which are termed as Agenda 2030. It ensures healthy living and well-being for all.

ACTIVITY Time

ACTIVITY 1

Create a Garden in School or Plant Trees

Material required

Seeds, garden waste, sprinkler, gardening tools

Procedure

- Form groups depending on the number of students available. Ask teacher to allot a piece of land in the school premises.
- Assign different tasks to different groups of students.
- The tasks can be ploughing, sowing seeds, making manure using vermicomposting and setting up a sprinkler system to water the plants.

ACTIVITY 2

Discussion on How to Prevent Wastage.

Procedure

- Form groups depending on the number of students available.
- Every student in the group will name way in which wasting of water and food can be stopped or prevented.
- Make a list and share it with the rest of the class.

ACTIVITY 3

Group Discussion

Procedure

- Form groups depending on the number of students available.
- Every student will describe one way in which they can work to conserve and protect the environment.
- Make a list and share it with the rest of the class.

ACTIVITY 4

Make art project using waste

Material required

Plastic bags, used bottles, papers cups, paper, wire, etc.

Procedure

- Form groups depending on the number of children available. Make a list of waste material that is thrown away. Now think of creative ideas in which you can use the waste material to make something useful.
- If time permits, every student can get some waste material from home, such as old newspapers, plastic bottles, old cloth, etc., and make the best out of waste (a painting, wall decoration or a bag). Have an exhibition at the front gate of your school.

NCERT FOLDER

Complete Explanations of all NCERT's Questions

A. Multiple Choice Questions

Q.1 How many sustainable development goals are given by the United Nations?

(a) 18 (b) 17
(c) 15 (d) 20

Q.2 Choose the option which defines sustainable development.

(a) Taking care of future generations
(b) Taking care of only ourselves
(c) Taking care of ourselves and the future generations
(d) Well-being of all

Q.3 Which organisation has made the Sustainable Development Goals.

(a) United Nations
(b) League of Nations
(c) UNICEF
(d) World Health Organisation

Q.4 Which of the following sources of energy is from a renewable source?

(a) Solar energy (b) Wood
(c) Coals (d) Petrol

Q.5 Choose the option which is not a sustainable development goal according to United Nations.

(a) Clean Water and Sanitation
(b) Gender Equality
(c) Population
(d) Reduced Inequalities

Answers

1. (b) 2. (c) 3. (a) 4. (a) 5. (c)

B. Subjective Questions

Q.1 What is the meaning of sustainable development?

Ans. Sustainable development refers to a mode of development that meets the needs of the present generation without compromising the ability of future generations to meet their own needs. It involves achieving economic growth, social inclusion, and environmental protection in a balanced and integrated manner.

Q.2 Why do you think the United Nations has made the 17 Sustainable Development Goals?

Ans. The United Nations has made the 17 Sustainable Development Goals (SDGs) to provide a comprehensive framework for addressing the world's most pressing economic, social, and environmental challenges in a coordinated and integrated manner. These goals aim to guide global efforts towards achieving sustainable development by 2030 by addressing issues such as poverty, inequality, climate change, environmental degradation, and social injustice. In short, the SDGs serve as a roadmap for international cooperation and action to build a more sustainable and equitable future for all.

Q.3 List some ways in which we can use resources sensibly.

Ans. Here are some ways to use resources sensibly

- Reduce, reuse, recycle
- Conserve energy and water
- Opt for sustainable transportation
- Support sustainable agriculture
- Protect natural habitats
- Practice mindful consumption
- Raise awareness through education

Q.4 Explain the importance of education towards sustainable development.

Ans. Education plays a crucial role in advancing sustainable development by raising awareness, fostering critical thinking, and empowering individuals and communities to take action towards a more sustainable future. In short, education promotes understanding of sustainability issues, equips people with the knowledge and skills to address them, and inspires collective action to achieve environmental, social, and economic goals in a balanced manner.

EXAM PATTERN EXERCISE

Including Competency Based Questions

Part I

Multiple Choice Questions

1 Sustainable development requires the judicious use of

(a) natural resources (b) human resources
(c) man-made resources (d) None of the above

2 Sustainable development is necessary because

(a) it helps to promote and conserve the environment
(b) it aware the people for effective use of natural resources
(c) it aims at achieving the goal of economic and social development
(d) All of the above

3 To save water as a resources which techniques must be adopted?

(a) Rainwater Harvesting (b) Sprinkler Irrigation
(c) Recycling of Waste (d) Both (a) and (b)

4 Energy demand is developing countries will increase to ...... times the current levels by 2030.

(a) four (b) five (c) six (d) eight

5 The biggest problem related to sustainable development is

(a) to safeguard forests (b) to safeguard fisheries
(c) to safeguard croplands (d) All of these

6 If sustainable development is neglected then

(a) we shall have a safe and secure environment.
(b) it will destroy ecology and environment endangering the survival of future generation.
(c) mankind will continue to live and prosper.
(d) All of the above

7 "Efforts are made to increase the solar power generation so that our electricity needs are met and at the same time we do not pollute the environment or use up natural resources".
Which SDG can you relate this statement to?

SQP 2024-25, Competency Based Ques.

(a) Life on land
(b) Clean water and sanitation
(c) Affordable and clean energy
(d) Reduced inequalities

8 .... is caused when natural or a man-made disturbance disrupts the natural balance of an ecosystem.

(a) Pollution (b) Damage
(c) Natural disaster (d) Ecological Imbalance

Answers

1. (a) 2. (d) 3. (d) 4. (c) 5. (d)
6. (b) 7. (c) 8. (d)

Statement Based Questions

1 Statement 1 Everything around us forms our environment and our lives depend on the natural world around us.
Statement 2 Over the years, with economic development, there has been an increase in environmental pollution.

(a) Both Statement1 and Statement 2 are correct
(b) Both Statement1 and Statement 2 are incorrect
(c) Statement 1 is correct but Statement 2 is incorrect
(d) Statement 2 is correct but Statement 1 is incorrect

2 Statement 1 Sustainable Development Goals (SDGs) were launched at the United Nations Sustainable Development Summit in New York in September 2015.
Statement 2 It has set targets that the countries have to should work towards and achieve by 2040.

(a) Both Statement 1 and Statement 2 are correct
(b) Both Statement 1 and Statement 2 are incorrect
(c) Statement 1 is correct but Statement 2 is incorrect
(d) Statement 2 is correct but Statement 1 is incorrect

3 Statement 1 Increasing population and development has led to the increase in consumption of the natural resources.
Statement 2 The more the population, the more food, energy and water we need.

(a) Both Statement 1 and Statement 2 are correct
(b) Both Statement 1 and Statement 2 are incorrect
(c) Statement 1 is correct but Statement 2 is incorrect
(d) Statement 2 is correct but Statement 1 is incorrect

Answers

1. (a) 2. (c) 3. (a)

Assertion & Reason Based Questions

1 Assertion (A) Organic farming technique is an example of a green skill that is essential for sustainable agriculture.
Reason (R) Organic farming technique prioritise environment friendly and sustainable practices such

as using natural fertilisers, avoiding synthetic pesticides and promoting soil health. **2024**

(a) Both A and R are true and R is the correct explanation for A.
(b) Both A and R are true and R is not the correct explanation of A.
(c) A is true, but R is false.
(d) A is false, but R is true.

2 Assertion (A) : Sustainable agriculture is environment friendly. **2025**

Reason (R): It prevents use of chemical fertilizers to protect soil.

(a) Both A and R are true and R is the correct explanation for A.
(b) Both A and R are true and R is not the correct explanation of A.
(c) A is true, but R is false.
(d) A is false, but R is true.

Answers

1. (a) **2.** (a)

Part II

Very Short Answer Type Questions

1 Write any one challenges to sustainable development.

Ans. Rise in population level would lead to severe environmental degradation in the future.

2 Give any one practice/sustainable process that is being used to help preserve the environment.

Ans. One practice/sustainable process that is being used to help preserve the environment is organic farming.

3 The achievement of sustainable development requires what?

Ans. The achievement of sustainable development requires the integration of economic, environmental and social components at all levels.

4 'Reduced Inequalities' is one of the sustainable development goals set by the UN. Give any two ways to reduce inequalities. **Competency Based Ques.**

Ans. Two easy ways to reduce inequalities are as follows

(i) We should help everyone in spite of caste, religion, rich or poor, etc.
(ii) It doesn't matter, who they are or what they do, treat everyone the same way with kindness and respect.

5 What is sustainable development?

Ans. Sustainable development is the development that satisfies the needs of the present without compromising the capacity of future generations, guaranteeing the balance between economic growth, care for the environment and social well-being.

6 How many sustainable development goals were formulated by the United Nations?

Ans. There are 17 sustainable development goals formulated by the United Nations.

Short Answer Type Questions

1 Mention any two human activities that lead to environmental degradation. **SQP 2023-24, SQP 2024-25**

Ans. (i) Use of fertilisers, pesticides, etc for increasing the production of crops.
(ii) Cutting down of forests for personal use such as construction of buildings, factories etc.

2 Discuss the following problems related to sustainable development **2025**
(i) Water **(ii) Fuel**

Ans. Problems Related to Sustainable Development:

(i) **Water**
- **Scarcity** Depletion of freshwater resources due to overuse and pollution.
- **Access** Unequal access to clean water, affecting health and sanitation.

(ii) **Fuel**
- **Fossil Fuel Dependence** Leads to greenhouse gas emissions and climate change.
- **Depletion** Finite resources are being consumed at unsustainable rates.

3 Give any two examples of how individual choices and behaviours can contribute in achieving sustainable development. **2024**

Ans. (i) Waste less food and support local farmers
(ii) Get yourselves and your family vaccinated

4 Why there is a need for sustainable development? Give reasons. **Competency Based Ques.**

Ans. There is a need of sustainable development because of the following reasons:

(i) Sustainable development teaches people to make use of means and resources for the maximum benefit without wastage.
(ii) Sustainable development brings about changes in people's knowledge, attitude and skill.
(iii) Sustainable development aims at achieving the goal of economic and social development without destroying the Earth's means and resources.

SELF ASSESSMENT

Multiple Choice Questions

1. The concept of sustainable development was popularised in
   (a) 1985 (b) 1986
   (c) 1987 (d) 1988
2. Sustainable development requires proper use of
   (a) natural resources (b) man-made resources
   (c) human resources (d) Both (a) and (b)
3. Sustainable Forest Management which were development in Europe during the ……… centuries.
   (a) 16th and 18th (b) 17th and 18th
   (c) 18th and 19th (d) 19th and 20th
4. The focus of sustainable development is correcting the policies that are the ……… of adverse environment.
   (a) results (b) root cause
   (c) solutions (d) none of these
5. Development is a term used to describe political goals and ……… progress.
   (a) Social (b) Economics
   (c) Environmental (d) All of these

Very Short Answer Type Questions

6. Give the definition of sustainable development as suggested by Brundtland Report.
7. When did the idea of sustainable development become popular?
8. Mention any one serious problem relating to sustainable development.

Short Answer Type Questions

9. Why do you think the United Nations has made the 17 Sustainable Development Goals?
10. What are the main principle of sustainable development?
11. Explain the long-term solution related to sustainable development.
12. Write down the global development goals set up the United Nation Sustainable Development Summit (2015).

PART B
SUBJECT SPECIFIC SKILLS

Revisiting AI Project Cycle & Ethical Frameworks for AI

CHAPTER 01

This chapter will guide you through the fundamental stages of the AI project cycle, including problem identification, data acquisition, model development, evaluation, and deployment. Additionally, it will explore prominent ethical frameworks that help mitigate risks associated with AI systems.

1.1 AI Project Cycle

It is a step-by-step process that a person should follow to develop an AI Project to solve a problem. AI Project Cycle provides us with an appropriate framework which can lead us to achieve our goal.

The AI project cycle is a structured roadmap for developing and deploying artificial intelligence projects to solve real-world problems.

This systematic approach helps define objectives, collect relevant data, uncover hidden insights, create models for AI systems, and assess their performance.

Different Stages of AI Cycle

The AI project cycle mainly has 5 stages

(i) **Problem Scoping** understanding the problem

(ii) **Data Acquisition** collecting accurate and reliable data

(iii) **Data Exploration** arranging the data uniformly

(iv) **Modelling** creating models from the data

(v) **Evaluation** evaluating the project

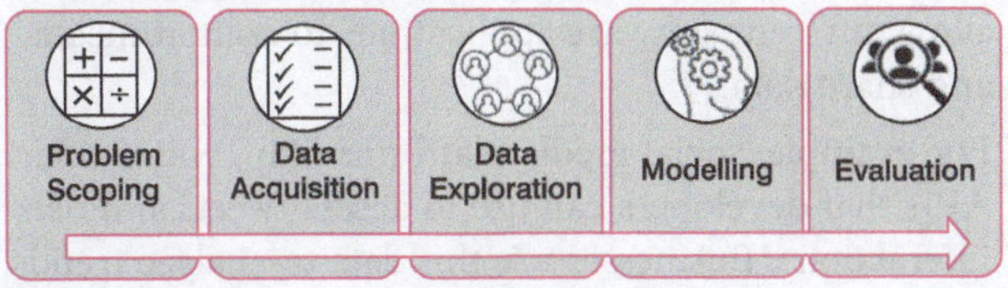

1.2 Problem Scoping

Problem scoping is the process of identifying the scope the problem that need to be solved. Problem scoping is a critical initial phase in the AI project cycle where the focus is on defining the problem or opportunity that the AI solution aims to address. This stage sets the foundation for the entire project and significantly influences its success.

> **Sustainable Development Goals**
>
> The Sustainable Development Goals (SDGs) are a set of 17 goals, defined by the United Nations (UN) in 2015 and to be implemented by 2030. The SDGs are also known as the **Global Goals**. The SDGs are a blueprint for sustainable future and address global challenges such as poverty, inequality, climate change and environmental degradation.

We use the 4Ws Problem Canvas to understand the problem in a better way.

The 4Ws Problem Canvas

The 4W problem canvas helps in identifying the key elements related to the problem.

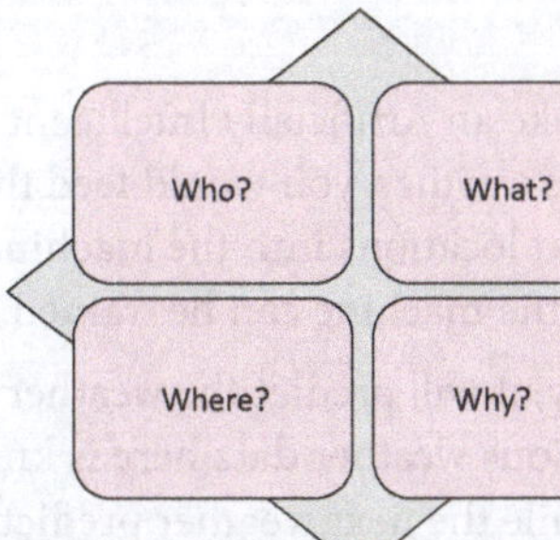

The 4Ws are

1. **Who?** This block helps in analysing the people who are getting affected directly or indirectly due to a problem. Under this, we find out who are the 'Stakeholders' to this problem?

2. **What?** This block helps to determine the nature of the problem. Under this block, we also gather evidence to prove that the problem you have selected actually exists.
3. **Where?** This block will help us to look into the situation in which the problem arises, and the locations.
4. **Why?** In this block, we think about the benefits which the stakeholders would get from the solution and how it will benefit them as well as the society.

Problem Statement Template

The problem statement template takes the information gathered from the 4Ws problem canvas (Who, What, When, Why) and Condenses it into a clear, concise statement. This process refines a broad problem into a well-defined one, allowing you to focus your efforts on a specific issue and develop targeted solution.

Try These 1.1

1 **Name the five stages of AI project cycle.**

2 **Explain a project life cycle with the help of an example.**

3 **The sustainable development goals aim is to achieve by the end of year**

(a) 2025 (b) 2030

(c) 2035 (d) 2040

4 **What should be the characteristics of a good problem statement template?**

1.3 Data Acquisition

Data Acquisition is the process of collecting the required data from reliable sources. This is the second phase of the AI project cycle, which is focused on obtaining the necessary data for the project. Data needs to be accurate and reliable.

For example, To make an Artificially Intelligent system which can predict the weather, you would feed the data of previous days for that locations into the machine. This is the data with which the machine can be trained.

Now, once it is ready, it will predict the weather conditions efficiently. The previous weather data here is known as "**Training Data**" while the next weather prediction data set is known as the "**Testing Data**".

Data Features

Data features refer to the individual characteristics of a dataset that provide information for analysis. These attributes can be numerical, categorical, or textual. They serve as the input variables for machine learning models, influencing the model's ability to make predictions or classifications based on patterns within the data.

Data Sources

Data source is where does one get data from? It's essential to consider data quality, relevance, and ethical considerations when choosing and handling data from these sources.

Some important ways to collect data are

- **Surveys** Surveys involve gathering data by asking questions directly to individuals or groups of people.
- **Web Scraping** Web scraping involves extracting data from websites and web pages.
- **Sensors** Sensors are devices that collect data from the physical world and convert it into a form that computers can understand. For example, temperature sensors in weather stations measure the ambient temperature, and this data is used to predict weather conditions. In smartphones, accelerometers detect the phone's movement and orientation, allowing for automatic screen rotation and activity tracking.
- **Cameras** Cameras capture visual data in the form of images or videos. They can be used to collect data in fields such as surveillance, computer vision, image processing, and object recognition.
- **Observations** Observations involve collecting data by monitoring or measuring phenomena. In agriculture, for example, farmers observe crop health using drones equipped with cameras. These drones take high-resolution images of fields, which are then analyzed to detect issues like pest infestations or water stress, helping farmers make better decisions about crop management.
- **API (Application Programming Interface)** APIs (Application Programming Interfaces) are tools that allow different software applications to communicate and share data.

  For example, social media platforms like Twitter offer APIs that developers can use to access tweets and user interactions. Businesses use this data to analyze trends, monitor brand reputation, and engage with customers in real-time.

One of the most dependable and trustworthy sources for data is government-hosted open-access websites. Examples of such government portals include data.gov.in and india.gov.in.

1.4 Data Exploration

Data exploration is the process of visualisation of collected data in a graphical format for better understanding to build the project. The data is a complex entity, full of numbers. Hence, to get some sense out of it, data visualization is a must.

Data Visualization

Data visualization is the graphical representation of data. It involves the use of visual elements such as charts, graphs, maps, and infographics to communicate insights, patterns, and trends hidden within the data.

Data visualization helps in

- Understanding complex data more easily.
- Identifying trends, patterns, and correlations.
- Communicating insights clearly and concisely.
- Spotting anomalies and outliers quickly.
- Exploring data interactively.
- Supporting evidence-based decision-making.

Different Ways to Visualize Data

There are some ways to visualize the data as follows

Bar Chart It is used to compare categorical data, where the length or height of bars represents the value of each category. It can be vertical or horizontal.

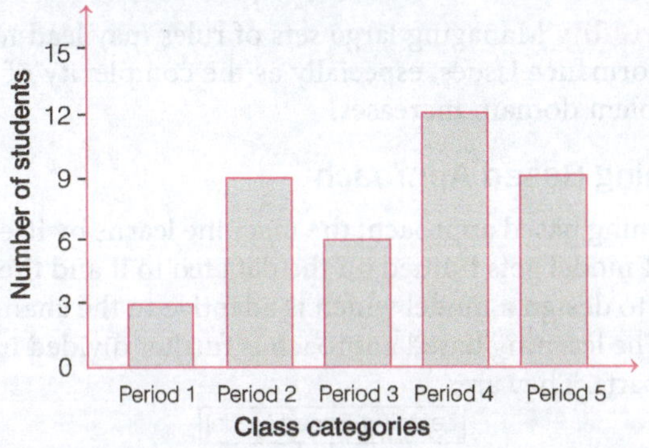

Line Chart It shows trends over time or relationships between variables by connecting data points. It is ideal for displaying continuous data.

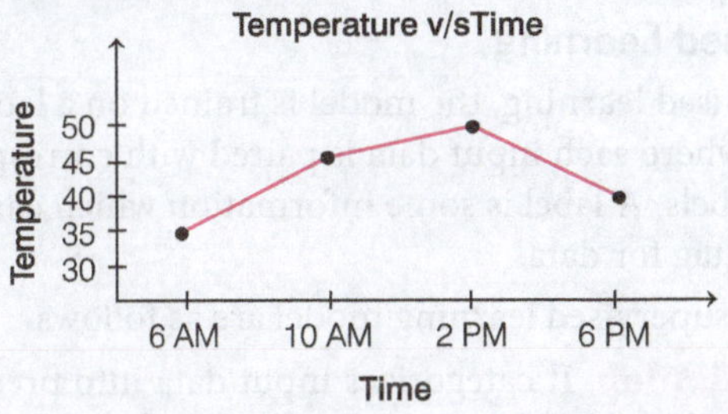

Pie Chart It displays parts of a whole, where each segment represents a proportion of the total. It is useful for illustrating percentages or proportions.

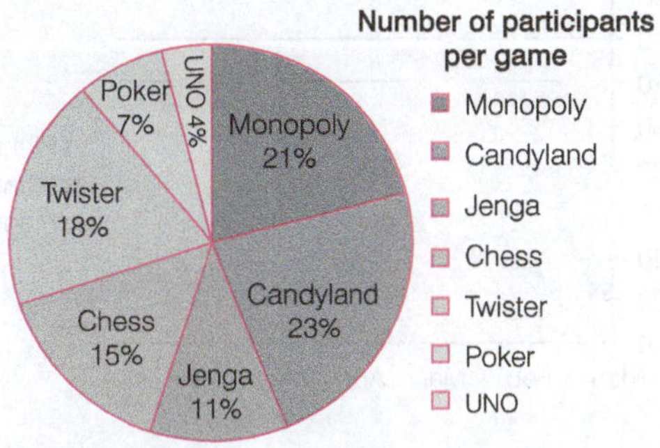

Scatter chart It represents individual data points as dots on a two-dimensional graph, with one variable on each axis. It is used to show relationships and correlations between variables.

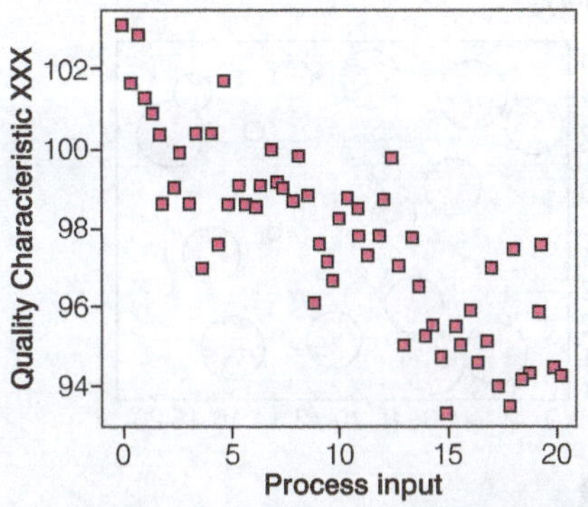

Scatterplot for quality characteristic XXX

Histogram It represents the distribution of numerical data by dividing it into intervals, or bins, and displaying the frequency or count of data points falling within each interval. It shows the distribution of values within predefined intervals (bins).

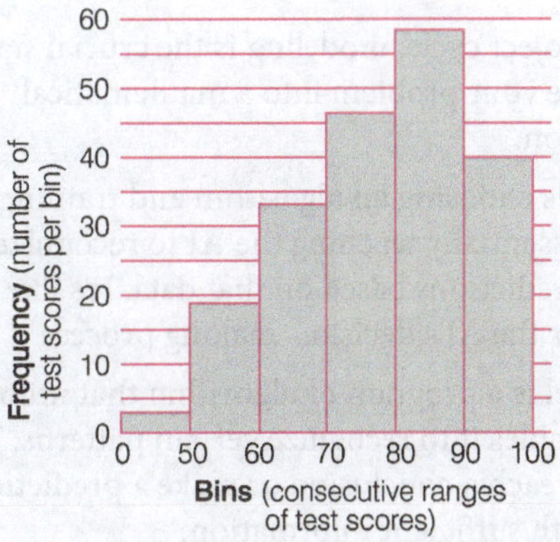

Area Chart It is similar to a line chart but with the area beneath the lines filled in. It is useful for visualizing cumulative totals over time.

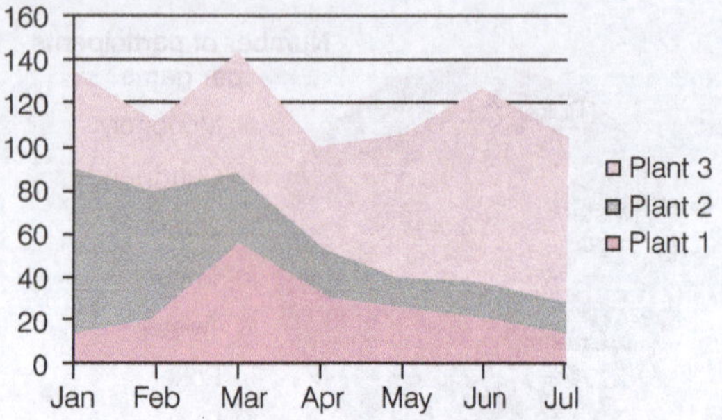

Bubble Chart It is similar to a scatter plot but with additional dimensions represented by the size and/or color of bubbles.

It allows for the visualization of three or more variables simultaneously.

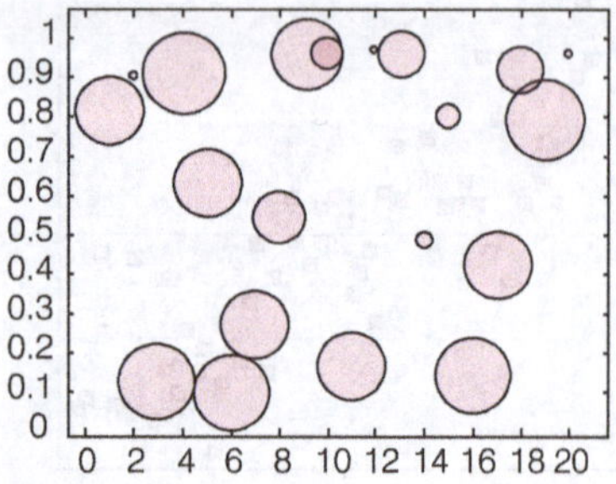

Try These 1.2

1. **Mention any two data visualization tools.**
2. **Why data visualization is important?**
3. **How chart helps in getting clear picture about the data?**
4. **What is testing data?**

1.5 Modelling

In the AI project cycle, modeling is the crucial stage where you translate your problem into a mathematical representation.

This involves choosing an algorithm and training it on your data, essentially teaching the AI to recognize patterns and make predictions based on that data. It's like creating a blueprint for the AI's decision-making process.

An AI model is a program or algorithm that utilizes a set of data that enables it to recognize certain patterns. This allows it to reach a conclusion or make a prediction when provided with sufficient information.

AI models can be classified into

Rule Based Approach

It refers to the AI modelling where the rules are defined by the developer. The machine follows the rules mentioned by the developer and performs its task accordingly.

These rules are typically expressed in the form of "if-then" statements, where specific actions or decisions are taken based on the satisfaction of certain conditions. Rule-based systems are often used in expert systems, decision support systems, and business process automation.

Rule-based approaches offer several advantages, including:

- **Interpretability** Rule-based systems are often highly interpretable, as the decision-making process is based on explicit rules that can be easily understood and inspected by humans.
- **Transparency** Reason behind the system's decisions is transparent, making it easier to diagnose errors or understand why a particular decision was made.
- **Ease of Maintenance** Rules can be modified or updated relatively easily, allowing for quick adjustments to accommodate changes in the problem domain.

However, rule-based approaches also have limitations, including:

- **Limited Expressiveness** Rule-based systems may struggle to capture complex patterns or relationships in the data that cannot be easily expressed as rules.
- **Scalability** Managing large sets of rules may lead to performance issues, especially as the complexity of the problem domain increases.

Learning Based Approach

In learning based approach, the machine learns by itself. The AI model gets trained on the data fed to it and then it is able to design a model which is adaptive to the change in data. The learning based approach is further divided into three parts. They are:

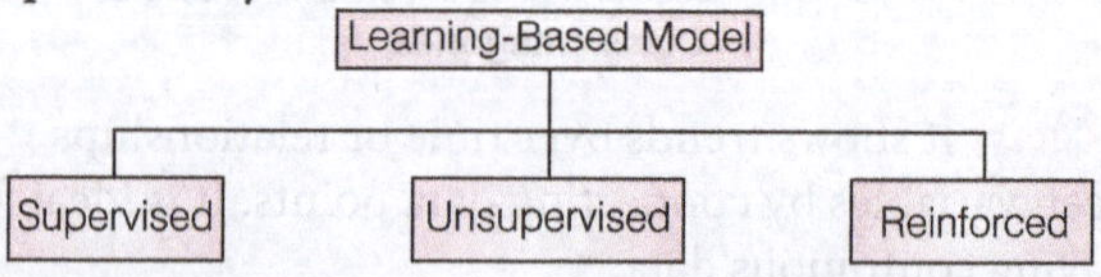

Supervised Learning

In supervised learning, the model is trained on a labelled dataset, where each input data is paired with corresponding output labels. A label is some information which can be used as a tag for data.

Types of supervised learning model are as follows

- **Classification** It categorizes input data into predefined labels. Classification works on discrete dataset which means the data need not be continuous.

For example, classifying emails as spam or not.

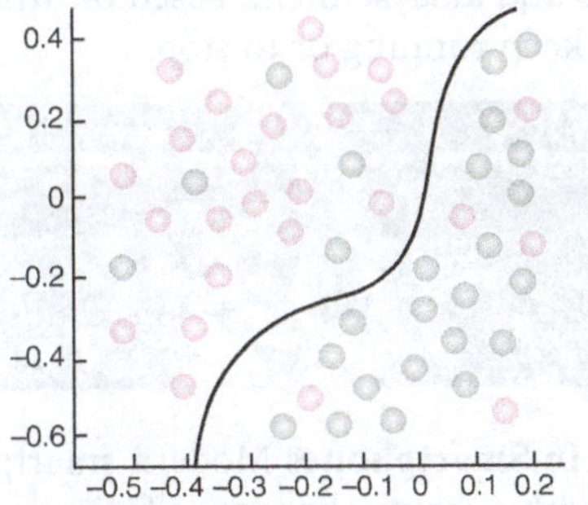

- **Regression** It is used to predict continuous numerical values based on input features. It aims to establish a functional relationship between independent variables and a dependent variable.

  For example, predicting house prices based on features like size, bedrooms, and location.

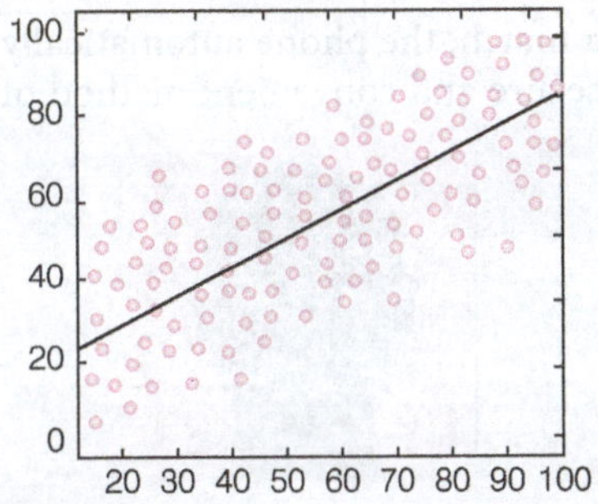

Unsupervised Learning

Unsupervised learning deals with unlabelled data. It does not receive any information regarding the output. The system by itself evaluates and finds out how different elements are related to it.

Types of unsupervised learning model are as follows

- **Clustering** Clustering is the process of grouping unlabelled data into clusters based on their similarities. The goal of clustering is to identify patterns and relationships in the data without any prior knowledge of data. This technique is applied to group data based on different patterns, such as similarities or differences.

  For example, finding out which customers made similar product purchases.

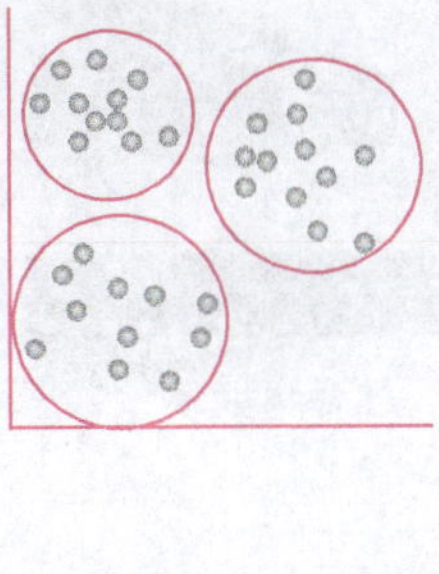

- **Dimensionality Reduction** It reduces the number of features, or dimensions, in a dataset. Dimensionality reduction extracts important features from the dataset, reducing the number of irrelevant or random features present.

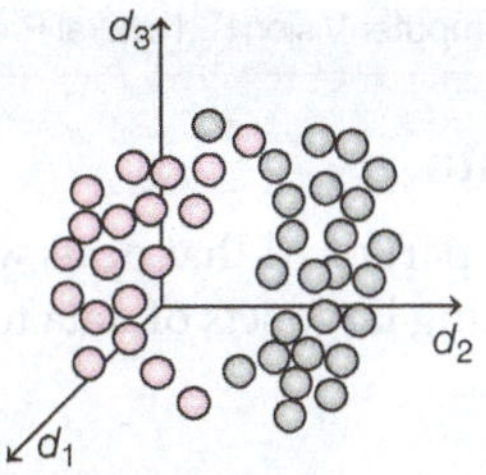

Reinforcement Learning

Reinforcement learning involves an agent learning to make decisions by interacting with an environment. The agent receives feedback in the form of rewards or punishments based on its actions.

1.6 Evaluation

The process of testing the project/machine like performance or capabilities and finding faults etc. is known as evaluation. Once a model has been made and trained, it needs to go through proper testing so that one can calculate the efficiency and performance of the model. Hence, the model is tested with the help of Testing Data and the efficiency of the model is calculated on the basis of the parameters mentioned below:

1. **Accuracy** Accuracy is a measure of the overall correctness of the model.
2. **Precision** Precision is the ratio of correctly predicted positive instances to the total predicted positive instances (true positives divided by true positives plus false positives).
3. **Recall** Recall, also known as sensitivity or true positive rate, is the ratio of correctly predicted positive instances to the total actual positive instances (true positives divided by true positives plus false negatives).
4. **F1 Score** The F1 score is the harmonic mean of precision and recall, providing a balanced measure between the two. It is calculated as

$$2 \times \frac{\text{Precision} \times \text{Recall}}{\text{Precision} + \text{Recall}}$$

1.7 Introduction to AI Domains

Artificial Intelligence (AI) becomes intelligent based on the training it receives. Training involves feeding the machine with datasets. The type of data provided depends on the application being developed. Based on the kind of data used, AI models can be grouped into three main domains:

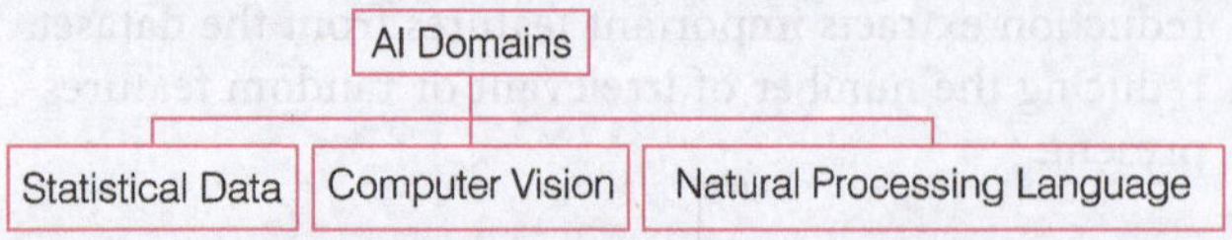

1. Statistical Data

Statistical Data is a part of AI that deals with collecting, storing, and analyzing large sets of data to find patterns and make decisions.

For example,

- **Price Comparison Websites** These websites collect data from various vendors to help users compare prices of products in one place. Popular examples include PriceGrabber, Shopzilla, and Junglee.
  Price comparison tools are used in many industries like technology, travel, and shopping.

2. Computer Vision (CV)

Computer Vision is a branch of AI that allows machines to understand and interpret visual information from the world, such as images and videos. The process includes capturing, analyzing, and understanding images to help the machine make decisions.

For example,

- **Agricultural Monitoring** Drones with cameras capture images of farmland. These images are analyzed to monitor crop health, detect pests, and estimate yields.

- **Surveillance Systems** Cameras equipped with AI monitor public places to detect suspicious activities and send real-time alerts to security teams.

- **Self-Driving cars/ Automatic Cars** CV systems scan live objects and analyse them, based on whether the car decides to keep running or to stop.

- **Face Lock in Smartphones** Modern smartphones come equipped with a feature known as face recognition, which allows users to unlock their phones using their facial features.
  During the setup process, the smartphone's front camera captures and stores details of the user's face. Once saved, the next time the user tries to unlock the phone, the camera detects the face and compares it with the stored features.
  If there is a match, the phone automatically unlocks, offering a secure and convenient method of access.

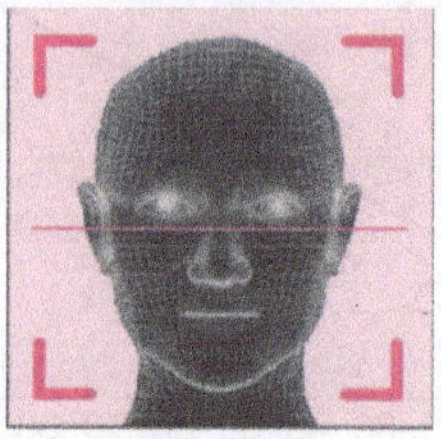

3. Natural Language Processing (NLP)

Natural Language Processing is the area of AI that enables computers to understand and process human language, both spoken and written.

The primary objective of Natural Language Processing (NLP) is to enable computers to understand, interpret, and generate human language, bridging the gap between human and machine communication.

For example,

- **Email Filters** Email services use NLP to detect and filter out spam messages automatically.

- **Machine Translation** Tools like Google Translate use NLP to translate text from one language to another by understanding sentence structures and meanings.

- **Smart Assistants** Smart assistants, such as Apple's Siri and Amazon's Alexa, are designed to recognize patterns in speech, understand the context, and generate appropriate responses.

  They use advanced algorithms to analyze voice commands, infer the meaning behind them, and provide helpful answers or perform tasks. Over time, these smart assistants can improve their accuracy by learning from user interactions, offering more personalized and efficient responses.

1.8 Frameworks

Frameworks are step-by-step guides that help us solve problems in an organized way. They help us think clearly and cover all important points while solving a problem.

For example, when you follow steps to solve a math problem or a science experiment, you are using a framework.

Ethical Frameworks

Ethics are values or morals that help us decide what is right or wrong. Ethical frameworks are step-by-step methods that help us make choices that do not cause harm. They help us solve problems while thinking about what is fair, honest, and good for everyone.

Need of Ethical Frameworks for AI

AI (Artificial Intelligence) is used to make decisions. But sometimes, AI can make unfair choices. For example, a hiring program might select fewer women because of biased data.

Ethical frameworks help prevent such problems by guiding AI to make fair and moral decisions. By using ethical frameworks, we can avoid mistakes before they happen.

Types of Ethical Frameworks for AI

There are two main types of ethical frameworks for AI:

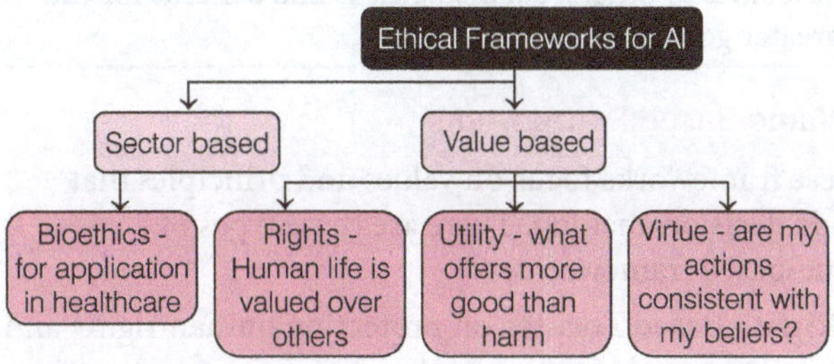

1. Sector-Based Frameworks

These frameworks are made for specific industries like healthcare, finance, or education. For example, in healthcare, the framework is called Bioethics, which ensures patient privacy, data security, and fairness in medical decisions.

Other sectors include finance, education, transportation, and law enforcement.

Example Bioethics in Healthcare

Bioethics is an ethical framework for healthcare. It guides the use of AI in medicine to protect patients and ensure fairness.

The four main principles of bioethics are:

- **Respect for Autonomy** Letting patients make their own choices.
- **Do Not Harm** Ensuring AI systems do not hurt people.
- **Ensure Maximum Benefit** Using AI to help as many people as possible.
- **Give Justice** Treating everyone fairly and equally.

Non-maleficence "Do no harm." This principle urges individuals and organizations to avoid actions that could cause harm or suffering to others. It requires minimizing harm whenever possible.

Maleficence The opposite of non-maleficence, this principle involves causing harm or engaging in wrongful actions. It's generally something to avoid in ethical decision-making.

Beneficence This principle encourages promoting the welfare of others. It involves actions aimed at contributing to the overall well-being and positive outcomes of others, balancing risks and benefits for the greater good.

2. Value-Based Frameworks

These frameworks focus on values and principles that guide decision-making. There are three types of value-based frameworks:

- **Rights-Based** Focuses on protecting human rights and treating people with respect.

  For example, ensuring that an AI chatbot does not use harmful language.
- **Utility-Based** Focuses on choosing actions that create the most good and the least harm.

  For example, using AI to reduce traffic accidents.
- **Virtue-Based** Focuses on honesty, compassion, and doing the right thing.

  For example, making sure AI developers act responsibly.

1.9 Case Study

This case study illustrates the significant impact that ethical frameworks, such as the bioethics principles, can have on the development and implementation of AI technologies, particularly in healthcare.

Let's break down the application of the bioethics framework and how it can lead to better outcomes:

Respect for Autonomy

Ensuring transparency and providing stakeholders (e.g., patients, healthcare providers) with a clear understanding of how the AI algorithm works is crucial. In this case, patients and healthcare professionals should know:

- How the algorithm functions, the data it uses, and the criteria for risk classification.
- The potential biases in the data and the limitations of the algorithm.
- In case of errors or concerns, being able to review the model's predictions, data labels, and methodology fosters accountability.

This respects the autonomy of healthcare providers and patients by enabling informed decision-making and trust in the system.

Do Not Harm

The principle of non-maleficence emphasizes that the AI system should not inadvertently cause harm. In the case study, the AI algorithm was inadvertently harmful because it misclassified patients based on biased data, prioritizing healthcare resources for those who didn't require as much attention:

- The algorithm, by using healthcare expense data, overlooked the actual healthcare needs of patients from the western region, causing them to be misclassified as lower-risk.
- It's crucial that the AI system is designed and trained on unbiased data that reflects a comprehensive view of health, ensuring that resources are allocated justly and appropriately to those most in need.

Maximum Benefit

While avoiding harm is critical, the AI system should also strive to maximize benefits for all groups:

- The solution should not only address the disparities in healthcare allocation but also actively benefit patients from all regions, including those from the western region.
- Using more representative, unbiased datasets would help achieve maximum benefit by ensuring that the AI's predictions align with patients' true healthcare needs. For example, using a more accurate and inclusive dataset could allow the algorithm to recognize the severity of illnesses in different regions, optimizing resource distribution.

Justice

The principle of justice ensures that the benefits and burdens of an AI solution are fairly distributed, without perpetuating societal biases such as racism or discrimination:

- The algorithm, as designed, resulted in unequal healthcare outcomes for patients from the western region due to biases in the dataset.
- To promote justice, the AI should consider the social determinants of health and be designed to eliminate systemic biases, ensuring equitable care for all patients.

Try These 1.3

1. **What is the primary purpose of an ethical framework in AI development?**
2. **Name two main categories of ethical frameworks for AI.**
3. **What are the four principles of Bioethics?**
4. **What was the main issue with the AI algorithm used in the case study provided?**

Glossary

Problem Scoping Understanding the Problem.

Data Acquisition Collecting accurate and reliable data.

Data Exploration Arranging the data uniformly.

Modelling Creating Models from the data.

Evaluation Evaluating the project.

Ethical Framework Ethical frameworks are frameworks which help us ensure that the choices we make do not cause unintended harm.

Ethical frameworks for AI can be categorized into two main types: sector-based and value- based frameworks.

Sector- based These are frameworks tailored to specific sectors or industries.

Value-based Value-based frameworks focus on fundamental ethical principles and values guiding decision- making.

Bioethics Bioethics is an ethical framework used in healthcare and life sciences.

Principles of bioethics Respect for Autonomy, Do not harm, Ensure maximum benefit for all and Give justice.

ACTIVITY Time

ACTIVITY 1 : My Goodness

Purpose To understand how our decisions get influenced by our personal morals, values, and ethics.

Instructions for Students

1. **Visit the Website** https://www.my-goodness.net/

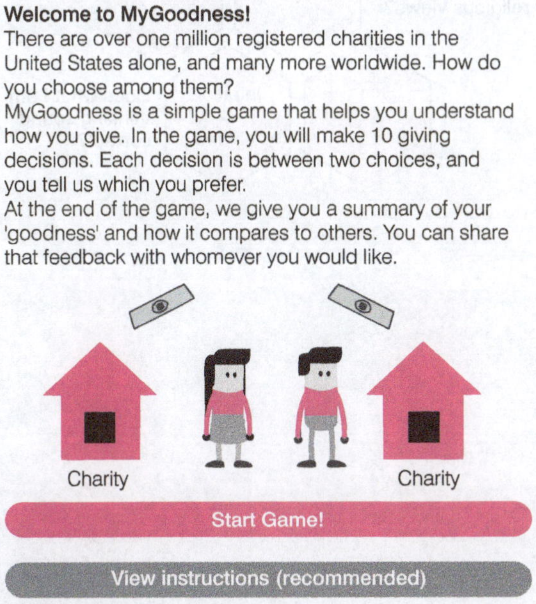

2. **Watch the Video** Take a quick look at the video to understand how the game works.

3. **Play the Game**
   - You will make 10 decisions on how you would like to donate to different causes.
   - You will see details about the recipients and the intended use of your donation.
   - In some cases, information about the recipients may be hidden, but you can choose to reveal it.

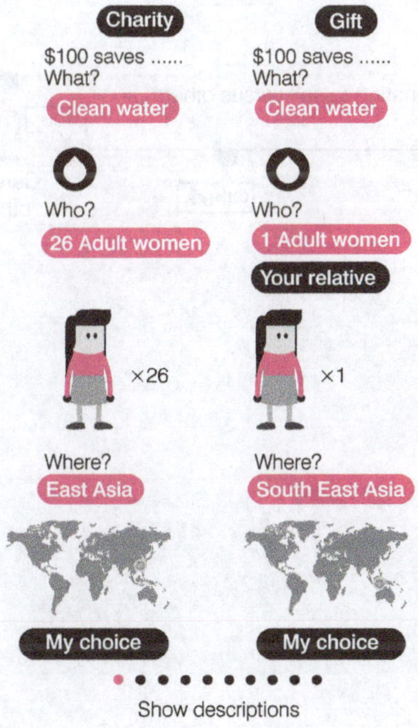

4. **Survey** After completing your decisions, fill out the short survey provided.

Would you like to help us better understand your judgement?

Yes No

5. **Insights** Once you finish, you will receive feedback and insights about your decision-making patterns.

Factors which could influence your decisions without you realizing it include

- Identity of the charity recipient (e.g., age, gender, background)
- Location of the recipient (e.g., local vs. international)
- Bias towards people with whom you relate (e.g., relatives, familiar causes)
- Uncovering or withholding information (e.g., choosing to reveal hidden details)

Which preferences may have reduced your effectiveness?

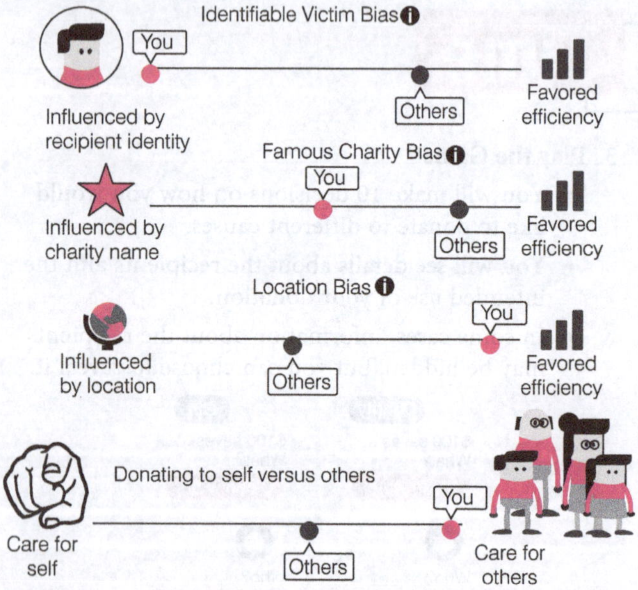

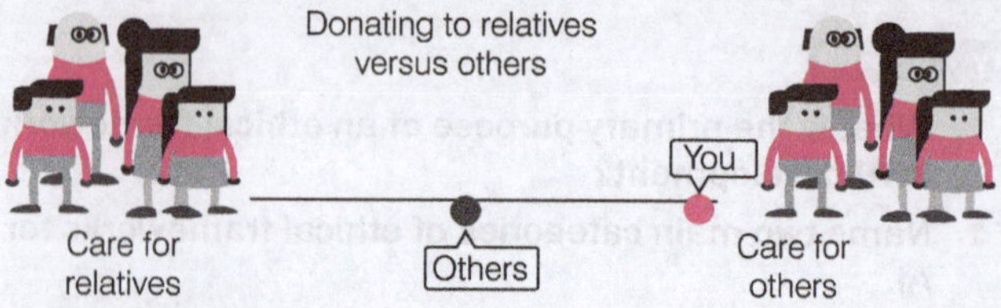

Do it yourself

- Did you discover any internal biases while making your decisions?
- Do you agree with the results shared by the game? Why or why not?

List at least 3 factors that knowingly or unknowingly influence your decision-making:

1. **Culture** Does my cultural background influence who I want to help?
2. **Religious Views** Is my decision aligned with my religious beliefs?
3. **Intuition & Values** Does what I am thinking feel ethically correct?

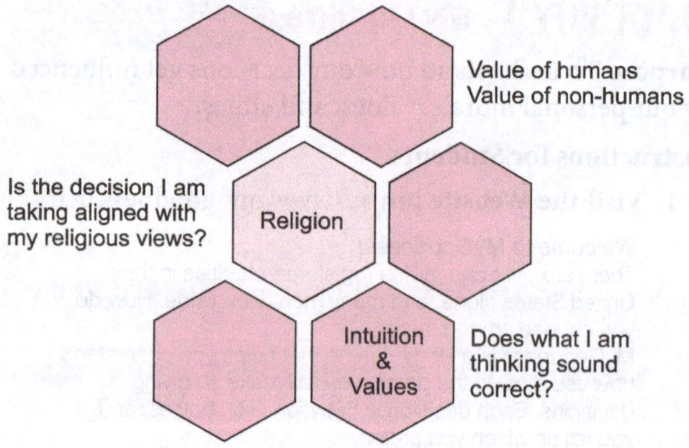

NCERT FOLDER

Complete Explanations of all NCERT's Questions

A. Multiple Choice Questions

1. What is the purpose of defining the problem statement during the Problem Scoping stage in an AI project cycle?
(a) To collect data
(b) To understand the aim and objective of the project
(c) To train the model
(d) To process data

2. In what ways can AI models be categorized based on the type of data fed into them?
(a) Two domains
(b) Four domains
(c) Three domains
(d) Five domains

3. In Statistical Data, what is the primary function of the system in relation to data?
(a) Generating large datasets
(b) Analyzing data to extract insights
(c) Converting data into images
(d) Distributing data across networks

4. What is the main goal of Computer Vision projects?
(a) Translating audio data into visual descriptions
(b) Converting digital data into analogue signals
(c) Teaching machines to understand textual information
(d) Converting digital visual data into computer-readable language

5. What is the primary focus of NLP?
(a) Analyzing computer languages
(b) Interacting between computers and humans using artificial language
(c) Dealing with the interaction between computers and humans using natural language
(d) Enhancing human-to-human communication

6. What do frameworks provide in the context of problem-solving?
(a) Random solutions
(b) Step-by-step guidance
(c) Legal advice
(d) Ethical justifications

7. How are Ethical Frameworks for AI categorized?
(a) Into legal and illegal frameworks
(b) Into sector-based and value-based frameworks
(c) Into historical and contemporary frameworks
(d) Into theoretical and practical frameworks

8. What is the central focus of virtue-based value-based frameworks?
(a) Maximizing utility
(b) Protecting human rights
(c) Aligning actions with ethical principles and beliefs
(d) Ensuring compliance with legal regulations

9. Which of the following best describes rights-based value-based frameworks?
(a) Prioritizing human rights and dignity, valuing human life over other considerations
(b) Evaluating actions based on maximizing overall good and minimizing harm
(c) Centering on the character of the decision-maker and the alignment of actions with personal or societal virtues
(d) Focusing on achieving outcomes that offer the greatest benefit

10. What is the primary domain of application for Bioethics?
(a) Agriculture
(b) Healthcare and life sciences
(c) Information technology
(d) Environmental conservation

11. Assertion (A) Ethics provide guidance in distinguishing right from wrong.
Reason (R) Ethics consist of a set of values and morals that aid individuals in making moral judgments and decisions.
(a) Both Assertion and Reasoning are true, and Reasoning is the correct explanation of the Assertion.
(b) Assertion is true, but Reasoning is false.
(c) Both Assertion and Reasoning are true, but Reasoning is not the correct explanation of the Assertion.
(d) Assertion is false, but Reasoning is true.

12. Assertion (A) Value-based frameworks in ethics provide guidance by focusing on fundamental ethical principles and values.
Reason (R) These frameworks effect different moral philosophies guiding ethical reasoning and are concerned with assessing the moral worth of actions.
(a) Both Assertion and Reasoning are true, and Reasoning is the correct explanation of the Assertion.
(b) Assertion is true, but Reasoning is false.
(c) Both Assertion and Reasoning are true, but Reasoning is not the correct explanation of the Assertion.
(d) Assertion is false, but Reasoning is true.

Answers

1. (b)	2. (c)	3. (b)	4. (d)	5. (c)
6. (b)	7. (b)	8. (c)	9. (a)	10. (b)
11. (a)	12. (a)			

B. Reflection Time

1. Outline the main steps in the AI Project Cycle briefly.

Ans. The AI Project Cycle consists of five main steps:

- **Problem Scoping** understanding the problem.
- **Data Acquisition** collecting and processing relevant data.
- **Data Exploration** arranging the data uniformly.
- **Modelling** creating models from the data.
- **Evaluation** evaluating the project.

2. What roles does computer vision play in agricultural monitoring systems?

Ans. Computer vision enhances agricultural monitoring by enabling crop health assessment, weed detection, yield estimation, soil moisture analysis, livestock monitoring, automated harvesting, and precision farming. It improves efficiency, reduces manual labor, and optimizes resource use in farming.

3. Mention the factors which knowingly or unknowingly influence our decision-making.

Ans. Factors influencing decision-making include:

- Cognitive biases (e.g., confirmation bias, anchoring bias)
- Emotions and psychological state
- Social influences and peer pressure
- Past experiences and learned behavior
- Availability of information and misinformation
- Time constraints and urgency
- Personal values and ethics

4. What is the necessity for Ethical Frameworks in AI development?

Ans. Ethical frameworks in AI development are necessary to ensure fairness, accountability, transparency, and security. They help mitigate bias, protect privacy, prevent misuse, and promote responsible AI applications that align with human rights and societal values.

5. Mention the key characteristics of sector-based frameworks.

Ans. Sector-based frameworks are:

- **Industry-Specific** Tailored to particular sectors (e.g., healthcare, finance, education).
- **Regulatory Compliant** Align with laws and policies governing the sector.
- **Risk-Oriented** Address industry-specific risks and challenges.
- **Guideline-Driven** Provide structured guidelines for implementation.
- **Stakeholder-Focused** Consider the needs of businesses, consumers, and regulators.

6. What do you mean by Bioethics?

Ans. Bioethics is the study of ethical issues related to biological sciences, medicine, and biotechnology. It addresses concerns like medical ethics, genetic engineering, euthanasia, and research ethics.

7. What is Natural Language Processing? Explain any two real-life applications of NLP.

Ans. Natural Language Processing (NLP) is a field of AI that enables computers to understand, interpret, and generate human language.

Two real-life applications:

1. **Chatbots (e.g., Siri, Alexa)** Assist users by processing voice commands.
2. **Sentiment Analysis** Helps businesses analyse customer opinions from reviews.

8. How do value-based frameworks contribute to ethical decision-making by emphasizing fundamental principles and values?

Ans. Value-based frameworks emphasize honesty, fairness, accountability, and respect, ensuring that decisions align with ethical principles rather than just legal compliance.

C. Case-Based Questions

1. In a corporate setting, a multinational company is facing scrutiny over its environmental practices, particularly regarding the disposal of industrial waste. The company has historically prioritized profit maximization and cost-cutting measures, leading to practices that result in environmental harm and negative impacts on local communities. As public awareness and concern about environmental sustainability grow, stakeholders, including investors, customers, and advocacy groups, are calling for the company to adopt more responsible and sustainable business practices.

Drawing from the case presented, analyze the ethical considerations surrounding the company's environmental practices through the lens of value-based frameworks in ethics.

Ans. The company's environmental practices raise ethical concerns related to sustainability, corporate responsibility, and social impact. A value-based ethical framework emphasizes fundamental principles like fairness, accountability, and environmental stewardship.

- **Accountability & Transparency** The Company must take responsibility for its environmental impact and disclose its waste management practices.

- **Sustainability & Environmental Ethics** Ethical business practices prioritize long-term ecological balance over short-term profit maximization.
- **Stakeholder Responsibility** The company must address concerns from investors, customers, and advocacy groups by adopting sustainable solutions.
- **Moral Obligation** The company should adopt sustainable practices, such as eco-friendly waste disposal and green technologies, aligning with ethical and legal standards.

  By integrating value-based ethics, the company can build trust, enhance its reputation, and contribute to a sustainable future while maintaining profitability.

2. In a rural farming community, a group of small-scale farmers is faced with a dilemma regarding the use of pesticides on their crops. The farmers have traditionally relied on chemical pesticides to control pests and maximize crop yields.

However, concerns have been raised about the potential environmental and health impacts of pesticide use, including soil contamination, water pollution, and adverse effects on human health. Additionally, neighboring communities and environmental advocacy groups have expressed opposition to the widespread use of pesticides, citing ecological damage and risks to biodiversity.

Using the case provided, examine the ethical considerations surrounding pesticide use in the agricultural sector, applying ethical frameworks to analyze the competing interests and values at stake.

Ans. The ethical considerations surrounding pesticide use in agriculture involve balancing economic benefits, environmental sustainability, and public health. Applying ethical frameworks, we can analyse the competing interests as follows:

- **Utilitarianism (Greatest Good for the Majority)** While pesticides increase crop yields and economic stability for farmers, their long-term harm to the environment and human health outweighs the short-term benefits. Sustainable alternatives should be explored.
- **Deontological Ethics (Duty-Based Ethics)** Farmers have a moral duty to protect human health and the environment. Continuing pesticide use despite known risks violates ethical responsibilities to the community and future generations.
- **Environmental Ethics (Sustainability & Stewardship)** Ethical farming requires responsible resource management to prevent soil and water contamination, ensuring biodiversity conservation and ecological balance.

EXAM PATTERN EXERCISE

Including Competency Based Questions

Part I

Multiple Choice Questions

1. Choose the five stages of AI project cycle in correct order 2024

(a) Evaluation → Problem Scoping → Data Exploration → Data Acquisition → Modelling
(b) Problem Scoping → Data Exploration → Data Acquisition → Evaluation → Modelling
(c) Data Acquisition → Problem Scoping → Data Exploration → Modelling → Evaluation
(d) Problem Scoping → Data Acquisition → Data Exploration → Modelling → Evaluation

2. ________ helps us to summarise all the key points into one single outline so that in future, whenever there is need to look back at the basis of the problem, we can take a look at it and understand the key elements of it.

(a) 4Ws Problem canvas (b) Problem Statement Template
(c) Data Acquisition (d) Algorithm

3. The ________________canvas helps you in identifying the key elements related to the problem.

(a) Problem scoping (b) 4Ws Problem
(c) Project cycle (d) Algorithm

4. Name any two methods of collecting data.

(a) Surveys and Interviews
(b) Rumors and Myths
(c) AI models and applications
(d) Imagination and thoughts

5. Give two examples of Supervised Learning models.

(a) Classification and Regression
(b) Clustering and Dimensionality Reduction
(c) Rule Based and Learning Based
(d) Classification and Clustering

6. Which of the following is not part of the AI Project Cycle?
(a) Data Exploration (b) Modelling
(c) Testing (d) Problem Scoping

7. .... is the last stage of the AI project life cycle.
(a) Problem Scoping (b) Evaluation
(c) Modelling (d) Data Acquisition

8. What is the primary need for evaluating an AI model's performance in the AI Model Development process? 2024
(a) To increase the complexity of the model.
(b) To visualize the data.
(c) To assess how well the chosen model will work in future.
(d) To reduce the amount of data used for training.

9. The 4 W's Problem Canvas helps in identifying the key elements related to the given problem.
Which of the following is not one of the blocks of the Problem Canvas? 2024
(a) When (b) What (c) Where (d) Why

10. During Data Acquisition, feeding previous data into the machine is called: 2023
(a) Training Data (b) Testing Data
(c) Predicting Data (d) Evaluating Data

11. Aditi, a student of class XII developed a chatbot that clarifies the doubts of Economics students. She trained the software with lots of data sets catering to all difficulty levels. If any student would type or ask questions related to Economics, the software would give an instant reply. Identify the domain of AI in the given scenario. Competency Based Que.
(a) Computer Vision
(b) Data Science
(c) Natural Language Processing
(d) None of the above

12. Search engines not only predict what popular searches may apply to your query as you start typing, but it looks at the whole picture and recognizes what you're trying to say rather than the exact search words. This is an example of SQP 2022-23
(a) Computer Vision
(b) Data Sciences
(c) Natural Language Processing
(d) Natural Language Understanding

13. .... is a domain of AI that depicts the capability of a machine to get and analyse visual information and afterwards predict some decisions about it.
(a) NLP (b) Data Science
(c) Augmented Reality (d) Computer Vision

14. .... is the sub-field of AI that is focused on enabling computers to understand and process human languages.
(a) Deep Learning (b) Machine Learning
(c) NLP (d) Data Science

15. Email filters, spam filters, smart assistants are the examples of 2023
(a) Pocket Assistants (b) CV
(c) NLP (d) Evaluation

16. .... is a concept to unify statistics, data analysis, machine learning and their related methods in order to understand and analyze actual phenomena with data. 2024
(a) Computer Vision
(b) Natural Language Processing
(c) Data Science
(d) Computer Science

17. Which of the following applications is not associated with Natural Language Processing (NLP)? 2024
(a) Sentiment Analysis
(b) Speech Recognition
(c) Spam Filtering in emails
(d) Stock Market Analysis

18. The concept of media platforms is used to apply face filters on various social 2024
(a) NLP
(b) Computer Vision
(c) Data Science
(d) Block chain Technology

19. Which domain of AI is used for interacting with virtual assistants such as Siri and Alexa? 2024
(a) Machine Learning (ML)
(b) Computer Vision (CV)
(c)Natural Language Processing (NLP)
(d) Technical Vision (TV)

20. Which of the following is NOT a commonly recognized ethical principle in AI frameworks?
(a) Accountability (b) Transparency
(c) Bias (d) Fairness

21. Which ethical framework emphasizes AI systems being understandable and explainable to humans?
(a) Responsibility (b) Transparency
(c) Privacy (d) Fairness

22. In the context of AI, which of the following is an example of bias that should be addressed in ethical AI development?
(a) An AI system that only uses data from one demographic group
(b) An AI system with clear, transparent decision-making
(c) An AI system that uses diverse datasets from multiple regions
(d) An AI system that follows a set of predetermined rules

23. Which domain of AI is involved in analyzing large datasets to identify patterns and make decisions?
(a) Computer Vision
(b) Natural Language Processing
(c) Statistical Data
(d) Ethical Frameworks

24. Which of the following is an example of Computer Vision?

(a) Email spam filtering
(b) Price comparison websites
(c) Drones analyzing crop health
(d) Translating text from one language to another

25. What is the primary function of Natural Language Processing (NLP)?

(a) Detecting objects in images
(b) Understanding and processing human language
(c) Comparing prices of online products
(d) Storing and analyzing large datasets

26. What is the role of frameworks in problem-solving?

(a) They collect data for AI training
(b) They help in solving problems step-by-step
(c) They translate human language into machine code
(d) They store images and videos for analysis

27. Why are ethical frameworks important for AI systems?

(a) To increase the speed of AI models
(b) To ensure AI systems can solve mathematical problems
(c) To guide AI in making fair and moral decisions
(d) To improve the storage capacity of datasets

28. Which type of ethical framework is specific to industries such as healthcare or education?

(a) Rights-Based Framework
(b) Utility-Based Framework
(c) Sector-Based Framework
(d) Virtue-Based Framework

29. What is the focus of a Rights-Based ethical framework?

(a) Maximizing benefits for the majority
(b) Protecting human rights and treating people with respect
(c) Reducing costs in AI development
(d) Enhancing the speed of AI models

30. Which principle of bioethics is violated if an AI system causes harm due to biased data?

(a) Justice
(b) Do Not Harm (Non-maleficence)
(c) Maximum Benefit (Beneficence)
(d) Respect for Autonomy

31. What is the principle of justice in AI ethics?

(a) Giving the majority more benefits
(b) Ensuring fairness and equal treatment for all
(c) Prioritizing the fastest algorithms
(d) Protecting AI from cyber-attacks

32. Platforms such as Spotify, Facebook, Instagram, Amazon, Netflix etc. shows recommendation on the basis of what you like. Which is the technology behind this? 2025

(a) Human Intelligence (b) Platform Intelligence
(c) Artificial Intelligence (d) Application Intelligence

33. Which form of learning-based approach does the following diagram indicate? 2025

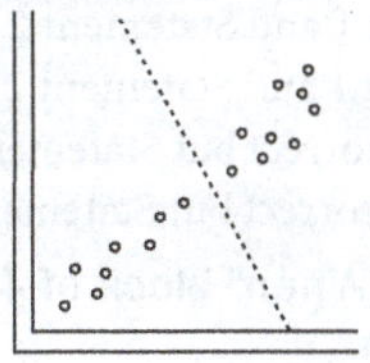

(a) Clustering (b) Classification
(c) Regression (d) Dimensionally Reduction

Answers

1. (d)	2. (b)	3. (b)	4. (a)	5. (a)
6. (c)	7. (b)	8. (c)	9. (a)	10. (a)
11. (c)	12. (c)	13. (d)	14. (c)	15. (c)
16. (c)	17. (d)	18. (b)	19. (c)	20. (c)
21. (b)	22. (a)	23. (c)	24. (c)	25. (b)
26. (b)	27. (c)	28. (c)	29. (b)	30. (b)
31. (b)	32. (c)	33. (b)		

Statement Based Questions

1. Statement 1 Unsupervised learning uses labeled datasets to train algorithms to predict outcomes and recognize patterns.

Statement 2 In unsupervised learning, the training data provided to the machines work as the supervisor.

(a) Both Statement 1 and Statement 2 are correct
(b) Both Statement 1 and Statement 2 are incorrect
(c) Statement 1 is correct but Statement 2 is incorrect
(d) Statement 2 is correct but Statement 1 is incorrect

2. Statement 1 Clustering is a machine learning technique, which groups the unlabeled dataset.

Statement 2 It is helpful for predicting numerical values based on different data points, such as sales revenue projections for a given business.

(a) Both Statement 1 and Statement 2 are correct
(b) Both Statement 1 and Statement 2 are incorrect
(c) Statement 1 is correct but Statement 2 is incorrect
(d) Statement 2 is correct but Statement 1 is incorrect

3. Statement 1 Healthcare Industries are applying AI to make a better and faster diagnosis than humans.

Statement 2 AI can help doctors with diagnoses and can inform when patients are worsening so that medical help can reach to the patient before hospitalization.

(a) Both Statement 1 and Statement 2 are correct
(b) Both Statement 1 and Statement 2 are incorrect
(c) Statement 1 is correct but Statement 2 is incorrect
(d) Statement 2 is correct but Statement 1 is incorrect

4. Statement 1 AI accountability means that developers and organizations should take responsibility for the consequences of AI decisions.

Statement 2 AI systems should be allowed to operate without any human oversight to ensure efficiency.

(a) Both Statement 1 and Statement 2 are correct
(b) Both Statement 1 and Statement 2 are incorrect
(c) Statement 1 is correct but Statement 2 is incorrect
(d) Statement 2 is correct but Statement 1 is incorrect

5. Statement 1 In "When" block of 4Ws canvas we find the stakeholders. 2025

Statement 2 Stakeholders are the people who face a particular problem and would be benefitted with the solution.

(a) Both Statement 1 and Statement 2 are correct.
(b) Both Statement 1 and Statement 2 are incorrect.
(c) Statement 1 is correct but Statement 2 is incorrect.
(d) Statement 2 is correct but Statement 1 is incorrect.

Answers

1. (b) 2. (a) 3. (b) 4. (c) 5. (a)

Assertion & Reason Based Questions

1. Assertion (A) Supervised learning is a type of machine learning where the model is trained on labeled data.

Reason (R) In supervised learning, the model learns from input-output pairs, where each input data point is associated with a corresponding output label.

(a) Both A and R are correct and R is the correct explanation of A
(b) Both A and R are correct but R is not the correct explanation of A
(c) A is correct but R is not correct
(d) A is not correct but R is correct

2. Assertion (A) Artificial intelligence (AI) has the potential to significantly enhance decision-making processes in various domains.

Reason (R) AI algorithms can analyze large datasets, identify complex patterns, and generate insights to inform better decision-making.

(a) Both A and R are correct and R is the correct explanation of A
(b) Both A and R are correct but R is not the correct explanation of A
(c) A is correct but R is not correct
(d) A is not correct but R is correct.

3. Assertion (A) Computer Vision (CV) is a branch of AI that helps machines analyze visual information to make decisions.

Reason (R) Computer Vision is commonly used in applications like agricultural monitoring and surveillance systems to interpret images and detect patterns.

(a) Both A and R are correct, and R is the correct explanation of A.
(b) Both A and R are correct, but R is not the correct explanation of A.
(c) A is correct, but R is not correct.
(d) A is not correct, but R is correct.

4. Assertion (A) Face lock in smartphones uses Computer Vision to unlock the phone.

Reason (R) The smartphone's front camera captures and stores the user's facial features, which are then compared during unlocking attempts.

(a) Both A and R are correct, and R is the correct explanation of A.
(b) Both A and R are correct, but R is not the correct explanation of A.
(c) A is correct, but R is not correct.
(d) A is not correct, but R is correct.

5. Assertion (A) Smart assistants like Siri and Alexa can understand and respond to human speech.

Reason (R) Smart assistants use Natural Language Processing (NLP) to analyze speech patterns, understand context, and generate appropriate responses.

(a) Both A and R are correct, and R is the correct explanation of A.
(b) Both A and R are correct, but R is not the correct explanation of A.
(c) A is correct, but R is not correct.
(d) A is not correct, but R is correct.

6. Assertion (A) Ethical frameworks are important for AI to ensure fairness and prevent harm in decision-making.

Reason (R) Sector-based frameworks focus on applying ethics to specific industries, such as bioethics in healthcare, which ensures patient privacy and fairness in medical decisions.

(a) Both A and R are correct, and R is the correct explanation of A.
(b) Both A and R are correct, but R is not the correct explanation of A.
(c) A is correct, but R is not correct.
(d) A is not correct, but R is correct.

7. Assertion (A) When a machine is able to mimic human traits, it is said to be artificially intelligent.

Reason (R) A fully automatic washing machine is artificially intelligent. 2025

(a) Both A and R are correct and R is the correct explanation of A.
(b) Both A and R are correct and R is not the correct explanation of A.
(c) A is correct but R is not correct.
(d) A is not correct but R is correct.

Answers

1. (a) 2. (d) 3. (a) 4. (a) 5. (a)
6. (a) 7. (c)

Part II

Very Short Answer Type Questions

1. It helps us to summarise all the key points into one single Template so that in future, whenever there is a need to look back at the basis of the problem, we can take a look at this and understand the key elements of it. **SQP 2022-23**

Ans. Problem Statement Template

2. It is a type of supervised learning model where the goal is to predict a continuous value output based on the input features. **2023**

Ans. Regression

3. In this learning model, the data set which is fed to the machine is labelled. Name the model.

Ans. The learning model where the dataset fed to the machine is labeled is called "Supervised Learning".

4. It refers to the unsupervised learning algorithm which can cluster the unknown data according to the patterns or trends identified out of it.

Ans. Clustering

5 Priya went to her hometown. Her hometown does not have all the facilities that are available in the urban area. She basically is working on selecting a problem which she will solve. In the project cycle, which step is required for selecting a problem to solve? **Competency Based Ques.**

Ans. Problem scoping

6 Mention any four sources of data sources.

Ans. The sources of data are – Surveys & questionnaire, web scrapping, sensors and API.

7 Mention the types of learning based approaches for AI modeling.

Ans. Supervised, Unsupervised and Reinforced.

8 With reference to AI domain, expand the term CV. **2023**

Ans. Computer Vision

9 Write about 'What' block of 4Ws problem. **2023**

Ans. The "What" block of the 4W problem canvas addresses the core issue or problem at hand. It requires a concise and clear articulation of what the problem is.

10 What is an ethical framework in AI?

Ans. A set of principles guiding the responsible development and use of AI.

11 Define AI transparency.

Ans. The ability to understand how an AI system makes decisions.

12. Identify the logo of an application of AI given below. It helps us to navigate to places. **2025**

Ans. Google maps

Short Answer Type Questions

1. Sirisha and Divisha want to make a model which will organise the unlabeled input data into groups based on features. Which learning model should they use and why? **Competency Based Ques.**

Ans. Clustering model/Unsupervised learning is used to organise the unlabelled input data into groups based on features.

Clustering is an unsupervised learning algorithm which can cluster unknown data according to the patterns or trends identified out of it. The patterns observed might be the ones which are known to the developer or it might even come up with some unique patterns out of it.

2. Suhana works for a company wherein she was assigned the task of developing a project using AI project cycle. She knew that the first stage was scoping the problem. Help her list the remaining stages that she must go through to develop the project. **Competency Based Ques.**

Ans. List the remaining stages of AI project cycle that she must go through to develop the project

1. Data Acquisition
2. Data Exploration
3. Modelling
4. Evaluation

3. Differentiate between Classification and Regression.

Ans.

Classification	Regression
This model works on a discrete dataset which means the data need not be continuous.	This model works on continuous data.
For example, in the grading system, students are classified on the basis of the grades they obtain with respect to their marks in the examination.	For example, if you wish to predict your next salary, then you would put in the data of your previous salary, any increments, etc and would train the model.

4. What is F1 Score in Evaluation?

Ans. F1 score can be defined as the measure of balance between precision and recall.

$$\text{F1 Score} = 2 \times \frac{\text{Precision} \times \text{Recall}}{\text{Precision} + \text{Recall}}$$

5. What do you mean by Evaluation of an AI model ? Also explain the concept of overfitting with respect to AI model Evaluation. 2024

Ans. Evaluation of an AI model refers to the process of assessing its performance and effectiveness in solving a particular task or problem.

One critical concept in the evaluation of AI models is overfitting. Overfitting occurs when a model learns the training data too well, capturing noise or random fluctuations in the data rather than the underlying patterns.

6. What does Computer Vision aim to do?

Ans. Computer Vision aims to teach computers to interpret and understand visual information, such as images and videos, in a similar way humans do. Common applications of Computer Vision include facial recognition, object detection, medical image analysis, and autonomous vehicles.

7. Describe the principle of privacy in AI and its ethical implications.

Ans. Privacy in AI involves safeguarding personal data and respecting individuals' right to control their information. Ethical implications include protecting users from data breaches, unauthorized surveillance, and ensuring that AI systems do not violate privacy laws or personal boundaries.

8. What is the importance of inclusivity and diversity in designing ethical AI systems?

Ans. Inclusivity and diversity ensure that AI systems are representative of various demographic groups, experiences, and perspectives. This helps avoid bias, fosters fairness, and ensures that the benefits of AI are shared equitably across society.

9. Differentiate between Computer Vision (CV) and Natural Language Processing (NLP). 2025

Ans. The differentiate between Computer Vision (CV) and Natural Language Processing (NLP):

- **Computer Vision (CV)** Focuses on enabling computers to "see" and interpret images or videos, extracting meaningful information.
- **Natural Language Processing (NLP)** Focuses on enabling computers to understand, interpret, and generate human language (text or speech).

10. Define the following term with respect to AI project cycle:
(I) Data Exploration
(ii) Data Features 2025

Ans. (i) **Data Exploration** The initial phase of analyzing and understanding the dataset. This involves summarizing data, identifying patterns, and visualizing relationships to gain insights relevant to the project's goals.

(ii) **Data Features** The individual measurable properties or characteristics of the data used as input for the AI model. They are the variables that the model uses to make predictions or decisions.

11. What is the use of problem statement template with respect to 4Ws pf problem scoping? Draw a problem statement template depicting all key elements. 2025

Ans. Use of Problem Statement Template with 4Ws:

Purpose Provides a structured way to define a problem, ensuring clarity and focus for AI projects.

4Ws (What, Who, Where, Why):

- **What** What is the problem?
- **Who** Who is affected?
- **Where** Where does it occur?
- **Why** Why is it a problem?

Template (Example):

- **Problem** [Clearly state the problem]
- **Who** [Target audience or affected group]
- **Where** [Context or location]
- **Why** [Impact and consequences]

Long Answer Type Questions

1. Akhil wants to learn how to scope the problem for an AI Project. Explain him the following:
(a) 4Ws Problem Canvas
(b) Problem Statement Template

Competency Based Ques.

Ans. (a) The 4Ws Problem canvas helps in identifying the key elements related to the problem. The 4Ws are

- The "Who" block helps in analysing the people getting affected directly or indirectly due to the problem.
- The "What" block helps us to determine the nature of the problem.
- The "Where" block helps us to look into the situation in which the problem arises, the context of it, and the locations where it is prominent.
- The "Why" block suggests to us the benefits which the stakeholders would get from the solution and how it will benefit them as well as to the society.

(b) **Problem Statement Template**

Our	Stakeholders	Who?
Have a problem that	Issues, problem, need	What?
When/ while	Context, situation	Where?
An ideal solution would be	Solution	Why?

2. Your grandmother watches you use AI applications. She wants to understand more about it. Help her understand the term artificial intelligence by giving the right definition and explain to her with an example how machines become artificially intelligent. 2025 improve on its own, it is said to have artificial intelligence. In other words, you can say that a machine is artificially intelligent when it can accomplish tasks by itself - collect data, understand it, analyse it, learn from it, and improve it.

Machines become intelligent once they are trained with some data which helps them achieve their tasks. AI machines also keep updating their knowledge to optimise their output. For example, Netflix gives us recommendations on the basis of what we like. Whenever we start liking a new genre, it updates and gives better suggestions.

3. Consider the following graphs (Figure 1 and Figure 2) that demonstrate the two types of Supervised Learning Models of Artificial Intelligence. Identify and explain each model giving suitable examples of each. **2024**

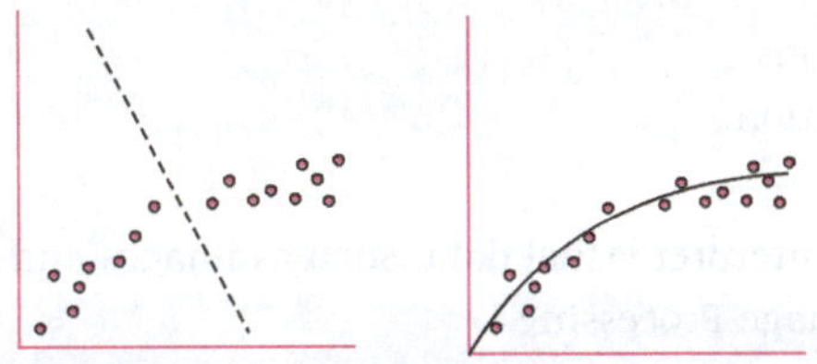

Figure 1 Figure 2

Ans. Figure 1 refers to classification and figure 2 refers to regression.

Classification In classification, the goal is to predict which category or class the input data belongs to. The output variable is categorical. Examples include:

- **Binary Classification** The output variable has two classes. For instance, predicting whether an email is spam or not spam.
- **Multi-class Classification** The output variable has more than two classes. For example, classifying images of animals into categories such as dog, cat, or bird.

Regression In regression, the goal is to predict a continuous numerical value based on input features. The output variable is numerical. Examples include:

- **Linear Regression** Predicting house prices based on features such as size, number of bedrooms, and location.
- **Polynomial Regression** Predicting the temperature based on historical weather data.

4. What is the significance of AI project cycle? Also explain in detail about how Data Acquisition is different from data exploration. **2023**

Ans. The AI (Artificial Intelligence) project cycle is a structured approach to developing and deploying AI solutions. It encompasses various stages from problem identification and data collection to model development, deployment, and monitoring. The significance of the AI project cycle lies in its ability to guide teams through a systematic process, ensuring that AI projects are well-planned, executed efficiently, and yield meaningful results.

Data Acquisition differs from Data Exploration as

Data Acquisition	Data Exploration
Data Acquisition is the process of gathering raw data from various sources, such as databases, APIs, sensors, or external datasets.	Data exploration is the process of analyzing and understanding the characteristics, patterns, and relationships within the collected data.
It involves identifying and accessing relevant datasets that contain information necessary for solving the problem at hand.	It involves visualizing and summarizing the data to gain insights into its structure, distribution, and potential biases.
Data Acquisition focuses on obtaining the required data in its raw form, without significant manipulation or analysis.	Data exploration aims to uncover hidden patterns, anomalies, or interesting trends that may inform subsequent modeling decisions.
Data Acquisition ensures that the collected data is of sufficient quantity, quality, and diversity to support subsequent analysis and modeling tasks.	Data exploration helps identify data preprocessing steps, feature engineering strategies, and suitable modeling approaches based on the observed patterns in the data.

5. Samarth attended a seminar on Artificial Intelligence and has now been asked to write a report on his learnings from the seminar. Being a non-technical person, he understood that the AI enabled machine uses data of different formats in many of the daily based applications but failed to sync it with the right terminologies and express the details. Help Samarth define Artificial Intelligence, list the three domains of AI and the data that is used in these domains. **Competency Based Que.**

Ans. Artificial Intelligence (AI) refers to any technique that enables computers to mimic human intelligence i.e., make decisions, predict the future, learn and improve on its own.

With respect to the type of data fed in the AI model, AI models can be broadly categorised into three domains:

1. Statistical data
2. Computer vision
3. Natural Language Processing

Data Science takes input in the form of numeric and alphanumeric data. Computer Vision takes input in the form of images and videos. Natural Language Processing takes input in the form of text and speech.

6. Explain the three domains of AI model with example.

Ans. Refer to text on page no. 75-77 (Introduction to AI Domains).

SELF ASSESSMENT

Multiple Choice Questions

1. Which of the following is not an ethical question in AI?
   (a) Autonomy and responsibility (b) Data privacy
   (c) Personal growth (d) Job displacement

2 Which of the following is an example of unsupervised learning model?
   (a) Regression (b) Clustering (c) Classification (d) Rule-based

3 Vijender has to maintain inventory on a daily basis, it is usually taking 3-4 hours for a helper to take out raw material, which in turns delays the production cycle and also delays the updation of stock. His manager has identified the problem and looking for a possible solution. This is the task under
   (a) Problem scoping (b) Data exploration (c) Data evaluation (d) Neural network

4. Which of the following best defines the principle of AI accountability?
   (a) Ensuring AI systems are efficient in processing data
   (b) Holding developers and organizations responsible for AI decisions
   (c) Making AI systems fully autonomous without human intervention
   (d) Reducing the cost of AI implementation

5. Which domain of AI involves teaching machines to recognize and interpret visual data, such as images and videos?
   (a) Computer Vision (b) Natural Language Processing
   (c) Machine Learning (d) Robotics

6. What is the primary focus of Natural Language Processing (NLP)?
   (a) Analyzing and interpreting human speech (b) Enabling machines to process and understand human languages
   (c) Detecting objects in images (d) Identifying patterns in large data sets

7. Which of the following is a key application of Computer Vision in the healthcare industry?
   (a) Sentiment Analysis Of Doctor-Patient Interactions
   (b) Image-based diagnosis and medical imaging
   (c) Voice recognition for health assistants
   (d) Data analysis of patient records

Very Short Answer Type Questions

8. What is model evaluation in the AI project cycle?
9. What does accountability in AI refer to?
10. What is statistical data?
11. What is the final step of the AI project cycle?

Short Answer Type Questions

12. Differentiate between supervised learning and unsupervised learning.
13. What is the significance of data evaluation stage in AI project cyle?
14. Explain the concept of data visualization in AI. Why is it important?
15. What is the purpose of clustering in Machine Learning?

Long Answer Type Questions

16. Differentiate between data acquisition and data exploration with an example.
17. Describe the field of computer vision and its importance in AI. How does computer vision enable machines to interpret and understand visual data?
18. Discuss the importance of ethical frameworks in the development and deployment of AI systems. How can ethical guidelines ensure that AI technologies are developed responsibly and are used for the greater good of society?

Advanced Concepts of Modeling in AI

CHAPTER 02

In this chapter, readers will gain a comprehensive understanding of how advanced AI models are designed, trained, and applied, along with insights into their strengths, limitations, and future prospects.

2.1 Revisiting AI, ML, DL

Artificial Intelligence

The process of transferring data, knowledge, and human intelligence to machines is known as **artificial intelligence**, or AI. The creation of autonomous machines with human-like thinking and behavior is the primary objective of artificial intelligence. These machines can mimic human behavior and carry out duties by studying and solving problems. The majority of AI systems mimic natural intellect to handle challenging issues.

Machine Learning

Machine Learning (ML) is a subset of AI that allows machines to improve their performance on tasks through experience. In ML, the system learns from new data during testing and applies this knowledge to make better decisions in future iterations. Additionally, ML considers errors and exceptions to fine-tune its performance over time.

Deep Learning

Deep Learning (DL) is a specialized area within Machine Learning that involves training software to handle vast amounts of data. With access to large datasets, deep learning systems utilize multiple machine learning algorithms working together to tackle complex tasks, making them highly efficient for tasks like image recognition and natural language processing.

Relationship Between AI, ML and DL

AI is the overarching concept that encompasses both Machine Learning and Deep Learning. Deep Learning is a specific approach within Machine Learning that uses a large set of algorithms to process data. The relationship can be visualized as a funnel: there are many applications of AI, of which some fall under ML, and only a few advanced tasks go into DL.

Thus, while all Deep Learning is Machine Learning, not all Machine Learning is Deep Learning.

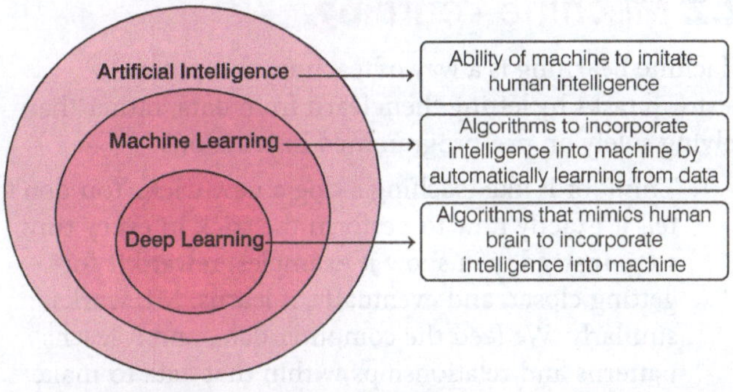

Differentiate between AI, ML and DL

Artificial Intelligence (AI)	Machine Learning (ML)	Deep Learning (DL)
AI simulates human intelligence to perform tasks and make decisions.	ML is a type of AI that uses algorithms to learn from data patterns.	DL is a type of ML that uses neural networks for complex tasks.
AI can use predefined rules and may not always need large data.	ML needs labelled data for training and predictions.	DL needs large datasets and works well with big data.
AI may need human programming and can handle various tasks.	ML automates learning from data with minimal human help.	DL reduces the need for manual programming with automatic feature extraction.

Artificial Intelligence (AI)	Machine Learning (ML)	Deep Learning (DL)
AI can be used for both simple and complex tasks.	ML is used for tasks like classification and regression.	DL is great for tasks like image recognition and speech processing.
AI algorithms can be simple or complex.	ML uses algorithms like decision trees and SVM.	DL uses deep neural networks with multiple layers for learning.
AI can require less training time, especially with rule-based systems.	ML training time depends on the complexity and dataset.	DL needs more time and computing power for training.
AI results are often interpretable based on rules.	ML models can be interpretable or complex, depending on the algorithm.	DL models are harder to interpret due to complex structures.
AI is used in virtual assistants and recommendation systems.	ML is used in tasks like spam filtering and image recognition.	DL is used in advanced AI applications like autonomous vehicles.

2.2 Machine Learning

Machine Learning is a way of teaching computers to perform tasks by letting them learn from data, rather than relying solely on pre-programmed instructions.

1. Think of it like teaching a dog a new trick. You don't tell it exactly how to perform the trick in every tiny step. Instead, you show it examples, reward it for getting closer, and eventually, it learns. ML works similarly. We feed the computer data, and it learns patterns and relationships within that data to make predictions or decisions.
2. It learns from its "mistakes" and uses that knowledge to improve its performance in the future.
3. Essentially, it improvises based on its own experiences.

Working of Machine Learning

Here's a simple way to visualize the process:

Input Data (Past Experiences) → Machine Learning Model → Output (Predictions/Decisions)

We give the ML model a bunch of data (this could be anything - images, numbers, text, etc.), and the model learns from this data. Once it has learned, we can give it new data, and it will use its learning to generate an output, like a prediction or a classification.

Think of a machine learning model as a student preparing for an exam.

1. **Data Collection** The student gathers practice questions and answers. This is our data. The more varied and relevant the questions, the better the student will learn.
2. **Training the Model** The student studies the questions and tries to find patterns and relationships between the questions and answers. This is called training. The model learns from the data.
3. **Testing the Model** The student is given a new set of questions they haven't seen before. This is the test data. The student uses what they learned during training to answer these questions.
4. **Evaluation** We check the student's answers. If they get some wrong, we can provide more practice questions or explain the concepts better. This is like tuning the model.

Examples of Machine Learning

1. **Object Classification** Machine Learning can be used to identify and classify objects within an image or data point.

   For example, an ML model can look at a picture of fruit and determine whether it is an apple, orange, or banana. It assigns a label to the object based on its features (such as color, size, or shape). This process is used in applications like facial recognition, image search engines, and automatic tagging in social media.
2. **Anomaly Detection** Anomaly detection is used to identify unusual patterns or outliers in data that do not fit expected behavior.

   For example, if you are monitoring your heart rate, ML can detect a sudden spike or drop, which could indicate a medical issue. This is used in various fields, such as fraud detection in banking (spotting unusual transactions) or monitoring equipment performance in industries to identify potential malfunctions.

2.3 Deep Learning

Deep Learning uses artificial neural networks with many layers (hence "deep"). These networks are made up of interconnected nodes (like neurons in the brain) that process information. Think of it as a team of experts working together to solve a problem, where each expert focuses on a different aspect.

Need of Deep Learning

Traditional machine learning methods can struggle with complex data like images, audio, and text. Deep learning, with its multiple layers, can automatically learn complex patterns and features from this data, leading to better accuracy and performance.

Working of Deep Learning

Imagine a deep learning network as a multi-story building. Each floor represents a layer of the network

1. **Input Layer** The ground floor receives the raw data (e.g., an image of a cat).
2. **Hidden Layers** The middle floors are where the magic happens. Each layer learns different features of the data.

   For example, one layer might learn edges and corners, another might learn shapes, and another might learn combinations of shapes.

   The deeper the layers, the more complex the features they can learn.
3. **Output Layer** The top floor gives the final result (e.g., "cat").

Examples of Deep Learning

1. **Object Identification** In deep learning, object classification involves identifying and labeling objects within an image. Deep learning uses powerful algorithms, such as convolutional neural networks (CNNs), to analyze the features in the image and categorize them.

   For example, a deep learning model can identify objects like a cat, dog, or car in a picture and label them accordingly.

2. **Digit Recognition** Digit recognition in deep learning focuses on training computers to recognize handwritten digits (0-9) in images.
   This technology is widely used in applications like reading postal addresses on mail, analyzing forms, and recognizing numbers in check payments. A deep learning model can be trained to correctly identify and process digits, even if the handwriting varies across different images.

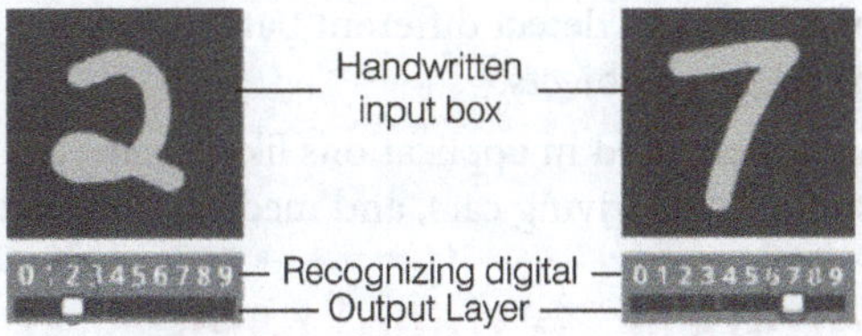

3. **Facial Recognition** Another example of deep learning is facial recognition, where the system identifies individuals based on their facial features. Using deep learning models, such as CNNs, the system can learn to recognize specific facial features like the shape of the eyes, nose, and mouth, allowing it to match faces in images or videos. This technology is used in security systems, social media apps, and smartphones for user identification and authentication.

Sub Categories of Deep Learning

Deep Learning is a type of machine learning where computers learn to perform tasks by studying large amounts of data. In deep learning, the machine trains itself using this data and becomes capable of solving complex problems without human instructions.

There are two main types of Deep Learning models:

Artificial Neural Networks (ANN)

- Artificial Neural Networks are inspired by the human brain and nervous system.
- They can automatically find patterns and features in data without needing detailed instructions from a programmer.
- Each node (neuron) in the network acts like a small machine learning program.
- ANN is useful for solving problems where there is a large amount of data, such as recognizing handwriting or detecting spam emails.

Convolutional Neural Networks (CNN)

- Convolutional Neural Networks are a type of deep learning model commonly used for analyzing images.

- CNNs can identify patterns such as shapes, colors, and textures in images.
- They use layers to detect different parts of an image, such as edges or objects.
- CNN is widely used in applications like facial recognition, self-driving cars, and medical image analysis.

2.3 Common Terminologies used with Data

Data

- Data refers to information in any form.
- For example, a table containing information about fruits can be considered data.
- Each row in the table represents different fruits, and the columns provide various details about each fruit.

Features

- Features are the columns in a table.
- In the example of fruits, features might include name, color, size, etc.
- Some of these features play a more important role in prediction, and they are referred to as labels.

Labels

- Data labeling is the process of giving meaning to the data.
- The label depends on the problem you're solving.
- For example, in predicting the fruit type based on its color, the color is the feature, and the fruit name (like "Apple" or "Banana") is the label.

Example Data Table (Fruits Dataset)

Name	Color	Size	Weight (g)	Fruit Type
Apple	Red	Medium	180	Fruit
Banana	Yellow	Medium	120	Fruit
Tomato	Red	Small	90	Fruit
Cucumber	Green	Large	300	Vegetable
Grape	Purple	Small	50	Fruit

In this table:

- **Features** Name, Color, Size, Weight
- **Label** Fruit Type (whether it is a "Fruit" or "Vegetable")

Data can either be **labeled** (with a known output) or **unlabeled** (where the output is not known).

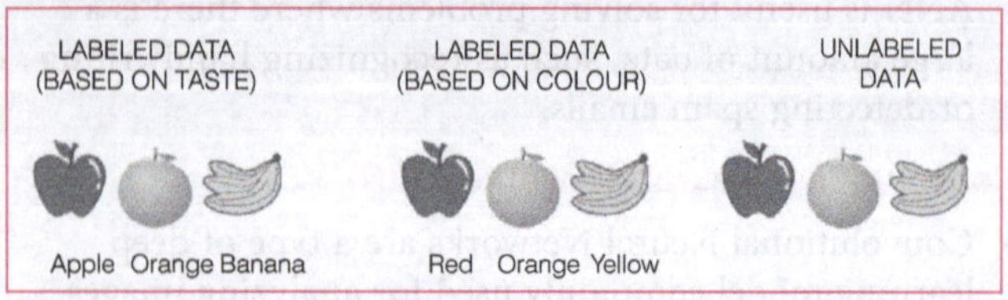

Training Data Set

- A training data set is a collection of examples provided to the machine learning model so it can learn and make predictions.
- Just like how a teacher uses many examples to teach a subject, labeled data is used to train the AI model, allowing it to learn how to identify patterns and make predictions.

Testing Data Set

- A **testing data set** is used to evaluate the performance of the trained model.
- Similar to how a teacher gives a test to check students' understanding, the testing data set is used to check the model's accuracy.
- The model makes predictions based on the testing data (which is unlabeled) and then the predictions are compared with the actual labels to verify the model's performance.

2.4 Modeling

AI Modeling refers to the process of developing algorithms, or models, that can be trained to produce intelligent outputs.

In simple terms, it involves writing code to make a machine behave intelligently by learning from data and experiences.

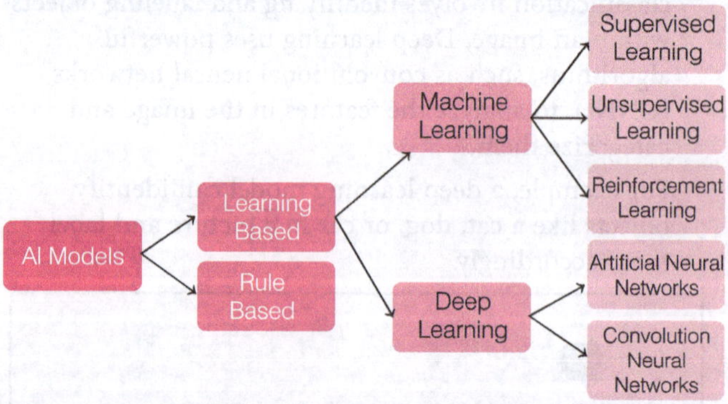

In AI, Rule-Based and Learning-Based approaches are two main ways to build intelligent systems. Let's explore these approaches with examples and scenarios to understand how they work.

Rule-Based Approach

A Rule-Based Approach refers to AI systems that are driven by predefined rules created by a human developer. These rules define how the machine should respond to different inputs. The machine doesn't learn from experience or data but follows the rules given to it.

How It Works

- The machine follows explicit rules defined by the developer to perform specific tasks.
- The system reacts based on these rules to deliver the desired output.
- **Example** If a user asks a rule-based chatbot a question, the system looks for keywords in the input and uses predefined rules to provide an answer.

Scenario: Rule-Based Chatbot for Order Tracking

Imagine a clothing website with a chatbot to help customers track their orders.

1. **Data** The chatbot doesn't require a large dataset. Instead, it relies on a set of predefined questions and answers for order tracking.
2. **Rules** The chatbot follows these rules:

   Rule 1 If the user's message contains keywords like "track order," "shipment status," or "delivery," proceed to order tracking options.

   Rule 2 Under order tracking options:

   - If the user asks for their order number, prompt them to enter it.
   - If the user enters a valid order number, retrieve the tracking info from the database and display it.
   - If the order number is invalid, display an error and ask the user to re-enter it.

   Rule 3 If the user's query doesn't match any predefined rules, provide a message like "Sorry, I can't help with that. Please check our FAQs or contact customer support."
3. **Interaction** The chatbot analyzes the user's query based on the rules and provides an answer. If the query matches one of the rules, it follows the corresponding action. If not, it directs the user to other options.

Advantages

- Easy to understand and debug.
- Works well for well-defined problems with clear rules.
- Can be very accurate if the rules are well-defined.

Disadvantages

- Difficult to create rules for complex or uncertain situations.
- Not adaptable to new information or changes in the environment.
- Can be brittle – if one rule is wrong, the whole system can be affected.

Learning-Based Approach

The **Learning-Based Approach** uses machine learning algorithms that allow the system to learn patterns from data. Instead of following predefined rules, the machine is trained on large datasets and develops its own rules to make predictions or decisions.

How It Works

- The system is fed with labeled data (inputs and outputs) and uses algorithms to learn patterns in the data.
- Over time, the system improves its performance and can generalize to new, unseen data.

Example: Email Spam Filter

A learning-based approach can be used in an email spam filter.

1. **Data** The system is fed with thousands of emails, labeled as either spam or not spam.
2. **Learning Process** The machine learns from these examples. It might identify patterns such as certain words, sender email addresses, or formats associated with spam emails.
3. **Prediction** When a new email arrives, the system uses what it has learned to predict whether the email is spam or not.

Advantages

- Can handle complex and uncertain situations.
- Adaptable to new information and changes in the environment.
- Can achieve high accuracy with enough data.

Disadvantages

- Requires a large amount of data for training.
- Can be difficult to understand how the system makes decisions (black box).
- May not work well if the data is biased or incomplete.

Differences between Rule-Based and Learning-Based Approaches

Aspect	Rule-Based Approach	Learning-Based Approach
How It Works	Uses predefined rules for decision-making.	Learns patterns from data to make predictions.
Data Requirement	Requires a set of clear rules and limited data.	Needs large datasets for training and learning.
Adaptability	Fixed, doesn't adapt unless rules are manually updated.	Adapts and improves as it gets more data.

Aspect	Rule-Based Approach	Learning-Based Approach
Example	Rule-based chatbot, expert systems	Email spam filters, self-driving cars
Advantages	Easy to understand and implement for simple tasks.	Can handle complex and dynamic data patterns.
Disadvantages	Doesn't learn from new data; limited flexibility.	Requires large amounts of labeled data for training.

Categories of Machine Learning Based Models

Learning based approaches are inded a broad category that encompass both machine learning and deep learning. Machine learning can further be divided into three parts:

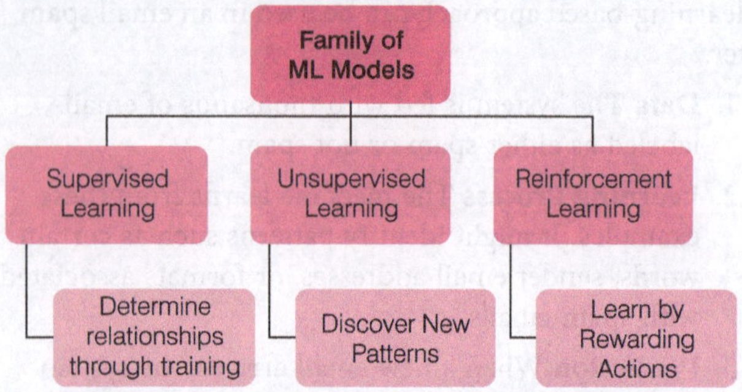

Supervised Learning

In Supervised Learning, the model is trained using a labeled dataset. This means that each piece of data in the training set is paired with a correct output (label).

The system learns to map inputs to the correct outputs by looking at these labeled examples. It's like having a teacher supervise the learning process, guiding the machine to make accurate predictions or classifications.

How It Works

- The system is trained using a dataset where both the inputs and outputs are known.
- Labels are the correct answers or categories associated with the data.
- The machine uses these labeled examples to understand patterns in the data.
- Once trained, the model can predict the labels of new, unseen data.

Example 1 : Predicting House Prices

Imagine we are trying to predict house prices based on certain features like square footage, number of rooms, location, and age of the house.

1. **Data** A dataset with information about different houses is given. Each house is described by several features (like size, number of rooms, location) and its price (label).

House Size (sq ft)	No. of Rooms	Location	Age (Years)	Price (in $)
1500	3	Downtown	5	350,000
2000	4	Suburban	10	450,000
1200	2	City Center	2	300,000
2500	5	Suburban	20	550,000

2. **Training** The machine is trained using the dataset above, where the features (size, rooms, location, age) are inputs, and the price is the label.
3. **Learning Process** The machine looks at the relationship between the inputs (features) and the output (price) to develop a model.
4. **Prediction** Once trained, the model can predict the price of a new house given its size, number of rooms, location, and age.

For example, if a new house is 1800 sq ft, has 3 rooms, is located in a suburban area, and is 10 years old, the trained model will predict its price based on the patterns learned from the training data.

Example 2

Let's consider the example of currency coins.

- **Problem Statement** Build a model to predict the coin based on its weight.
- Assume that we have different currency coins (dataset) having different weights.
- 1 Euro weighs 5 grams
- 1 Dirham weighs 7 grams
- 1 Dollar weighs 3 grams
- 1 Rupee weighs 4 grams and so on
- Feature – Weights
- Label – Currency

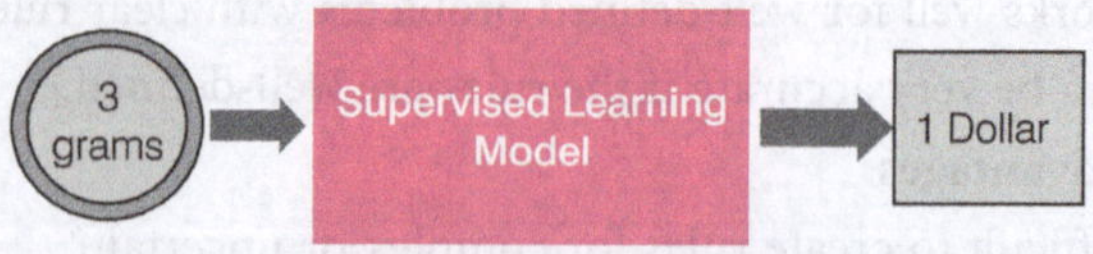

Sub Categories of Supervised Learning

Supervised learning is a type of machine learning where the model is trained on labeled data, meaning that each input is paired with the correct output.

There are two primary types of supervised learning models: Classification and Regression.

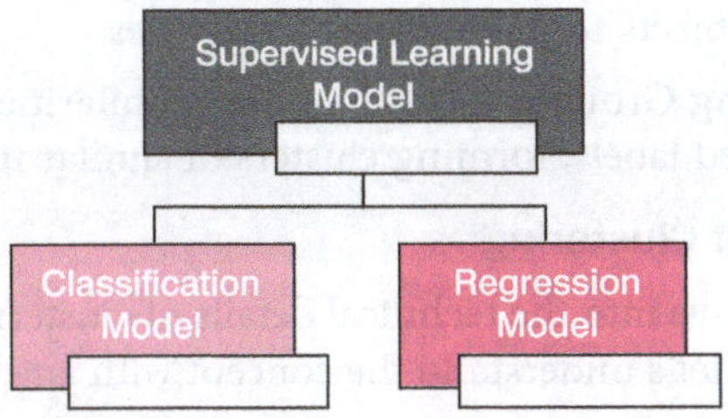

1. Classification Model

A classification model is used to predict discrete labels or categories for a given input. It works with data that is discrete in nature, where the output variable falls into distinct classes or categories.

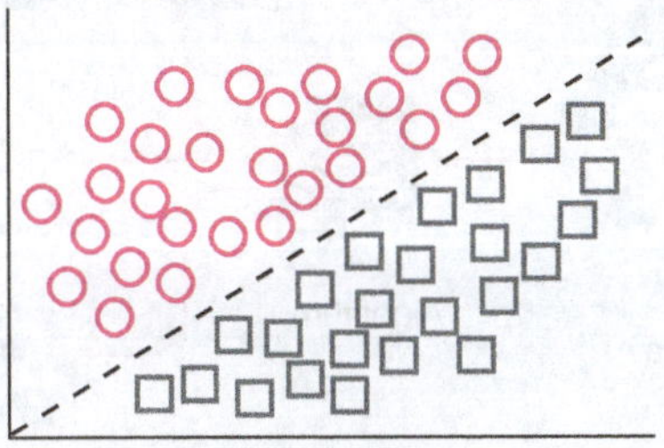

Classification

Examples of a Classification Model

1. **Weather Prediction** In this example, a classification model is used to predict whether the weather will be "hot" or "cold" based on various features.

   For example,

   Features (Independent Variables)

   - Location (temperature varies geographically)
   - Season (summer vs. winter)
   - High and low temperatures
   - Humidity

   Label (Dependent Variable)

   - The classification categories are "hot" or "cold" weather.

   The model would be trained on historical weather data, and once trained, it can predict whether the weather tomorrow will be "hot" or "cold" by analyzing these features.

2. **Spam Email Classification** In this case, a model is trained to classify emails as either spam or not spam. The model learns patterns based on features like:

   - The sender's email address
   - Keywords in the subject line (e.g., "free," "discount," etc.)
   - The frequency of certain phrases or links

   Once trained, the model can analyze new emails and classify them as either spam or not spam, helping email systems filter out unwanted content.

   Other email classification models have evolved to categorize messages into more categories like social, promotions, notifications, etc.

2. Regression Model

A regression model is used to predict continuous values. The output is continuous and can take any value within a range, such as temperature, price, or age.

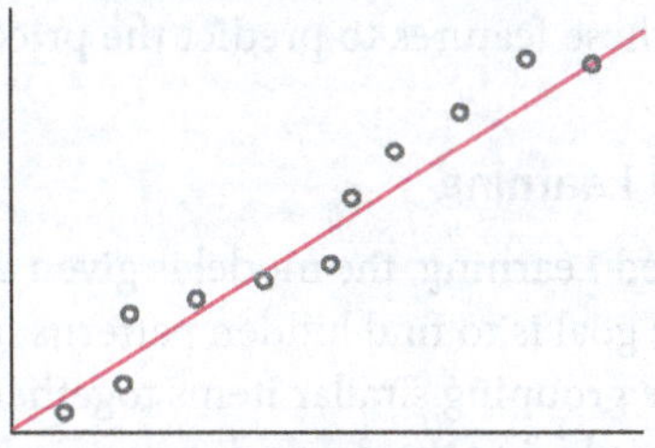

Regression

Examples of a Regression Model

1. **Predicting Temperature** Since temperature is a continuous variable, regression models can be used to predict future temperatures based on past weather data.

   The model may use features like:

   - Historical temperature data
   - Time of year (season)
   - Location

2. **Used Car Price Prediction** In this case, the goal is to predict the selling price of a used car based on various features. The output (price) is a continuous value.

   Features (Independent Variables)

   - Fuel type (petrol, diesel, electric)
   - Years of service (age of the car)
   - Number of previous owners
   - Kilometers driven
   - Transmission type (manual/automatic)

   Label (Dependent Variable)

   - Price (the predicted price is continuous).

   A regression model would predict the car's price based on the values of these features, such as predicting the price for a 5-year-old diesel car with 50,000 km driven.

3. **House Price Prediction** In this example, a regression model predicts the price of a house based on various features:

Features (Independent Variables)
- Number of bedrooms
- Carpet size
- Garage area
- Location

Label (Dependent Variable)
- House price (the predicted price is continuous).

The model would analyze historical housing prices and use these features to predict the price of a new house.

Unsupervised Learning

In Unsupervised Learning, the model is given data without any labels. The goal is to find hidden patterns or structures in the data, like grouping similar items together (clustering) or reducing the data's dimensionality.

Example,

Consider an e-commerce website that has thousands of products. The system uses unsupervised learning to group similar products together, such as grouping all shoes, shirts, and pants into separate clusters based on their features (e.g., color, material, size) without knowing which products belong to which category.

Sub Categories of Unsupervised Learning

Unsupervised learning models can be further divided into two categories:

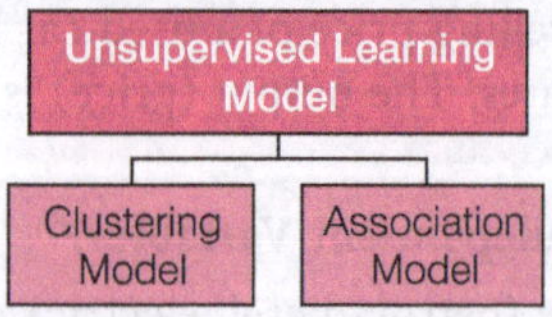

1. Clustering

The task of grouping data points based on their similarity with each other is called **Clustering** or **Cluster Analysis.** This method is defined under the branch of unsupervised learning, which aims at gaining insights from unlabelled data points.

Think of it as you have a dataset of customers shopping habits. Clustering can help you group customers with similar purchasing behaviors, which can then be used for targeted marketing, product recommendations, or customer segmentation.

Difference Between Clustering and Classification

- **Classification** Uses predefined categories (labels) and assigns objects to these known categories.
- **Clustering** Groups objects based on similarities without predefined labels, forming clusters of similar items.

Example of Clustering

Before we dive into the technical details of clustering algorithms, let's understand the concept with an easy example.

Imagine you have a large collection of fruit images. The collection includes three types of fruits:

1. Strawberries 2. Pears 3. Apples

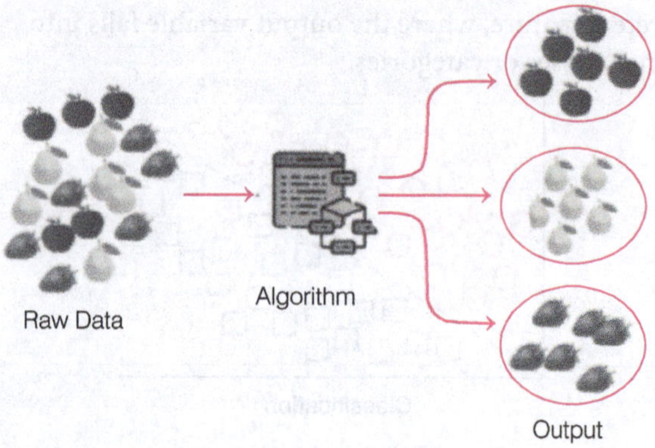

However, the images are all mixed up, and your task is to group similar fruits together. In other words, you need to create three groups:

- One group with only strawberry images
- One group with only pear images
- One group with only apple images

This is exactly what a clustering algorithm does! It organizes or clusters similar items together without knowing their labels beforehand.

So, without anyone telling the machine which images are strawberries, pears, or apples, it will analyze the features (such as color, shape, or size) and automatically create three groups based on similarities.

Info Wall Clustering techniques are used by platforms like Netflix or Spotify to recommend content based on viewing or listening patterns.

2. Association

Association rule learning is a type of unsupervised learning where the computer finds relationships between different items in a dataset. It helps identify patterns and connections between items that often appear together.

This method is commonly used in:

- **Market Basket Analysis** Retailers use this technique to understand which items customers often buy together.
- **Web Usage Mining** Websites recommend content based on what users view together.
- **Production Management** Factories use it to improve workflows by grouping related tasks.

Market Basket Analysis Example

Imagine you are at a supermarket. If you buy bread, you are likely to buy butter, eggs, or milk. To increase sales, the store places these items on nearby shelves.

For example,

- If Bread → Then Butter (80% chance)
- If Milk → Then Cookies (70% chance)

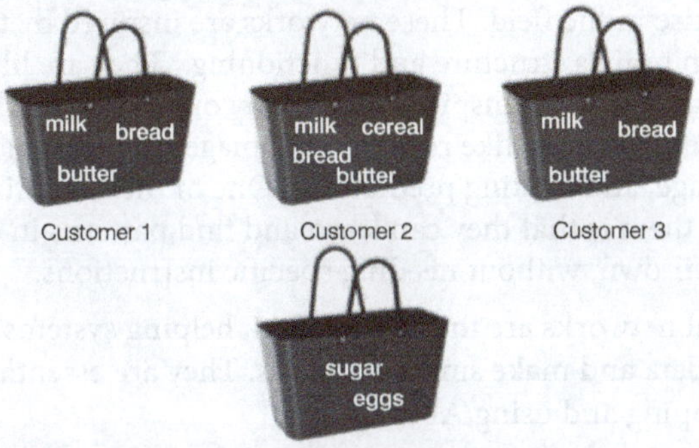

This is how association rule learning helps businesses make smart decisions using patterns from customer behavior.

Reinforcement Learning

Reinforcement Learning (RL) is an approach where an agent (machine) learns to perform tasks by interacting with an environment. It learns through trial and error, receiving feedback in the form of rewards or penalties based on the actions it takes. The agent's goal is to maximize the cumulative reward over time. Unlike supervised learning, where the correct answers are given, in RL, the agent is not explicitly told what to do but must explore and find out the best actions on its own.

Example : Fruit Recognition

Let's consider a scenario where a machine is trained to recognize fruits using reinforcement learning:

1. **Task** The machine is shown an image of a fruit and asked to predict what fruit it is.
2. **Initial Prediction** The machine sees an image of an apple and predicts it as 'cherry.'
3. **Negative Feedback** Since the prediction is incorrect, you provide negative feedback, signaling that the guess is wrong.
4. **Learning** The machine now understands that the fruit in the image is not a cherry and learns that it must explore other possibilities.
5. **Second Attempt** The machine is shown the same image of an apple again and predicts it as 'apple' this time.
6. **Positive Feedback** You provide positive feedback, confirming that the prediction is correct.
7. **Reinforcement** The machine reinforces this behavior, associating the image of an apple with the label "apple" and understanding that this is the correct output for future attempts.

Through this process of trial, error, feedback, and learning, the machine can gradually improve its accuracy in predicting fruits.

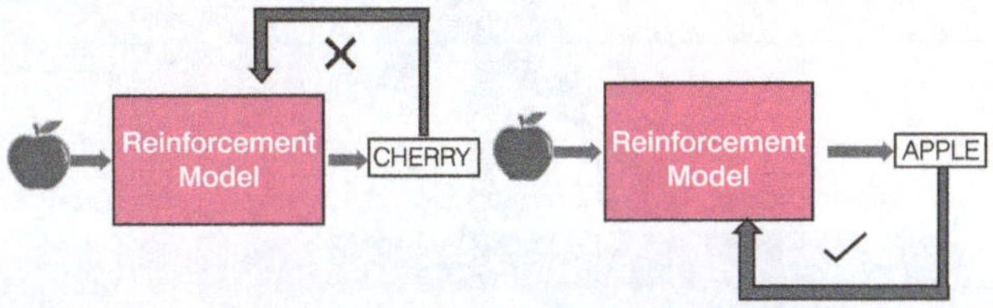

Some more examples of Reinforcement Learning

1. Parking a Car

Imagine training a self-driving car to park in a tight spot.

- **Agent** The self-driving car.
- **Environment** The parking lot with other cars, lines, and obstacles.
- **Actions** Steering, accelerating, braking.
- **Rewards** Parking successfully within the lines.
- **Penalties** Crashing into another car, hitting a curb, or failing to park within the lines.

The car learns by trial and error. It tries different steering and braking maneuvers. If it parks successfully, it gets a reward. If it crashes, it gets a penalty.

Over time, it learns the optimal way to park in different situations.

2. Humanoid Walking

Training a robot to walk like a human is a complex task.

Agent The humanoid robot.

Environment The ground with its uneven terrain and obstacles.

Actions Moving its legs, adjusting its balance.

Rewards Walking smoothly and stably without falling.

Penalties Falling down or stumbling.

The robot learns by trying different walking motions. If it walks smoothly, it gets a reward. If it falls, it gets a penalty. Through this process, it learns to coordinate its movements and maintain balance.

Try These 2.1

1. **Identify the model: Supervised or Unsupervised?** NCERT

   Case 1 Social Media platforms identify your friend in a picture from an album of tagged Photographs

   Case 2 OTT platform Recommendations based on someone's watch history

   Case 3 Analyze bank data for suspicious-looking transactions and flag the fraud transactions

2. **Identify the model: Classification or Regression?** NCERT

   Case 1 Predicting whether a customer is eligible for a bank loan or not?

   Case 2 Predicting weather for next 24 hours

3. **Let's have knowledge check based on learning approaches and its types** NCERT

   (A) Which learning approach uses labelled data for training?
   - Supervised Learning
   - Reinforcement Learning
   - Unsupervised Learning

   (B) The target variable is categorical in....... Problem?
   - Regression
   - Clustering
   - Classification

   (C) Which algorithmic model would you use when you have to predict a continuous valued output?
   - Regression
   - Clustering
   - Classification

   (D) Which of the following is false about Reinforcement Learning?
   - Uses Reward Mechanism
   - Target is to Maximize the Reward
   - Predicts a continuous value as output

   (E) Clustering is........ learning and its goal is to...... ?
   - Supervised, Classify data points into different classes
   - Unsupervised, Divide the data points into different groups
   - Unsupervised, Predict the output based on input data points

2.5 Neural Networks

Neural networks are a fundamental concept in artificial intelligence and machine learning, aligning with your expertise in the field. These networks are inspired by the human brain's structure and functioning. They are like computer systems inspired by the way our brains work. We use them for tasks like recognizing images, understanding language, and making predictions. One of the best things about them is that they can learn and find patterns in data on their own, without needing specific instructions.

Neural networks are the brains of AI, helping systems learn from data and make smart decisions. They are essential for developing and using AI solutions.

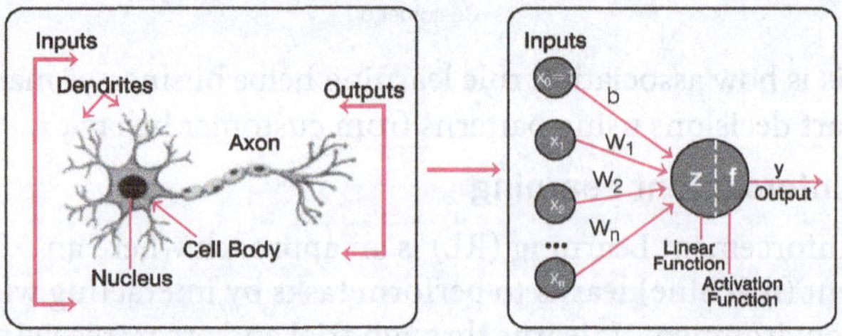

Biological Neural Network | Artificial Neural Network (ANN)

How Neural Network Functions?

Neural networks, simplified into three primary layers—input, hidden, and output—work through interconnected nodes, mimicking the human brain's functioning.

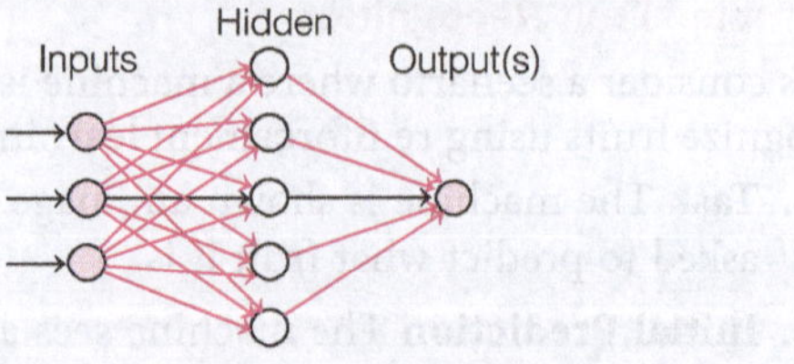

- **Input Layer** This layer receives the initial data. Each node represents a feature of the input data. For instance, in image recognition, each node might represent a pixel's intensity.

- **Hidden Layers** These layers process the input data through weighted connections. Each node applies a transformation to the data it receives, passing it on to the next layer. This layer performs complex calculations to identify patterns in the data.
- **Output Layer** This layer produces the final result or prediction based on the processed information from the hidden layers. The nodes here represent the possible outcomes or classifications. For instance, in a binary classification problem (e.g., spam detection), there might be two nodes representing "spam" or "not spam".

During the training process, the network adjusts the weights of connections between nodes to minimize the difference between the predicted output and the actual output. This adjustment is done using optimization algorithms like gradient descent. By iteratively adjusting these weights based on the error, neural networks learn to recognize patterns and make predictions. This process is known as training. Once trained, the network can be used to make predictions on new, unseen data.

Fact BoT

The first Artificial Neural Network was invented in 1958 by American psychologist Frank Rosenblatt.

Features of Neural Network

Some of the features of a Neural Network are listed below:

- They are able to automatically extract features without feeding the input by programmer.
- Every node of layer in a Neural network is compulsorily a machine learning algorithm.
- It is very useful to implement when solving problems for very huge datasets.

How Does AI Make a Decision?

Imagine you want to decide whether to go for a run this morning. What factors would you consider?

For most people, one of the main concerns might be the weather. No one wants to run in the rain or during extremely hot conditions, right? So, let's break it down into factors that could affect your decision:

- Is it sunny right now?
- What's the temperature?
- Will it rain later?
- Do I have enough time to run?

Just like a human, an AI makes decisions by analyzing multiple factors. However, not all factors are equally important. Some are more influential than others. For instance, "Is it sunny right now?" might be more important than "Do I have time to run?"

Let's rank them in order of importance:

1. Is it sunny right now? (More important)
2. What's the temperature?
3. Will it rain later?
4. Do I have enough time to run? (Less important)

Now, let's convert this decision-making process into a simple AI model, similar to a perceptron.

Inputs and Weights

For AI to make this decision, it looks at four main factors (inputs):

- **X1** Is it sunny right now? (1 for yes, 0 for no)
- **X2** What's the temperature? (1 for good temperature, 0 for bad)
- **X3** Will it rain later? (1 for yes, 0 for no)
- **X4** Do I have enough time to run? (1 for yes, 0 for no)

Each input has a **weight** that indicates its importance:

- **W1** Weight for "Is it sunny right now?"
- **W2** Weight for "What's the temperature?"
- **W3** Weight for "Will it rain later?"
- **W4** Weight for "Do I have enough time?"

Additionally, there's a **bias (B)** that adjusts the decision process based on personal preference. The **bias weight (WB)** influences whether the decision favors staying in or going out.

How Weights Work

Weights can come from previous experiences or personal preferences. For example, if you've had great runs when it was sunny, the weight for "Is it sunny right now?" will be high. If you're less concerned about time, the weight for "Do I have enough time?" will be low.

Example 1: Decision to Run

Let's say you're ready to make the decision to run:

- Is it sunny right now? Yes → 1
- What's the temperature? Good → 1
- Will it rain later? No → 0
- Do I have enough time to run? Yes → 1

Now, let's assign some weights (these could be based on your past experiences):

- **W1 = 2** (Sunshine is very important to you)
- **W2 = 1** (Temperature is moderately important)
- **W3 = -2** (Rain is very important to avoid)
- **W4 = 0.5** (Time is less important)

And the **bias (B)** is set to **1** for this example.

Calculation

Output = (X1 * W1) + (X2 * W2) + (X3 * W3) + (X4 * W4) + B

Output = (1 * 2) + (1 * 1) + (0 * -2) + (1 * 0.5) + 1

Output = 2 + 1 + 0 + 0.5 + 1

Output = 4.5

Now, let's compare the output to the threshold. If the output is greater than **0**, the decision is to **run**. So, in this case, **you decide to go for a run.**

Example 2: Decision Not to Run

Let's try another scenario:

- Is it sunny right now? No → 0
- What's the temperature? Hot → 0
- Will it rain later? Yes → 1
- Do I have enough time to run? No → 0

We'll use the same weights as before:

- W1 = 2
- W2 = 1
- W3 = -2
- W4 = 0.5
- Bias (B) = 1

Calculation

Output = (X1 * W1) + (X2 * W2) + (X3 * W3) + (X4 * W4) + B

Output = (0 * 2) + (0 * 1) + (1 * -2) + (0 * 0.5) + 1

Output = 0 + 0 - 2 + 0 + 1

Output = -1

Since the output is **less than 0**, the decision is **not to run.**

Try These 2.2

1. **Define the role of input layer in a neural network.**
2. **Write about training data feature of neural network.**
3. **How does the bias term (B) influence AI decision-making?**

Glossary

Artificial Intelligence (AI) AI enables machines to mimic human intelligence, making decisions, solving problems, and performing tasks autonomously.

Machine Learning (ML) ML is a subset of AI that allows computers to learn from data and improve performance without explicit programming.

Deep Learning (DL) DL is a type of ML that uses neural networks with multiple layers to analyze complex data patterns and make predictions.

Rule-Based Approach This approach relies on predefined rules and logic to make decisions, without learning from data.

Learning-Based Approach Machines learn patterns from data instead of following fixed rules, making them adaptable to new scenarios.

Supervised Learning A type of ML where models are trained using labeled data to make predictions or classifications.

Unsupervised Learning ML models analyze unlabeled data to find hidden patterns or structures, such as clustering and association.

Reinforcement Learning An ML technique where an agent learns by interacting with an environment and receiving rewards or penalties.

Neural Networks A deep learning model inspired by the human brain, consisting of layers of interconnected nodes (neurons) that process data.

ACTIVITY Time

ACTIVITY 1 : Human Neural Network-The Game

Objective

To help students understand how a neural network works by participating in a hands-on activity that simulates the functioning of a neural network, with different layers of nodes (students) processing and passing information.

Materials Required

- **Images (To be kept with the facilitator)** 2 images of a particular object, person, or scene (only shown to the input layer).
- **Post-It Notes** 80 notes, for each student to write their chosen words.
- **Sketch-pens** 40 pens for students to write on the Post-It notes.

Game Structure

Layer	Number of Students	Number of Chits
Input Layer	7	6
Hidden Layer 1	6	4
Hidden Layer 2	6	2
Output Layer	1	-
TOTAL	20	-

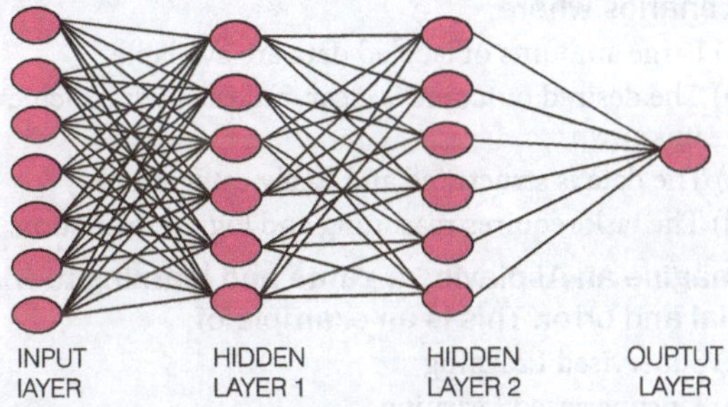

Ground Rules

1. **No Communication** No two nodes can communicate. Each student must rely on their own discretion.
2. **Silent Process** The game is played silently; there should be no verbal communication between students at any point.
3. **Processing Time** Each student should quickly write down the word(s) representing their layer's task. They should not take too long to make decisions.
4. **Individual Discretion** Each student must choose their words independently, based on the image shown to them.
5. **Completion** Once a layer has finished their task, they sit aside quietly without disturbing the other layers.

Instructions for Each Layer

Input Layer (7 Students)

- Each of the 7 students in the input layer will see an image and choose 6 words that best describe the image. The words can be repeated if needed.
- After writing their words on Post-Its, each student passes one chit to each of the 6 students in Hidden Layer 1.

Hidden Layer 1 (6 Students)

- The students in this layer will receive 7 chits from the input layer, each containing words from the input layer's students.
- Each student in Hidden Layer 1 will write 4 different words on 4 new chits based on the words they received. They can either repeat words from the input layer or introduce new ones based on their understanding of the image.
- After writing the words, they pass one chit to each of 4 nodes in Hidden Layer 2.

Hidden Layer 2 (6 Students)

- The students in this layer will receive the chits from Hidden Layer 1. They must review the words and write 2 words each on 2 new chits, again based on their interpretation of the image.
- They pass the chits to the Output Layer.

Output Layer (1 Student)

- The student in the output layer receives all 12 chits. Based on the words provided, they must deduce the image shown to the Input Layer and write a summary explaining the reasoning behind their guess.
- The summary must not exceed 5 lines. The output layer must then present the summary to the class.
- If the summary is correct, the network wins. If not, the network loses.

Example to Clarify the Process

- **Input Layer's Task** A student in the Input Layer sees an image of a cat and writes words like "fur," "tail," "whiskers," "purring," "ears," and "claws."

- **Hidden Layer 1's Task** The students in Hidden Layer 1 receive words like "fur," "tail," "ears," and write new words based on these, such as "animal," "pet," "meow," "cute."
- **Hidden Layer 2's Task** Hidden Layer 2 students then receive words like "animal," "pet," and write their own such as "domestic," "friendly."
- **Output Layer's Task** The Output Layer student receives words like "animal," "cute," "meow," "tail," and finally guesses the image is of a cat and writes a summary like:
"The words like 'tail,' 'whiskers,' and 'meow' suggest it's an animal. The words 'fur' and 'cute' indicate it's a domestic pet. Therefore, the image is most likely a cat."

NCERT FOLDER

Complete Explanations of all NCERT's Questions

A. Multiple Choice Questions

1. In which type of machine learning is the data labeled with the desired output?
(a) Supervised Learning
(b) Unsupervised Learning
(c) Reinforcement Learning
(d) Deep Learning

2. An email spam filter that learns to identify spam emails based on labeled examples is an application of:
(a) Supervised Learning
(b) Unsupervised Learning
(c) Reinforcement Learning
(d) Transfer Learning

3. A machine learning algorithm that groups similar customer purchases into clusters for recommendation systems uses:
(a) Supervised Learning
(b) Unsupervised Learning
(c) Reinforcement Learning
(d) Neural Networks

4. An AI agent playing a game and learning from its rewards and penalties is an example of:
(a) Supervised Learning
(b) Unsupervised Learning
(c) Reinforcement Learning
(d) Evolutionary Learning

5. Which of the following statements is NOT true about supervised learning?
(a) Requires labeled data for training.
(b) Used for classification and regression tasks.
(c) Can be less efficient for large datasets.
(d) Often used in image recognition applications.

6. In an unsupervised learning scenario, the goal is to:
(a) Predict a specific output based on labeled data.
(b) Identify patterns and relationships within unlabeled data.
(c) Train an AI agent through rewards and penalties.
(d) Develop complex neural network architectures.

7. Clustering algorithms are commonly used in unsupervised learning for:
(a) Spam filtering
(b) Image classification
(c) Stock price prediction
(d) Grouping similar data points

8. Reinforcement learning is particularly useful for scenarios where:
(a) Large amounts of labeled data are available.
(b) The desired outcome is clear, but the path to achieve it is unknown.
(c) The data is structured and easily categorized.
(d) The task requires reasoning and logical deduction.

9. Imagine an AI playing a game and learning to win by trial and error. This is an example of:
(a) Supervised Learning
(b) Unsupervised Learning
(c) Reinforcement Learning
(d) Natural Language Processing

10. Artificial neural networks are inspired by the structure and function of:
(a) The human brain
(b) Quantum computers
(c) Complex mathematical models
(d) High-speed processors

11. The process of adjusting the weights in a neural network to improve performance is called:
(a) Activation (b) Learning
(c) Optimization (d) Training

12. **A neural network with multiple layers of interconnected neurons is called a:**
(a) Single-layer network
(b) Deep Neural Network
(c) Linear network
(d) Perceptron

13. **Neural networks are particularly well-suited for tasks involving:**
(a) Simple calculations and mathematical operations
(b) Recognizing patterns in complex data like images and text
(c) Performing logical deductions and reasoning tasks
(d) Storing and retrieving large amounts of information

14. **Training a neural network often requires:**
(a) A small set of labeled data samples
(b) A significant amount of data and computational resources
(c) A specific set of programming instructions
(d) A human expert to guide the learning process

Answers

1. (a)	2. (a)	3. (b)	4. (c)	5. (c)
6. (b)	7. (d)	8. (b)	9. (c)	10. (a)
11. (d)	12. (b)	13. (b)	14. (b)	

B. Assertion and Reason Based Questions

1. **Assertion (A) Unsupervised Learning is a type of learning without any guidance.**

Reason (R) Unsupervised learning models work on unlabeled datasets, where the data fed into the machine is random and the person training the model may not have any prior information about it.
(a) Both A and R are true and R is the correct explanation for A
(b) Both A and R are true and R is not the correct explanation for A
(c) A is True but R is False
(d) A is false but R is True

2. **Assertion (A) Information processing in a neural network relies on weights and biases assigned to nodes.**

Reason (R) These weights and biases determine how strongly a node is influenced by its inputs and its overall contribution to the next layer.
(a) Both A and R are true and R is the correct explanation for A
(b) Both A and R are true and R is not the correct explanation for A
(c) A is True but R is False
(d) A is false but R is True

Answers

1. (a) 2. (a)

C. Subjective Questions

1. **Give difference between rule based and learning based AI models.**

Ans.
- **Rule-Based AI Models** Use predefined rules and logic to make decisions. They don't learn from data and require manual updates.
- **Learning-Based AI Models** Learn from data, adapt over time, and improve performance by recognizing patterns from large datasets.

2. **What is supervised, unsupervised and reinforcement learning? Explain with examples.**

Ans. **Supervised Learning** In supervised learning the model is trained with labeled data to predict outputs (e.g., email spam filtering).

Unsupervised Learning In unsupervised learning the model finds hidden patterns or structures in unlabeled data (e.g., customer segmentation).

Reinforcement Learning In this the agent learns by receiving rewards or penalties based on actions taken in an environment (e.g., AI playing a game).

3. **What is clustering and how is it different from classification?**

Ans. **Clustering** It is an unsupervised learning method that groups similar data points together based on their features. No predefined labels are used.

Example Grouping customers based on purchasing behavior.

Classification It is a supervised learning method that assigns data points to predefined categories based on labeled data.

Example Classifying emails as spam or not.

Difference Clustering finds natural groupings in data without labels, while classification assigns data to predefined categories based on labeled data.

4. **Explain neural networks. Also give functions of three layers of neural networks.**

Or **What is neural network? Give the functioning of its three layers?**

Ans. A neural network is a machine learning model inspired by the human brain. It consists of layers of neurons that process data and learn patterns from it. Neural networks are used in tasks like image recognition and speech processing.

Functions of Three Layers
- **Input Layer** Receives raw data and passes it to the next layer. Each neuron represents a feature of the data.
- **Hidden Layer(s)** Processes data by applying weights and activation functions to extract features and learn patterns.
- **Output Layer** Produces the final prediction or classification based on the learned data.

5. Differentiate between classification and regression model.

	Classification Model	Regression Model
Purpose	It predicts labels or categories for data.	It predicts a number or a continuous value.
Output	The result is a category or class, like "yes" or "no," "spam" or "not spam."	The result is a numerical value, like a price or temperature.
Example	Deciding whether an email is spam or not.	Predicting the price of a house based on its size and location.

6. Identify the type of learning (supervised, unsupervised, reinforcement learning) are the following case studies most likely based on?

(a) A company wants to predict customer churn based on past purchasing behavior, demographics, and customer interactions. They have a dataset with labeled examples of customers who churned and those who did not.

(b) A social media platform wants to group users based on their interests and behavior to recommend relevant content. They have a large dataset of user interactions but no predefined categories. Which type of learning isthis case study most likely based on?

(c) An autonomous vehicle is learning to navigate through a city environment. It receives feedback in the form of rewards for reaching its destination safely and penalties for traffic violations. Which type of learning is this case study most likely based on?

(d) A healthcare provider wants to identify patterns in patient data to personalize treatment plans. They have a dataset with various patient attributes but no predefined labels indicating specific treatment plans. Which type of learning is this case study most likely based on?

(e) A manufacturing company wants to optimize its production process by detecting anomalies in sensor data from machinery. They have a dataset with examples of normal and anomalous behavior. Which type of learning is this case study most likely based on?

Ans. (a) Supervised Learning
(b) Unsupervised Learning
(c) Reinforcement Learning
(d) Unsupervised Learning
(e) Supervised Learning

7. Identify the type of model (classification, regression, clustering, association model) are the following case studies most likely based on?

(a) A bank wants to predict whether a loan applicant will "default" or "non-default" on their loan payments. They have a dataset containing information such as income, credit score, loan amount, and employment status.

(b) A real estate agency wants to predict the selling price of houses based on various features such as size, location, number of bedrooms, and bathrooms. They have a dataset containing historical sales data.

(c) A marketing company wants to segment its customer base into distinct groups based on purchasing behavior for targeted marketing campaigns. They have a dataset containing information such as purchase history, frequency of purchases, and amount spent.

(d) A grocery store wants to identify associations between different products purchased by customers to understand which products are commonly bought together. They have a transaction dataset containing records of items purchased together during each transaction.

Ans. (a) Classification (b) Regression
(c) Clustering (d) Association Model

8. A healthcare provider wants to improve patient care by predicting the length of hospital stays for different medical conditions. They have a dataset containing patient demographics, medical history, and treatment details. The task involves:

(a) To predict whether a patient will have a short or long hospital stay.

(b) To predict the number of days a patient will stay in the hospital.

(c) To segment patients into groups with similar characteristics for personalized treatment plans.

(d) To identify patterns in patient treatments and outcomes.

Identify the type of model (classification, regression, clustering, and association model) in the above tasks.

Ans. (a) Classification (b) Regression
(c) Clustering (d) Association

9. Convert the following scenarios to perceptron:

(a) Context: A manager is deciding whether to approve a work-from-home request from an employee.

Factors:

- **Does the employee perform well when working remotely?**
- **Are there any upcoming team meetings or collaborative projects?**
- **Does the company's policy support remote work?**

- **Is it beneficial for both the employee and the company?**

(b) Context: A homeowner is deciding whether to invest in solar panels for their house.

Factors:

- **Do I have a sufficient average amount of sunlight in my area?**
- **Are there any available incentives or rebates for installing solar panels?**
- **Does installing solar panels impact the value of my home?**
- **Does solar energy lead to environmental benefits?**

Ans. To convert these scenarios into perceptron models, we need to represent them using binary inputs, weighted sums, and an activation function.

(a) Work-from-Home Decision Model

Let's define the following binary inputs (1 for "Yes", 0 for "No"):

x1 : Employee performs well remotely

x2 : No upcoming team meetings/collaborative projects

x3 : Company's policy supports remote work

x4 : Beneficial for both employee and company

Perceptron Model:

$y=f(w1\times1+w2\times2+w3\times3+w4\times4-\theta)$

Where:

- w1,w2,w3,w4 are the weights assigned to each factor based on importance
- θ is the threshold

Activation function: $f(x)=1$ if $x \geq 0$, otherwise $f(x)=0$

Output:

y=1(Approve Work-from-Home request)

y=0 (Deny Work-from-Home request)

(b) Solar Panel Investment Model

Binary Inputs:

x1 : Sufficient sunlight in the area

x2 : Incentives/rebates available

x3 : Increases home value

x4 : Provides environmental benefits

Perceptron Model:

$y=f(w1\times1+w2\times2+w3\times3+w4\times4-\theta)$

Where:

- Weights w1,w2,w3,w4 reflect importance
- θ is the threshold

Activation function: $f(x)=1$ if $x \geq 0$, otherwise $f(x)=0$

Output:

y=1 (Invest in Solar Panels)

y=0(Do Not Invest)

EXAMPLE PATTERN EXERCISE

Including Competency Based Questions

Part I

Multiple Choice Questions

1. Identify the incorrect statement(s) from the following: SQP 2022-23

(i) Deep learning is a subset of Machine Learning

(ii) Machine Learning is a subset of Deep Learning

(iii) Artificial Intelligence is a subset of Deep Learning

(iv) Deep Learning is the advanced form of AI and ML

(a) only (i) (b) (ii) and (iii)

(c) (i) and (ii) (d) Only (iii)

2. .... refers to the AI Modeling where the machine learns by itself.

(a) Learning Based (b) Rule Based

(c) Machine Learning (d) Data Science

3. What is the primary objective of Artificial Intelligence (AI)?

(a) To replace human intelligence completely

(b) To create autonomous machines with human-like thinking and behavior

(c) To eliminate the need for programming

(d) To store large amounts of data

4. How does Machine Learning (ML) improve its performance over time?

(a) By using predefined rules for decision-making

(b) By learning from new data and experiences

(c) By relying only on manual programming

(d) By increasing computing power

5. **Which of the following statements is true about Deep Learning (DL)?**
(a) Deep Learning is a type of Machine Learning that uses neural networks
(b) Deep Learning requires less data compared to Machine Learning
(c) Deep Learning does not use algorithms for pattern recognition
(d) Deep Learning is the same as Artificial Intelligence

6. **What is an example of Machine Learning application?**
(a) Virtual assistants like Alexa and Siri
(b) Anomaly detection in banking transactions
(c) Self-driving cars analyzing real-time road conditions
(d) All of the above

7. **In Deep Learning, what is the role of hidden layers?**
(a) To directly produce the final output
(b) To store and retrieve training data
(c) To learn different features of the input data step by step
(d) To reduce the complexity of computations

8. **What is the primary difference between labeled and unlabeled data?**
(a) Labeled data contains missing values, while unlabeled data is complete.
(b) Labeled data has predefined output (labels), while unlabeled data does not.
(c) Labeled data is always structured, while unlabeled data is unstructured.
(d) Labeled data cannot be used in machine learning models, while unlabeled data can.

9. **In the given fruit dataset, which of the following is considered a feature?**
(a) Fruit Type
(b) Name
(c) Labeled Data
(d) Training Data

10. **Which of the following best describes a Rule-Based Approach in AI?**
(a) It learns from patterns in data and makes predictions.
(b) It uses predefined rules created by a developer to make decisions.
(c) It continuously adapts and improves over time with more data.
(d) It is a type of reinforcement learning model.

11. **In supervised learning, what is the role of a training data set?**
(a) To evaluate the model's performance
(b) To teach the model by providing labeled examples
(c) To help the model interact with its environment and learn from feedback
(d) To group similar data points into clusters

12. **Which learning approach is used by an email spam filter to classify emails as spam or not spam?**
(a) Rule-Based Approach (b) Supervised Learning
(c) Unsupervised Learning (d) Reinforcement Learning

Answers

1. (b)	2. (a)	3. (b)	4. (b)	5. (a)
6. (d)	7. (c)	8. (b)	9. (b)	10. (b)
11. (b)	12. (b)			

Statement Based Questions

1. **Statement 1 Ml (Machine Learning) Deals With Structured And Semi-Structured Data.**
Statement 2 The Goal Of Machine Learning Is To Solve The Complex Problems As The Human Brain Does, Using Various Algorithms.
(a) Both Statement 1 and Statement 2 are correct
(b) Both Statement 1 and Statement 2 are incorrect
(c) Statement 1 is correct but Statement 2 is incorrect
(d) Statement 2 is correct but Statement 1 is incorrect

2. **Statement 1 There Are Four Layers In A Neural Network.** SQP 2024-25
Statement 2 The first layer of the neural network is known as the output layer.
(a) Both Statement 1 and Statement 2 are correct.
(b) Both Statement 1 and Statement 2 are incorrect.
(c) Statement 1 is correct but Statement 2 is incorrect.
(d) Statement 2 is correct but Statement 1 is incorrect.

3. **Statement 1: Features in a dataset refer to the columns that provide specific details about the data.**
Statement 2: In a dataset used for predicting fruit type based on its color, the fruit name is a feature.
(a) Both Statement 1 and Statement 2 are correct.
(b) Both Statement 1 and Statement 2 are incorrect.
(c) Statement 1 is correct but Statement 2 is incorrect.
(d) Statement 2 is correct but Statement 1 is incorrect.

4. **Statement 1: A training data set is used to teach the AI model by providing labeled data.**
Statement 2: A testing data set contains only labeled data to help improve the model's learning.
(a) Both Statement 1 and Statement 2 are correct.
(b) Both Statement 1 and Statement 2 are incorrect.
(c) Statement 1 is correct but Statement 2 is incorrect.
(d) Statement 2 is correct but Statement 1 is incorrect.

5. **Statement 1: A rule-based approach in AI follows predefined rules to make decisions and does not learn from data.**
Statement 2: A learning-based approach adapts to new data and improves over time by recognizing patterns.
(a) Both Statement 1 and Statement 2 are correct.
(b) Both Statement 1 and Statement 2 are incorrect.

(c) Statement 1 is correct but Statement 2 is incorrect.
(d) Statement 2 is correct but Statement 1 is incorrect.

6. Statement 1: Neural networks are inspired by the structure and functioning of the human brain.
Statement 2: A neural network consists of layers of interconnected nodes called neurons.
(a) Both Statement 1 and Statement 2 are correct.
(b) Both Statement 1 and Statement 2 are incorrect.
(c) Statement 1 is correct but Statement 2 is incorrect.
(d) Statement 2 is correct but Statement 1 is incorrect.

7. Statement 1: The input layer of a neural network receives data and passes it to hidden layers for processing.
Statement 2: The output layer of a neural network generates the final result based on the learned patterns.
(a) Both Statement 1 and Statement 2 are correct.
(b) Both Statement 1 and Statement 2 are incorrect.
(c) Statement 1 is correct but Statement 2 is incorrect.
(d) Statement 2 is correct but Statement 1 is incorrect.

Answers

1. (c) 2. (b) 3. (c) 4. (c) 5. (a)
6. (a) 7. (a)

Assertion and Reason Based Questions

1. Assertion (A): Machine Learning (ML) is a subset of Artificial Intelligence (AI) that enables machines to learn from data and improve their performance over time.
Reason (R): Deep Learning (DL) is a specific branch of Machine Learning that uses neural networks with multiple layers to process vast amounts of data efficiently.
(a) Both A and R are true, and R is the correct explanation of A.
(b) Both A and R are true, but R is not the correct explanation of A.
(c) A is true, but R is false.
(d) A is false, but R is true.

2. Assertion (A): Deep Learning (DL) models require large datasets and high computational power for training.
Reason (R): DL models rely on predefined rules rather than learning from patterns in data.
(a) Both A and R are true, and R is the correct explanation of A.
(b) Both A and R are true, but R is not the correct explanation of A.
(c) A is true, but R is false.
(d) A is false, but R is true.

3. Assertion (A): Features in a dataset refer to the columns that provide various details about the data.
Reason (R): Features play an essential role in making predictions, and the most significant ones are referred to as labels.
(a) Both A and R are true, and R is the correct explanation of A.
(b) Both A and R are true, but R is not the correct explanation of A.
(c) A is true, but R is false.
(d) A is false, but R is true.

4. Assertion (A): A testing dataset is used to train a machine learning model so that it can learn patterns in the data.
Reason (R): A testing dataset is used to evaluate the performance of a trained model by comparing predictions with actual labels.
(a) Both A and R are true, and R is the correct explanation of A.
(b) Both A and R are true, but R is not the correct explanation of A.
(c) A is true, but R is false.
(d) A is false, but R is true.

5. Assertion (A): The rule-based approach in AI relies on predefined rules and does not adapt to new data.
Reason (R): Learning-based approaches require large datasets and can improve accuracy by identifying patterns from the data.
(a) Both A and R are true, and R is the correct explanation of A.
(b) Both A and R are true, but R is not the correct explanation of A.
(c) A is true, but R is false.
(d) A is false, but R is true.

Answers

1. (a) 2. (c) 3. (c) 4. (d) 5. (b)

Part II

Very Short Answer Type Questions

1. Srishti learnt about AI terminologies but was not able to recollect the term that is used to refer to machines that perform tasks with vast amounts of data using neural networks. Help her with the correct term. **Competency Based Que.**

Ans. Deep Learning

2. What is the primary goal of Artificial Intelligence (AI)?

Ans. The primary goal of AI is to create machines that mimic human thinking and behavior.

3. How does Machine Learning (ML) improve its performance?

Ans. ML improves performance by learning from new data and past mistakes.

4. What type of data does Deep Learning (DL) require for effective training?

Ans. DL requires large datasets to train deep neural networks for complex tasks.

5. What is the main difference between labeled and unlabeled data?

Ans. Labeled data has known outputs (labels), while unlabeled data lacks predefined labels.

6. How does a rule-based AI system respond to new, unseen inputs?

Ans. It follows predefined rules and cannot adapt unless manually updated.

7. Why does a learning-based approach require large datasets?

Ans. It learns patterns from data and needs many examples to make accurate predictions.

8. What type of AI learning is used in self-driving cars, and why?

Ans. Learning-based approach, as it adapts to new situations and improves with more data.

9. Srishti learnt about AI terminologies but was not able to recollect the term that is used to refer to machines that perform tasks with vast amounts of data using neural networks. Help her with the correct term. CBSE 2024-25

Ans. Deep Learning

Short Answer Type Questions

1. How does deep learning differ from traditional machine learning in handling complex data?

Ans. Deep learning uses multiple neural network layers to automatically extract complex patterns, while traditional machine learning often requires manual feature selection and struggles with large, unstructured data like images or audio.

2. Why is labeled data important for machine learning, but not always necessary for artificial intelligence?

Ans. Machine learning relies on labeled data for training models to recognize patterns, whereas artificial intelligence can use predefined rules and logic to perform tasks without always needing labeled data.

3. How does an AI system decide whether a flame in an image is real or just a photograph?

Ans. An AI system can analyze temperature, movement, and other physical properties, using deep learning models trained to distinguish between real flames and static images.

4. What is the primary function of hidden layers in a deep learning model?

Ans. Hidden layers in a deep learning model extract and refine features from input data, gradually identifying patterns such as edges, shapes, and complex structures to improve classification accuracy.

5. Define the term Machine Learning. Also give two applications of Machine Learning in our daily lives.

Ans. Machine Learning is a subset of Artificial Intelligence which enables machines to improve at tasks with experience (data).

Applications of Machine Learning

- The intention of Machine Learning is to enable machines to learn by themselves using the provided data and make accurate Predictions/ Decisions.
- Machine Learning is used in Snapchat Filters, NETFLIX recommendation system.

6. Differentiate between Machine Learning (ML) and Deep Learning (DL). 2024

Ans.

Machine Learning (ML)	Deep Learning (DL)
ML is an artificial intelligence (AI) methodology. Not all ML is deep learning.	Deep learning is an advanced ML methodology. All deep learning is ML.
You have to manually select and extract features from raw data and assign weights to train an ML model.	Deep learning models can self-learn using feedback from known errors.

7. All of us use smartphones. When we install a new app, it asks us for several permissions to access our phone's data in different ways. Why do apps collect such data? CBSE 2024-25

Ans.
- To deliver personalized notifications and suggestions based on user preferences.
- To enhance the app's performance, ensuring faster response times and more accurate results.

Long Answer Type Questions

1. Ms. Sooji is a beginner in the field of artificial intelligence. She got confused among the core terms like artificial intelligence, machine learning and deep learning. Many a times, these terms are used interchangeably but are they the same? Justify your answer. Help her in understanding these terms by drawing a well labelled diagram to depict the interconnection of these three fields. 2023

Ans. No, artificial intelligence (AI), machine learning (ML), and deep learning (DL) are not the same, although they are related.

Artificial Intelligence (AI) This is the broader concept of machines performing tasks in a way that we would consider "smart" if done by humans. It encompasses a wide range of techniques aimed at enabling computers to perform tasks that normally require human intelligence.

Machine Learning (ML) ML is a subset of AI. It focuses on the development of algorithms that allow computers to learn from and make predictions or decisions based on data. ML algorithms improve their performance on a task as they are exposed to more data over time.

Deep Learning (DL) DL is a subset of ML that specifically deals with neural networks containing many layers (hence "deep"). These neural networks are capable of learning complex representations of data. DL has gained popularity due to its remarkable performance in various tasks, such as image recognition and natural language processing.

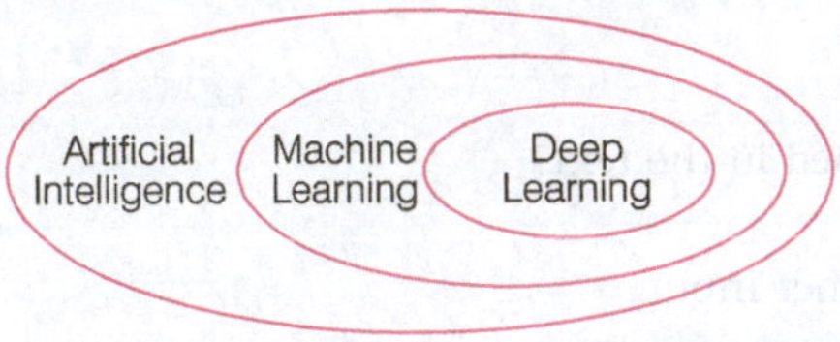

2. Identify and explain the types of the learning-based approaches in the figures given below. **SQP 2024-25**

Ans. Learning-Based Approaches: Supervised and Unsupervised Learning

Figure 1: Supervised Learning

In supervised learning, the dataset provided to the machine is labeled. The person training the model knows the dataset and assigns labels, which act as tags for the data.

For example, labeled images of a dog and a cat are used to train the model. After training, the model correctly identifies an input image as a dog based on its learning.

Figure 2: Unsupervised Learning

In unsupervised learning, the dataset is unlabeled and unstructured. The person training the model may have no prior information about the data. The model identifies patterns, relationships, and trends without labeled guidance.

For example, when fed with images of various animals, the model groups them into clusters based on similar features, helping users understand patterns and key characteristics within the data.

This comparison highlights how supervised learning uses known data for classification, while unsupervised learning discovers hidden patterns in unknown data.

3. What is a neural network, and how does it work?

Ans. A neural network is a computer system modeled after the human brain. It consists of layers of artificial neurons that process data and recognize patterns. A neural network has three main layers: the input layer, which receives data; the hidden layers, which process information using mathematical operations; and the output layer, which produces the final result. Each neuron in these layers is connected and assigned a weight, which determines its importance. When data passes through the network, these weights are adjusted to improve accuracy through a process called training. Neural networks learn from large datasets and improve their performance over time. They are widely used in applications like image recognition, language translation, and medical diagnosis. Due to their ability to analyze complex data efficiently, neural networks are considered a key technology in artificial intelligence (AI).

SELF ASSESSMENT

Multiple Choice Questions

1. Which of the following is a common example of a supervised learning task?
   (a) Customer segmentation based on purchase history.
   (b) Anomaly detection in network traffic.
   (c) Image classification (e.g., identifying cats vs. dogs).
   (d) Reducing the dimensionality of a dataset.
2. Which of the following is a common example of an unsupervised learning task?
   (a) Predicting stock prices based on historical data.
   (b) Sentiment analysis of customer reviews.
   (c) Clustering documents based on their content.
   (d) Spam email detection.
3. What is the primary advantage of using neural networks as described in the text?
   (a) They always provide perfectly accurate results.
   (b) They can automatically extract data features without programmer input.
   (c) They are simpler to program than traditional algorithms.
   (d) They require very small datasets to function effectively.
4. Which of the following best describes the function of the hidden layers in a neural network?
   (a) To acquire and feed data into the network.
   (b) To present the final processed information to the user.
   (c) To perform computations on the input data using weights and biases.
   (d) To store the raw input data for later use.

Very Short Answer Type Questions

5. Write the name of unsupervised category of learning model.
6. Give examples of data features.

Short Answer Type Questions

7. Explain Convolutional Neural Network (CNN) in short.
8. What do you understand by Machine Learning?
9. What is Learning Based model?

Long Answer Type Questions

10. What do you understand by AI, ML & DL? How are they different from each other?
11. What is clustering and how is it different from classification?
12. Differentiate between classification and regression model.

Evaluation

CHAPTER 03

Evaluation in artificial intelligence (AI) is like giving AI systems a report card to understand how well they're performing. AI models undergo evaluation to see if they're making accurate predictions and decisions. This evaluation helps us ensure that AI systems are trustworthy, reliable, and ready for real-world use. .

3.1 Introduction

So far, we have learned about the four stages of the AI project cycle: Problem Scoping, Data Acquisition, Data Exploration, and Modeling. While modeling allows us to create different types of models, how do we determine which one performs best? This is where Evaluation comes into play.

In the Evaluation stage, we explore various methods to assess an AI model's effectiveness. Model Evaluation is a crucial part of the development process, helping us identify the best model that accurately represents the data and ensures its reliability for future predictions.

Importance of Model Evaluation

- Model evaluation is the process of using different metrics to assess a machine learning model's performance.
- An AI model improves with constructive feedback from evaluation metrics.
- The process involves building a model, analyzing its performance using metrics, making improvements, and repeating the cycle until achieving the desired accuracy.

Think of model evaluation as a school report card:

- Just as students are assessed using grades, percentages, percentiles, and ranks, AI models are evaluated using various performance metrics.
- Academic evaluation helps students identify areas for improvement, just as model evaluation helps refine AI models for better accuracy and reliability.

Need of Model Evaluation

Model evaluation is like giving your AI model a report card—it helps assess its strengths, weaknesses, and overall suitability for the given task. This feedback loop is crucial for building trustworthy and reliable AI systems.

Now that we understand the importance of model evaluation, let's explore how to begin the process. The evaluation technique used depends on the type and purpose of the model, ensuring that the chosen method effectively measures its performance.

3.2 Splitting the Training Set Data for Evaluation

Train-Test Split

- The train-test split is a commonly used technique for evaluating the performance of a machine learning model.
- It applies to any supervised learning algorithm and helps assess model accuracy.
- The process involves dividing a dataset into two subsets:
  - Training set: Used to train the model.
  - Testing set: Used to evaluate the model's performance on unseen data.
- The train-test split approach is most effective when a sufficiently large dataset is available.

Need of Train-Test Split

- The training dataset is used to help the model learn patterns from the data.
- The test dataset consists of new input elements that are fed into the trained model to make predictions. These predicted values are then compared to the actual (expected) values.

- The main objective of the train-test split is to estimate the performance of the machine learning model on unseen data—data that was not used during training. This simulates real-world usage, where the model is trained on known data and later makes predictions on new, unknown examples.

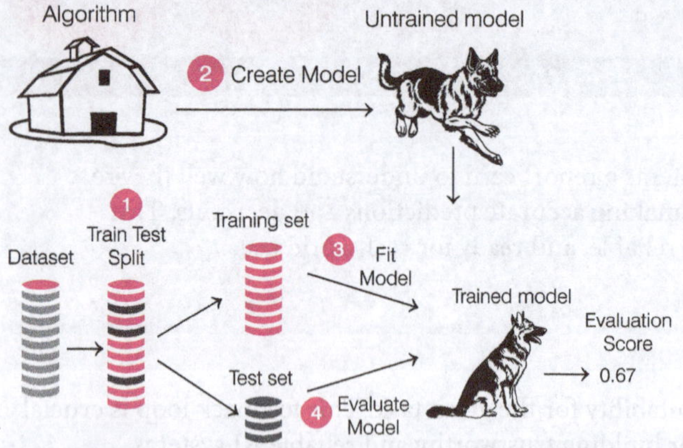

Info Wall

Why Not Use the Training Data for Evaluation?
It is not recommended to evaluate a model using the same data it was trained on. Doing so may lead to overfitting, where the model memorizes the training data instead of learning generalizable patterns. As a result, it will always predict the correct label for training samples but may perform poorly on new data.

As you progress to higher classes, you will learn more about key concepts such as train-test split and cross-validation, which help in properly evaluating a model's performance.

Try These 3.1

1 **What is model evaluation?**
2 **Why is the train-test split used?**
3 **What happens if we evaluate a model using training data?**
4 **How does model evaluation help AI models?**

3.3 Accuracy and Error

Accuracy

- Accuracy is a metric used to measure the total number of correct predictions made by a model.
- The higher the accuracy, the better the model's performance, as accurate predictions indicate better learning.

Error

- Error refers to an incorrect or inaccurate prediction.
- In Machine Learning, error helps evaluate how well a model can predict new, unseen data.
- Choosing the right model depends on minimizing error for a given dataset.

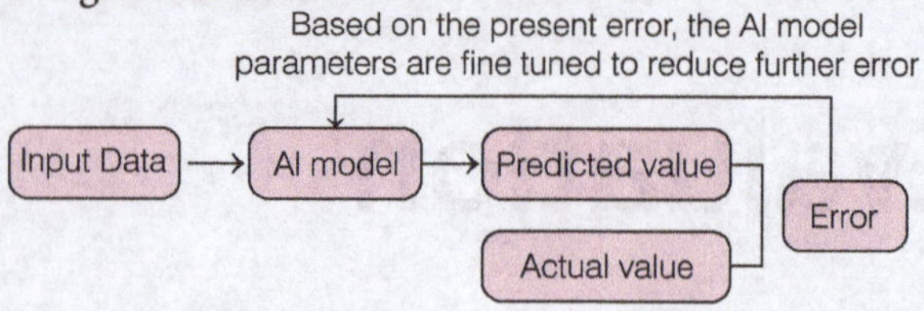

Imagine you're training a model to predict whether a person has a certain disease. This is a classification task where the model's predictions can have significant real-world consequences.

Key Concepts

- **Error** If the model predicts that a person is disease-free when they actually have the disease, this is an error. Errors quantify how far the prediction deviates from reality.
- **Accuracy** If the model correctly predicts the presence or absence of a disease over a given period, it achieves 100% accuracy for that period.

Important Considerations

- The goal is to minimize errors and maximize accuracy for reliable predictions.
- Real-world data is often messy, and even the best models make mistakes.
- Focusing solely on accuracy may not always be ideal. In medical diagnosis, a model with slightly lower accuracy but a better ability to minimize false negatives (failing to detect a real case) can be more valuable.
- Choosing the right metric for evaluating the model depends on the specific task and its impact. In healthcare, precision, recall, and false positive/negative rates are often just as important as accuracy.

3.4 Classification

Imagine you go to a supermarket and are given two trolleys. One trolley is designated for fruits and vegetables, while the other is for grocery items such as bread, oil, eggs, etc. In this scenario, you are essentially categorizing or classifying the items into two distinct groups:

- Fruits and Vegetables
- Grocery Items

Classification is a type of problem where the goal is to predict a specific class label from a given set of input data.

For example, in our vegetable-grocery classifier model, the task is to predict whether an item in the supermarket belongs to the "vegetable" class or the "grocery" class.

Classification Metrics

Popular metrics used for classification model

- Confusion matrix
- Classification accuracy
- Precision
- Recall

Confusion Matrix

A confusion matrix is a table used to evaluate the performance of a classification model. It compares the actual values (ground truth) with the predicted values (model output).

Confusion Matrix

	Actually Positive(1)	Actually Negative(0)
Predicted Positive(1)	True Positives (TPs)	False Positives (FPs)
Predicted Negative(0)	False Negatives (FNs)	True Negatives (TNs)

Structure of a Confusion Matrix

For a binary classification problem (where the model predicts either 1 (infected) or 0 (not infected)), the confusion matrix is structured as follows:

Actual / Predicted	1 (Predicted Infected)	0 (Predicted Not Infected)
1 (Actual Infected)	True Positive (TP)	False Negative (FN)
0 (Actual Not Infected)	False Positive (FP)	True Negative (TN)

Explanation of Each Term

1. **True Positive (TP)** The model correctly predicts infected (1) when the person is actually infected.
2. **False Negative (FN)** The model incorrectly predicts not infected (0) when the person is actually infected.

   A false negative is dangerous in medical diagnoses, as an infected person may go untreated.
3. **False Positive (FP)** The model incorrectly predicts infected (1) when the person is actually not infected.

   This can lead to unnecessary treatments or anxiety.
4. **True Negative (TN)** The model correctly predicts not infected (0) when the person is actually not infected.

Let's understand each cell of the matrix in details.

Imagine that you have come up with an AI based prediction model which has been deployed in a forest which is prone to forest fires. Now, the objective of the model is to predict whether a forest fire has broken out in the forest or not. There exist two conditions which we need to ponder upon Prediction and Reality. The prediction is the output which is given by the machine has been made. Now let us look at the various combinations that we can have with these two conditions.

Case 1: Is there a forest fire?

Here, we can see in the picture that a forest fire has broken out in the forest. The model predicts a Yes which means there is a forest fire. The prediction matches with the Reality. Hence, this condition is termed as **True Positive**.

Case 2: Is there a forest fire?

Here there is no fire in the forest hence the Reality is No. In this case, the machine too has predicted it correctly as a No. Therefore, this condition is termed as **True Negative**.

Case 3: Is there a forest fire?

Here the reality is that there is no forest fire. But the machine has incorrectly predicted that there is a forest fire. This case is termed as **False Positive.**

Case 4: Is there a forest fire?

Prediction: No

Reality : Yes

False Negative

Here, a forest fire has broken out in the forest because of which the Reality is Yes but the machine has incorrectly predicted it as a No. which means the machine predicts that there is no Forest Fire. Therefore, this case becomes False Negative.

Let us once again take a look at the four conditions that we went through in the Forest Fire scenario:

FN
- False Negative
- Prediction & Reality do not matches (False)
- Prediction is False (Negative)

FP
- False Positive
- Prediction & Reality do not matches (False)
- Prediction is True (Positive)

TN
- True Negative
- Prediction & Reality matches (True)
- Prediction is False (Negative)

TP
- True Positive
- Prediction & Reality matches (True)
- Prediction is True (Positive)

Info Wall

The confusion matrix was invented in 1904 by Karl Pearson. He used the term Contingency Table, which appeared in Karl Pearson, F.R.S. (1904).

Try These 3.2

1 **Which of this is a classification use case example?** NCERT

(a) House price prediction

(b) Credit card fraud detection

(c) Salary prediction

2 **What is True positive?**

3 **Give an example of True negative and False positive.**

4 **Difference between prediction and reality.**

Accuracy from Confusion Matrix

Classification accuracy is a measure of how well a model predicts the correct outcomes. It is calculated as:

$$\text{Accuracy} = \frac{\text{Number of Correct Predictions}}{\text{Total Predictions}}$$

Using values from the confusion matrix:

$$\text{Accuracy} = \frac{TP + TN}{TP + TN + FP + FN}$$

where,

- **TP (True Positives)** Correctly predicted positive cases
- **TN (True Negatives)** Correctly predicted negative cases
- **FP (False Positives)** Incorrectly predicted positive cases
- **FN (False Negatives)** Incorrectly predicted negative cases

Limitations of Accuracy

- Accuracy is only suitable when there is an equal number of observations in each class, i.e., a balanced dataset (which is rarely the case). It assumes that all predictions and prediction errors are equally important, which is often not true.
- The reason for this limitation will be better understood in the next activity.

Precision from Confusion Matrix

- Precision is the ratio of the total number of correctly classified positive examples to the total number of predicted positive examples.
- A precision score of 0.843 means that when the model predicts a patient has heart disease, it is correct around 84% of the time.

$$\text{Precision} = \frac{\text{Correct positive predictions}}{\text{Total positive predictions}} = \frac{TP}{TP + FP}$$

Use of Precision

Precision is generally used for unbalanced datasets when False Positives (FPs) are critical, and the model needs to minimize them.

Use Case Example: Satellite Launch

- In predicting a good day for launching a satellite based on weather conditions, a favorable weather day is considered a Positive class, and a non-favorable day is considered a Negative class.
- Missing out on predicting a good weather day (low recall) is acceptable, but predicting a bad weather day as

a good one (False Positive) can lead to disastrous consequences.

- In this case, reducing False Positives is crucial to avoid incorrect satellite launches.

Recall from Confusion Matrix

- Recall measures the model's ability to correctly identify True Positives.
- For patients who actually have heart disease, recall indicates how many are correctly identified as having the disease. A recall score of 0.86 means that 86% of the total heart disease cases are correctly detected.

  Recall is also called **Sensitivity** or **True Positive Rate (TPR).**

$$\text{Recall} = \frac{\text{Correct positive predictions}}{\text{Total actual positive values}} = \frac{TP}{TP + FN}$$

Use of Recall

Recall is generally used for unbalanced datasets where False Negatives (FNs) are critical, and the model needs to minimize them.

Use Case Example: COVID-19 Detection

- In a COVID-19 prediction classifier, detecting an affected case is considered a Positive class, and detecting a non-affected case is considered a Negative class.
- If a COVID-19 positive person is falsely predicted as negative, they may not receive treatment and could unknowingly spread the virus.
- In such cases, reducing False Negatives is crucial. **Recall is the preferred metric** for such scenarios.

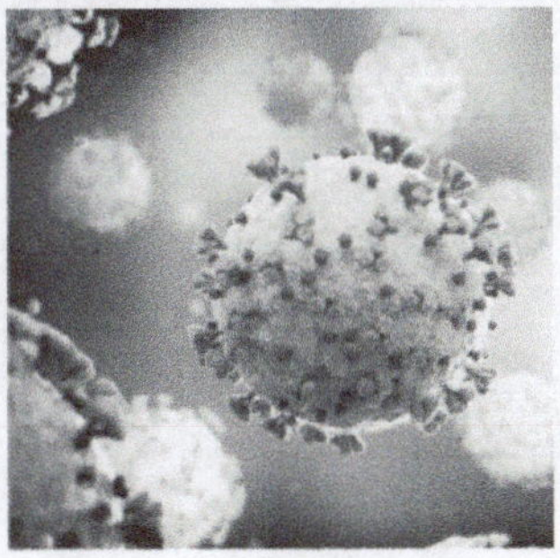

F1 Score

- The F1 Score combines both Precision and Recall into a single metric, providing a balanced measure of a model's performance.
- It is calculated using the formula:

$$\text{F1 Score} = 2 \times \frac{\text{Precision} \times \text{Recall}}{\text{Precision} + \text{Recall}}$$

Use of F1 Score

- The F1 Score is useful in cases where the dataset is imbalanced, and it is unclear whether False Positives (FPs) or False Negatives (FNs) are more important.
- It ensures a balance between Precision (minimizing FPs) and Recall (minimizing FNs), making it a suitable metric when both aspects are equally critical.

3.6 Ethical Concerns Around Model Evaluation

When evaluating an AI model, it is important to consider several ethical concerns to ensure fairness, accuracy, and responsible use. Some key ethical concerns include:

1. Bias

- AI models can develop biases based on the data they are trained on.
- If the training data is not diverse or representative, the model may make unfair predictions.
- **Example** A hiring AI system trained on past data that favors a particular gender may unfairly reject qualified candidates.

2. Transparency

- Users and developers should understand how an AI model makes decisions.
- If the model is too complex or lacks documentation, it becomes difficult to trust its outputs.
- **Example** A loan approval AI should clearly state why a person was denied a loan.

3. Accountability

- AI systems should have clear responsibility assigned in case of errors or unethical outcomes.
- Developers, companies, or policymakers must ensure the AI is used ethically.
- **Example** If an AI-driven self-driving car causes an accident, it should be clear who is responsible.

Try These 3.3

1 Write the formula to calculate Precision.
2 Write the formula to calculate Accuracy.
3 What is Recall?
4 What is a major ethical concern in AI models related to data?
5 Why is transparency important in AI model evaluation?

Glossary

Evaluation It is basically to check the performance of your AI model. This is done by mainly two things "Prediction" & "Reality".

Accuracy It measures the proportion of correctly classified instances out of the total instances in the dataset.

Precision It evaluates the accuracy of positive predictions made by a model.

Recall It also known as sensitivity or true positive rate, measures the proportion of actual positive instances that were correctly identified by the model.

F1 Score It is a hormonic mean of precision and recall, providing a single metric that balances both measures.

ACTIVITY Time

ACTIVITY 1 : Find the Accuracy of the AI Model

Calculate the accuracy of the House Price Prediction AI model by completing the table below using the given formulas.

Formulae:

Error (Absolute Value) (Actual-Predicted)

Error Rate $\frac{\text{Error}}{\text{Actual}}$

Accuracy 1-Error Rate

Accuracy %Accuracy×100

Predicted House Price (USD)	Actual House Price (USD)	Error Abs (Actual - Predicted)	Error Rate (Error / Actual)	Accuracy (1 - Error Rate)	Accuracy % (Accuracy × 100)
391k	402k	11k	0.027	0.973	97.3%
453k	488k	35k	0.072	0.928	92.8%
125k	97k	28k	0.289	0.711	71.1%
871k	907k	36k	0.040	0.960	96.0%
322k	425k	103k	0.242	0.758	75.8%

$$\text{Mean Accuracy} = \frac{(0.973 + 0.928 + 0.711 + 0.960 + 0.758)}{5}$$

$$= 0.866$$

$$= 86.6\%$$

Thus, the AI model's accuracy is 86.6%.

ACTIVITY 2 : Build the Confusion Matrix from Scratch

Duration 10 minutes

Activity Guidelines

1. Assume we are predicting the presence of a disease.
   "Yes" means the person has the disease.
   "No" means the person does not have the disease.
2. The AI model outputs either "Yes" or "No" as predictions.
3. Below is a table showing actual values and predicted values.
4. Construct a confusion matrix based on the given data.
5. Count how many predictions were correct among all predictions.

Given Data

Actual Value	Predicted Value
Yes	Yes
No	No
No	Yes
Yes	No
No	No
Yes	Yes
Yes	No
No	No
No	No
No	No

Step 1 Count the occurrences

- **True Positives (TP)** Cases where the actual value is "Yes" and the predicted value is also "Yes".
- **False Negatives (FN)** Cases where the actual value is "Yes" but the predicted value is "No".
- **False Positives (FP)** Cases where the actual value is "No" but the predicted value is "Yes".
- **True Negatives (TN)** Cases where the actual value is "No" and the predicted value is also "No".

Step 2 Fill in the Confusion Matrix

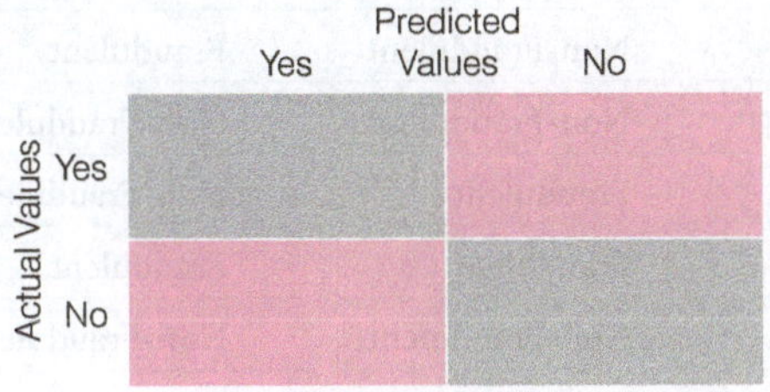

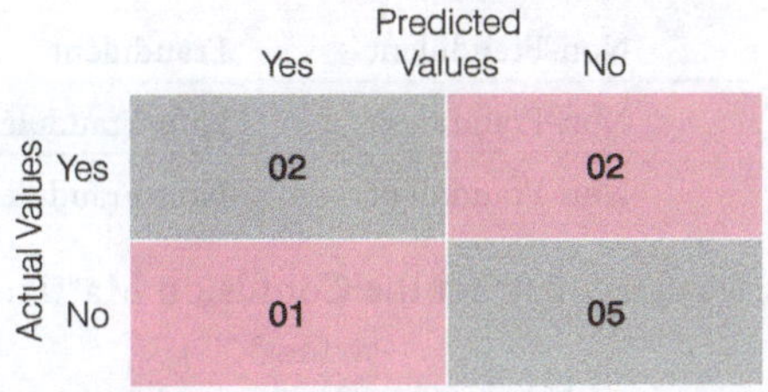

Step 3 Correct Predictions Count

Total correct predictions = TP + TN = 2 + 5 = 7

Step 4 Incorrect Predictions Count

Total incorrect predictions = FP + FN = 1 + 2 = 3

Final Notes

- The confusion matrix helps analyze model performance.
- Correct predictions are 7 out of 10.
- Incorrect predictions are 3 out of 10.
- A high TN count indicates the model is good at detecting negatives, but FN and FP should be minimized for better performance.

ACTIVITY 3 : Calculate the Accuracy of the Classifier Model

Duration 20 minutes

Activity Guidelines

- Assume you are testing your model on 1000 total test data points.
- The actual values consist of 900 'Yes' (positive class) and 100 'No' (negative class), making it an unbalanced dataset.
- The classifier is a faulty model that predicts 'Yes' for all inputs, regardless of the actual values.

Step 1 Construct the Actual vs Predicted Table

Actual Values	Predicted 'Yes'	Predicted 'No'
Yes (900)	900	0
No (100)	100	0

Step 2 Construct the Confusion Matrix

A confusion matrix helps visualize the performance of the classifier.

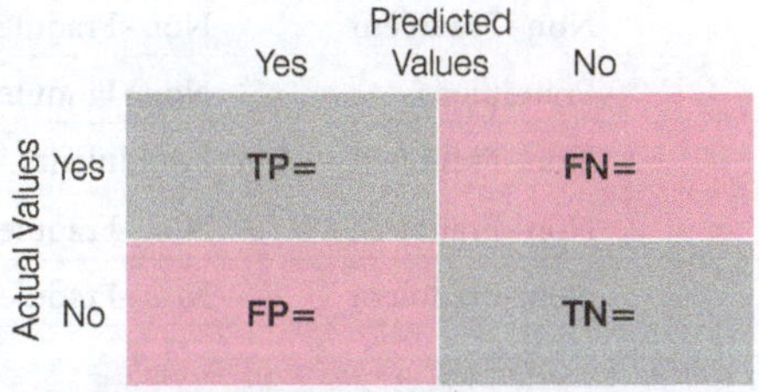

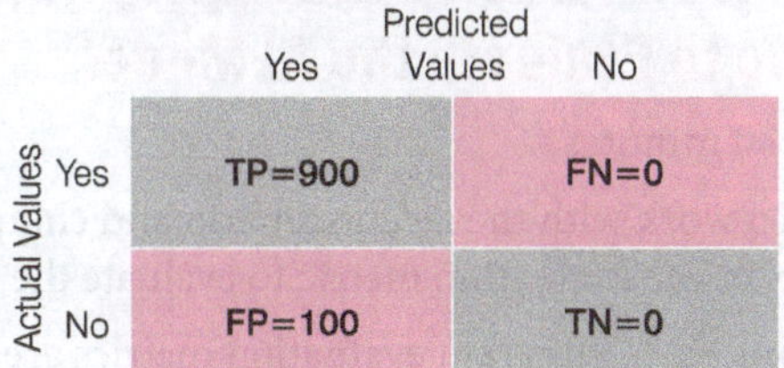

Where:

- **TP (True Positive)** 900 (Correctly predicted 'Yes')
- **FN (False Negative)** 0 (Incorrectly predicted 'No' instead of 'Yes')
- **FP (False Positive)** 100 (Incorrectly predicted 'Yes' instead of 'No')
- **TN (True Negative)** 0 (Correctly predicted 'No')

Step 3 Calculate Classification Accuracy

The formula for classification accuracy is:

$$\text{Accuracy} = \frac{TP + TN}{TP + TN + FP + FN}$$

Substituting values:

$$\text{Accuracy} = \frac{900 + 0}{900 + 0 + 100 + 0} = \frac{900}{1000} = 0.9$$

Step 4 Convert Accuracy to Percentage

$\text{Classification Accuracy} = 0.9 \times 100 = 90\%$

Does this Accuracy Make Sense?

Although the model shows a high 90% accuracy, it is misleading because it fails to correctly classify any of the negative class ('No').

This highlights a problem with accuracy in unbalanced datasets.

Transaction ID	Actual value	Predicted Value
1	Non-Fraudulent	Non -Fradulent
2	Non-Fraudulent	Fraudulent
3	Non -Fradulent	Non -Fradulent
4	Fraudulent	Non -Fradulent
5	Fraudulent	Fraudulent
6	Non -Fradulent	Non -Fradulent
7	Fraudulent	Non -Fradulent
8	Non -Fradulent	Fraudulent
9	Non -Fradulent	Non -Fradulent
10	Non -Fradulent	Non -Fradulent

ACTIVITY 4 : Decide the Appropriate Metric to Evaluate the AI Model

Duration 30 minutes

Purpose To work with the given scenario and choose the most appropriate evaluation metric to evaluate the model.

Instructions Say: "Different evaluation metrics are used for evaluation in different scenarios, and it is important that we realize how to choose the correct one."

Scenario Flagging Fraudulent Transactions

- You have designed a model to detect fraudulent transactions with a credit card.
- You are testing your model with a highly unbalanced dataset.
- What is the metric to be considered in this case?
    - It is okay to classify a legitimate transaction as fraudulent—it can always be re-verified by passing through additional checks.
    - But it is definitely not okay to classify a fraudulent transaction as legitimate (false negative).
    - So here, false negatives should be reduced as much as possible.
    - Hence, in this case, Recall is more important.

Confusion Matrix Construction

Using the given transaction data:

Transaction ID	Actual Value	Predicted Value
1	Non-Fraudulent	Non-Fraudulent
2	Non-Fraudulent	Fraudulent
3	Non-Fraudulent	Non-Fraudulent
4	Fraudulent	Non-Fraudulent
5	Fraudulent	Fraudulent
6	Non-Fraudulent	Non-Fraudulent
7	Fraudulent	Non-Fraudulent
8	Non-Fraudulent	Fraudulent
9	Non-Fraudulent	Non-Fraudulent
10	Non-Fraudulent	Non-Fraudulent

From this, we can construct the Confusion Matrix:

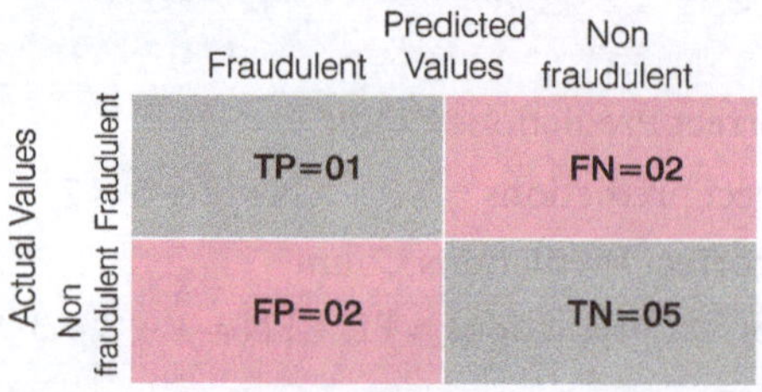

Recall is calculated using the formula

$$\text{Recall} = \frac{\text{True Positives (TP)}}{\text{True Positives (TP) + False Negatives (FN)}}$$

Now, applying the recall formula for the fraudulent class

$$\text{Recall} = \frac{1}{1+2} = \frac{1}{3} \approx 0.3333 \text{ or } 33.33\%$$

So, the recall for detecting fraudulent cases is 33.33%

NCERT FOLDER

Complete Explanations of all NCERT's Questions

A. Multiple Choice Questions

1. In a medical test for a rare disease, out of 1000 people tested, 50 actually have the disease while 950 do not. The test correctly identifies 40 out of the 50 people with the disease as positive, but it also wrongly identifies 30 of the healthy individuals as positive. What is the accuracy of the test?

(a) 97% (b) 90% (c) 85% (d) 70%

2. A student solved 90 out of 100 questions correctly in a multiple-choice exam. What is the error rate of the student's answers?

(a) 10% (b) 9%
(c) 8% (d) 11%

3. In a spam email detection system, out of 1000 emails received, 300 are spam. The system correctly identifies 240 spam emails as spam, but it also marks 60 legitimate emails as spam. What is the precision of the system?

(a) 80% (b) 70%
(c) 75% (d) 90%

4. In a binary classification problem, a model predicts 70 instances as positive out of which 50 are actually positive. What is the recall of the model?

(a) 50% (b) 70%
(c) 80% (d) 100%

5. In a sentiment analysis task, a model correctly predicts 120 positive sentiments out of 200 positive instances. However, it also incorrectly predicts 40 negative sentiments as positive. What is the F1 score of the model?

(a) 0.8 (b) 0.75
(c) 0.72 (d) 0.82

6. A medical diagnostic test is designed to detect a certain disease. Out of 1000 people tested, 100 have the disease, and the test identifies 90 of them correctly. However, it also wrongly identifies 50 healthy people as having the disease. What is the precision of the test?

(a) 90% (b) 80%
(c) 70% (d) 60%

7. A teacher's marks prediction system predicts the marks of a student as 75, but the actual marks obtained by the student are 80. What is the absolute error in the prediction?

(a) 5 (b) 10
(c) 15 (d) 20

8. The goal when evaluating an AI model is to:

(a) Maximize error and minimize accuracy
(b) Minimize error and maximize accuracy
(c) Focus solely on the number of data points used
(d) Prioritize the complexity of the model

9. A high F1 score generally suggests:

(a) A significant imbalance between precision and recall
(b) A good balance between precision and recall
(c) A model that only performs well on specific data points
(d) The need for more training data

10. How is the relationship between model performance and accuracy described?

(a) Inversely proportional (b) Not related
(c) Directly proportional (d) Randomly fluctuating

Answers

1. (a)	2. (a)	3. (a)	4. (d)	5. (c)
6. (c)	7. (a)	8. (b)	9. (b)	10. (c)

B. Subjective Questions

1. What will happen if you deploy an AI model without evaluating it with known test set data?

Ans. If an AI model is deployed without evaluation, it may produce inaccurate predictions and fail in real-world applications. The model might overfit training data, leading to biased and unreliable decisions. This can result in financial losses, security risks, or ethical issues.

2. Do you think evaluating an AI model is that essential in an AI project cycle?

Ans. Yes, evaluating an AI model is crucial to ensure accuracy, reliability, and fairness. It helps detect overfitting, optimize performance, and validate the model's applicability to real-world scenarios. Without evaluation, the model may fail to generalize to new data.

3. Explain train-test split with an example.

Ans. The train-test split is a method used to evaluate machine learning models by dividing the dataset into two parts:

Training Set Used to train the model.

Test Set Used to evaluate the model's performance on unseen data.

Example

Suppose we have a dataset of 10,000 customer transactions for fraud detection. We split the dataset into:

80% (8000 transactions) as the training set to teach the model.

20% (2000 transactions) as the test set to assess its accuracy.

If the model performs well on the test set, it is likely to work well in real-world scenarios.

4. "Understanding both error and accuracy is crucial for effectively evaluating and improving AI models." Justify this statement.

Ans. Accuracy alone may be misleading, especially in imbalanced datasets. Analyzing errors (false positives and false negatives) helps identify weaknesses and improve precision, recall, and F1-score. A balanced evaluation ensures better real-world performance of AI models.

5. What is classification accuracy? Can it be used all times for evaluating AI models?

Ans. Classification accuracy is the percentage of correct predictions made by the model. However, it is not always reliable, especially for imbalanced datasets. In such cases, metrics like precision, recall, and F1-score provide a better evaluation of model performance.

C. Assertion and Reason Based Questions

1. Assertion (A) Accuracy is an evaluation metric that allows you to measure the total number of predictions a model gets right.
Reason (R) The accuracy of the model and performance of the model is directly proportional, and hence better the performance of the model, the more accurate are the predictions.
Choose the correct option:

(a) Both A and R are correct and R is the correct explanation of A
(b) Both A and R are correct but R is not the correct explanation of A
(c) A is correct but R is not correct
(d) A is not correct but R is correct

2. Assertion (A) The sum of the values in a confusion matrix's row represents the total number of instances for a given actual class.
Reason (R) This enables the calculation of class-specific metrics such as precision and recall, which are essential for evaluating a model's performance across different classes.
Choose the correct option:

(a) Both A and R are correct and R is the correct explanation of A
(b) Both A and R are correct but R is not the correct explanation of A
(c) A is correct but R is not correct
(d) A is not correct but R is correct

Answers

1. (c) **2.** (a)

D. Case Study Based Questions

1. Identify which metric (Precision or Recall) is to be used in the following cases and why?

(a) Email Spam Detection
(b) Cancer Diagnosis
(c) Legal Cases (Innocent until proven guilty)
(d) Fraud Detection
(e) Safe Content Filtering (like Kids YouTube)

Ans. (a) Precision (False positives (important emails marked as spam) should be minimized to avoid losing crucial messages.)

(b) Recall (False negatives (missed cancer cases) must be minimized to ensure no patient with cancer goes undiagnosed.)

(c) Precision (False positives (wrongful convictions) should be minimized to avoid punishing innocent people.)

(d) Recall (False negatives (missed fraud cases) must be minimized to prevent fraud from going undetected.)

(e) Recall (False negatives (unsafe content passing through) should be minimized to ensure children's safety.)

2. Examine the following case studies. Draw the confusion matrix and calculate metrics such as accuracy, precision, recall, and F1-score for each one of them.

(a) A spam email detection system is used to classify emails as either spam (1) or not spam (0). Out of 1000 emails:

- **True Positives (TP)** 150 emails were correctly classified as spam.
- **False Positives (FP)** 50 emails were incorrectly classified as spam.
- **True Negatives (TN)** 750 emails were correctly classified as not spam.
- **False Negatives (FN)** 50 emails were incorrectly classified as not spam.

(b) A credit scoring model is used to predict whether an applicant is likely to default on a loan (1) or not (0). Out of 1000 loan applicants:

- **True Positives (TP)** 90 applicants were correctly predicted to default on the loan.
- **False Positives (FP)** 40 applicants were incorrectly predicted to default on the loan.
- **True Negatives (TN)** 820 applicants were correctly predicted not to default on the loan.
- **False Negatives (FN)** 50 applicants were incorrectly predicted not to default on the loan.

(c) A fraud detection system is used to identify fraudulent transactions(1) from legitimate ones (0). Out of 1000 transactions:

- **True Positives (TP)** 80 transactions were correctly identified asfraudulent.
- **False Positives (FP)** 30 transactions were incorrectly identified asfraudulent.
- **True Negatives (TN)** 850 transactions were correctly identified aslegitimate.
- **False Negatives (FN)** 40 transactions were incorrectly identified aslegitimate.

(d) A medical diagnosis system is used to classify patients as having a certain disease (1) or not having it (0). Out of 1000 patients:

- **True Positives (TP)** 120 patients were correctly diagnosed with the disease.
- **False Positives (FP)** 20 patients were incorrectly diagnosed with the disease.
- **True Negatives (TN)** 800 patients were correctly diagnosed as not having the disease.
- **False Negatives (FN)** 60 patients were incorrectly diagnosed as not having the disease.

(e) An inventory management system is used to predict whether a product will be out of stock (1) or not (0) in the next month. Out of 1000 products:

- **True Positives (TP)** 100 products were correctly predicted to be out of stock.
- **False Positives (FP)** 50 products were incorrectly predicted to be out of stock.
- **True Negatives (TN)** 800 products were correctly predicted not to be out of stock.
- **True Negatives (TN)** 800 products were correctly predicted not to be out of stock.
- **False Negatives (FN)** 50 products were incorrectly predicted not to be out of stock.

Ans. (a) Confusion Matrix:

	Predicted Spam (1)	Predicted Not Spam (0)
Actual Spam (1)	TP= 150	FN= 50
Actual Not Spam (0)	FP= 50	TN= 750

- Accuracy = (TP + TN) / (TP + TN + FP + FN) = (150 + 750) / 1000 = 90%
- Precision = TP / (TP + FP) = 150 / (150 + 50) = 75%
- Recall = TP / (TP + FN) = 150 / (150 + 50) = 75%
- F1-Score = 2 × (Precision × Recall) / (Precision + Recall) = 0.75 or 75 %

(b) Confusion Matrix:

	Predicted Default (1)	Predicted Not Default (0)
Actual Default (1)	TP= 90	FN= 50
Actual Not Default (0)	FP= 40	TN= 820

- Accuracy = (90 + 820) / 1000 = 91%
- Precision = 90 / (90 + 40) = 69.23%
- Recall = 90 / (90 + 50) = 64.29%
- F1-Score = 2 × (0.6923 × 0.6429) / (0.6923 + 0.6429) = 0.6667 or 66.67 %

(c) Confusion Matrix:

	Predicted Fraud (1)	Predicted Not Fraud (0)
Actual Fraud (1)	TP= 80	FN = 40
Actual Not Fraud (0)	FP = 30	TN = 850

- Accuracy = (80 + 850) / 1000 = 93%
- Precision = 80 / (80 + 30) = 72.73%
- Recall = 80 / (80 + 40) = 66.67%
- F1-Score = 2 × (0.7273 × 0.6667) / (0.7273 + 0.6667) = 0.70 or approx 69.57 %

(d) Confusion Matrix:

	Predicted Disease (1)	Predicted No Disease (0)
Actual Disease (1)	TP = 120	FN = 60
Actual No Disease (0)	FP= 20	TN= 800

- Accuracy = (120 + 800) / 1000 = 92%
- Precision = 120 / (120 + 20) = 85.71%
- Recall = 120 / (120 + 60) = 66.67%
- F1-Score = 2 × (0.8571 × 0.6667) / (0.8571 + 0.6667) = 0.75 = 75%

(e) Confusion Matrix:

	Predicted Out of Stock (1)	Predicted In Stock (0)
Actual Out of Stock (1)	TP = 100	FN = 50
Actual In Stock (0)	FP = 50	TN = 800

- Accuracy = (100 + 800) / 1000 = 90%
- Precision = 100 / (100 + 50) = 66.67%
- Recall = 100 / (100 + 50) = 66.67%
- F1-Score = 2 × (0.6667 × 0.6667) / (0.6667 + 0.6667) = 0.6667 or 66.67 %

EXAM PATTERN EXERCISE

Including Competency Based Questions

Part I

Multiple Choice Questions

1. .... is defined as the percentage of correct predictions out of all the observations.

(a) Predictions (b) Accuracy
(c) Reality (d) F1 Score

2. Raunak was learning the conditions that make up the confusion matrix. He came across a scenario in which the machine that was supposed to predict an animal was always predicting not an animal. What is this condition called? Competency Based Ques.

(a) False Positive (b) True Positive
(c) False Negative (d) True Negative

3. Differentiate between Prediction and Reality.

(a) Prediction is the input given to the machine to receive the expected result of the reality.
(b) Prediction is the output given to match the reality.
(c) The prediction is the output which is given by the machine and the reality is the real scenario in which the prediction has been made.
(d) Prediction and reality both can be used interchangeably.

4. Which two evaluation methods are used to calculate the F1 score? SQP 2023-24, 2022-23

(a) Precision & Accuracy (b) Precision & Recall
(c) Accuracy & Recall (d) Precision & F1 score

5. What will be the outcome, if the Prediction is "Yes" and it matches with the Reality? What will be the outcome, if the Prediction is "Yes" and it does not match with the Reality?

(a) True Positive, True Negative
(b) True Negative, False Negative
(c) True Negative, False Positive
(d) True Positive, False Positive

6. Which of the following scenario result in a high false positive cost? SQP 2023-24

(a) Viral outbreak (b) Forest fire
(c) Flood (d) Spam filter

7. Priya was confused with the terms used in the evaluation stage suggest her the term used for the percentage of correct predictions out of all the observations. Competency Based Ques.

(a) Accuracy (b) Precision
(c) Recall (d) F1 score

8. Recall – Evaluation method is

(a) defined as the fraction of positive cases that are correctly identified.
(b) defined as the percentage of true positive cases versus all the cases where the prediction is true.
(c) defined as the percentage of correct predictions out of all the observations.
(d) comparison between the prediction and reality.

9. Which of the following statements is true for the term Evaluation?

(a) Helps in classifying the type and genre of a document.
(b) It helps in predicting the topic for a corpus.
(c) Helps in understanding the reliability of any AI model.
(d) Process to extract the important information out of a corpus.

10. Prediction and Reality can be easily mapped together with the help of

(a) Prediction (b) Reality
(c) Accuracy (d) Confusion Matrix

11. The last stage of an AI Project Life Cycle is

(a) Problem Scoping (b) Data Exploration
(c) Modelling (d) Evaluation

12. Which of the following is defined as the measure of balance between precision and recall? 2023

(a) Accuracy (b) F1 Score
(c) Reliability (d) Punctuality

13. ....is one of the parameter for evaluating a model's performance and is defined as the fraction of positive cases that are correctly identified. 2024

(a) Precision (b) Accuracy (c) Recall (d) F1

14. In spam email detection, which of the following will be considered as "False Negative"? 2024

(a) When a legitimate email is accurately identified as not spam.
(b) When a spam email is mistakenly identified as legitimate.
(c) When an email is accurately recognised as spam.
(d) When an email is inaccurately labelled as important.

15. Whenever we want an AI project to be able to predict an output, we need to 2025

(a) first test it using the data.
(b) first train it using the data.
(c) Both (a) and (b)
(d) Neither (a) nor (b)

16. **Which condition of evaluation does the following diagram indicate ?** 2025

Prediction : No	Reality: Yes

(a) False Positive (b) False Negative
(c) True Positive (d) True Negative

17. **It is one of the parameters for evaluating a model's performance and is defined as the percentage of true positive cases versus all the cases where the prediction is true.** 2025

Which of the following evaluation parameter is this?
(a) Precision (b) Recall
(c) F1 score (d) Accuracy

18. **With respect to evaluation, for which of the following does the prediction and reality match?** 2025
(a) True positive and False positive
(b) True positive and True negative
(c) False positive and False negative
(d) True positive and False negative

19. **Which of the following scenarios might have a high False Negative (FN) cost?** 2025
(a) Viral Disease Outbreak
(b) Spam
(c) Mining
(d) Image Search

Answers

1. (b)	2. (c)	3. (c)	4. (b)	5. (d)
6. (d)	7. (a)	8. (a)	9. (c)	10. (d)
11. (d)	12. (b)	13. (c)	14. (b)	15. (b)
16. (b)	17. (a)	18. (b)	19. (a)	

Statement Based Questions

1. **Statement 1 The output given by the AI model is known as reality.**
Statement 2 The real scenario is known as prediction. SQP 2023-24
(a) Both Statement 1 and Statement 2 are correct.
(b) Both Statement 1 and Statement 2 are incorrect.
(c) Statement 1 is correct but Statement 2 is incorrect.
(d) Statement 2 is correct but Statement 1 is incorrect.

2. **Statement 1 Confusion matrix is an evaluation metric.** 2024

Statement 2 Confusion matrix is a record which helps in evaluation.
(a) Both Statement 1 and Statement 2 are correct.
(b) Both Statement 1 and Statement 2 are incorrect.
(c) Statement 1 is correct and Statement 2 is incorrect.
(d) Statement 2 is correct and Statement 1 is incorrect.

3. **Statement 1 To evaluate a models' performance, we need either precision or recall.** 2024

Statement 2 When the value of both Precision and Recall is 1, the F1 score is 0.
(a) Both statement 1 and statement 2 are correct.
(b) Both statement 1 and statement 2 are incorrect.
(c) Statement 1 is correct, but statement 2 is incorrect.
(d) Statement 1 is incorrect, but statement 2 is correct.

4. **Statement 1 Overfitting is not recommended for evaluation of a model.** 2025

Statement 2 This is because the model will simply remember the whole training set, and will therefore always predict the correct label for any point in the training set.
(a) Both Statement 1 and Statement 2 are correct.
(b) Both Statement 1 and Statement 2 are incorrect.
(c) Statement 1 is correct but Statement 2 is incorrect.
(d) Statement 2 is correct but Statement 1 is incorrect.

Answers

1. (b) 2. (a) 3. (b) 4. (a)

Assertion & Reason Based Questions

1. **Assertion (A) Precision helps us understand how good the model is at avoiding false alarms.**

Reason (R) It measures the proportion of correctly predicted positive cases out of all the positive predictions the model made.
(a) Both A and R are correct and R is the correct explanation of A
(b) Both A and R are correct but R is not the correct explanation of A
(c) A is correct but R is not correct
(d) A is not correct but R is correct

2. **Assertion (A) The F1 score is a special metric that combines precision and recall.**
Reason (R) It calculates the percentage of correct predictions (both true positives and true negatives) over the entire dataset.
(a) Both A and R are correct and R is the correct explanation of A
(b) Both A and R are correct but R is not the correct explanation of A
(c) A is correct but R is not correct
(d) A is not correct but R is correct

3. **Assertion (A) The confusion matrix is a matrix used to determine the performance of the classification models for a given set of test data.**
Reason (R) It can only be determined if the true values for test data are known.
(a) Both A and R are correct and R is the correct explanation of A
(b) Both A and R are correct but R is not the correct explanation of A
(c) A is correct but R is not correct
(d) A is not correct but R is correct

4. **Assertion (A) Accuracy helps us to evaluate the recall and precision at the same time.**

Reason (R) Accuracy defines how often the model predicts the correct output.

(a) Both A and R are correct and R is the correct explanation of A

(b) Both A and R are correct but R is not the correct explanation of A

(c) A is correct but R is not correct

(d) A is not correct but R is correct

Answers

1. (a) 2. (c) 3. (a) 4. (d)

Part II

Very Short Answer Type Questions

1. **With reference to evaluation process of understanding the reliability of any AI model, define the term True Positive.** **2022**

Ans. True Positive refers to the instances where the model correctly identifies the positive class or outcome.

2. **Give an example where high precision is not useful.**

Ans. Too many false negative will make the spam filter in effective but false positive may cause important mails to be must and hence precession is not usable.

3. **What is Recall?**

Ans. Recall refers to the ability of a model to correctly identify all relevant instances from a dataset.

4. **Define accuracy.**

Ans. Accuracy is a measure of the overall correctness of a model's predictions. It represents the proportion of correct predictions out of the total number of predictions made by the model.

5. **In which form confusion matrix is recorded?**

Ans. The confusion matrix is recorded in tabular form, typically with actual class labels represented by rows and predicted class labels represented by columns.

6. **Give one reason for the inefficiency of the AI model.**

Ans. AI model could be insufficient or low-quality training data. If the model is not trained on a diverse and representative dataset, it may fail to generalise well to unseen data, leading to poor performance and inefficiency.

7. **Give the formula for calculating Precision.**

Ans. $\text{Precision} = \dfrac{\text{True Positives}}{\text{True Positives} + \text{False Positives}}$

8. **Why should we avoid using the training data for evaluation?**

Ans. This is because our model will simply remember the whole training set, and will therefore always predict the correct label for any point in the training set.

9. **What should be the value of F1 score if the model needs to have 100% accuracy?**

Ans. The model will have an F1 score of 1 if it has to be 100% accurate.

10. **Which evaluation parameter takes into consideration all the correct predictions?** **SQP 2023-24**

Ans. Accuracy

Short Answer Type Questions

1. **With reference to evaluation stage of AI project cycle, explain the term Accuracy. Also give the formula to calculate it.** **2022**

Ans. In the evaluation stage of an AI project cycle, accuracy is a key metric used to assess the performance of a machine learning model. It measures the proportion of correctly classified instances out of all instances examined. In other words, accuracy indicates how often the model is correct in its predictions.

$$\text{Accuracy} = \frac{(TP + TN)}{(TP + TN + FP + FN)} \times 100$$

2. **What is F1 Score in Evaluation?**

Ans. F1 score can be defined as the measure of balance between precision and recall.

$$\text{F1 Score} = 2 \times \frac{\text{Precision} \times \text{Recall}}{\text{Precision} + \text{Recall}}$$

3. **Give an example of a situation where in false positive would have a high cost associated with it.**

Ans. Let us consider a model that predicts that a mail is spam or not. If the model always predicts that the mail is spam, people would not look at it and eventually might lose important information. Here False Positive condition (Predicting the mail as spam while the mail is not spam) would have a high cost.

4. **What is a confusion matrix? What is it used for?**

Or

Define Confusion Matrix. **2023**

Ans. The confusion matrix is used to store the results of comparison between the prediction and reality. From the confusion matrix, we can calculate parameters like recall, precision, F1 score which are used to evaluate the performance of an AI model.

5. **Draw the confusion matrix for the following data** **SQP 2023-24**

- **The number of true positive = 100**

- The number of true negative= 47
- The number of false positive = 62
- The number of false negative = 290

Ans.

Confusion Matrix		Reality	
		Yes	No
Prediction	Yes	100	62
	No	290	47

6. People of a village are totally dependent on the farmers for their daily food items. Farmers grow new seeds by checking the weather conditions every year. An AI model is being deployed in the village which predicts the chances of heavy rain to alert farmers which helps them in doing the farming at the right time. Which evaluation parameter out of precision, recall and F1 Score is best to evaluate the performance of this AI model? Explain. **Competency Based Ques.**

Ans. Let us take each of the factor into consideration at once,

- If precision is considered, FN cases will not be taken into account, so it will be of great loss as if the machine will predict there will be no heavy rain, but if the rain occurred, it will be a big monetary loss due to damage to crops.
- If only recall is considered, then FP cases will not be taken into account. This situation will also cause a big amount of loss, as all people of the village are dependent on farmers for food, and if the model predicts there will be heavy rain and the farmers may not grow crops, it will affect the basic needs of the people.

  Hence F1 Score is the best suited parameter to test this AI model, which is the balance between Precision and Recall.

7. Suppose you are developing an AI model to detect fraudulent financial transaction risk. Describe False Positives and False Negatives in this context. **2025**

Ans. False Positives and False Negatives in Fraudulent Financial Transaction Detection:

False Positive The AI model flags a legitimate transaction as fraudulent (incorrectly identifying a non-fraudulent transaction as fraudulent).

False Negative The AI model fails to detect a fraudulent transaction (incorrectly identifying a fraudulent transaction as non-fraudulent).

Long Answer Type Questions

1. Traffic Jams have become a common part of our lives nowadays. Living in an urban area means you have to face traffic each and every time you get out on the road. Mostly, school students opt for buses to go to school. Many times, the bus gets late due to such jams and the students are not able to reach their school on time. Thus, AI model is created to predict explicitly if there would be traffic jam on their way to school or not. The Confusion Matrix for the same is: **Competency Based Ques.**

The Confusion Matrix	Actual 1	Actual 0
Predicted 1	50	50
Predicted 0	0	0

Explain the process of evaluating F1 score for the given problem.

Ans. From the confusion matrix provided:

Now, let's calculate the precision, recall, and F1 score:

$$\text{Precision} = \frac{TP}{TP+FP} = \frac{50}{50+50} = \frac{50}{100} = 0.5$$

$$\text{Recall} = \frac{TP}{TP+FN} = \frac{50}{50+0} = \frac{50}{50} = 1$$

$$\text{F1 Score} = 2 \times \frac{\text{Precision} \times \text{Recall}}{\text{Precision} + \text{Recall}}$$

$$= 2 \times \frac{0.5 \times 1}{0.5+1} = 2 \times \frac{0.5}{1.5} = 0.67$$

2. Automated trade industry has developed an AI model which predicts the selling and purchasing of automobiles during testing the AI model game with the following predictions. **SQP 2022-23**

To Confusion Matrix		Reality	
		Yes	No
Predicated	Yes	60	25
	No	05	10

(a) How many total tests have been performed in the above scenario?

(b) Calculate precision, recall and F1 score.

Ans. From the confusion matrix:

TP = 60

FP = 25

TN = 10

FN = 5

(a) Total tests performed: The total number of tests is the sum of all entries in the confusion matrix:

Total tests = TP + FP + TN + FN

= 60 + 25 + 10 + 5 = 100

(b) Now, let's calculate precision, recall and F1 score:

1. Precision (P) = TP/(TP + FP)

= 60/(60 + 25) = 60/85 = 0.706

2. Recall (R) = TP/(TP + FN) = 60/(60 + 5)

= 60/65 = 0.923

3. F1 Score $= 2 \times (P \times R)/(P + R)$
$= 2 \times (0.706 \times 0.923)/(0.706 + 0.923)$
$= 2 \times (0.651/1.629)$
$= 2 \times 0.399 = 0.799$

3. Imagine that you have come up with an AI based prediction model which has been deployed on the roads to check traffic jams. Now, the objective of the model is to predict whether there will be a traffic jam or not. Now, to understand the efficiency of this model, we need to check if the predictions which it makes are correct or not. Thus, there exist two conditions which we need to ponder upon: Prediction and Reality.

Traffic Jams have become a common part of our lives nowadays. Living in an urban area means you have to face traffic each and every time you get out on the road. Mostly, school students opt for buses to go to school. Many times, the bus gets late due to such jams and the students are not able to reach their school on time.

Considering all the possible situations make a Confusion Matrix for the above situation.

Competency Based Ques.

Ans. Case 1: Is there a traffic Jam?
Prediction: Yes Reality: Yes
True Positive
Case 2: Is there a traffic Jam?
Prediction: No Reality: No
True Negative
Case 3: Is there a traffic Jam?
Prediction: Yes Reality: No
False Positive
Case 4: Is there a traffic Jam?
Prediction: No Reality: Yes
False Negative

Confusion Matrix		Reality	
		Yes	No
Prediction	Yes	True Positive	False Positive
	No	False Negative	True Negative

4. Take a look at the confusion matrix:

Confusion Matrix		Reality	
		Yes	No
Prediction	Yes	True Positive (TP)	False Positive (FP)
	No	False Negative (FN)	True Negative (TN)

How do you calculate F1 score?

Ans. We begin the calculation by first using the formula to calculate Precision

Precision is defined as the percentage of true positive cases versus all the cases where the prediction is true. That is, it takes into account the True Positives and False Positives.

$$\text{Precision} = \frac{\text{True Positive}}{\text{All Predicted Positives}} \times 100\%$$

$$\text{Precision} = \frac{TP}{TP + FP} \times 100\%$$

Next, we calculate recall as the fraction of positive cases that are correctly identified.

$$\text{Recall} = \frac{\text{True Positive}}{\text{True Positive} + \text{False Negative}}$$

$$\text{Recall} = \frac{TP}{TP + FN}$$

Finally, we calculate the F1 score as the measure of balance between precision and recall.

$$\text{F1 score} = 2 \times \frac{\text{Precision} \times \text{Recall}}{\text{Precision} + \text{Recall}}$$

5. An AI model made the following sales prediction for a new mobile phone which they have recently launched: **SQP 2023-24**

Confusion Matrix		Reality	
		Yes	No
Prediction	Yes	50	40
	No	12	10

(i) Identify the total number of wrong predictions made by the model.
(ii) Calculate precision, recall and F1 Score.

Ans. (i) The total number of wrong predictions made by the model is the sum of false positive and false negative.

FP + FN = 40 + 12 = 52

(ii) Precision = TP/(TP+FP)
=50/(50+40) =50/90 =0.55
Recall =TP/(TP+FN)
=50/(50+12) =50/62 =.81
F1 Score = $2 \times$ Precision $\times$ Recall/(Precision+Recall)
$=2 \times 0.55 \times .81/(.55+.81)$
=.891/1.36 =0.65

6. What do you understand by AI Bias and AI Access ? Give one example of each to support your answer. **2025**

Ans. AI Bias and AI Access:

- **AI Bias** Systematic and repeatable errors in an AI system that create unfair outcomes.

Example Facial recognition software trained primarily on lighter skin tones may perform poorly on darker skin tones.

- **AI Access** The ability of individuals and groups to use and benefit from AI technologies.

  Example Lack of internet access or digital literacy in rural areas hinders AI adoption.

7. An AI model has been developed to test specimens of blood/urine/cough etc., to diagnose ailments (diabetes/liver infection etc.). The model was tested on a data-set of about 630 tests and the resulting confusion matrix is as follows: **2025**

Confusion Matrix		Reality	
		Yes	No
Prediction	Yes	110 (TP)	60 (FP)
	No	50 (FN)	410 (TN)

(A) How many total cases are True Negative in the above scenario?

(B) Calculate Precision, Recall and F1 Score.

Ans. (A) 410 (found directly in the TN cell of the matrix)

(B) Given,

True Positives (TP) = 110

False Positives (FP) = 60

False Negatives (FN) = 50

True Negatives (TN) = 410

Precision = TP / (TP + FP) = 110 / (110 + 60) = 110 / 170 ≈ 0.647

Recall (Sensitivity) = TP / (TP + FN) = 110 / (110 + 50) = 110 / 160 ≈ 0.6875

F1 Score = 2 * (Precision * Recall) / (Precision + Recall)

= 2 * (0.647 * 0.6875) / (0.647 + 0.6875)

≈ 2 * 0.4458 / 1.3345

≈ 0.8916 / 1.3345 ≈ 0.668

SELF ASSESSMENT

Multiple Choice Questions

1 In a confusion matrix, which quadrant represents instances where the model predicted positive but the actual value was negative?

(a) True Positive (b) False Positive
(c) True Negative (d) False Negative

2 What does precision measure in the context of classification models?

(a) Ability of the model to identify true positive cases
(b) Ability of the model to avoid false positive predictions
(c) Ability of the model to identify true negative cases
(d) Ability of the model to avoid false negative predictions

3 F1 Score is 1 when

(a) Recall and Precision is 100% (b) Recall is 100%
(c) Precision is 0 (d) Recall and Precision is 0

4 In a confusion matrix handing data for a model predicting breast cancer, what does False Positive refer to?

(a) Model predicted positive and the person has breast cancer in reality.
(b) Model predicted positive and the person does not have breast cancer in reality.
(c) Model predicted negative and the person has breast cancer in reality
(d) Model predicted negative and the person does not have breast cancer in reality.

Very Short Answer Type Questions

5 What is the importance of evaluation in machine learning?

6 Define accuracy in the context of classification models.

Short Answer Type Questions

7 What are the four permutations used in confusion matrix?

8 Accuracy is very important evaluation method. Explain in brief.

Long Answer Type Questions

9 How recall is different from precision? Explain in details with an example.

10 A lot of times people face the problem of sudden downpower. People wash clothes and put them out to dry but due to unexpected rain, their work gets wasted. Thus, an AI model has been created which predicts if there will be rain or not. The confusion matrix for the same is:

The Confusion Matrix	Actual 1	Actual 0
Predicted 1	0	3
Predicted 0	3	94

Find the F1 score for the above problem.

Statistical Data

CHAPTER 04

Statistical data provides us with meaningful insights by summarizing complex real-world phenomena through numbers and patterns. It transforms raw information into structured formats that allow us to observe relationships, make predictions, and draw conclusions with confidence.

Data science is a journey of exploration and discovery. Artificial Intelligence (AI) is a technology that relies entirely on data to make machines intelligent. Based on the type of data used, AI can be categorized into three broad domains: Data Science, Computer Vision, and Natural Language Processing.

Understanding Data Science

Data Science is an interdisciplinary field that combines statistics, data analysis, machine learning, and computational techniques to extract meaningful insights from data.

It integrates principles from Mathematics, Statistics, Computer Science, and Information Science to analyze real-world phenomena and drive data-driven decisions.

4.1 Applications of Data Science

1. **Internet Search** Search engines like Google make use of data science algorithms to deliver the most relevant search results within seconds.

   With Google processing over 20 petabytes of data daily, data science plays a crucial role in ensuring efficiency and accuracy in search results.

2. **Targeted Advertising** Digital marketing relies heavily on data science to display relevant ads to users. Whether it's website banners, social media ads, or digital billboards, these advertisements are optimized based on user behavior.

   This results in significantly higher Click-Through Rates (CTR) compared to traditional advertising.

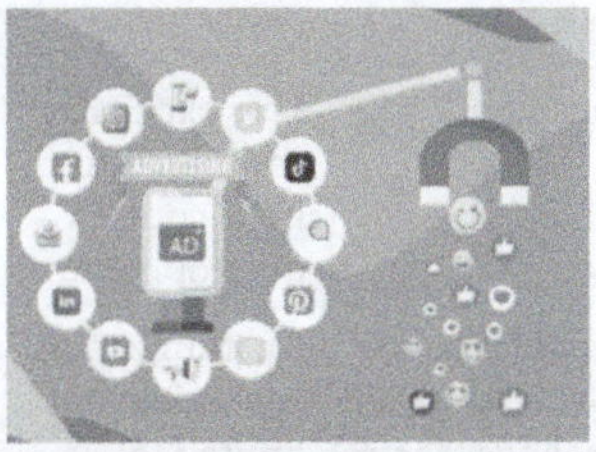

3. **Website Recommendations** Platforms like Amazon, Netflix, Google Play, LinkedIn, and IMDB use recommendation systems to suggest relevant products, movies, or content based on previous user interactions. This enhances the user experience while driving engagement and sales.

4. **Genetics & Genomics** Data science has revolutionized personalized medicine by integrating genomic data with other medical research. This allows for a deeper understanding of genetic predispositions to diseases, improving drug responses and treatment plans. As personal genome data advances, healthcare will become more individualized and precise.

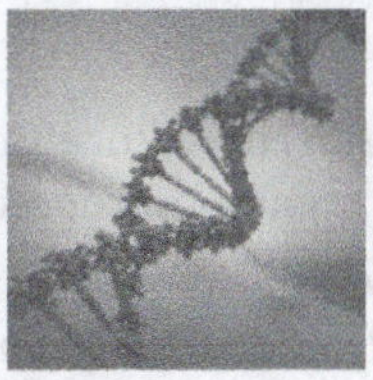

4.2 Introduction to Low/No-Code AI Approach for Statistical Data

AI development can be categorized into three approaches based on the level of coding required: High Code, Low Code, and No Code.

High Code *versus* Low Code *versus* No Code

Aspect	High Code	Low Code	No Code
Definition	Involves traditional software development where programmers manually write code using languages like Java, Python, C#, etc.	Utilizes platforms or tools with visual interfaces and pre-built components to simplify application development.	Extends low-code principles by enabling application creation without any coding or scripting knowledge.
Coding Requirement	A team of software developers writes all the code manually.	Some manual coding is required by programmers.	No coding knowledge is needed, allowing anyone to create applications.
Cost	Expensive.	Less expensive compared to high-code development.	More affordable than low-code development.
Customization & Ownership	Companies have full ownership and control over their product, allowing complete customization.	Customization is possible but limited to coding capabilities within the platform. Example: Custom chatbot.	Limited customization options, as No-Code AI tools are restricted to predefined functions and rely on drag-and-drop features.

No-Code AI

- **Drag and drop** AI models in seconds.
- No coding knowledge is required to implement complex machine learning (ML) algorithms.
- Simple visual interface with an easy-to-use drag-and-drop feature.

Need of No-Code AI

- **Eliminates Coding Errors** Since there's no coding involved, we avoid common programming mistakes.
- **Cost-Effective** Saves businesses from high costs associated with fully coded AI systems.
- **No AI Expertise Required** Companies can implement AI without hiring specialized AI professionals.
- **User-Friendly** Even middle school students can build AI models!
- **Real-Time Visualization** Users can see what they are building as they work.

Use of No-Code AI

- Non-technical professionals like doctors, architects, and musicians can build AI models effortlessly.
- Businesses and startups can integrate AI into their systems without a dedicated AI team.
- Educators and students can explore AI concepts without needing programming expertise.

Benefits of No-Code Tools

- **Accessibility** No-code tools make AI and application development available to non-technical users, allowing professionals from various fields to build AI models without coding knowledge.
- **Fast** With drag-and-drop functionality, AI models and applications can be created in minutes, significantly reducing development time compared to traditional coding methods.
- **Ease of Use** The intuitive interface eliminates the complexity of coding, enabling users to focus on functionality rather than syntax errors or debugging.
- **Innovation** No-code tools empower individuals and businesses to experiment, prototype, and implement AI solutions quickly, fostering creativity and technological advancement.

Disadvantages of No-Code Tools

- **Lack of Flexibility** No-code platforms restrict customization, as users are limited to predefined drag-and-drop elements, reducing control over application functionality.
- **Automation Bias** Users may overly trust automated decisions, ignoring contradicting but accurate information, leading to potential errors.
- **Security Issues** No-code tools lack advanced security controls, making them unsuitable for handling sensitive data, as security best practices are not always enforced.

Try These 4.1

1. **What are the key components of Data Science?**
2. **How does Google use Data Science in internet search?**
3. **What is the main advantage of No-Code AI?**
4. **Mention one disadvantage of No-Code AI tools.**

Popular No-Code AI Tools

No-Code Tool	Details	Release Year
Azure Machine Learning	Cloud-based AI service by Microsoft.	July 2014
Google Cloud AutoML	Cloud-based AI service by Google for building ML models.	January 2018
Orange Data Mining	Open-source toolkit for data visualization, ML, and data mining.	October 1996
Lobe AI	Visual interface platform for creating custom ML models.	2015
Teachable Machine	Web-based tool for fast and easy ML model creation.	November 2017

Azure Machine Learning

Azure Machine Learning is a cloud-based AI service by Microsoft designed to simplify the machine learning process.

Key Features

- **No-Code Development** Users can build ML models without writing code.
- **Data Processing** Provides an easy interface for cleaning and preparing data.
- **Model Training & Evaluation** Enables users to train, test, and fine-tune ML models.
- **Deployment** Allows seamless integration and deployment of models into production.

Azure Machine Learning is ideal for businesses and individuals looking for a user-friendly ML platform with minimal coding requirements.

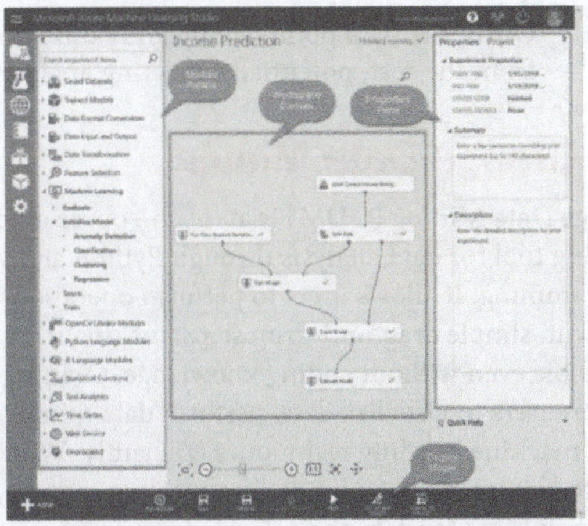

Google Cloud AutoML

Google Cloud AutoML is a cloud-based machine learning platform designed for users with limited ML expertise to build high-quality custom models with minimal effort.

Key Features

- **Easy to Use** Enables businesses to train ML models without deep technical knowledge.
- **Fast Model Creation** Allows users to build custom ML models in minutes.
- **Seamless Integration** Models can be deployed directly into applications and websites.

Google Cloud AutoML makes AI accessible by automating complex ML processes, allowing businesses to leverage AI without extensive coding.

Google's AutoML

Orange Data Mining

Orange Data Mining is an open-source tool for data visualization, machine learning, and data mining, designed for users with no coding experience.

Key Features

- **Data Visualization** Provides interactive and beautiful visuals for easy analysis.
- **No-Code Interface** Users can perform data mining and ML tasks without writing code.
- **Ease of Use** Offers a drag-and-drop workflow, making analysis simple and accessible.

Orange is ideal for researchers, educators, and businesses looking for an intuitive and visually-driven ML tool.

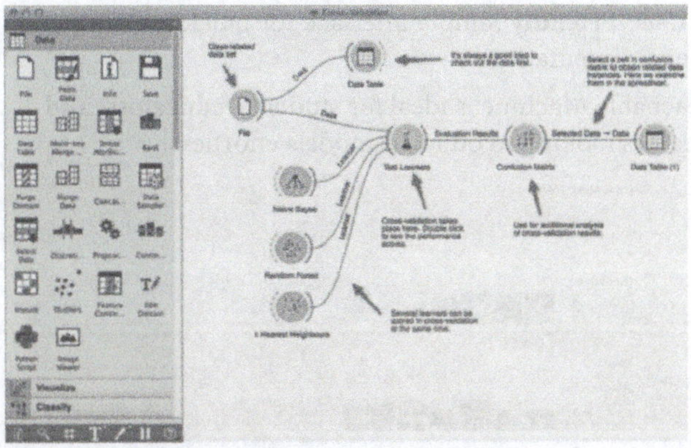

Other No code AI Tools

Lobe

Lobe AI simplifies machine learning by providing an intuitive and free tool for training models.

Key Features

- **No-Code Training** Users can train ML models without writing code.
- **Easy-to-Use Interface** Drag-and-drop functionality makes ML accessible.
- **Automatic Model Training** Lobe automatically trains a custom ML model.
- **Seamless Integration** Trained models can be easily exported and used in applications.

Lobe AI is perfect for beginners and professionals looking to quickly build ML models without technical expertise

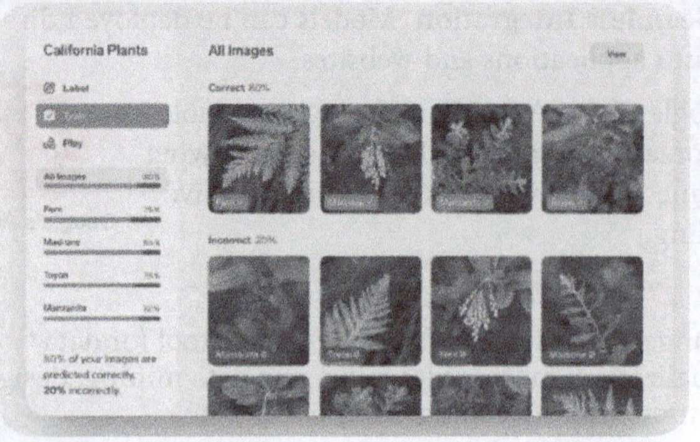

Teachable Machine

Teachable Machine is a web-based tool designed to make machine learning fast, easy, and accessible to everyone.

Key Features

- **No Coding Required** Anyone can train ML models without programming knowledge.
- **Custom Model Training** Can recognize images, sounds, and poses.
- **User-Friendly** Simple interface for quick learning and experimentation.

Teachable Machine is ideal for students, educators, and creators looking to build AI models effortlessly.

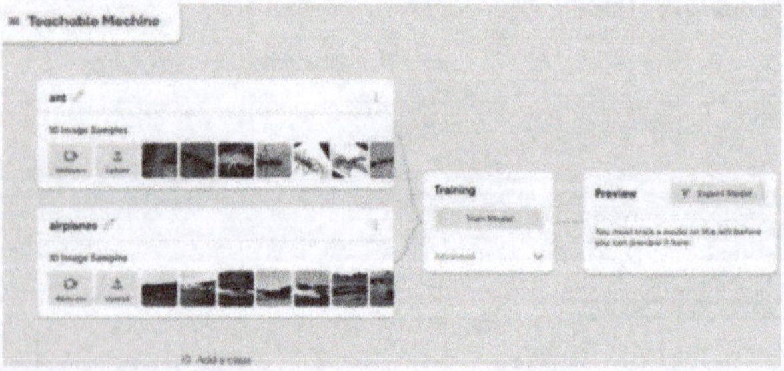

4.3 Statistical Data: Use Case Walkthrough

Before we start with Orange data mining, let's discuss some important concepts of Statistical Analysis

Important Concepts in Statistics

1. Statistical Sampling

- The population refers to the complete dataset available for a study.
- Since analyzing the entire population is impractical, a sample (subset of the population) is selected for analysis.

2. Descriptive Statistics

- **Mean** The average value of the dataset.
- **Median** The middle value when data is arranged in order.
- **Mode** The most frequently occurring value in the dataset.

3. Distributions

- Graphs or charts showing the frequency of values in a dataset.
- Normal distribution – A symmetrical curve where most values cluster around the central peak.
- Skewed distributions occur when some values are significantly larger or smaller than others.

4. Probability

- The likelihood of an event occurring.
- **Independent events** Do not influence each other.
- **Dependent events** The outcome of one affects the other.

5. Variance & Standard Deviation

- **Variance** Measures the spread of data points from the mean.
- **Standard Deviation** A derived metric that quantifies data dispersion.
- **Outlier** A data point significantly different from the rest, potentially affecting analysis.

4.4 Orange Data Mining

Orange Data Mining (ODM) is an open-source machine learning tool for data analysis through Python and visual programming. It allows users to perform operations on data with simple drag-and-drop steps, making it accessible even without coding knowledge. Orange enables users to visualize data, perform data mining, and apply machine learning techniques efficiently. With its easy-to-use interface and visually appealing outputs, it is a powerful tool for data analysis.

Key Features of Orange Data Mining

1. Data Loading Widgets

These widgets help import data into Orange from various sources:

- **File** Loads data from files in formats like CSV, Excel, and SQL.
- **URL** Loads data directly from a URL.

- **Data Table** Displays loaded data in a tabular format for easy inspection.

2. Data Exploration Widgets

These widgets allow users to explore data using visual tools:

- **Scatter Plot** Visualizes relationships between two variables.
- **Data Table** Enables manual inspection and exploration of data.
- **Distributions** Displays histograms and other statistical distributions.

3. Preprocessing Widgets

These widgets help clean and prepare data for analysis:

- **Impute** Handles missing values in the dataset.
- **Normalize** Scales data to a common range.
- **Select Columns** Allows users to choose specific columns from the dataset.

4. Feature Selection Widgets

These widgets help identify the most important features for analysis:

- **Select Columns** Lets users choose relevant columns/features.
- **Select Best Features** Automatically selects the best features based on mutual information or correlation.

5. Modeling Widgets

These widgets build models from data using machine learning algorithms:

- **Classification Tree** Constructs a decision tree classifier.
- **k-Means** Performs k-means clustering.
- **Support Vector Machine** Trains an SVM classifier.
- **Logistic Regression** Builds a logistic regression model.

6. Evaluation Widgets

These widgets assess model performance:

- **Test & Score** Evaluates predictive models on a test dataset.
- **Cross Validation** Performs cross-validation to assess accuracy.
- **ROC Curve** Plots the receiver operating characteristic curve for binary classifiers.

7. Visualization Widgets

These widgets generate visual representations of data for better understanding:

- **Bar Chart** Displays data as bar graphs.
- **Heat Map** Represents data using color intensity.
- **Scatter Plot** Shows relationships between two variables.

Getting Started with Orange Data Mining

1. Open the Software

- Download and install Orange from the official website.
- Launch the Orange application to access the workspace.

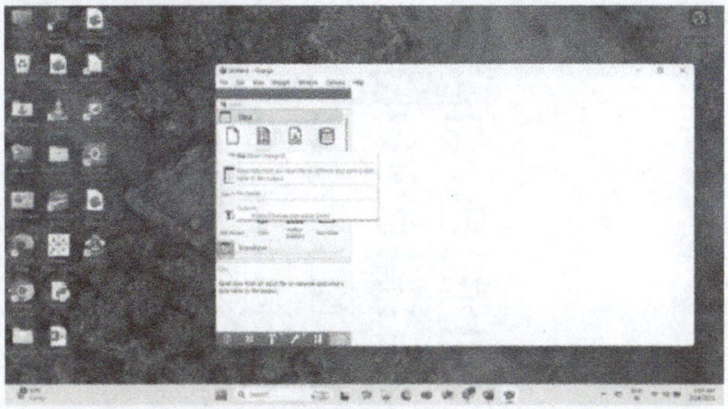

2. Exploring the Canvas

- **Canvas** The main workspace where widgets are added and connected to create workflows.
- **Widget Toolbox** Provides various tools categorized for data handling, preprocessing, modeling, and visualization.

Data Acquisition

Data Widgets

- **File Widget** Loads data from files in formats like CSV, Excel, and SQL.
- **CSV File Import Widget** Specifically imports CSV files.
- **Datasets Widget** Provides access to preloaded datasets.
- **Data Info Widget** Displays metadata about the dataset, such as the number of rows and columns.

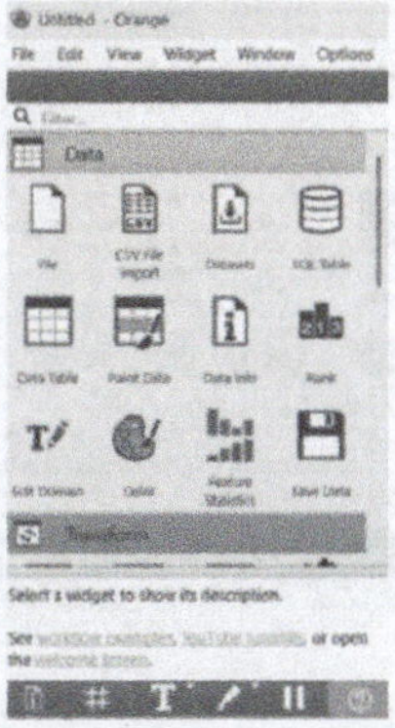

Data Exploration

Transform Widgets

- **Data Sampler Widget** Selects a subset of data for analysis.
- **Select Columns Widget** Allows users to choose specific columns from the dataset.

- **Impute Widget** Handles missing values by filling them with appropriate values.
- **Discretize Widget** Converts continuous numerical data into discrete categories.

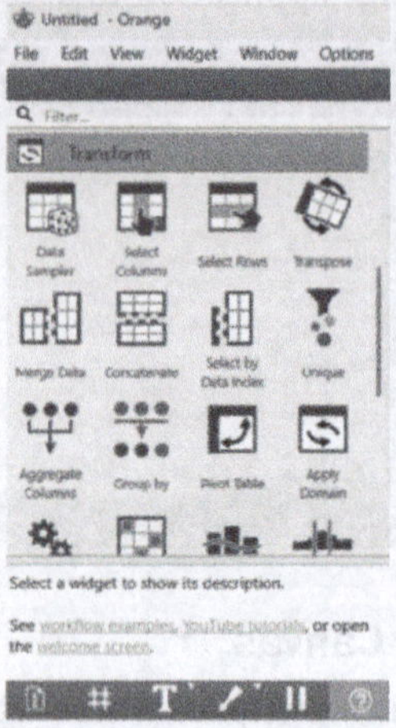

Visualize Widgets

- **Tree Viewer Widget** Displays decision trees graphically.
- **Box Plot Widget** Visualizes the distribution of data using box plots.
- **Scatter Plot Widget** Shows relationships between two numerical variables.
- **Bar Plot Widget** Displays categorical data using bar charts.

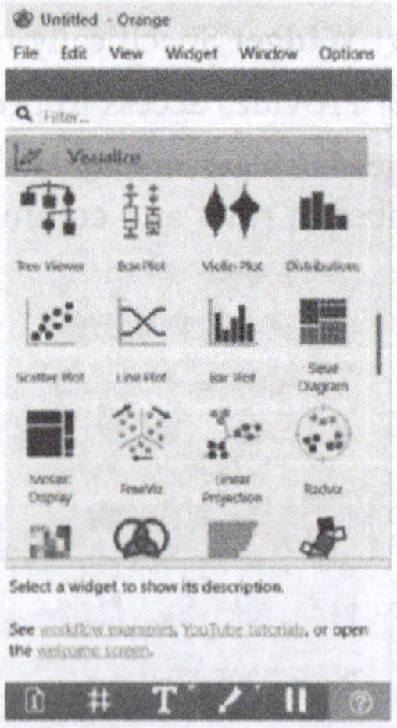

Modeling

Model Widgets

- **Tree Widget** Constructs decision tree models for classification.
- **Random Forest Widget** Implements random forest classification.
- **Linear Regression Widget** Builds a linear regression model for prediction.
- **Logistic Regression Widget** Constructs a logistic regression model for classification.

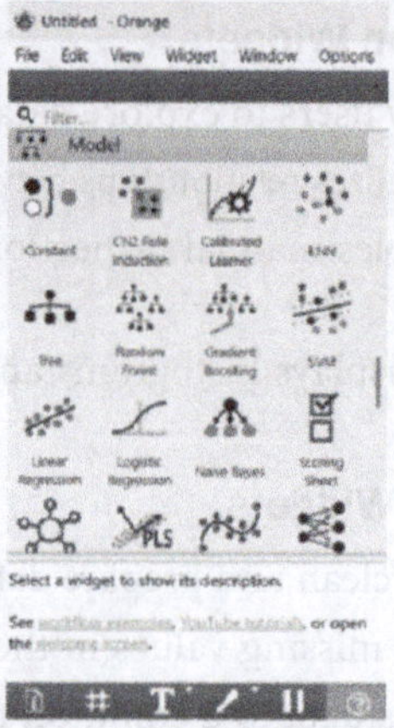

Unsupervised Widgets

- **Distance Matrix Widget** Computes distance matrices for clustering analysis.
- **t-SNE Widget** Reduces the dimensionality of data for visualization.
- **Correlations Widget** Computes correlations between variables.
- **k-Means Widget** Performs k-means clustering on the data.

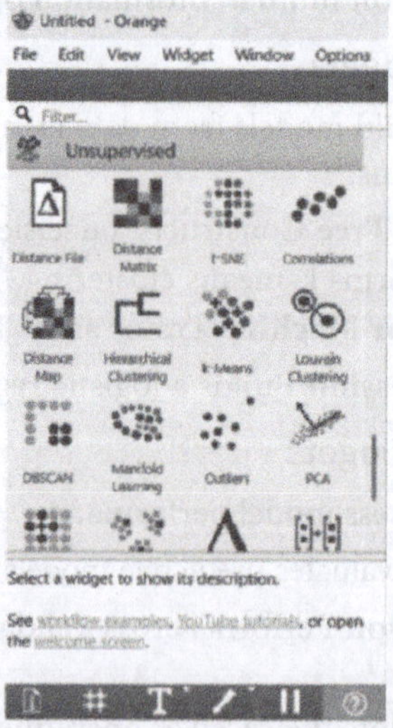

Evaluation

Evaluate Widgets

- **Test and Score Widget** Evaluates predictive models based on test datasets.
- **Predictions Widget** Generates predictions based on trained models.
- **Confusion Matrix Widget** Displays the performance of classification models.

- **ROC Analysis Widget** Plots ROC curves to evaluate classifier performance.

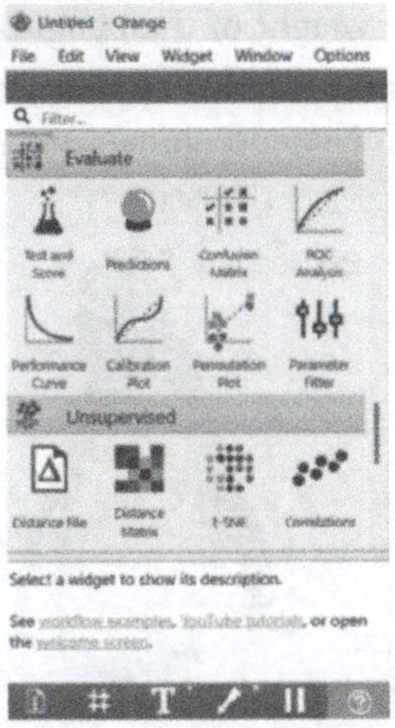

Let's understand how we can apply the AI Project Cycle in Orange **Data Mining.**

Data acquisition

Step 1 Upload data

Data exploration

Step 2 Clean missing data

Step 3 Select columns

Step 4 Data sampler

Modeling

Step 5 Train model

Evaluation

Step 6 Evaluate model

Step 7 Predictions

Thus, all the stages of AI project cycle can be mapped in Orange data mining tool.

Try These 4.2

1. **Which company developed Azure Machine Learning?**
2. **What is the main purpose of Orange Data Mining?**
3. **Which No-Code AI tool allows users to train models using images, sounds, and poses?**
4. **What is the release year of Google Cloud AutoML?**

4.5 Case Study

The Palmer Penguins dataset is a popular dataset for statistical and machine learning analysis, often compared to the famous Iris dataset. It contains measurements of three penguin species (Adelie, Chinstrap, and Gentoo) collected from three islands in the Palmer Archipelago, Antarctica.

Dataset Features

The dataset includes the following attributes:

- Species (Adelie, Chinstrap, Gentoo)
- Island (Biscoe, Dream, Torgersen)
- Bill Length (mm)
- Bill Depth (mm)
- Flipper Length (mm)
- Body Mass (g)
- Sex (Male/Female)

Potential Case Study Analysis

1. **Species Classification**
   - Predict the species of a penguin based on its physical attributes using machine learning models.
2. **Impact of Climate Change**
   - Analyze trends in penguin populations over time and their habitat preferences.
3. **Feature Correlations**
   - Study relationships between different features, such as the correlation between flipper length and body mass.
4. **Data Visualization**
   - Use scatter plots, histograms, and boxplots to explore species distributions across islands.

4.5 Palmer Penguins Model Index

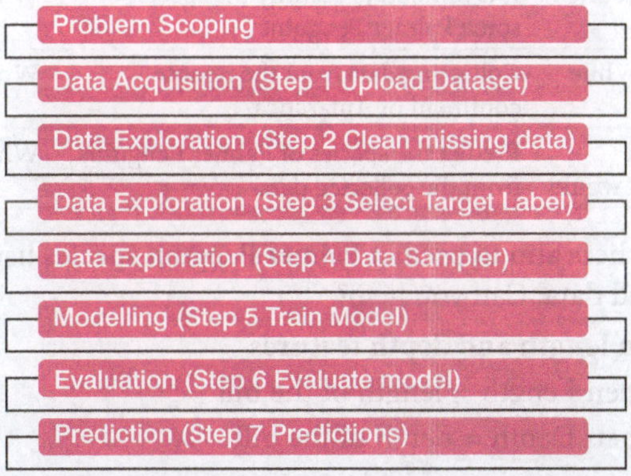

The above image shows the index of this case study.

Scan the QR code for all files of PALMER PENGUINS.

Short link https://bit.ly/4atlCN7

Long Link

https://drive.google.com/drive/folders/1fmcRVb-ilTyUhmUv4DWT1BFsaCoQ2BmF?usp=drive_link

The Palmer Penguins

- **Palmer station** Antarctica collects data from the remote continent of **Antarctica**.
- **Researchers** from **this institute** have **collected** data on **penguins** at the **Palmer Archipeiago.**

The data set is called **Palmer Archipelago (Antarctica) penguin dataset**. It consists of information on various features of three penguin species.

Problem Scoping

Our	Research Community	Who
Has a problem that	It is difficult to identify the species of some Palmer Penguins	What
When/While	Collecting data from the remote continent of Antarctica	Where
An ideal solution would	Predict the species of Palmer Penguins from the collected data	Why

Researchers aim to predict Palmer Penguin species using collected data. Can you help?

Culmen length and depth features

- Culmen Length = length of the bill
- Culmen Depth = depth of the bill

Note *In the raw data, bill dimensions are recorded as " culmen length" and "culmen depth". The culmen is the dorsal ridge atop the bill.*

Flipper Length and Body Mass feature

- Flipper Length is the length of the flippers of a penguin
- Body Mass is the weight of the penguin
- In picture: Gentoo penguin flippers are the shortest in comparison to Adelie and chinstrap

Orange Data Mining is an excellent tool for building machine learning models without extensive coding.

If you're using Orange Data Mining to train an AI model for predicting penguin species, you'll likely follow these steps:

1. **Load the Dataset** Import the Palmer Penguins dataset into Orange.
2. **Data Preprocessing** Handle missing values, normalize data, and select relevant features (beak length, flipper length, etc.).
3. **Model Training** Use classification models like Decision Trees, k-NN, or Naive Bayes to predict the penguin species.
4. **Model Evaluation** Check accuracy using cross-validation or confusion matrices.
5. **Visualization** Use scatter plots and heatmaps to analyze the patterns in penguin species.

Glossary

Data Science Combines statistics, machine learning, and computing to extract insights from data, used in search engines, ads, and healthcare.

No-Code AI Enables AI model building without coding using drag-and-drop tools, ideal for non-technical users and businesses.

Low-Code AI Requires minimal coding with visual interfaces, allowing faster AI development with some customization.

Orange Data Mining An open-source tool for data visualization and machine learning with an easy drag-and-drop interface.

ACTIVITY Time

ACTIVITY 1 : Word Scramble–AI Applications

Purpose Recall key AI-related terms by unscrambling the words.

1. VANAGTOINI APP → NAVIGATION APP
2. UALTIRV SSISATANT → VIRTUAL ASSISTANT
3. AGEGUALAN TIONSLATRAN → LANGUAGE TRANSLATION

ACTIVITY 2 : Mind Map Structure

Central Topic Descriptive Statistics in Real Life

Main Branches

1. Mean (Average) Applications
   - **Education** Calculating students' average scores
   - **Business** Finding average sales per month
   - **Healthcare** Average patient recovery time
2. Median Applications
   - **Real Estate** Finding the median house price
   - **Income Analysis** Median salary in a profession
   - **Data Science** Handling skewed distributions
3. Mode Applications
   - **Fashion Industry** Identifying the most popular clothing size
   - **Marketing** Determining the most sold product
   - **Sports** Identifying the most frequent score in a game

Tools for Mind Mapping

- **Offline** XMind, FreeMind, Microsoft Visio
- **Online** MindMeister, Canva, Coggle, Miro

ACTIVITY 3 : Excel for Statistical Analysis

Purpose To use Excel tool for Simple linear regression of cars speed and distance

Say Download the template and follow the instructions

Short Link https://bit.ly/43SIq6K

Long Link https://docs.google.com/spreadsheets/d/1f5GJXyP7EV2fy1hax47YVaH5gyq8KZy/edit?usp=drive_link&ouid=109928090180926267402&rtpof=true&sd =true

Solution Performing Simple Linear Regression in Excel

Follow these steps to analyze the relationship between Speed and Distance using Excel's Analysis ToolPak.

Step 1 Enable the Analysis ToolPak Add-in

1. Go to File → Options → Add-ins.
2. Under Inactive Application Add-ins, select Analysis ToolPak.
3. At the bottom, find Manage → Select Excel Add-ins → Click Go.
4. In the pop-up window, check Analysis ToolPak → Click OK.
5. The Data Analysis option will now appear in the Data menu.

Step 2 Load the Speed versus Distance Data

1. Open the provided Excel template.
2. Identify Independent Variable (X): Speed and Dependent Variable (Y): Distance.

Step 3 Create a Scatter Plot

1. Select both columns (Speed and Distance).
2. Go to Insert → Charts → Scatter.
3. Edit the chart title to "Distance versus Speed".

Step 4 Add a Regression Line

1. Click on the Scatter Plot.
2. Go to Chart Design → Add Chart Element → Trendline.
3. Click on More Trendline Options → Select Linear.
4. Check the boxes for:
   - Display Equation on Chart
   - Display R-squared Value on Chart

Step 5 Perform Linear Regression Analysis

1. Click on Data → Data Analysis → Select Regression → Click OK.
2. Y Range: Select the Distance column (including the column name).
3. X Range: Select the Speed column (including the column name).
4. Check Labels (since we included column names).
5. Select an Output Range where the results will be displayed.
6. Click OK to generate the regression summary output.

Step 6 Find the distance using the generated linear equation as per Y= MX + C (where, m= slope, C= intercept and x=speed value).

NCERT FOLDER

Complete Explanations of all NCERT's Questions

A. Multiple Choice Questions

1. Orange data mining is an example of
(a) Custom coding (b) Low code
(c) No code (d) None of these

2. Select Which is not the feature of No code approach.
(a) visual (b) Highly expensive
(c) code free (d) drag and drop

3. .... assembly relies on developers to write and deploy code.
(a) High code (b) Low code
(c) No code (d) None of these

4. Flexibility is often limited in ....
(a) High code (b) High code and Low code
(c) No code (d) High code and No code

5. The organisation is heavily dependent on developer resources. This statement is true for
(a) High code approach (b) Low code approach
(c) No code approach (d) All of the above

6. What type of tool is Orange?
(a) Open-source (b) Closed-source
(c) Paid software (d) Hardware

7. Which of the following tasks can be performed using Orange?
(a) Classification (b) Regression
(c) Clustering (d) All of these

8. What type of data can be imported into Orange?
(a) CSV (b) Excel
(c) SQL databases (d) All of these

9. What does the Data Table widget in Orange primarily facilitate?
(a) Loading and viewing datasets
(b) Performing clustering analysis
(c) Running machine learning algorithms
(d) Evaluating

10. Which component in Orange enables users to evaluate the performance of machine learning models?
(a) Test & Score
(b) Data Table
(c) Data Projection
(d) Data Exploration

Answers

1. (c)	2. (b)	3. (a)	4. (c)	5. (a)
6. (a)	7. (d)	8. (d)	9. (a)	10. (a)

B. Subjective Questions

1. Name any two cloud-based No-code AI tools?

Ans. 1. Google AutoML
2. Microsoft AI Builder

2. How accessible are no-code AI tools for non-technical users?

Ans. No-code AI tools are highly accessible for non-technical users as they provide intuitive interfaces, drag-and-drop functionality, and pre-built AI models, allowing users to create AI solutions without coding knowledge.

3. What types of tasks can be accomplished with no-code AI tools?

Ans. No-code AI tools can be used for tasks like image recognition, text analysis, chatbots, predictive analytics, speech-to-text conversion, and data visualization.

4. Can no-code AI tools be used for advanced projects? Justify.

Ans. Yes, no-code AI tools can handle moderately complex projects like automated customer support, sentiment analysis, and machine learning-based predictions. However, for highly customized or large-scale AI applications, coding-based solutions may offer more flexibility and control.

5. Do no-code AI tools require prior programming knowledge? Justify.

Ans. No, prior programming knowledge is not required as these tools are designed with user-friendly interfaces, templates, and automation features, enabling users to build AI models without writing code.

6. What are the benefits of using No-code AI tools?

Ans. No-code AI tools provide several advantages, making AI accessible to a broader audience:

1. **Ease of Use** They offer drag-and-drop interfaces, templates, and pre-trained models, eliminating the need for programming skills.
2. **Faster Development** Businesses can deploy AI models quickly without spending months on development.
3. **Cost-Effective** Reduces the need for hiring AI developers, making it affordable for startups and small businesses.
4. **Accessibility** Allows non-technical users, such as marketers and business analysts, to build AI-driven solutions.

5. **Integration** Many no-code AI platforms integrate seamlessly with existing software, automating workflows efficiently.
6. **Scalability** Enables organizations to scale AI applications without extensive infrastructure investment.

7. What are the challenges faced in using No-code AI tools?

Ans. Despite their benefits, no-code AI tools come with some limitations:

1. **Limited Customization** Users can only work within the predefined templates and configurations, making it difficult to create unique AI models.
2. **Data Dependency** The quality and quantity of data determine the effectiveness of AI models, and poor data can lead to inaccurate results.
3. **Scalability Issues** For highly complex projects, no-code AI may lack the necessary flexibility and computational power.
4. **Security Concerns** Cloud-based no-code AI tools may pose risks related to data privacy and security.
5. **Integration Challenges** Some platforms may not integrate well with custom enterprise systems.

8. Differentiate Low-Code and No-Code AI Tools with Examples.

Ans.

Feature	No-Code AI	Low-Code AI
Target Users	Business users, marketers, analysts	Developers, IT professionals
Coding Requirement	No coding required	Minimal coding required
Customization	Limited to predefined options	Allows more customization and flexibility
Use Cases	Chatbots, sentiment analysis, data classification	Advanced machine learning models, enterprise AI applications
Examples	Google AutoML, Microsoft AI Builder	DataRobot, H2O.ai

9. As the CEO of a small e-commerce startup, you're eager to leverage artificial intelligence to enhance your platform's user experience and drive sales. However, your team lacks the technical expertise to develop and deploy AI-powered solutions. What would be your recommendations for the CEO?

Ans. As the CEO of a small e-commerce startup, leveraging AI without technical expertise can be achieved by:

1. **Using No-Code AI Tools** Platforms like Google AutoML, Microsoft AI Builder, or Teachable Machine can help in tasks like customer segmentation, product recommendations, and sales forecasting.
2. **Implementing AI Chatbots** Tools like Dialogflow or IBM Watson Assistant can improve customer service without requiring programming.
3. **Automating Marketing & Personalization** AI-driven tools like Pimcore or Phrasee can help in automating email marketing and personalized product recommendations.
4. **Data Analysis with AI** Platforms like MonkeyLearn can help analyze customer feedback and predict trends.
5. **Seeking AI Consulting** Partnering with AI-as-a-Service providers can help the business scale AI solutions efficiently.

By utilizing no-code AI tools, the startup can enhance user experience, automate operations, and drive sales without hiring an AI development team.

10. Samarth attended a seminar on Artificial Intelligence and has now been asked to write a report on his learnings from the seminar. Being a non-technical person, he understood that the AI enabled machine uses data of different formats in many of the daily based applications but failed to sync it with the right terminologies and express the details.

Help Samarth define Artificial Intelligence, list the three domains of AI and the data that is used in these domains.

Ans. **Definition of Artificial Intelligence (AI)** AI is the branch of computer science that enables machines to simulate human intelligence, allowing them to perform tasks such as learning, reasoning, problem-solving, and decision-making.

Three Domains of AI and Their Data Usage

1. Data Science & Machine Learning

   Used in Predictive analytics, recommendation systems, fraud detection.

   Data Used Numerical data, structured data, unstructured text.

2. Computer Vision

   Used in Face recognition, medical image analysis, autonomous vehicles.

   Data Used Images, videos, pixel-based data.

3. Natural Language Processing (NLP)

   Used in Chatbots, sentiment analysis, language translation.

   Data Used Text data, speech data, social media content.

11. Would you like to explore the Orange Data Mining tool to build No-Code AI projects? How?

Ans. Yes, Orange Data Mining is an excellent no-code AI tool for data visualization, machine learning, and predictive analytics. To explore it, one can:

- **Download & Install** Get Orange from its official website and install it on a computer.
- **Use Built-in Widgets** Utilize its drag-and-drop interface to perform tasks like classification, clustering, and data visualization.
- **Load and Analyze Data** Import datasets (CSV, Excel, etc.) and apply machine learning models without coding.
- **Explore AI Applications** Use Orange for sentiment analysis, medical diagnostics, or recommendation systems.
- **Take Online Tutorials** Learn from Orange's documentation and video tutorials to enhance AI project development.

12. Are you aware of any other tools or platforms used for low-code or No-Code AI Projects? List them.

Ans. Yes, several tools enable no-code and low-code AI development, including:

- **Google AutoML** For building machine learning models without coding.
- **Microsoft AI Builder** Integrated with PowerApps for AI-driven automation.
- **Teachable Machine** Google's tool for training image and sound recognition models.
- **IBM Watson Studio** A cloud-based AI platform for data science and ML.
- **DataRobot** A low-code AI platform for automating predictive analytics.
- **H2O.ai** Provides AutoML and ML capabilities with minimal coding.
- **Lobe.ai** A no-code tool for training custom machine learning models.

13. Define No-Code and Low-Code AI.

Ans. No-Code AI refers to AI development platforms that allow users to build and deploy AI models without writing any programming code. These platforms provide drag-and-drop interfaces, pre-built machine learning models, and automated workflows, making AI accessible to non-programmers.

Low-Code AI involves minimal coding, allowing users to customize AI solutions while reducing the complexity of manual programming. It is ideal for those with some technical knowledge who want more flexibility than No-Code AI.

14. Identify the differences between Code and No-Code AI concerning Statistical Data.

Ans.

Feature	Code AI	No-Code AI
Data Handling	Requires manual data processing and feature engineering using Python, R, etc.	Provides pre-built tools for automatic data handling and preprocessing.
Statistical Analysis	Users must implement statistical methods like mean, median, standard deviation manually.	Built-in statistical tools simplify analysis with drag-and-drop features.
Flexibility	Offers complete control for advanced statistical modeling.	Limited customization, as predefined statistical methods are used.
Learning Curve	Requires knowledge of statistics and programming.	User-friendly, suitable for non-programmers.
Example Tools	Python (pandas, NumPy), R, TensorFlow.	Orange, KNIME, Google AutoML.

15. Relate AI project stages to the stages of No-Code AI projects.

Ans. Given below is a direct mapping of AI project stages to No-Code AI stages:

AI Project Stages	No-Code AI Project Stages
Define the problem to be solved using AI (e.g., predicting sales, detecting fraud).	Choose the type of problem (classification, regression, clustering) using No-Code AI tools.
Gather data from sources such as databases, APIs, or online repositories.	Upload data from CSV, Excel, or connect to databases using built-in import features.
Clean, normalize, and handle missing values using programming libraries like pandas or NumPy.	Use No-Code tools with built-in widgets for data cleaning, filtering, and transformation.
Choose an appropriate algorithm (e.g., Decision Tree, SVM, Neural Networks).	Drag and drop machine learning models like Decision Trees, SVM, or Neural Networks.
Write and execute code to train models, adjust hyperparameters, and optimize performance.	Train the selected model using built-in No-Code AI features with automated settings.
Assess model accuracy using performance metrics like accuracy, precision, recall, and F1-score.	Use built-in evaluation tools that display performance metrics and visualizations.
Convert the trained model into an API or integrate it into applications.	Export the trained model or integrate it into other systems with one-click deployment options.

16. Orange Data Mining is a machine learning tool for data analysis where we can perform operations through simple drag-and-drop steps.

Ans. Orange is an open-source data mining tool that allows users to analyze data without writing code. It provides a visual workflow where users can connect different widgets to import data, preprocess it, apply machine learning models, and visualize results through simple drag-and-drop interactions.

17. Descriptive statistics – Mean, Median, Mode – help us to describe the data and its underlying characteristics.

Ans. Descriptive statistics summarize and interpret data:

- **Mean (Average)** The sum of all values divided by the total number of values.
- **Median** The middle value in an ordered dataset.
- **Mode** The most frequently occurring value in a dataset.
- These statistics help in understanding data distribution and patterns.

18. No code tools for AI projects.

Ans. Some popular No-Code AI tools include:

- **Orange** Drag-and-drop tool for machine learning and data visualization.
- **Google AutoML** Automated ML model building with minimal effort.
- **Teachable Machine** Google's tool for creating AI models using images, sounds, and text.
- **DataRobot** Enterprise-level automated machine learning platform.
- **KNIME** Open-source tool for data science and machine learning workflows.
- **Lobe.ai** Microsoft's tool for training deep learning models with no code.

EXAM PATTERN EXERCISE

Including Competency Based Questions

Part I

Multiple Choice Questions

1. Which of the following fields does Data Science integrate?

(a) Mathematics and Statistics
(b) Computer Science and Information Science
(c) Machine Learning and Data Analysis
(d) All of the above

2. Which application of Data Science helps in delivering the most relevant search results?

(a) Website Recommendations
(b) Internet Search
(c) Targeted Advertising
(d) Genomics

3. How do platforms like Amazon and Netflix use Data Science?

(a) To improve video quality
(b) To recommend relevant products or content
(c) To monitor website performance
(d) To create social media campaigns

4. What is a major advantage of No-Code AI over Traditional AI development?

(a) Requires expertise in AI programming
(b) Eliminates coding errors
(c) Needs manual debugging
(d) Takes more time to implement

5. Which of the following is NOT a key feature of Azure Machine Learning?

(a) No-code development
(b) Manual coding required for every model
(c) Model training & evaluation
(d) Seamless deployment of models

6. Which No-Code AI tool is an open-source toolkit for data visualization, ML, and data mining?

(a) Google Cloud AutoML
(b) Azure Machine Learning
(c) Orange Data Mining
(d) Teachable Machine

7. Which statistical concept measures the spread of data points from the mean?

(a) Median
(b) Mode
(c) Variance
(d) Probability

8. What does the 'Select Best Features' widget in Orange Data Mining do?
(a) Automatically selects the most relevant features
(b) Removes missing values
(c) Normalizes the data
(d) Generates scatter plots

9. What is a major disadvantage of No-Code AI tools?
(a) Requires expertise in programming
(b) High flexibility for customization
(c) Limited security controls
(d) Takes longer development time

10. Which No-Code AI tool allows users to train models by simply dragging and dropping images?
(a) Lobe AI
(b) Google Cloud AutoML
(c) Azure Machine Learning
(d) Orange Data Mining

11. Which of the following data science application is not associated with genetics and genomics? **2025**
(a) To understand the impact of DNA on health.
(b) To analyze reaction of drugs and diseases.
(c) To finds individual biological connections.
(d) To search the house address of a relative on the Internet.

Answers

1. (d) 2. (b) 3. (b) 4. (b) 5. (b)
6. (c) 7. (c) 8. (a) 9. (c) 10. (a)
11. (d)

Statement Based Questions

1. Statement 1: Data Science integrates principles from Mathematics, Statistics, Computer Science, and Information Science to analyze real-world phenomena.

Statement 2: Data Science is limited to only machine learning techniques and does not involve data analysis.
(a) Both Statement 1 and Statement 2 are correct
(b) Both Statement 1 and Statement 2 are incorrect
(c) Statement 1 is correct but Statement 2 is incorrect
(d) Statement 2 is correct but Statement 1 is incorrect

2. Statement 1: No-Code AI tools allow users to develop AI models without any coding knowledge.

Statement 2: No-Code AI is best suited for highly complex AI applications requiring deep customization.
(a) Both Statement 1 and Statement 2 are correct
(b) Both Statement 1 and Statement 2 are incorrect
(c) Statement 1 is correct but Statement 2 is incorrect
(d) Statement 2 is correct but Statement 1 is incorrect

3. Statement 1: Search engines like Google use data science algorithms to process and deliver relevant search results efficiently.

Statement 2: Data Science has no role in targeted advertising and digital marketing strategies.
(a) Both Statement 1 and Statement 2 are correct
(b) Both Statement 1 and Statement 2 are incorrect
(c) Statement 1 is correct but Statement 2 is incorrect
(d) Statement 2 is correct but Statement 1 is incorrect

4. Statement 1: Orange Data Mining is an open-source tool that enables users to perform data analysis using a drag-and-drop interface.

Statement 2: Orange Data Mining requires advanced programming skills and cannot be used by non-technical users.
(a) Both Statement 1 and Statement 2 are correct
(b) Both Statement 1 and Statement 2 are incorrect
(c) Statement 1 is correct but Statement 2 is incorrect
(d) Statement 2 is correct but Statement 1 is incorrect

Answers

1. (c) 2. (c) 3. (c) 4. (c)

Assertion and Reason Type Questions

1. Assertion (A): Data Science integrates principles from Mathematics, Statistics, Computer Science, and Information Science to analyze real-world phenomena.

Reason (R): Data Science is solely based on machine learning algorithms.
(a) Both A and R are true, and R is the correct explanation of A.
(b) Both A and R are true, but R is not the correct explanation of A.
(c) A is true, but R is false.
(d) A is false, but R is true.

2. Assertion (A): No-code AI tools allow users to build AI models without any programming knowledge.

Reason (R): No-code AI tools eliminate the need for coding by providing a drag-and-drop interface.
(a) Both A and R are true, and R is the correct explanation of A.
(b) Both A and R are true, but R is not the correct explanation of A.
(c) A is true, but R is false.
(d) A is false, but R is true.

3. Assertion (A): Google Cloud AutoML is a cloud-based machine learning platform that allows users to build custom models with minimal effort.

Reason (R): Google Cloud AutoML requires advanced programming skills to implement machine learning models.
(a) Both A and R are true, and R is the correct explanation of A.
(b) Both A and R are true, but R is not the correct explanation of A.
(c) A is true, but R is false.
(d) A is false, but R is true.

4. Assertion (A): No-code AI tools are cost-effective because they eliminate the need for AI specialists.

Reason (R): No-code AI tools require users to have expertise in programming and machine learning.

(a) Both A and R are true, and R is the correct explanation of A.

(b) Both A and R are true, but R is not the correct explanation of A.

(c) A is true, but R is false.

(d) A is false, but R is true.

Answers

1. (c) **2.** (a) **3.** (c) **4.** (c)

Part II

Very Short Answer Type Questions

1. What is Data Science?

Ans. Data Science is an interdisciplinary field that combines statistics, data analysis, machine learning, and computational techniques to extract insights from data.

2. How does Google use Data Science in internet searches?

Ans. Google leverages data science algorithms to deliver relevant search results efficiently by processing over 20 petabytes of data daily.

3. What is the role of Data Science in targeted advertising?

Ans. Data Science helps display relevant ads based on user behavior, improving Click-Through Rates (CTR) compared to traditional advertising.

4. What are No-Code AI tools?

Ans. No-Code AI tools allow users to create AI models without coding knowledge using drag-and-drop features.

5. Name two disadvantages of No-Code AI tools.

Ans. Lack of flexibility and security issues due to predefined drag-and-drop elements and weak security controls.

6. What is Orange Data Mining used for?

Ans. Orange Data Mining is an open-source tool for data visualization, machine learning, and data mining without coding.

7. What does the Test & Score widget in Orange do?

Ans. It evaluates predictive models on a test dataset to assess their performance.

Short Answer Type Questions

1. How does data science enhance targeted advertising?

Ans. Data science analyzes user behavior to display personalized ads, improving Click-Through Rates (CTR). It ensures relevant content reaches the right audience through predictive modeling.

2. What role does data science play in genomic research?

Ans. Data science integrates genomic data with medical research to identify genetic predispositions. This improves drug response predictions and personalizes treatment plans.

3. How does Google Cloud AutoML make AI accessible to non-experts?

Ans. Google Cloud AutoML automates model building, requiring minimal technical expertise. Users can train and deploy machine learning models quickly without coding.

4. Why is variance important in statistical analysis?

Ans. Variance measures how data points spread from the mean, indicating data consistency. A high variance suggests greater dispersion, while a low variance indicates clustering.

5. What is the major drawback of using no-code AI tools?

Ans. No-code AI tools limit customization since they rely on predefined functions. This reduces flexibility in developing complex, tailored AI applications.

6. How do modeling widgets in Orange Data Mining help in data analysis?

Ans. Modeling widgets apply machine learning techniques like classification and clustering. They enable users to train, test, and evaluate predictive models visually.

7. One of the application of Data Science is Airline Route Planning. List any two tasks that airline companies can do using Data Science. 2025

Ans. Two tasks airlines can do using Data Science in Route Planning:

- **Predicting Flight Demand** Analyze historical data to forecast passenger numbers for different routes, optimizing flight schedules.
- **Optimizing Fuel Efficiency** Use weather patterns and flight data to determine the most fuel-efficient routes, reducing costs and emissions.

Long Answer Type Questions

1. Discuss the role of Data Science in personalized medicine and genomics. How does it impact healthcare?

Ans. Data Science has revolutionized personalized medicine by integrating genomic data with medical research to improve diagnosis, treatment plans, and drug effectiveness. By analyzing vast genetic datasets, machine learning algorithms can identify genetic predispositions to diseases such as cancer, diabetes, and heart disorders.

One major application is precision medicine, where treatments are tailored to individual patients based on their genetic profiles. For instance, in oncology, AI-driven models predict how a specific cancer patient will respond to different treatments, reducing trial-and-error prescribing. Similarly, in pharmacogenomics, data science helps in designing drugs that work best for specific genetic variations, improving drug efficacy and minimizing side effects.

Additionally, wearable devices and health trackers collect real-time patient data, which, when analyzed using machine learning, can detect early warning signs of diseases. As genome sequencing becomes more affordable, healthcare providers can offer more personalized and predictive healthcare solutions, enhancing patient outcomes.

2. Compare and contrast No-Code AI and Traditional AI Development. What are the benefits and limitations of No-Code AI?

Ans. No-Code AI and Traditional AI Development differ significantly in terms of accessibility, cost, and complexity.

No-Code AI

- Uses drag-and-drop interfaces, eliminating the need for coding.
- Enables rapid AI model development, reducing implementation time.
- Suitable for non-technical users such as doctors, educators, and businesses.
- Cost-effective, as companies do not need to hire specialized AI engineers.
- Offers real-time visualization and ease of use.

However, No-Code AI has limitations

- Lack of Flexibility: Users are restricted to predefined algorithms and configurations.
- Automation Bias: Users may over-rely on AI-generated outputs without validation.
- Security Risks: No-Code platforms often lack advanced security controls, making them unsuitable for handling sensitive data.

Traditional AI Development

- Requires extensive coding in Python, Java, or C++.
- Provides complete control over AI model customization.
- Suitable for complex and large-scale AI applications.
- Involves high costs and the need for expert developers.

While No-Code AI is beneficial for quick, non-technical implementations, traditional AI remains essential for advanced, fully customizable AI applications.

3. Explain the importance of statistical concepts like Mean, Variance, and Standard Deviation in Data Science. How are these used in real-world applications?

Ans. Statistical concepts like Mean, Variance, and Standard Deviation are fundamental in Data Science for analyzing data distributions, detecting patterns, and making predictions.

- **Mean (Average)** It represents the central value of a dataset and is widely used in summarizing numerical data. For instance, in stock market analysis, the mean stock price helps investors understand market trends.
- **Variance** It measures how spread out data points are from the mean. A high variance indicates a wide spread, whereas a low variance suggests data is clustered around the mean. Variance is crucial in risk assessment, such as evaluating the stability of financial investments.
- **Standard Deviation** It quantifies data dispersion and helps in anomaly detection. In quality control, standard deviation ensures product consistency by identifying defects in manufacturing processes.

SELF ASSESSMENT

Multiple Choice Questions

1. What is the primary objective of Data Science?
   (a) Creating websites using HTML and CSS
   (b) Extracting meaningful insights from data using statistical and computational techniques
   (c) Writing programs in Java and Python
   (d) Managing databases in SQL
2. Which of the following is NOT an application of Data Science?
   (a) Internet Search (b) Targeted Advertising
   (c) Website Development (d) Genetics & Genomics
3. What is a key benefit of No-Code AI?
   (a) Requires expertise in programming languages like Python and Java
   (b) Eliminates coding errors and allows non-technical users to create AI models
   (c) Offers unlimited customization and full control over AI applications
   (d) Is only suitable for large enterprises with dedicated AI teams
4. Which of the following No-Code AI tools was developed by Microsoft?
   (a) Google Cloud AutoML (b) Orange Data Mining
   (c) Azure Machine Learning (d) Lobe AI
5. What does the "Descriptive Statistics" concept in data analysis include?
   (a) Mean, Median, Mode
   (b) Deep Learning, Neural Networks, Reinforcement Learning
   (c) File Handling, URL Data Import, Data Table Creation
   (d) Classification Trees, k-Means Clustering, Support Vector Machines
6. What is a major disadvantage of No-Code AI tools?
   (a) They provide high flexibility and complete customization
   (b) They require deep knowledge of programming languages
   (c) They may lack advanced security controls, making them unsuitable for handling sensitive data
   (d) They are exclusively available for large enterprises

Very Short Answer Type Questions

7. What role does data science play in internet search engines?
8. How does data science improve targeted advertising?
9. What is the main advantage of No-Code AI for businesses?
10. Why are No-Code AI tools considered user-friendly?

Short Answer Type Questions

11. What is a major disadvantage of No-Code AI platforms in terms of security?
12. How does Orange Data Mining help in feature selection for machine learning?
13. What is the significance of statistical sampling in Data Science?

Long Answer Type Questions

14. Explain the interdisciplinary nature of Data Science and its impact on real-world decision-making.
15. How do internet search engines utilize Data Science for efficient results? Explain with examples.

Computer Vision

CHAPTER 05

In our ever-changing world, the fusion of technology with human capabilities continues to redefine the boundaries of innovation. At the forefront of this technological revolution stands computer vision, a cutting-edge field dedicated to teaching machines to interpret and process visual information much like the human eye and brain.

5.1 Introduction

In the previous chapter, you explored the concepts of Artificial Intelligence (AI) for Data Science. AI unifies statistics, data analysis, machine learning, and related techniques to analyze and understand real-world phenomena using data.

Artificial Intelligence enables computers to mimic human intelligence. Humans can see, analyze, and take appropriate actions based on what they perceive. But can machines do the same? Can they "see" like humans?

The answer is yes! The Computer Vision domain of AI allows machines to interpret visual data, process images, and analyze them using algorithms. This capability enables machines to extract meaningful insights from images and make data-driven decisions.

Note *The Emoji Scavenger Hunt game is based on computer vision. It is developed by Google. This game challenges players to find real-world objects that match a given emoji within a limited time frame.*

https://emojiscavengerhunt.withgoogle.com/

5.2 Computer Vision and Artificial Intelligence

Computer Vision is a branch of Artificial Intelligence (AI) that enables machines to interpret and analyze visual data, such as images and videos. While AI allows computers to think and learn, Computer Vision empowers them to see, observe, and understand the visual world.

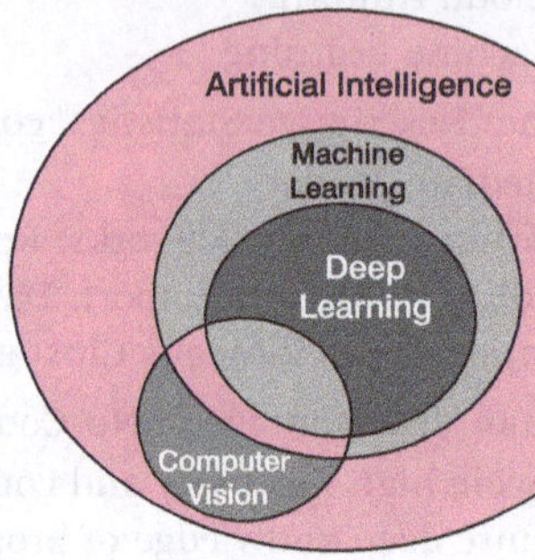

Computer Vision *versus* Image Processing

Computer Vision	Image Processing
Extracts meaningful information from images or videos to understand and predict visual input.	Focuses on processing raw images to enhance or prepare them for further tasks.
A superset of Image Processing.	A subset of Computer Vision.
Examples Object detection, handwriting recognition.	**Examples** Rescaling images, correcting brightness, changing tones.

Applications of Computer Vision

The applications of computer vision are as follows

Facial Recognition

Face recognition using Artificial Intelligence (AI) is a computer vision technology. It is used to enable a system to detect, recognize and verify faces in digital images or videos. The technology has become increasingly popular in a wide variety of applications such as unlocking a smartphone, unlocking doors, passport authentication, security systems, medical applications and so on.

There are even models that can detect emotions from facial expressions.

Face Filters

Face filters are digital overlays that can be applied to photos or videos in real-time to alter or enhance the appearance of a person's face. These filters can range from simple effects like adding glasses or hats to more complex transformations like changing facial features or applying makeup.

Face filters work by using computer vision algorithms to detect and track facial features such as eyes, nose, mouth, and contours. Once these features are identified, the filter is applied to the appropriate areas of the face, adjusting in real-time as the person moves. Popular apps for face filters include Snapchat, Instagram, TikTok, and FaceApp. These apps offer a wide variety of filters for users to express their creativity and have fun with their selfies and videos.

Image Based Search

Image based search is now possible by Google Images (previously Google Image Search) .Google search is a search service owned by Google that allows users to search the World Wide Web for images. It was introduced on July 12, 2001.Unlike traditional image retrieval, this feature removes the need to type in keywords and terms into the Google search box. Instead, users search by submitting an image as their query.

Results may include similar images, web results, pages with the image, and different resolutions of the image.

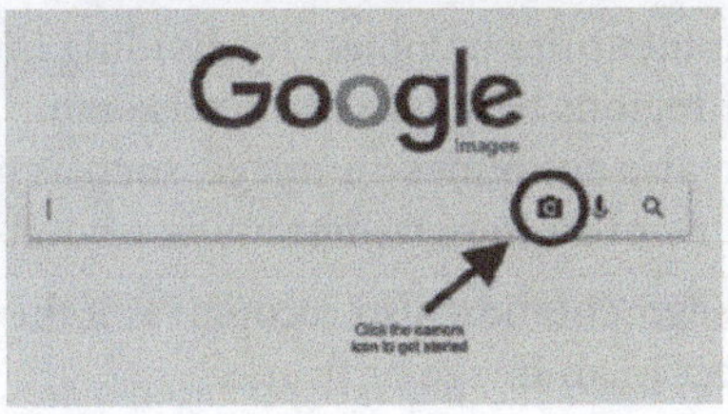

Users can upload an image from their device or provide a URL linking to an image, and Google will search for similar or related images across the web. This feature can be useful for identifying objects, locations, or people in images, finding higher-resolution versions of images, or discovering visually similar content.

Computer Vision in Retail

Computer vision in retail refers to the utilization of artificial intelligence and image processing techniques to extract insights and enhance various aspects of retail operations. Computer vision is transforming retail by giving machines the ability to see and understand the physical store environment. Imagine cameras that track inventory, analyze customer behavior, and even power cashierless shopping.

For example, Amazon Go stores use computer vision to automatically detect items a customer takes from shelves and adds to their virtual cart, eliminating the need for checkout lines. This technology also helps retailers understand customer traffic patterns, optimize store layout, and even deliver targeted advertising based on what products a customer lingers near. In short, computer vision is creating a smarter and more personalized shopping experience.

Self-Driving Cars

Self-driving cars also known as **autonomous vehicles**, rely on advanced computer vision. It is equipped with a multitude of sensors, including cameras, LiDAR, radar, and ultrasonic sensors, autonomous vehicles capture and analyse data about the environment, such as road markings, traffic signs, other vehicles, pedestrians, and obstacles for safety.

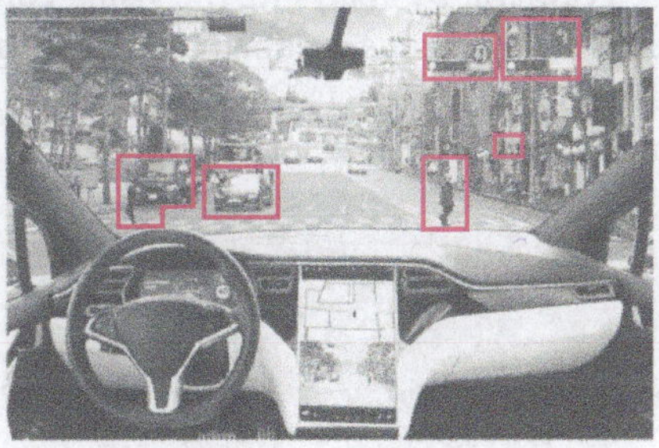

Medical Imaging

Over recent decades, computer-supported medical imaging applications have become invaluable tools for physicians. These technologies not only generate and analyze images but also assist doctors in their interpretation. For instance, advanced applications can convert 2D scan images into interactive 3D models, enabling medical professionals to gain a detailed understanding of a patient's health condition.

Artificial intelligence (AI) has further enhanced medical imaging by improving diagnostic accuracy and efficiency. AI-based diagnostic tools can rapidly interpret complex images, aiding in the early detection of diseases and facilitating personalized treatment plans.

Companies like Aidoc have developed AI-powered radiology platforms that streamline workflows, prioritize critical findings, activate care teams, and facilitate patient follow-up, thereby empowering radiologists to play a central role in patient care.

Furthermore, AI has been applied across various medical imaging domains, including radiology, pathology, and cardiology, revolutionizing the field by enhancing diagnostic accuracy, efficiency, and patient care.

In the image below, a portion has been highly magnified to reveal its composition of pixels. As shown, the pixels form an approximation of the actual image. The higher the number of pixels, the more accurately the image resembles the original.

Google Translate App

The Google Translate app utilises computer vision technology, to enable real-time translation of text captured by the device's camera. By analysing the visual content of images, such as signs, menus, or documents, Google Translate identifies and extracts text characters, which are then translated into the desired language.

5.3 Computer Vision Tasks

Although computer vision has been utilised in so many fields, there are a few common tasks for computer vision systems. These tasks are given below

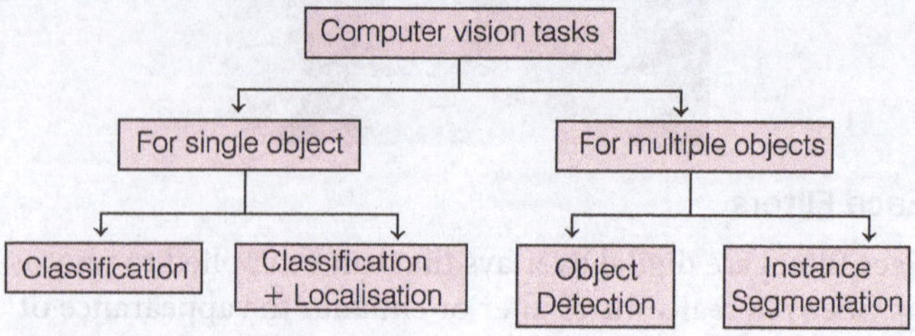

1. Classification

Image classification enables computers to see an image and accurately classify it in the class in which it falls. It requires training a model to recognise patterns and features within images to assign them to the correct class. Computer vision understands classes and labels them.

For example, distinguishing between different types of animals in image.

2. Classification + Localisation

It involves both processes of identifying the object present in the image and at the same time identifying the location at which the object is present in that image. So, this combined task of classification and localisation means processing the input image to identify its category along with the localisation of the object in the image. For example, classifying the animal shown as a dog, and localisation would be showing its position.

3. Object Detection

Object detection is the task of locating and classifying multiple objects within an image i.e., identifying where the object is in the image. It goes beyond image classification by not only identifying objects but also drawing bounding boxes around them.

For example, one dog, one cat and one duck can be easily detected and classified using the object detection technique.

4. Instance Segmentation

Segmentation identifies an object by dividing images of it into different regions based on the pixels seen.

Segmentation also simplifies an image, such as placing a shape or outline of an item to determine what it is.

By doing so, segmentation also recognizes if there is more than one object in an image or frame.

For example, if there are two animals in an image, instance segmentation will separately identify and highlight each animal, treating them as distinct instances.

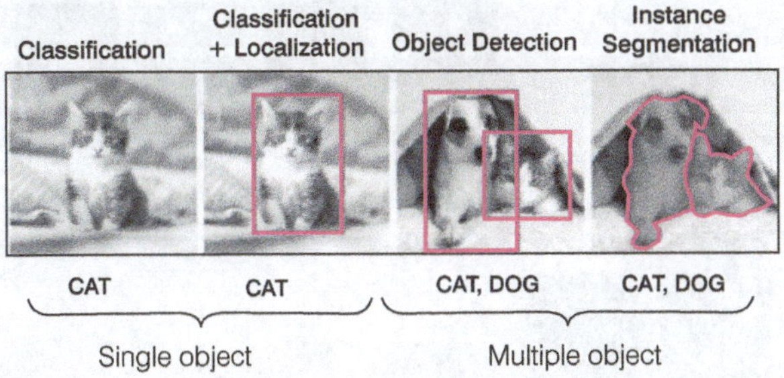

5.4 Basics of Images

Images are two-dimensional representations of visual data. Images are made up of different elements which are as follows

Pixels

Pixels are the smallest units of a digital image and stands for "picture element". They represent individual points of light and are typically arranged in a grid pattern. Each pixel is characterised by its position within the image and its color or intensity value. In the image below, a portion has been highly magnified to reveal its composition of pixels. As shown, the pixels form an approximation of the actual image. The higher the number of pixels, the more accurately the image resembles the original.

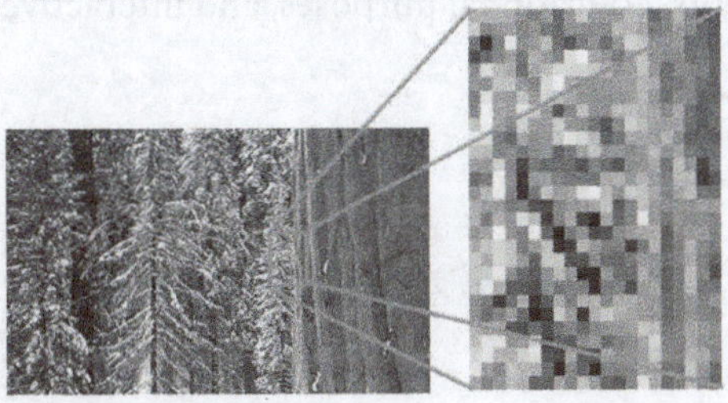

Resolution

Resolution refers to the number of pixels contained in an image, typically expressed as width × height in pixels. High resolutions result in greater detail and clarity while lower resolutions may appear pixelated or blurry.

High Resolution Image

Low Resolution Image

Example, a monitor resolution of 1280 × 1024. This means there are 1280 pixels from one side to the other, and 1024 from top to bottom.

Pixel Value

Pixel value refers to the numerical representation of the colour or intensity of a pixel. To determine the pixel value of an image, you would need to specify whether you are referring to a grayscale or color image and then examine the intensity values of the pixels at the desired location in the image.

Grayscale Images

Grayscale images consist of pixels that contain only shades of grey, ranging from black to white. Each pixel has a single intensity value representing its brightness level. Grayscale images are often used for simplicity or when colour information is not necessary.

A grayscale has each pixel of size 1 byte having a single plane of 2d array of pixels. The size of a grayscale image is defined as the Height × Width of that image.

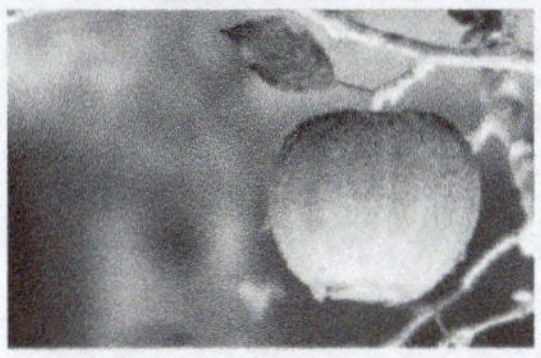

RGB Images

RGB (Red, Green, Blue) images consist of pixels that contain three primary colour channels: i.e. red, green, and blue. Each channel specifies the intensity of its respective colour component, and the combination of these channels produces a wide range of colours.

In most RGB images, each color is represented by an 8-bit integer, meaning each color channel have values ranging from 0 to 255 with 0 meaning zero light and 255 meaning maximum light.

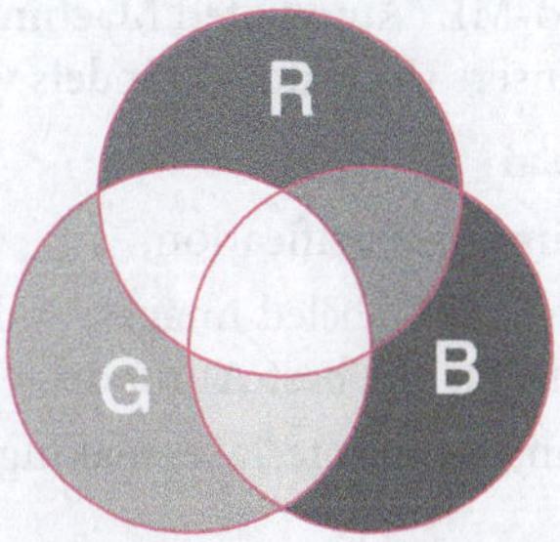

RGB page using the provided link (https://www.w3schools.com/colors/colors_rgb.asp) and explore the online tool available there.

RGB Color Tool allows users to adjust Red (R), Green (G), and Blue (B) values to create different colors. It provides a visual representation of how RGB color combinations work in digital displays.

Steps

1. Open the link in a web browser.
2. Experiment with the RGB sliders or enter specific values for Red, Green, and Blue to see how different colors are formed.
3. Use this understanding to answer the given questions related to RGB colors.

This activity helps in learning how colors are created using RGB values and how changing these values affects the final color output.

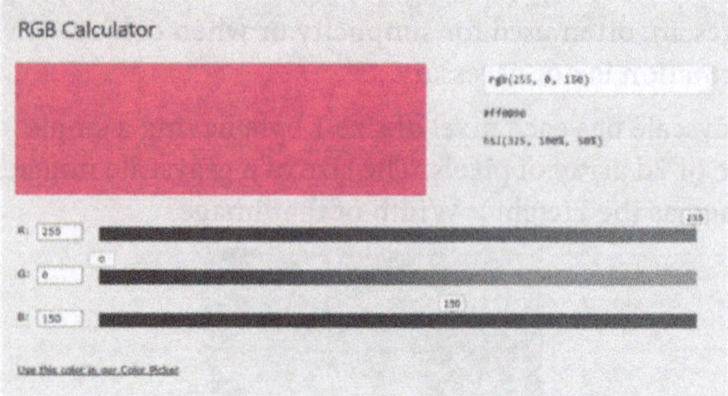

Try These 5.1

1. **How self-driving cars uses computer vision?**
2. **Give a brief account on how computer vision has evolved till now.**
3. **Write a short note on pixel value.**
4. **Differentiate between semantic segmentation and instance segmentation.**

5.5 No Code AI Tools

Lobe

Lobe.ai is an Auto-ML (Automated Machine Learning) tool that enables users to create AI models without coding.

Features of Lobe.ai

- Specializes in image classification.
- Users upload a set of labeled images, and Lobe automatically trains the best AI model.
- Simple, drag-and-drop interface, making it easy for beginners.
- Helps in quick AI model development without requiring technical expertise.

This makes Lobe.ai a great tool for educators, businesses, and non-programmers to explore AI effortlessly.

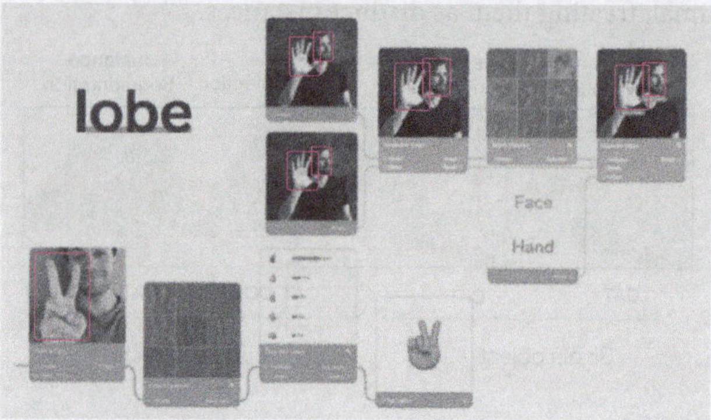

Teachable Machine

Teachable Machine is a web-based AI tool developed by Google in 2017 for Machine Learning and Deep Learning.

Key Features

- Built on TensorFlow.js, also developed by Google.
- Allows users to train AI models using images, audio, or poses as input.
- Supports input from a webcam, uploaded pictures, or audio files.
- No coding required, making it user-friendly for beginners and educators.

Teachable Machine is widely used for quick AI experiments, educational purposes, and interactive projects.

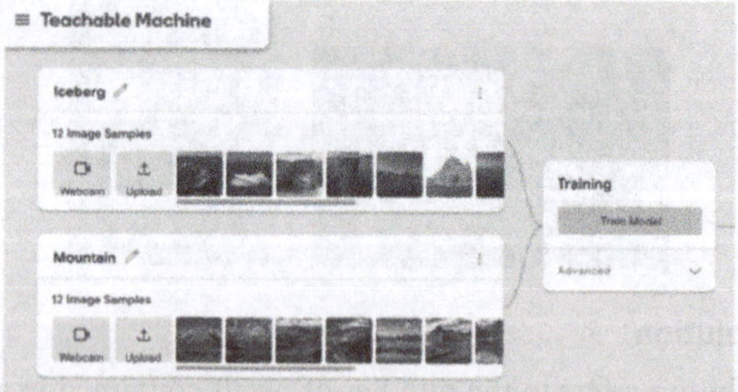

5.6 Image Features

In computer vision and image processing, an image feature is a key piece of information used to analyze and interpret an image. Features help in identifying patterns, structures, and important elements in an image.

Types of Image Features

1. **Edges** Boundaries between different regions in an image.

2. **Corners** Points where edges meet, often indicating key object structures.
3. **Textures** Patterns in an image, such as smoothness or roughness.
4. **Color Features** RGB or grayscale intensity variations in an image.
5. **Shape Features** Geometrical structures like circles, squares, or contours.

These features are extracted and used in AI models for image classification, object detection, and facial recognition.

5.7 Convolution

Convolution is a general purpose filter effect for images. It is a tool used for editing images. It involves applying a filter to an input image to extract features or perform operations such as blurring, sharpening, edge detection, etc.

It involves sliding the kernel over the input image and computing the element-wise multiplication between the kernel and the corresponding region of the image, followed by summing up the results to produce a single output value for each position.

Convolution Operator

The convolution operator involves three main components: the input image, the kernel (also known as a filter or mask), and the output feature map. Technically, convolution is defined as a simple Mathematical operation that multiplies two numeric arrays of the same dimensions but different sizes to produce a third numeric array of the same dimension.

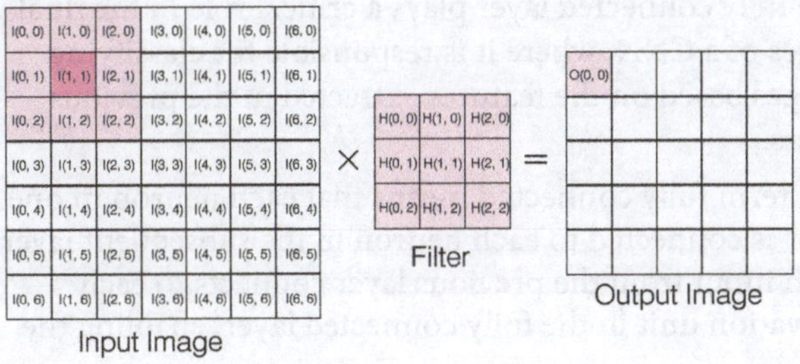

At each position of the input image, the kernel is applied by performing element-wise multiplication between the kernel values and the pixel values of the image at that position. The resulting products are then summed up to obtain the output value for that position in the feature map.

KERNEL

Kernel refers to the learnable parameters that are convolved with the input image to extract features. Kernels are small matrices typically with dimensions much smaller than the input image, and they are learned during the training process through backpropagation.

Each kernel specialises in detecting specific patterns or features within the input image, such as edges, textures, or shapes, depending on the task and the depth of the network.

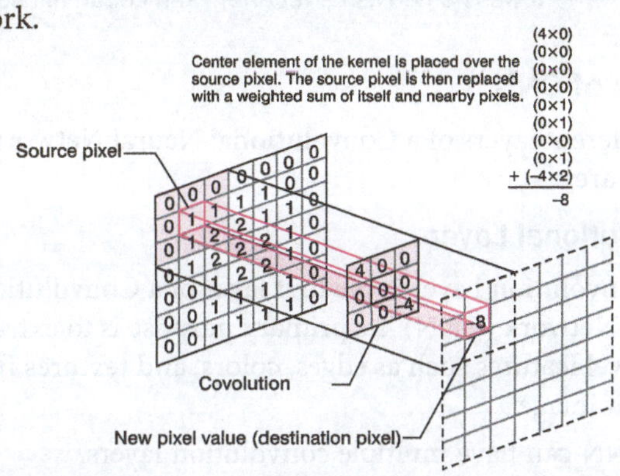

In image processing, we use convolution operation to extract the features from the images which can be later used for further processing. In this process, we overlap the centre of the image with the centre of the kernel to obtain the convolution output. The output image becomes smaller as the overlapping is done at the edge row and the column of the image.

Convolution Neural Network (CNN)

Neural networks are computational models inspired by the structure and functionality of the human brain. They consist of interconnected nodes, or neurons, organised into layers. Each neuron receives input, processes it using an activation function, and passes the result to the neurons in the next layer.

They are widely used in machine learning for tasks such as classification, regression, pattern recognition, and optimization.

A Convolution Neural Network (CNN) is a type of artificial neural network specifically designed for processing and analysing visual data, such as images and videos. CNNs consist of multiple layers, including convolutional layers, pooling layers, and fully connected layers, which work together to automatically learn hierarchical representations of input images.

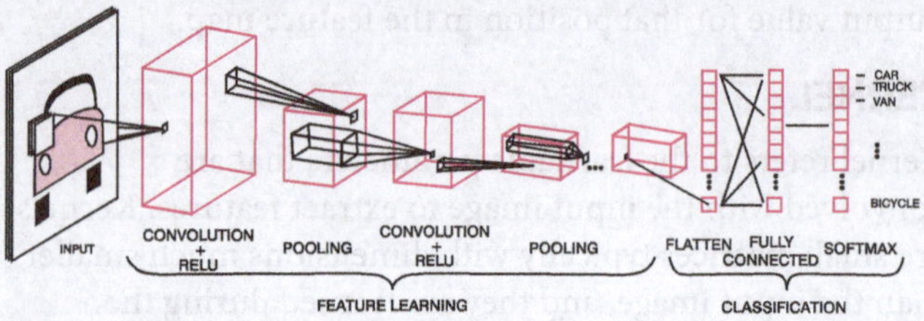

Info Wall

In the 1980s, the world saw its first CNN developed by postdoctoral computer science researcher Yann LeCun. It was built to recognize handwritten digits. It was named as LeNet after Yann LeCun himself.

Layers of CNN

The different layers of a Convolutional Neural Network (CNN) are:

Convolutional Layer

The Convolution Layer is the first layer of a Convolutional Neural Network (CNN). Its primary purpose is to extract high-level features such as edges, colors, and textures from an input image.

- A CNN can have multiple convolution layers.
- The first convolution layer captures low-level features like edges, colors, and gradients.
- Deeper layers extract high-level features, allowing the network to develop a comprehensive understanding of the image.

Working of Convolution Layer:

- The layer applies a convolution operation using multiple kernels (filters) to detect different features.
- The result of this operation is called a feature map (or activation map).

Uses of Feature Maps

- Reduces image size for efficient processing.
- Focuses on important features for better recognition (e.g., detecting eyes, nose, and mouth instead of the entire face).

Rectified Linear Unit (ReLU)

This is the second layer of CNN. After we get the feature map, it is then passed onto the ReLU layer. This layer simply gets rid of all the negative numbers in the feature map and lets the positive number stay as it is. The process of passing it to the ReLU layer introduces non-linearity in the feature map.

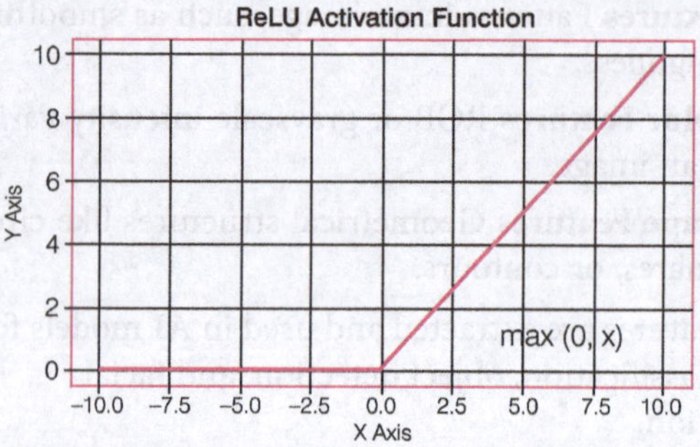

The ReLU graph starts with a horizontal straight line and then increases linearly as it reaches a positive number.

Pooling Layer

- Pooling layers are used to reduce the spatial dimensions of feature maps while preserving important information.
- Pooling layers help to make the representations more invariant to small translations or distortions in the input, while also reducing the computational cost and the risk of overfitting. It makes the image smaller and more manageable.

There are two types of pooling

(i) **Max pooling** returns the maximum value from the portion of the image covered by the Kernel.

(ii) **Average pooling** returns the average of all the values from the portion of the image covered by the Kernel.

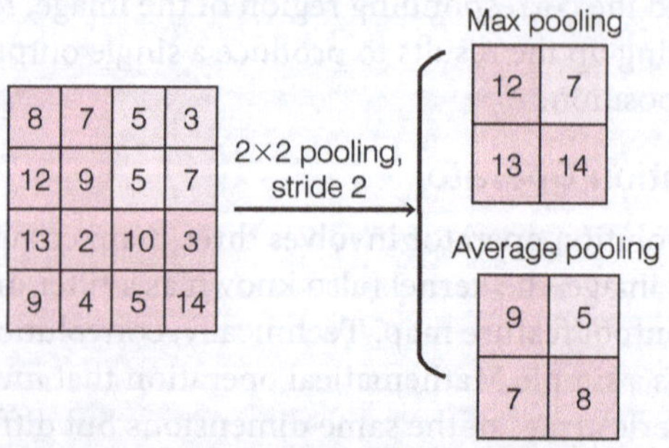

Fully Connected Layer

The fully connected layer plays a critical role in the final stages of a CNN, where it is responsible for classifying images based on the features extracted in the previous layers.

The term fully connected means that each neuron in one layer is connected to each neuron in the subsequent layer. Each input from the previous layer connects to each activation unit in the fully connected layer, enabling the

CNN to simultaneously consider all features when making a final classification decision.

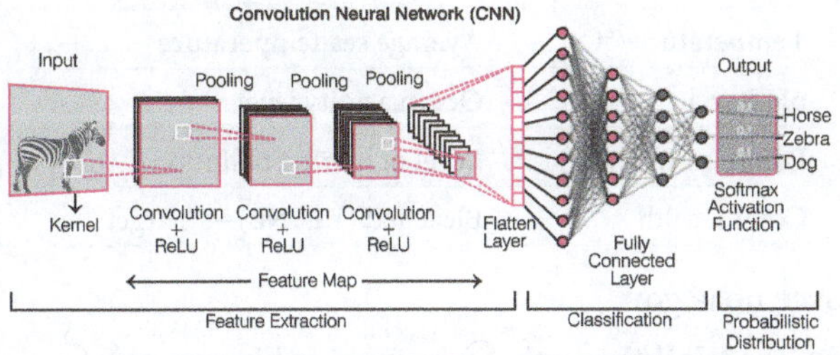

Each of these layers plays a crucial role in the overall architecture of a CNN, contributing to the network's ability to learn hierarchical representations of input data and make accurate predictions for various tasks in computer vision.

Try These 5.2

1. **Explain the various features of an image.**
2. **What is convolution?**
3. **Explain kernel in brief.**
4. **Write a short note on image processing.**

Glossary

Object detection It involves identifying and locating specific objects within an image or video frame.

Instance segmentation It is an extension of semantic segmentation that not only labels each pixel with a category but also distinguishes between individual object instances within the same category.

Resolution It refers to the number of pixels contained in an image, typically expressed as width × height in pixels.

Convolution It involves applying a filter or kernel to an input image to extract features or perform operations such as blurring, sharpening, edge detection, etc.

The **kernel** refers to the learnable parameters that are convolved with the input image to extract features.

Convolutional Neural Network (CNN) It is specifically designed for processing and analysing visual data, such as images and videos.

ACTIVITY Time

ACTIVITY 1 : Create Pixel Art & GIF Using Piskel

To understand RGB better, create pixel art and animate it using Piskel:

1. **Go to** www.piskelapp.com.
2. **Create pixel art** by drawing on the grid using different colors.
3. **Add frames** to animate your art.
4. **Preview the animation** to see how it looks.
5. **Export as GIF** to save your animated pixel art.

This task helps in understanding **how RGB colors work in digital images** and how pixels combine to form colorful visuals.

Activity Time Build a Smart Sorter

Purpose Use Computer Vision (CV) to automate sorting processes using a No-Code AI tool.

Steps to Complete the Activity:

1. **Form Groups** Create teams of 4 members.
2. **Collect Images** Find or capture images of Bottles, Cans, and Paper from the internet or surroundings.
3. **Use a No-Code AI Tool** Visit a No-Code AI platform like Teachable Machine or Lobe.ai.
4. **Create 3 Classes** Label and categorize images into three classes:
   - Bottles
   - Cans
   - Paper
5. **Train the Model** Upload the images and train the AI to recognize the objects.
6. **Test the Classifier** Upload new images to check if the model correctly identifies Bottles, Cans, and Paper.

   This activity helps in understanding how AI and CV can be used for automated sorting and classification!

ACTIVITY 2: Coral Bleaching Classification Model using Orange Data Mining Tool

Objective Use the Orange Data Mining Tool to build a classification model that predicts coral bleaching based on environmental factors.

Understanding Coral Reefs & Coral Bleaching

What Are Coral Reefs

- Found in tropical ocean waters.
- Composed of marine invertebrates called coral.
- Essential for aquatic life, providing habitat and biodiversity.

What Is Coral Bleaching

- Happens when corals lose their symbiotic algae (zooxanthellae) due to stress.
- **Common causes**
  - Rising sea temperatures (Global Warming)
  - Pollution (Chemicals, Plastics)
  - Ocean acidification (CO_2 Absorption)

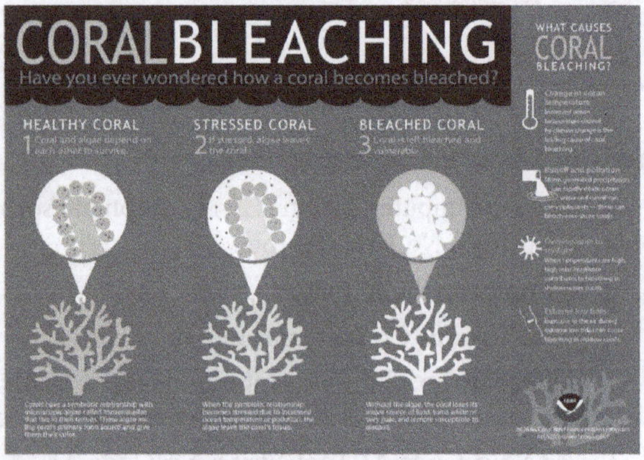

Steps to Build the Classification Model in Orange

- Install & Open Orange Data Mining Tool

Download & install Orange from: https://orangedatamining.com/

- Load Coral Bleaching Dataset

Use an existing dataset (or create one) with attributes like:

Feature	Description
Temperature (°C)	Average sea temperature
pH Level	Ocean acidity level
Pollution Index	Level of marine pollution
Coral Health	Bleached (Yes/No) → Target

Source noaa.gov

Use Case Walkthrough Steps involved in project development & required dataset can be checked using the links and QR code given below:

Short link https://bit.ly/orange_computer_vision

Long Link
https://drive.google.com/drive/folders/1ppJ4d-8yOFJ2G22rHHpjNrK0ejdIAe5Q?usp=sharing

or Scan the QR code below

- Build the Classification Workflow

Drag & connect the following widgets:

1. File Widget → Load dataset
2. Data Table → View dataset
3. Select Columns → Choose features & target
4. Data Sampler → Split data into training/testing
5. Classification Models (Choose any):
   - Logistic Regression
   - Decision Tree
   - Random Forest
6. Test & Score → Evaluate model accuracy
7. Confusion Matrix → Check classification performance

- Train & Test the Model
  - Run the model to classify coral as **"Healthy"** or **"Bleached"**.
  - Analyze results and accuracy.

This activity helps in understanding **AI-based environmental monitoring** and contributes to marine conservation.

NCERT FOLDER

Complete Explanations of all NCERT's Questions

A. Multiple Choice Questions

1. What is the primary objective of the Convolution Layer in a Convolutional Neural Network (CNN)?
(a) To flatten the input image
(b) To assign importance to various aspects/objects in the image
(c) To reduce the spatial size of the input image
(d) To perform element-wise multiplication of image arrays

2. Which of the following tasks is an example of computer vision?
(a) Rescaling an image
(b) Correcting brightness levels in an image
(c) Object detection in images or videos
(d) Changing tones of an image

3. How is resolution typically expressed?
(a) By the number of pixels along the width and height, such as 1280 ×1024
(b) By the brightness level of each pixel, ranging from 0 to 255
(c) By the total number of pixels, such as 5 megapixels
(d) By the arrangement of pixels in a 2-dimensional grid

4. What is the core task of image classification?
(a) Identifying objects and their locations in images
(b) Segmenting objects into individual pixels
(c) Assigning an input image one label from a fixed set of categories
(d) Detecting instances of real-world objects in images

5. What is the function of the Rectified Linear Unit (ReLU) layer in a CNN?
(a) To reduce the image size for more efficient processing
(b) To assign importance to various aspects/objects in the input image
(c) To get rid of negative numbers in the feature map and retain positive numbers
(d) To perform the convolution operation on the input image

6. Object detection and handwriting recognition are examples of tasks commonly associated with:
(a) Computer vision
(b) Image processing
(c) Both computer vision and image processing
(d) Neither computer vision nor image processing

7. What does the pixel value represent in an image?
(a) Width of the pixel
(b) Brightness or color of the pixel
(c) Height of the pixel
(d) Resolution of the pixel

8. In the byte image format, what is the range of possible pixel values?
(a) 0 to 10
(b) 0 to 100
(c) 0 to 1000
(d) 0 to 255

9. In a grayscale image, what does the darkest shade represent?
(a) Total presence of color
(b) Zero value of pixel
(c) Lightest shade of gray
(d) Maximum pixel value

10. In an RGB image, what does a pixel with an intensity value of 0 represent?
(a) Full presence of color
(b) No presence of color
(c) Maximum brightness level
(d) Minimum brightness level

Answers

1. (c)	2. (c)	3. (a)	4. (c)	5. (c)
6. (a)	7. (b)	8. (d)	9. (b)	10. (b)

B. Assertion and Reason Based Questions

1. Assertion (A) Object detection is a more complex task than image classification because it involves identifying both the presence and location of objects in an image.

Reason (R) Object detection algorithms need to not only classify the objects present in an image but also accurately localize them by determining their spatial extent.

Select the appropriate option for the statements given above.
(a) Both A and R are true and R is the correct explanation of A
(b) Both A and R are true and R is not the correct explanation of A
(c) A is true but R is false
(d) A is False but R is true

2. Assertion (A) Grayscale images consist of shades of gray ranging from black to white, where each pixel is represented by a single byte, and the size of the image is determined by its height multiplied by its width.

Reason (R) Grayscale images are represented using a three intensities per pixel, typically ranging from 0 to 255.

Select the appropriate option for the statements given above:

(a) Both A and R are true and R is the correct explanation of A

(b) Both A and R are true and R is not the correct explanation of A

(c) A is true but R is false

(d) A is False but R is true

Answers

1. (a) 2. (c)

C. Subjective Questions

1. Imagine you have a smartphone camera app that can recognize objects. When you point your camera at a dog, the app identifies it as a dog, analyzing patterns and features in the image. Behind the scenes, the app's software processes the image, detecting edges, shapes, and colors, then compares these features to a vast database to make accurate identifications."

Identify the technology used in the above scenario and explain the way it works.

Ans. The technology used in this scenario is Computer Vision with Deep Learning-based Object Recognition.

The app captures an image, processes it using a Convolutional Neural Network (CNN), and extracts important features like edges, textures, and patterns.

The extracted features are then compared with a pre-trained dataset to classify the object (e.g., recognizing a dog).

2. Enlist two smartphone apps that utilize computer vision technology? How have these apps improved your efficiency or convenience in daily tasks?

Ans. Two smartphone apps that utilize computer vision technology are:

1. **Google Lens** It recognizes objects, text, and landmarks.

   Efficiency It can instantly translates text, searches for objects, and identifies plants/animals.

2. **Face ID (Apple)** It uses facial recognition for unlocking devices.

   Convenience It provides fast and secure authentication without using passwords.

3. How an RGB image is different from a grayscale image?

Ans. Difference Between RGB and Grayscale Images

Feature	RGB Image	Grayscale Image
Color Channels	3 (Red, Green, Blue)	1 (Shades of Gray)
Pixel Representation	Each pixel has three values (R, G, B)	Each pixel has a single intensity value (0-255)
File Size	Larger due to three channels	Smaller as it stores only intensity values
Usage	Used in color-based image processing, graphics, and multimedia	Used in medical imaging, pattern recognition, and image preprocessing
Example	A full-color photo of a landscape	A black-and-white version of the same photo

In simple terms, an RGB image contains full-color details, while a grayscale image represents intensity variations without color information.

4. Determine the color of a pixel based on its RGB values mentioned below:

(i) R=0, B=0, G=0 (ii) R=255, B=255, G=255
(iii) R=0, B=0, G=255 (iv) R=0, B=255, G=0

Ans. (i) R=0, B=0, G=0 → Black

(ii) R=255, B=255, G=255 → White

(iii) R=0, B=0, G=255 → Blue

(iv) R=0, B=255, G=0 → Green

5. Briefly describe the purpose of the convolution operator in image processing.

Ans. The convolution operator is a mathematical function used in image processing to extract important features such as edges, textures, and patterns.

It works by applying a small filter (kernel) to an image, sliding over it pixel by pixel, and computing a weighted sum to enhance or detect specific characteristics.

Key Purposes of the Convolution Operator:

- **Edge Detection** Identifies object boundaries by highlighting intensity changes.
- **Blurring & Noise Reduction** Smoothens images by averaging neighboring pixel values.
- **Sharpening** Enhances edges and fine details in an image.
- **Feature Extraction in Deep Learning** Helps Convolutional Neural Networks (CNNs) recognize patterns like textures, shapes, and objects.

6. What are the different layers in Convolutional Neural Network? What features are likely to be detected by the initial layers of a neural network and how is it different from what is detected by the later layers?

Ans. A CNN consists of multiple layers that extract and process image features step by step. The key layers are:

- **Convolutional Layer** Applies filters (kernels) to extract low-level features like edges and textures.
- **Pooling Layer (Downsampling)** Reduces image size while retaining essential information, making processing more efficient.

- **Activation Function (ReLU)** Introduces non-linearity to help detect complex patterns.
- **Fully Connected (Dense) Layer** Combines extracted features to classify images.
- **Softmax/Output Layer** Converts the final outputs into probability scores for different categories.

Feature Detection: Initial *versus* Later Layers

Layer Stage	Features Detected	Purpose
Initial Layers	Basic features like edges, corners, textures, and color patterns.	Helps detect simple structures in an image.
Middle Layers	More complex features like shapes, patterns, and small parts of objects.	Helps recognize parts of objects (e.g., eyes, wheels).
Later Layers	High-level features like full objects, faces, and complex shapes.	Helps in classification (e.g., distinguishing between a dog and a cat).

In summary, initial layers detect simple patterns, while later layers identify entire objects, making CNNs effective for image recognition tasks.

7. "Imagine you're a researcher tasked with improving workplace safety in a manufacturing environment. You decide to employ computer vision technology to enhance safety measures."

Ans. As a researcher, you can integrate computer vision technology to improve workplace safety in a manufacturing environment. This can be achieved through real-time monitoring and automated detection of potential hazards. Two Key Applications of Computer Vision for Safety Enhancement are:

1. PPE (Personal Protective Equipment) Compliance Monitoring
   - **Objective** Ensure that workers wear required safety gear like helmets, gloves, and vests.
   - **Technique Used** Object Detection (YOLO, Faster R-CNN)

   Implementation
   - Cameras continuously monitor employees.
   - AI-based models detect PPE compliance.
   - Alerts are triggered when workers fail to wear safety equipment.

   Benefits
   - Reduces injury risks.
   - Ensures adherence to safety regulations.
2. Hazard and Anomaly Detection in Machinery
   - **Objective** Detect unsafe conditions like overheating machines, sparks, or unexpected movements.
   - **Technique Used** Thermal Imaging + Anomaly Detection (CNNs, Autoencoders)

   Implementation
   - AI-powered cameras inspect machinery in real-time.
   - Analyzes thermal patterns and movement irregularities.
   - Alerts are generated for potential failures or unsafe conditions.

   Benefits
   - Prevents machine failures and accidents.
   - Reduces downtime and improves operational efficiency.

8. How would you utilize computer vision in two distinct applications to promote safety within the manufacturing plant, ensuring both the physical well-being of employees and the efficiency of operations?

Provide detailed explanations for each application, including the specific computer vision techniques or algorithms you would employ, and how they would contribute to achieving your safety goals.

Ans. To enhance safety and efficiency in a manufacturing plant, computer vision can be implemented in various ways. Here are two distinct applications:

1. **Intrusion Detection in Restricted Areas**

   Objective Prevent unauthorized personnel from entering high-risk zones, such as areas with heavy machinery, hazardous chemicals, or robotic arms in operation.

   Computer Vision Techniques Used
   - **Motion Detection & Object Tracking** OpenCV with Background Subtraction
   - **Facial Recognition & Access Control** Deep Learning (FaceNet, MTCNN)

   Implementation
   - AI-powered cameras are installed in restricted zones and entry points.
   - The system continuously monitors movements and detects unauthorized access.
   - If an unregistered person is detected, an alert is sent to security personnel, and access can be automatically restricted (e.g., by locking doors).

   Safety Contribution
   - Prevents unauthorized personnel from entering dangerous areas.
   - Reduces the risk of accidents due to untrained workers accessing hazardous zones.
   - Enhances workplace security and compliance with regulations.

2. **Fatigue Detection in Workers Operating Heavy Machinery**

Objective Identify signs of worker fatigue to prevent accidents caused by drowsiness or lack of attention.

Computer Vision Techniques Used

- **Facial Recognition & Eye Tracking** CNN-based models like Dlib, OpenCV
- **Blink Detection & Head Movement Analysis** Haar Cascades, Deep Learning models

Implementation

- Cameras monitor workers' facial expressions and eye movement in real-time.
- If a worker blinks too slowly, closes eyes frequently, or shows signs of drowsiness, the system generates an alert.
- The system can trigger break reminders or temporarily halt machine operations for safety.

Safety Contribution

- Prevents accidents caused by worker fatigue (e.g., forklift or crane accidents).
- Improves worker well-being and reduces long-term health issues.
- Enhances overall productivity and ensures a safer work environment.

9. Explain the distinctions between image classification, classification with localization, object detection, and instance segmentation in computer vision tasks. Provide examples for each to support your answer.

Ans.

Task	Description	Example
Image Classification	Assigns an image a single label.	Identifying an image as "dog" or "cat."
Classification with Localization	Classifies an image and provides coordinates for a single object.	Detecting a "dog" and drawing a bounding box around it.
Object Detection	Detects multiple objects and their locations in an image.	Identifying and labeling all cars and pedestrians in a traffic image.
Instance Segmentation	Detects objects and outlines their precise shapes.	Separating different objects (like leaves in an image of a tree).

10. "Agriculture is an industry where precision and efficiency are crucial for sustainable production. Traditional farming methods often rely on manual labor and visual inspection, which can be time-consuming and error-prone. However, advancements in computer vision technology offer promising solutions to optimize various agricultural processes. Agricultural drones equipped with high-resolution cameras and computer vision algorithms are increasingly being used to monitor crop health, detect diseases, and assess crop yields."

Answer the following questions based on the case study mentioned above:

(a) How does the integration of computer vision technology with drones improve efficiency in agricultural practices compared to traditional methods?

(b) What are some key indicators or parameters that computer vision algorithms can analyze to assess crop health and detect diseases?

Ans. (a) How Drones Improve Agricultural Efficiency

- **Faster Monitoring** Drones scan large fields in minutes.
- **Early Disease Detection** AI identifies plant stress before visible symptoms appear.
- **Precision Agriculture** Resources (fertilizer, water) are applied exactly where needed.
- **Real-time Data Processing** Immediate insights help farmers make quick decisions.

(b) **Key Indicators for Crop Health Analysis**

- **Leaf Color & Texture** Detects diseases and nutrient deficiencies.
- **NDVI (Normalized Difference Vegetation Index)** Measures plant stress levels.
- **Pest Damage Patterns** Identifies areas affected by insects.
- **Moisture Levels** Detects water stress using thermal imaging.

11. You are tasked with developing a computer vision system for a self-driving car company. The system needs to accurately detect and classify various objects on the road to ensure safe navigation. Imagine you're working on improving the object detection algorithm for the self-driving car's computer vision system. During testing, you notice that the system occasionally misclassifies pedestrians as cyclists, especially in low-light conditions.

How would you approach addressing this issue? What steps would you take to enhance the accuracy of pedestrian detection while ensuring the system's overall performance and reliability on the road?

Ans. **Issue** Misclassification of pedestrians as cyclists in low-light conditions.

Steps to Enhance Accuracy:

1. **Enhancing Dataset**
   - Collect more low-light pedestrian images.
   - Use data augmentation (adjust brightness, contrast).
2. **Improving Object Detection Model**

- Use multi-scale object detection (YOLO, Faster R-CNN).
- Implement attention mechanisms to focus on finer details.

3. **Sensor Fusion for Better Recognition**
   - Combine LiDAR, radar, and thermal imaging with computer vision.
   - Detects heat signatures to differentiate pedestrians from cyclists.
4. **Uncertainty Estimation and Model Confidence**
   - If the model is uncertain, it flags the detection for extra caution.
   - Prioritizes pedestrian safety by reducing misclassifications.

EXAM PATTERN EXERCISE

Including Competency Based Questions

Part I

Multiple Choice Questions

1. The computer vision program is based on ________.

(a) Speaking
(b) Reading
(c) Understanding voice command
(d) Understanding the content of digital images

2. Which one of these is not an example of computer vision?

(a) Image classification (b) Speech segmentation
(c) Image segmentation (d) Object detection

3. Which of the following is an example of image classification in computer vision?

(a) Price prediction
(b) Photo albums in smartphones
(c) Trend setting
(d) Lock in smartphone

4. Which of the following is an Applications of Computer Vision?

(a) Robotics (b) Medicine
(c) Security (d) All of these

5. __________ is the process of finding instances of real-world objects in images or videos. SQP 2023-24

(a) Instance segmentation
(b) Object detection
(c) Classification
(d) Image segmentation

6. In computer vision which of the following tasks is used for multiple objects? 2024

(a) Classification (b) Classification + Localisation
(c) Instance Segmentation (d) Localisation

7. What is the primary function of Lobe.ai?

(a) Text translation (b) Image classification
(c) Speech recognition (d) Database management

8. ______ means a picture element which is the smallest unit of information that makes up a picture. SQP 2023-24

(a) Vision (b) Pics (c) Pixel (d) Piskel

9. The resolution of most images we use is measured in

(a) RGB (b) Pixels
(c) Grayscale (d) HSV

10. Which is the most common pixel format where this number is stored as an 8-bit integer giving a range of possible values from 0 to 255?

(a) Byte image (b) Resolution
(c) Pixel (d) Grayscale

11. Which technology is Teachable Machine built on?

(a) PyTorch (b) TensorFlow.js
(c) OpenCV (d) Keras

12. What is the primary purpose of a Convolutional Neural Network (CNN)?

(a) Object detection (b) Image classification
(c) Text generation (d) Reinforcement learning

13. Which of the following algorithms is commonly used for image classification?

(a) K-means clustering
(b) Decision trees
(c) Convolutional Neural Networks (CNN)
(d) Support Vector Machines (SVM)

14. Which layer type is typically used to extract local features in a CNN?

(a) Convolutional layer (b) Pooling layer
(c) Fully connected layer (d) Activation layer

15. What is the purpose of the filter/kernel in a convolutional layer?
(a) To determine the number of neurons in the layer
(b) To specify the size of the feature maps
(c) To extract local features from the input data
(d) None of the above

16. What is the purpose of the pooling layer in a CNN?
(a) To reduce the spatial dimensions of the feature maps
(b) To introduce non-linearity to the network
(c) To adjust the weights and biases of the network
(d) To compute the gradients for backpropagation

17. Which activation function is commonly used in the convolutional layers of a CNN?
(a) ReLU (Rectified Linear Unit)
(b) Sigmoid
(c) Tanh (Hyperbolic Tangent)
(d) Softmax

18. Which layer is CNN is responsible for increasing the non-linear properties of the trained networks?
(a) ReLU (b) Input layer
(c) Pooling layer (d) Output layer

19. Which layer type is responsible for making final predictions in a CNN?
(a) Convolutional layer (b) Pooling layer
(c) Fully connected layer (d) Activation layer

20. What does the term "image processing" refer to in Computer Vision ? **2025**
(a) Editing videos
(b) Extracting meaningful information from images
(c) Playing audio files
(d) Comiling codes

21. In Computer Vision, which of the following tasks is used for single object? **2025**
(a) Object Detection (b) Classification + Localization
(c) Instance Segmentation (d) Non – Localization

Answers

1. (d)	2. (b)	3. (b)	4. (d)	5. (b)
6. (c)	7. (b)	8. (c)	9. (b)	10. (d)
11. (b)	12. (b)	13. (c)	14. (a)	15. (c)
16. (a)	17. (a)	18. (a)	19. (c)	20. (b)
21. (b)				

Statement Based Questions

1. Statement 1 Computer vision is one of the most important fields of artificial intelligence (AI)
Statement 2 It is capable of extracting meaningful information from visual data like videos and images.
(a) Both Statement 1 and Statement 2 are correct
(b) Both Statement 1 and Statement 2 are incorrect
(c) Statement 1 is correct but Statement 2 is incorrect
(d) Statement 2 is correct but Statement 1 is incorrect

2. Statement 1 Computer vision has enabled machines to detect face images of people to verify their identity.
Statement 2 Facebook also use facial recognition to detect and tag users.
(a) Both Statement 1 and Statement 2 are correct
(b) Both Statement 1 and Statement 2 are incorrect
(c) Statement 1 is correct but Statement 2 is incorrect
(d) Statement 2 is correct but Statement 1 is incorrect

3. Statement 1 A pixel is defined as the smallest element of a digital image.
Statement 2 Pixel resolution is the total pixel count in a digital image.
(a) Both Statement 1 and Statement 2 are correct
(b) Both Statement 1 and Statement 2 are incorrect
(c) Statement 1 is correct but Statement 2 is incorrect
(d) Statement 2 is correct but Statement 1 is incorrect

4. Statement 1 A Convolutional Neural Network (CNN) is a type of deep learning algorithm that is particularly well-suited for image recognition and processing tasks.
Statement 2 Fully connected layer is the second layer of CNN.
(a) Both Statement 1 and Statement 2 are correct
(b) Both Statement 1 and Statement 2 are incorrect
(c) Statement 1 is correct but Statement 2 is incorrect
(d) Statement 2 is correct but Statement 1 is incorrect

5. Statement 1 Various search engines and e–commerce portals now how a new feature called image – based search using computer vision.
Statement 2 Image-based search helps in finding items, people and places by giving their sounds to the system. **2025**
(a) Both Statement 1 and Statement 2 are correct.
(b) Both Statement 1 and Statement 2 are incorrect.
(c) Statement 1 is correct but Statement 2 is incorrect.
(d) Statement 2 is correct but Statement 1 is incorrect.

Answers

1. (a)	2. (a)	3. (a)	4. (c)	5. (c)

Assertion & Reason Based Questions

1. Assertion (A) With the use of computer vision, autonomous vehicles can understand their environment.
Reason (R) The autonomous vehicle can navigate streets and highways on its own, swerve around obstructions, and get its passengers where they need to go safely.
(a) Both A and R are true and R is the correct explanation for A.
(b) Both A and R are true and R is not the correct explanation for A.
(c) A is true, but R is false.
(d) A is false, but R is true.

2. Assertion (A) Image Classification involves categorising images into predefined classes or categories, such as animals, vehicles, or buildings.
Reason (R) Image detection is identifying and classifying human actions within an image or video stream.

(a) Both A and R are true and R is the correct explanation for A.
(b) Both A and R are true and R is not the correct explanation for A.
(c) A is true, but R is false.
(d) A is false, but R is true.

3. Assertion (A) The term used to refer to the number of pixels in an image is resolution.
Reason (R) Resolution in an image denotes the total number of pixels it contains, usually represented as height × width. **2024**

(a) Both A and R are true and R is the correct explanation for A.
(b) Both A and R are true and R is not the correct explanation for A.
(c) A is true, but R is false.
(d) A is false, but R is true.

4. Assertion (A) Pooling layers down sample the spatial dimensions of the input, reducing the computational complexity and the number of parameters in the network.
Reason (R) Max pooling is a common pooling operation, selecting the maximum value from a group of neighboring pixels.

(a) Both A and R are true and R is the correct explanation for A.
(b) Both A and R are true and R is not the correct explanation for A.
(c) A is true, but R is false.
(d) A is false, but R is true.

Answers

1. (a) **2.** (c) **3.** (a) **4.** (a)

Part II

Very Short Answer Type Questions

1. With reference to AI domain, expand the term CV.

Ans. CV stands for Computer Vision.

2. Which app uses face filters?

Ans. Snapchat uses face filters.

3. Give an example of object recognition.

Ans. Object recognition is identifying specific instances of objects and associating them with known categories or concepts.

4. What is the process of detecting an instance of the object, categorising it and giving each pixel a label on that basis?

Ans. Instance segmentation

5. It is basically the dimensions through which you can measure how many pixels are there on a screen. What is it?

Ans. Resolution

6. How many channels does a color image have? **SQP 2023-24**

Ans. Three channels

7. Mention any 2 features of image based on which they are characterised.

Ans. Two features based on which images are characterised are – textures and edges.

8. What is a kernel?

Ans. A kernel, is a small matrix of numerical values that defines a specific operation to be performed on the input image.

Short Answer Type Questions

1. Name the real-life applications of computer vision.

Ans. The real-life applications of computer vision are:

- Facial recognition in smartphones
- Face filters
- Google translate app

2. How computer vision is helping in medical imaging?

Ans. Computer vision plays a pivotal role in medical imaging, facilitating tasks such as image analysis, diagnosis, treatment planning, and surgical guidance across various medical specialties. By analysing medical images, including X-rays, CT scans, MRIs, and ultrasound images, computer vision algorithms assist healthcare professionals in detecting abnormalities, quantifying disease progression, identifying anatomical structures, and guiding interventions.

3. How Google translate uses computer vision?

Ans. Google Translate employs computer vision to enable instant translation of text captured through a smartphone camera. Using optical character recognition (OCR) technology, the app recognises and extracts text from images, such as signs, menus, or documents. Then, machine translation algorithms process the extracted text to provide translations in real-time, facilitating communication across languages.

4. Face lock feature of a smartphone is an example of computer vision. Briefly discuss this feature. **2023**

Ans. The face lock feature of a smartphone is indeed an example of computer vision technology in action. It utilises the device's front-facing camera and sophisticated algorithms to recognise and authenticate the user's face before granting access to the device.

5. Can you define "digital image"?

Ans. A digital image is a picture that's made up of smaller parts, called pixels. These pixels are made of numerical components that represent their color codes and intensity. AI systems use these numbers to understand an image.

6. What programming languages does computer vision support?

Ans. Computer vision primarily utilizes these programming languages:

- **Python** Widely favored due to its simplicity and extensive libraries (like OpenCV, TensorFlow, and PyTorch).
- **C++** Used for performance-critical applications requiring speed and efficiency.
- **MATLAB** Common in research and academic settings.

7. Explain the term resolution with an example. SQP 2023-24

Ans. Resolution of an image refers to the number of pixels in an image, across the width and height. For example a monitor resolution of 1280×1024. This means there are 1280 pixels from one side to the other, and 1024 pixels from top to bottom.

8. How does the computer see an image?

Ans. In a digital image, every coloured image that is stored can be split into 3 different channels, i.e. Red (R), Green (G) and Blue (B), with different intensities. The computer identifies the value related to each pixel and determines the size and colour of the image.

9. What's the purpose of grayscaling?

Ans. Grayscale is the range of whiteness to blackness of a digital image. Programmers take an image that's in color and change it to grayscale, which is called grayscaling. This helps simplify the image data so a computer can more easily process the input.

10. Differentiate between grayscale and RGB images. 2024

Ans. Differentiate between grayscale and RGB images are as follows

Grayscale image	RGB image
Grayscale images contain shades of gray, ranging from black to white, with no color information.	RGB (Red, Green, Blue) images are composed of three color channels: red, green, and blue.
Each pixel in a grayscale image is represented by a single intensity value, typically an 8-bit value ranging from 0 (black) to 255 (white), where intermediate values represent varying shades of gray.	Each pixel in an RGB image is represented by a combination of three intensity values, one for each color channel. Typically, each intensity value is an 8-bit integer ranging from 0 to 255, resulting in 24 bits per pixel (8 bits per channel).

11. Name the four important layers in CNN.

Ans. The 4 layers in CNN are:

(i) Convolution layer
(ii) Rectified linear unit
(iii) Pooling layer
(iv) Fully connected layer

12. Differentiate between Max pooling and Average pooling.

Ans. The difference between max pooling and average pooling is:

Max pooling is the most commonly used method that selects the maximum value of the current image view and helps preserve the maximum detected features.

While, Average pooling finds out the average value of the current image view and thus down samples the feature map.

13. Give any two key impacts of Computer Vision on medical imaging. 2025

Ans. Two key impacts of Computer Vision on medical imaging:

- **Improved Diagnosis** Automated analysis of scans (X-rays, MRIs) to detect anomalies and assist in early disease detection.
- **Enhanced Surgical Precision** Real-time image guidance during surgeries for more accurate procedures.

Long Answer Type Questions

1. Define the computer vision task.

Ans. Refer to text on page 150-151 (Computer vision tasks)

2. What is image? Also, Explain the basics of image.

Ans. Image is a visual representation of an object, a scene or a concept.

Basics of image Refer to text on page 151-152 (Basics of images)

3. Explain the different layers of convolution neural network.

Ans. Refer to text on page 154-155 (Layers of CNN)

SELF ASSESSMENT

Multiple Choice Questions

1. Which of the following images will be the sharpest?

(a) 300 ppi (b) 100 ppi

(c) 600 ppi (d) 75 ppi

2. The task performed by computer vision for single object is:

(a) Classification and localisation (b) Object detection and instance segmentation

(c) Filtering (d) Both (a) and (b)

3. The task/s that facial recognition models perform is

(a) verification (b) recognition

(c) both (a) and (b) (d) image enhancement

4. The final layer of a CNN is called the

(a) fully connected layer (b) convolution layer

(c) pooling layer (d) None of these

5. Which among the following images around us are made up of 3 primary colors of Red, Green and Blue?

(a) Moving (b) Static

(c) Monochrome (d) Colored

6. Which of the following is commonly used in applications such as image retrieval and automated vehicle parking systems?

(a) Instance Segmentation (b) Object detection

(c) Localization (d) Classification

Very Short Answer Type Questions

7. How do computers store images?

8. Write the full form of ReLU.

9. What is object detection?

Short Answer Type Questions

10. What do you mean by image feature?

11. Mention any two functions of convolution operator.

Long Answer Type Questions

12. Explain three important applications of computer vision in details.

13. Explain the meaning of convolution. How does convolution works?

CHAPTER 06

Natural Language Processing

Natural Language Processing (NLP) bridges the gap between human language and machine understanding. It empowers computers to interpret, manipulate, and generate human language in meaningful ways. This field is essential for applications ranging from voice assistants to sentiment analysis, transforming how we interact with technology.

Computer languages are used to communicate with computers. Examples include Python, C++, Java, and HTML.

Computers do not understand human language directly. They require specific instructions, called programs, to process input. To bridge this gap, Natural Language Processing (NLP) helps convert human language into a format that computers can interpret.

Importance of NLP

Computers can only process electronic signals in binary form. Natural Language Processing (NLP) enables the conversion of human language into a digital format, making communication between humans and computer systems possible. It involves developing tools and techniques that enhance the interpretation of intent and context.

Demystifying Natural Language Processing (NLP)

Natural Language Processing (NLP) is a subfield of AI focused on enabling computers to analyze, understand, and process human language to extract meaningful information.

6.1 Applications of Natural Language Processing (NLP)

As Artificial Intelligence (AI) continues to integrate into our daily lives, Natural Language Processing (NLP) plays a crucial role in various real-world applications. Here are some key uses of NLP:

Voice Assistants

Voice assistants process natural speech, interpret it, and provide relevant responses. NLP enables these assistants to understand human language and perform tasks efficiently.

Examples

- Hey Google, set an alarm for 3:30 PM.
- Hey Alexa, play some music.
- Hey Siri, what's the weather today?

Auto-Generated Captions

NLP is used to convert spoken language into real-time text, improving accessibility for videos.

Examples

- Auto-generated captions on YouTube
- Live captions on Google Meet

Language Translation

NLP helps convert text or speech from one language to another, promoting seamless communication across languages.

Example

- Google Translate

Sentiment Analysis

Sentiment analysis determines whether a statement expresses a positive, negative, or neutral sentiment. Businesses use it to analyze customer emotions and improve services.

Applications of sentiment analysis is customer service (It helps in the automatic detections of emotions when customers interact with products, services or brands), voice of the customer (It measures the gap between what customers expect and what they actually experience when they use the products or services).

Now, let's understand Sentiment Analysis in detail using the Orange Data Mining tool.

Follow the given link to understand the technique.

Case Walkthrough Stepsinvolved in project development

Short Link https://bit.ly/OrangeNLP

Long Link
https://drive.google.com/drive/u/2/folders/1geFLXxV5890kfcakMfEg_KsH1LPcS_Iz

Or Scan the QR code provided along side.

Text Classification

This process categorizes documents or sentences into predefined groups such as News, Sports, or Politics. It helps in organizing large amounts of text-based information.

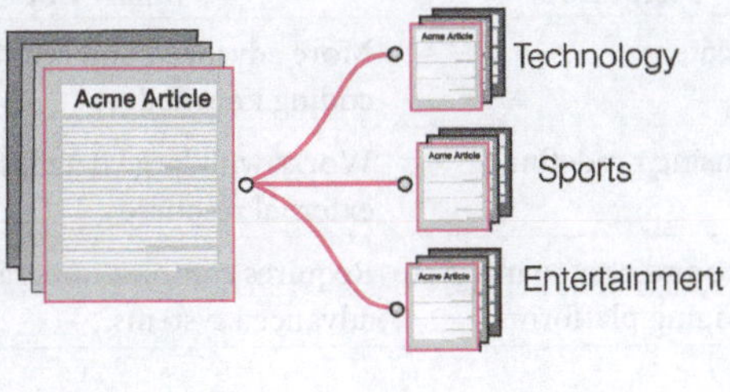

Keyword Extraction

Keyword extraction identifies the most relevant words or phrases in a text. Businesses use it to gain insights from customer feedback on social media, helping improve customer service. NLP continues to enhance human-computer interaction, making technology more intuitive and accessible.

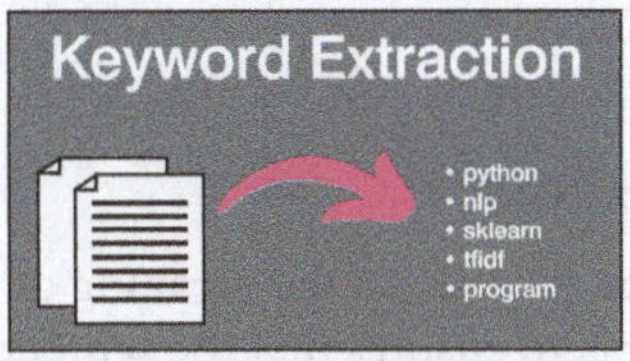

6.2 Stages of Natural Language Processing (NLP)

Natural Language Processing (NLP) consists of multiple stages, each playing a crucial role in analyzing and interpreting human language. The main stages include:

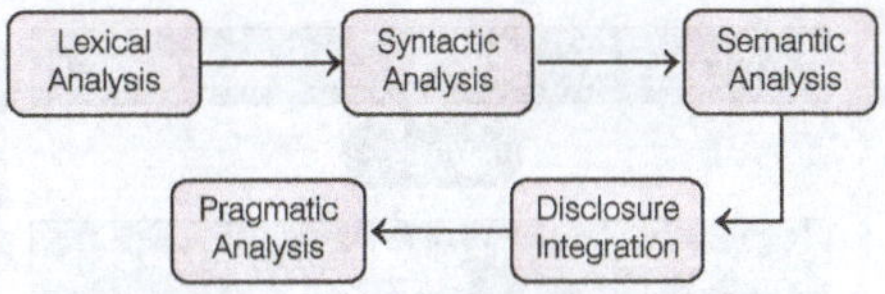

Lexical Analysis

This stage involves breaking down large chunks of text into meaningful units, such as sentences, words, and phrases. The lexicon refers to the vocabulary used in a language. By structuring the text, NLP can process it more efficiently.

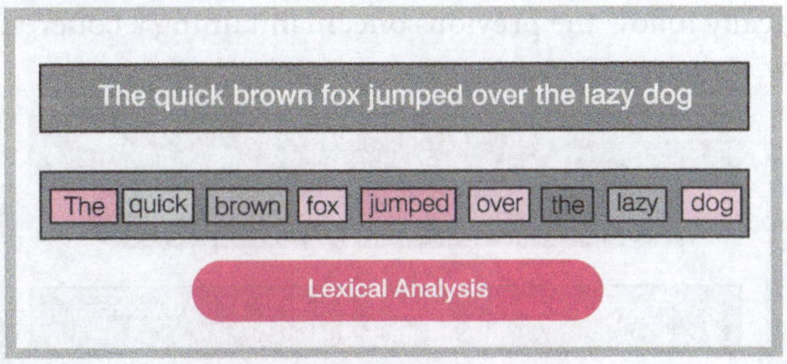

Lengthy text is broken down into **chunks**.

Syntactic Analysis (Parsing)

Here, the system checks whether a sentence follows grammatical rules. It examines the arrangement of words and their relationship within a sentence to ensure correctness. If a sentence is grammatically incorrect, it is discarded.

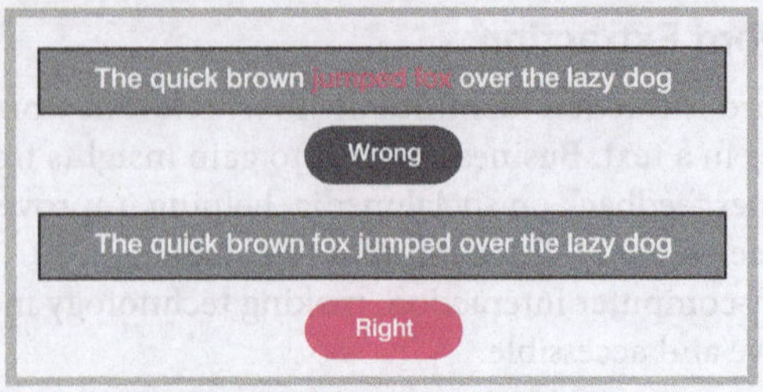

The grammar is correct.

Semantic Analysis

At this stage, the focus is on the meaning of words and phrases. The system ensures that the sentence conveys a meaningful message.

Example

- A phrase like "hot ice cream" would be rejected as it contradicts logical meaning.
- "The fox jumped into the dog" does not make sense and would be flagged as incorrect.

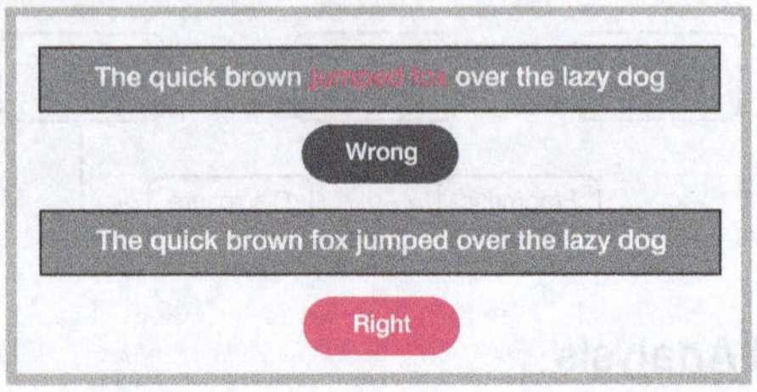

Sentence make actual sense.

Discourse Integration

This step ensures that sentences are connected and contribute to the overall context. Each sentence should logically follow the previous one, maintaining a coherent flow.

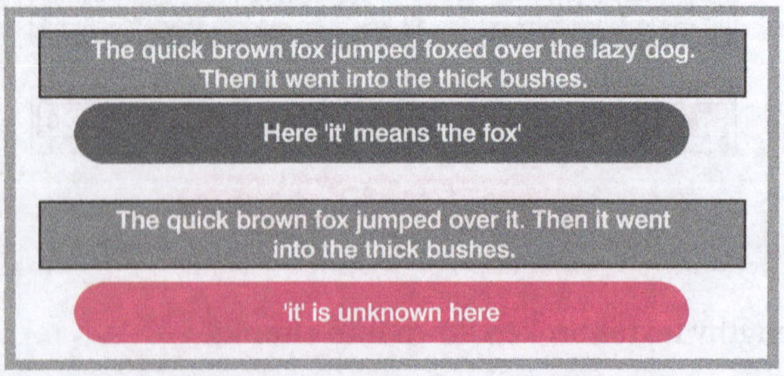

The flow of words makes sense.

Pragmatic Analysis

Finally, NLP evaluates the practical meaning of a sentence. It interprets the intended message rather than just the literal meaning. This stage helps determine whether the text is relevant and makes sense in real-world scenarios.

Each of these stages contributes to making NLP more effective in understanding and processing human language accurately.

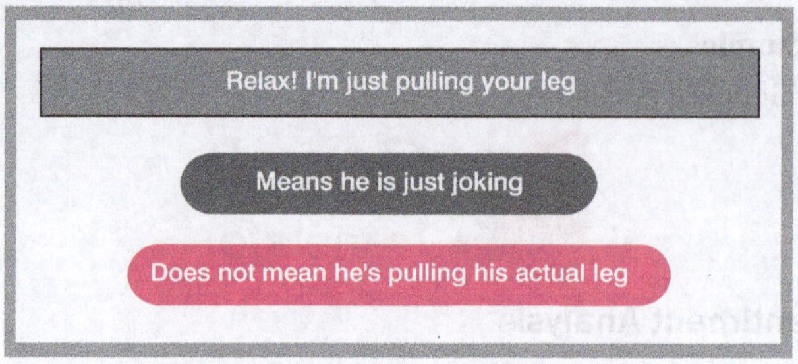

The intended meaning has been achieved.

Try These 6.1

1. I am so tired; I want to take a .... ? **NCERT**
   (a) break (b) brake
2. Let's .... her a letter **NCERT**
   (a) right (b) write
3. Syntax refers to the grammatical structure of a sentence.
   (a) Yes (b) No **NCERT**
4. Which technique is used to assess the meaningfulness of the input text? **NCERT**
   (a) Pragmatic analysis (b) Lexical analysis
   (c) Semantic analysis (d) Discourse integration

6.3 Chatbots

Chatbot is a computer program that simulates and processes human conversation (either written or spoken), allowing humans to interact with digital devices as if they were communicating with a real person.

Chatbots can be as simple as rudimentary programs that answer a simple query with a single-line response, or as sophisticated as digital assistants that learn and evolve to deliver increasing levels of personalization as they gather and process information.

Types of Chatbots

We can state that there are two types of chatbots around us which are as follows

Script Bot Vs Smart Bot

Script Bot	Smart Bot
Easy to create.	More advanced and requires coding knowledge.
Operates using predefined scripts.	Works with large databases and external resources.
Mostly free and easy to integrate with messaging platforms.	Requires complex integration with advanced systems.

Script Bot	Smart Bot
Has little to no natural language processing (NLP) capabilities.	Uses NLP and AI to improve interactions.
Limited functionality.	Offers wide and flexible functionality.
Does not learn from data.	Learns and improves over time with more data.
Example customer support chatbots and FAQ bots.	**Example** virtual assistants like Siri, Google, Assistant and advanced customer service chatbots.

Info Wall

Ruuh is an entertainment chatbot that focuses on humor, Bollywood, music, and other forms of entertainment. She is English-speaking and was created for an urban Indian audience.

6.4 Text Processing

Humans communicate effortlessly using natural languages, understanding and responding with ease. However, for computers, human languages are highly complex. As you have already explored some of the challenges in human language processing, let's now examine how Natural Language Processing (NLP) enables machines to interpret and generate human-like language.

Since computers operate using numerical data, the first step in NLP involves converting text into numerical form. This process requires multiple steps, beginning with Text Normalization.

Text Normalisation

It is a pre-processing step aimed at improving the quality of the text and making it suitable for machines to process.

Text Normalization involves a series of steps to transform raw text into a standardized format, suitable for downstream processing. This process operates on a corpus, which represents the aggregated textual data from multiple documents.

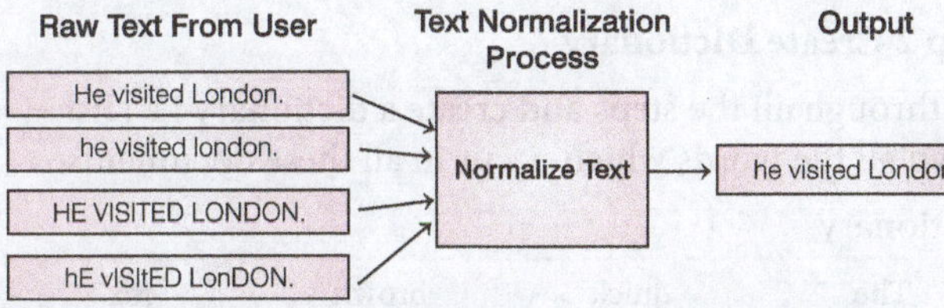

There are various steps in text normalisation as follows :

(i) **Sentence Segmentation** Sentence segmentation is the process of dividing a whole text into individual sentences. Sentence segmentation is crucial for various NLP tasks, including machine translation, text summarisation, and sentiment analysis, as it provides a foundational unit for analysis and processing.

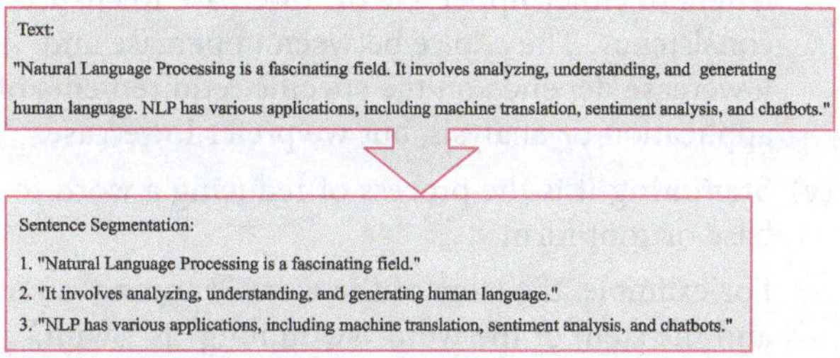

(ii) **Tokenization** Tokenization is the process of breaking down a piece of text into smaller units, such as words, phrases, symbols, or other meaningful elements.

Tokenisation is a fundamental step in various NLP tasks, enabling further analysis and processing of text data. It serves as the foundation for tasks like part-of-speech tagging, named entity recognition, and sentiment analysis.

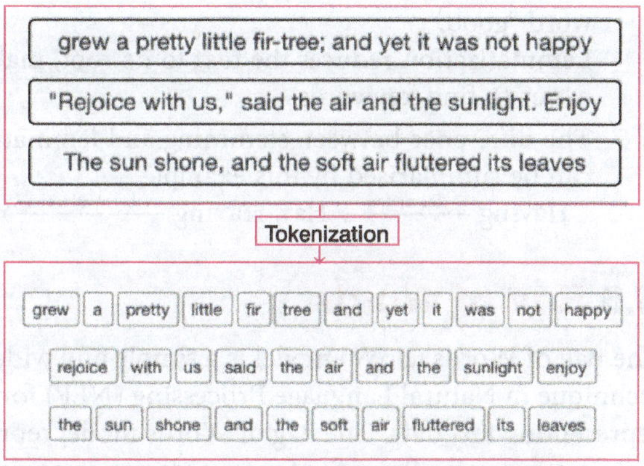

(iii) **Removing Stopwords, Special Characters and Numbers** By performing these steps, we can clean and prepare text data for further analysis or processing in natural language processing tasks, ensuring that only relevant information is retained.

Stopwords Stopwords are common words that often do not carry significant meaning in a sentence.

Examples of stopwords: "the", "is", "and", "to", "in", "a", "of", "that", "on".

Special Characters Special characters are symbols or punctuation marks that are not letters or numbers.

Examples of special characters: ".", ",", "!", "?", "(", ")", "-", "$", "%".

Numbers Numbers are numerical digits or sequences of digits.

Examples of numbers: "123", "3.14", "2024", "one", "two", "three".

(iv) **Converting Text to a Common Case** Converting text to a common case typically involves transforming all letters to either uppercase or lowercase to ensure consistency. The choice between uppercase and lowercase depends on the specific requirements of the application or analysis, but we prefer lowercase.

(v) **Stemming** It is the process of reducing a word to its base or root form.

For example, the stem of the word "running" is "run," and the stem of the word "swimming" is "swim." Stemming is often used in natural language processing tasks to standardise the text and improve the performance of algorithms.

(vi) **Lemmatization** It is the conversion of a word to its base form or lemma. This differs from stemming, which takes a word down to its root form by removing its prefixes and suffixes.
For example, the words "was," "is," and "will be" can all be lemmatized to the word "be." Similarly, the words "better" and "best" can be lemmatized to the word "good."
Lemmatization reduces the text to its root, making it easier to find keywords.

The difference between stemming and lemmatization can be summarised by this example

$$\text{Having} \xrightarrow{\text{Stemming}} \text{Hav, Having} \xrightarrow{\text{Lemmatization}} \text{Have}$$

6.5 Bag of Words

The Bag of Words (BoW) model is a simple and widely used technique in Natural Language Processing (NLP) for representing text data. The Bag of Words model represents text data as a collection of unique words, ignoring grammar, word order and convert the tokens into numbers.

The Bag of Words model provides a simple yet effective representation of text data, allowing for quantitative analysis and machine learning applications.

However, it's important to be aware of its limitations and consider enhancements or alternative models for text processing tasks.

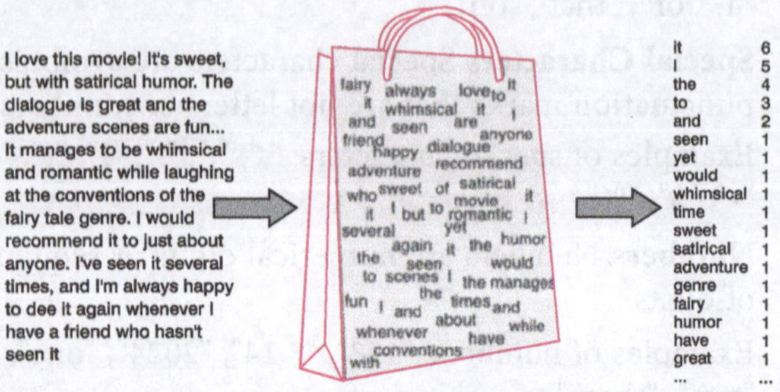

This image gives us a brief overview about how bag of words works. Let us assume that the text on the left in this image is the normalised corpus (a large set of text) which we have got after going through all the steps of text processing.

Now, as we put this text into the bag of words algorithm, the algorithm returns to us the unique words out of the corpus and their occurrence in it.

You can see at the right; it shows us a list of words appearing in the corpus and the numbers corresponding to it shows how many times the word has occurred in the text body. Thus, we can say that the bag of words gives us two things.

1. A vocabulary of words for the corpus.
2. The frequency of these words in the corpus.

The step-by-step approach to implement the Bag of Words algorithm as under :

(a) **Text Normalisation** Collect the data and pre-process it

(b) **Create Dictionary** Make a list of all the unique words occurring in the corpus

(c) **Create Document Vectors** For each document in the corpus, find out how many times the word from the unique list of words has occurred.

(d) Create document vectors for all the documents.

Example

Step 1 Collect data and pre-process it

Let's consider a simple corpus of two documents:

- **Document 1** "The quick brown fox"
- **Document 2** "The lazy dog jumps over the lazy fox"

After text normalisation, the text becomes

- **Document 1** [The, quick, brown, fox]
- **Document 2** [The, lazy, dog, jumps, over, the, lazy, fox]

Step 2 Create Dictionary

Go through all the steps and create a dictionary i.e., list down all the words which occur in all these documents.

Dictionary

The	quick	brown	fox
lazy	dog	jumps	over

There is a vocabulary of 8 words from the corpus containing 12 words. This is because some words though repeated in the documents are written just once while creating the dictionary.

Step 3 Create Document Vectors

In this step, the vocabulary is written in the first column. In the second column for each word in the document, if it matches the vocabulary, put a 1 in front of it and if the word appears again, increase the previous value by 1. If the word does not occur in that document put a 0 under it.

Create document vectors for all the documents. Hence, the table becomes:

	The	quick	brown	fox	lazy	dog	jumps	over
doc 1	1	1	1	1	0	0	0	0
doc 2	2	0	0	1	2	1	1	1

Now, the crucial step is converting the text tokens into numerical representations. This is often done using TF-IDF.

TF-IDF Term Frequency & Inverse Document Frequency

Term Frequency-Inverse Document Frequency (TF-IDF) is a numerical statistic used in information retrieval and text mining to evaluate the importance of a word in a document relative to a collection of documents. TF-IDF helps us identify the value of each word.

Term Frequency (TF)

Term Frequency measures the frequency of a term (word) in a document.

It's calculated as the ratio of the number of times a term appears in a document to the total number of terms in the document.

Inverse Document Frequency (IDF)

- Inverse Document Frequency measures the importance of a term across a collection of documents.
- It's calculated as the logarithm of the ratio of the total number of documents to the number of documents containing the term, adjusted by 1 to avoid division by zero for terms that appear in all documents.

$$\text{IDF}(t) = \log\left(\frac{\text{Total number of documents}}{\text{Number of documents containing term } t}\right) + 1$$

Example

- Total number of documents in the collection: 10,000
- Number of documents containing "brown": 3

Inverse Document Frequency of "brown": IDF

$$(\text{"brown"}) = \log\left(\frac{10000}{3}\right) + 1$$

Applications of TFIDF are as follows

- **Document Classification** Helps in classifying the type and genre of a document.
- **Topic Modelling** It helps in predicting the topic for a corpus.
- **Information Retrieval System** To extract the important information out of a corpus.
- **Stop word filtering** Helps in removing the unnecessary words out of a text body

Examples of Code and No-code NLP Tools

We have already explored sentiment analysis, an application of NLP, using the No-code tool Orange Data Mining. Now, let's delve into both Code and No-code tools for NLP.

Code NLP

1. **NLTK package** Natural Language Tool Kit or NLTK is a package readily available for text processing in Python. The package contains functions and modules which can be used for Natural Language Processing.
2. **SpaCy** SpaCy is an open-source natural language processing (NLP) library designed to build NLP applications. It offers various features such astokenization, part-of- speech tagging, named entity recognition, dependency parsing, and more.

No-Code NLP

1. **Orange Data Mining** It is a machine learning tool for data analysis through Python and visual programming. We can perform operations on data through simple drag-and-drop steps.
2. **MonkeyLearn** MonkeyLearn is a text analysis platform that offers NLP tools and machine learning models for text analysis, supporting tasks such as classification, sentiment analysis, and entity recognition. Users can create custom models or use pre- trained ones for tasks like social media monitoring and customer feedback analysis.

Try These 6.2

1 **What do you understand by the term text processing?**

2 **List down the application of NLTK.**

3 **Give examples of the following:**

(a) Sentence tokenisation

(b) Phrase tokenisation

(c) Lemmatisation

Glossary

Natural Language Processing (NLP) It is a branch of Artificial Intelligence (AI) that enables computers to understand, interpret, and generate human language.

Text classification It involves categorising text documents into predefined categories or classes based on their content.

Text summarisation It involves condensing large volumes of text into shorter summaries while preserving the most important information and key points.

Tokenisation It is the process of breaking down a piece of text into smaller units, such as words, phrases, symbols, or other meaningful elements.

Stemming It is the process of reducing words to their root or base form. It involves removing suffixes or prefixes from words to obtain the core meaning.

Bag of Words (BoW) It is a fundamental Natural Language Processing (NLP) technique used to convert text into numerical data for machine learning models.

Inverse Document Frequency (IDF) It measures how important a word is by reducing the weight of common words across documents.

Term Frequency (TF) It measures how after a word appears in a document.

ACTIVITY Time

ACTIVITY 1 : Keyword Extraction

Purpose

To understand how to use an API for keyword extraction from a website.

Introduction

Say

"Keyword extraction in NLP involves automatically identifying and extracting the most important words or phrases from a piece of text.

These keywords represent the main topics or themes within the text and are useful for tasks like document summarization, information retrieval, and content analysis."

Steps To perform the activity

Step 1 Visit the Website

Go to: Google Cloud Natural Language API

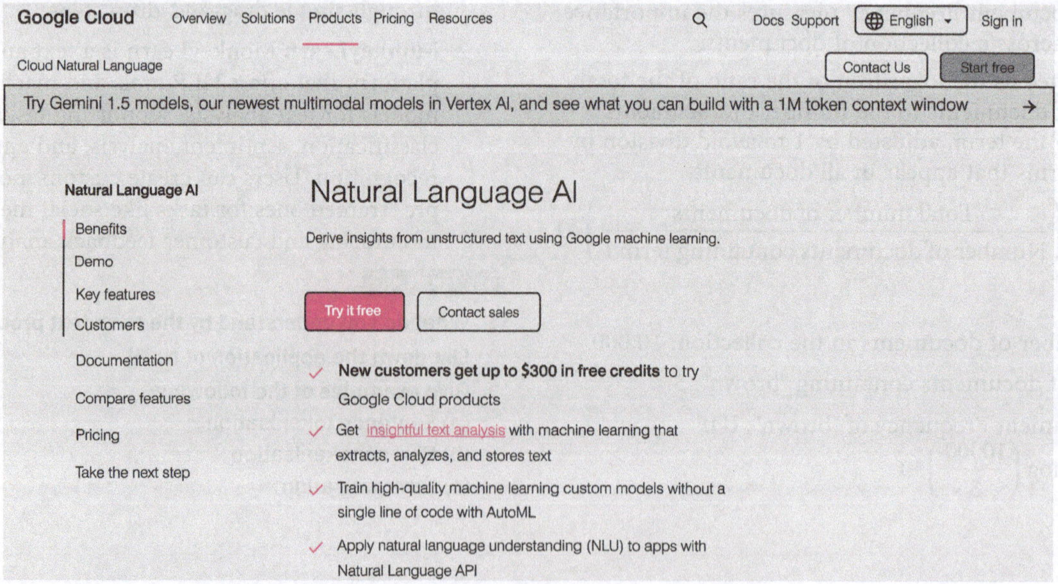

Step 2 Analyze the Text

1. Click on the "Analyze" button.

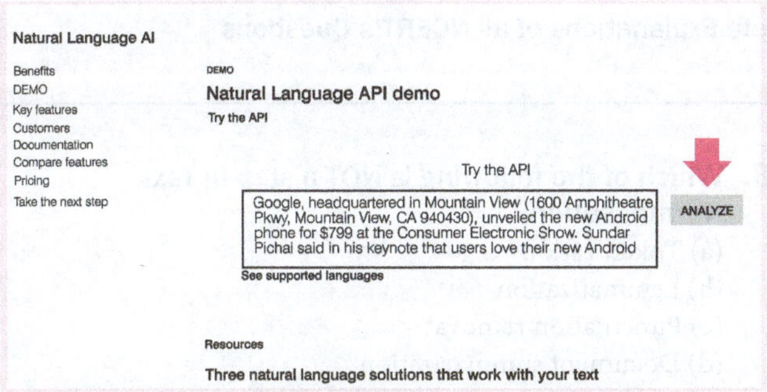

2. Observe the highlighted keywords in different colors (e.g., Google, Mountain View, etc.).
3. Try clicking on different options to see how the output changes.

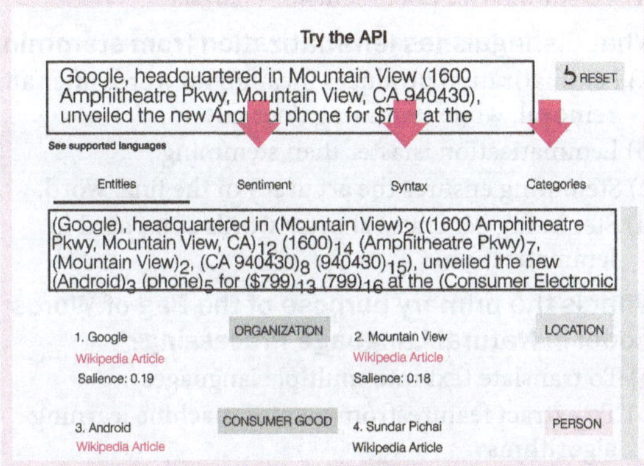

Step 3 Experiment with Your Own Text

1. Enter a custom paragraph in the text box.
2. Click "Analyze" again to check the extracted keywords.
3. Observe how the tool highlights key terms and identifies themes in your text.

By the end of this activity, you will understand how NLP-based keyword extraction works and how it helps in summarizing content efficiently.

ACTIVITY 2 : Play with Chatbots

One of the most widely used applications of Natural Language Processing (NLP) is a chatbot. A chatbot is a software program designed to simulate human conversation through text or voice interactions. Over time, it learns to improve its responses, making interactions more efficient.

Chatbots can

- Answer customer queries and troubleshoot problems.
- Qualify potential customers and generate leads.
- Assist in increasing sales on e-commerce platforms.

ELIZA

Mitsuku

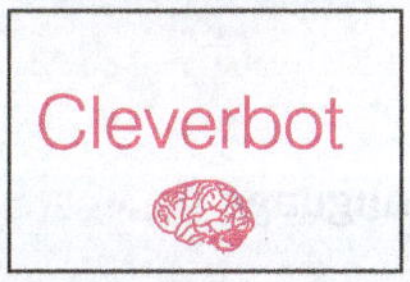

Cleverbot

Singtel

Try Out These Chatbots:

Elizabot https://www.masswerk.at/elizabot/

Mitsuki https://www.kuki.ai/

Cleverbot https://www.cleverbot.com/

Singtel https://www.singtel.com/personal/support

Discussion Questions

- Which chatbot did you try? Name one.
- What is the main purpose of this chatbot?
- How was your experience interacting with it?
- Did the chatbot feel more like a human or a robot? Why?
- Did you notice if the chatbot had a specific personality?

NCERT FOLDER

Complete Explanations of all NCERT's Questions

A. Multiple Choice Questions

1. Natural Language Processing majorly deals with ______ processing.
(a) Numeric data
(b) Textual data
(c) Image data
(d) Visual data

2. ______ is an NLP tool to express an opinion, whether the underlying sentiment is positive, negative, or neutral.
(a) Text Classification
(b) Machine Translation
(c) Sentiment Analysis
(d) Automatic Text Summarization

3. What is the first stage of Natural Language Processing (NLP)?
(a) Semantic Analysis
(b) Pragmatic Analysis
(c) Lexical Analysis
(d) Syntactic Analysis

4. Words that we want to filter out before doing any analysis of the text are called ______ .
(a) Rare words
(b) Stop words
(c) Frequent words
(d) Filter words

5. What does discourse integration involve in the context of sentence formation?
(a) Identifying individual words in a sentence
(b) Forming a coherent story within a sentence
(c) Establishing relationships between preceding and succeeding sentences
(d) Applying punctuation and grammar rules to a sentence

6. What is the primary challenge faced by computers in understanding human languages?
(a) Complexity of human languages
(b) Lack of computational power
(c) Incompatibility with numerical data
(d) Limited vocabulary

7. How do voice assistants utilize NLP?
(a) To analyze visual data
(b) To process numerical data
(c) To understand natural language
(d) To execute tasks based on computer code

8. Which of the following is NOT a step in Text Normalisation?
(a) Tokenization
(b) Lemmatization
(c) Punctuation removal
(d) Document summarization

9. In the context of text processing, what is the purpose of tokenisation?
(a) To convert text into numerical data
(b) To segmentsentencesinto smaller units
(c) To translate text into multiple languages
(d) To summarize documentsfor analysis

10. What distinguishes lemmatization from stemming?
(a) Lemmatization produces meaningful words after affix removal, while stemming does not.
(b) Lemmatization isfaster than stemming.
(c) Stemming ensures the accuracy of the final word.
(d) Stemming generates shorter words compared to lemmatization.

11. What is the primary purpose of the Bag of Words model in Natural Language Processing?
(a) To translate text into multiple languages
(b) To extract featuresfrom text for machine learning algorithms
(c) To summarize documentsfor analysis
(d) To remove punctuation marksfrom text

12. In the context of text processing, what are stop words?
(a) Words with the frequent occurrence in the corpus
(b) Words with negligible value that are often removed during preprocessing
(c) Words with the lowest occurrence in the corpus
(d) Words with the most value added to the corpus

13. What is the characteristic of rare or valuable words in the described plot?
(a) They have the highest occurrence in the corpus
(b) They are often considered stop words
(c) They occur the least but add the most value to the corpus
(d) They are typically removed during preprocessing

14. What information doesthe document vector table provide?
(a) The frequency of each word across all documents
(b) The frequency of each word in a single document
(c) The total number of words in the entire corpus
(d) The average word length in the entire corpus

15. What is the primary purpose of TFIDF in text processing?

(a) To identify the presence of stop wordsin documents
(b) To remove punctuation marksfrom text
(c) To identify the value of each word in a document
(d) To translate text into multiple languages

16. Assertion: Pragmatic analysis in natural language processing (NLP) involves assessing sentences for their practical applicability in real-world scenarios.

Reasoning: Pragmatic analysis requires understanding the intended meaning behind sentences and considering their practical or logical implications, rather than solely relying on literal word meanings obtained from semantic analysis.

(a) Both Assertion and Reasoning are true, and Reasoning is the correct explanation of the Assertion.
(b) Assertion is true, but Reasoning is false.
(c) Both Assertion and Reasoning are true, but Reasoning is not the correct explanation of the Assertion.
(d) Assertion is false, but Reasoning is true.

17. Assertion: Converting the entire text into lowercase following stop word removal is a crucial preprocessing step in natural language processing.

Reasoning: This process ensures uniformity in word representation, preventing the machine from treating words with different cases as distinct entities, thereby enhancing the accuracy of subsequent text analysis.

(a) Both Assertion and Reasoning are true, and Reasoning is the correct explanation of the Assertion.
(b) Assertion is true, but Reasoning is false.
(c) Both Assertion and Reasoning are true, but Reasoning is not the correct explanation of the Assertion.
(d) Assertion is false, but Reasoning is true.

Answers

1. (b)	2. (c)	3. (c)	4. (b)	5. (c)
6. (a)	7. (c)	8. (d)	9. (b)	10. (a)
11. (b)	12. (b)	13. (c)	14. (b)	15. (c)
16. (a)	17. (a)			

B. Subjective Questions

1. Mention a few features of natural languages.

Ans. Ambiguity, context-dependence, variability, evolution, and large vocabulary.

2. What is the significance of NLP?

Ans. NLP enables computers to understand and process human language, facilitating communication, automation, and information extraction.

3. What do you mean by lexical analysis in NLP?

Ans. Lexical analysis in NLP is the process of breaking down text into its smallest meaningful units (tokens), like words and phrases, to prepare it for further processing.

4. What do you mean by a chatbot?

Ans. Chatbot is a computer program that simulates and processes human conversation (either written or spoken). allowing humans to interact with digital devices as if they were communicating with a real person.

Chatbots can be as simple as rudimentary programs that answer a simple query with a single-line response, or as sophisticated as digital assistants that learn and evolve to deliver increasing levels of personalization as they gather and process information.

5. What does the term "Bag of Words" refer to in Natural Language Processing (NLP)?

Ans. It's a text representation that describes the occurrence of words within a document, disregarding grammar and word order, focusing on word frequency.

6. Describe two practical uses of Natural Language Processing in real-world scenarios.

Ans. **Sentiment Analysis** Analyzing customer reviews or social media posts to understand public opinion about products or services.

Chatbots/Virtual Assistants Providing automated customer support or answering queries through natural language conversations.

7. Explain the process of stemming and lemmatization in text processing, supported by an example.

Ans. **Stemming** Stemming is a rule-based process that removes prefixes or suffixes from words to obtain their root form. However, the stemmed word may not always be a valid dictionary word.

Example

- Words: "running," "runner," "runs"
- Stemmed Output: "run"

Lemmatization Lemmatization is a more accurate process that converts a word into its dictionary form (lemma) by considering its meaning and grammatical role.

Example

- Word: "better" → Lemmatized to: "good"
- Word: "mice" → Lemmatized to: "mouse"
- Word: "caring" → Lemmatized to: "care"

8. Describe any four applications of TFIDF.

Ans. **Applications of TFIDF are**

1. Document Classification
   - Helps in categorizing documents based on their content.
   - Example: Identifying whether a document belongs to "sports," "technology," or "politics" based on keyword importance.

2. Topic Modeling
   - Helps in identifying the main topics discussed in a large collection of texts (corpus).
   - Example: Grouping news articles into topics like "finance," "health," and "education" using TF-IDF scores.
3. Information Retrieval System
   - Extracts relevant documents based on user queries by ranking their importance.
   - Example: Search engines like Google use TF-IDF to find the most relevant web pages for a given search term.
4. Stop Word Filtering
   - Helps remove common, less meaningful words (e.g., "the," "is," "and") that do not contribute to understanding the document's content.
   - Example: In text summarization, TF-IDF helps focus on important words while ignoring common stop words.

9. Samiksha, a student of class X was exploring the Natural Language Processing domain. She got stuck while performing the text normalisation. Help her to normalise the text on the segmented sentences given below:
Document 1: Akash and Ajay are best friends.
Document 2: Akash likesto play football but Ajay prefers to play online games.

Ans. Text normalization is the process of transforming text into a standard format for Natural Language Processing (NLP). It includes lowercasing, tokenization, removing stop words, stemming/lemmatization, and handling punctuation.

Here's how Samiksha can normalize the given text:

Step 1 Convert to Lowercase
- **Document 1** akash and ajay are best friends.
- **Document 2** akash likes to play football but ajay prefers to play online games.

Step 2 Tokenization (Splitting into Words)
- **Document 1** ['akash', 'and', 'ajay', 'are', 'best', 'friends']
- **Document 2** ['akash', 'likes', 'to', 'play', 'football', 'but', 'ajay', 'prefers', 'to', 'play', 'online', 'games']

Step 3 Remove Stop Words (Common Words like 'and', 'are', 'to', 'but')
- **Document 1** ['akash', 'ajay', 'best', 'friends']
- **Document 2** ['akash', 'likes', 'play', 'football', 'ajay', 'prefers', 'play', 'online', 'games']

Step 4 Stemming or Lemmatization

Using lemmatization (more accurate than stemming):
- "likes" → "like"
- "prefers" → "prefer"
- "games" → "game"

Final normalized text:
- **Document 1** ['akash', 'ajay', 'best', 'friend']
- **Document 2** ['akash', 'like', 'play', 'football', 'ajay', 'prefer', 'play', 'online', 'game']

10. Through a step-by-step process, calculate TFIDF for the given corpus
Document 1: Johny Johny Yes Papa, **Document 2: Eating sugar? No Papa**
Document 3: Telling lies? No Papa **Document 4: Open your mouth, Ha! Ha! Ha!**

Ans. Step-by-Step Calculation of TF-IDF for the Given Corpus

Given Documents:
1. Document 1: Johny Johny, Yes Papa
2. Document 2: Eating sugar? No Papa
3. Document 3: Telling lies? No Papa
4. Document 4: Open your mouth, Ha! Ha! Ha!

1. Create Document Vectors (Term Frequency Table - TF)

Term	Johny	Yes	Papa	Eating	Sugar	No	Telling	Lies	Open	Your	Mouth	Ha
D1	2	1	1	0	0	0	0	0	0	0	0	0
D2	0	0	1	1	1	1	0	0	0	0	0	0
D3	0	0	1	0	0	1	1	1	0	0	0	0
D4	0	0	0	0	0	0	0	0	1	1	1	3

2. Document Frequency Table (DF)

The document frequency (DF) represents the number of documents in which a word appears.

Term	Johny	Yes	Papa	Eating	Sugar	No	Telling	Lies	Open	Your	Mouth	Ha
DF	1	1	3	1	1	2	1	1	1	1	1	1

3. Compute Inverse Document Frequency (IDF)

The inverse document frequency (IDF) is calculated using the formula:

$$\text{IDF}(W) = \log\left(\frac{N}{DF(W)}\right)$$

where N = 4 (total number of documents).

Term	Johny	Yes	Papa	Eating	Sugar	No	Telling	Lies	Open	Your	Mouth	Ha
IDF	4/1	4/1	4/3	4/1	4/1	4/2	4/1	4/1	4/1	4/1	4/1	4/1

4. Compute TF-IDF

The TF-IDF is calculated using the formula:

$$\text{TFIDF (W)} = \text{TF (W)} \times \log \text{(IDF (W))}$$

Term	Johny	Yes	Papa	Eating	Sugar	No	Telling	Lies	Open	Your	Mouth	Ha
D1	2×log(4/1)	1×log(4/1)	1×log(4/3)	0×log(4/1)	0×log(4/1)	0×log(4/2)	0×log(4/1)	0×log(4/1)	0×log(4/1)	0×log(4/1)	0×log(4/1)	0×log(4/1)
D2	0×log(4/1)	0×log(4/1)	1×log(4/3)	1×log(4/1)	1×log(4/1)	1×log(4/2)	0×log(4/1)	0×log(4/1)	0×log(4/1)	0×log(4/1)	0×log(4/1)	0×log(4/1)
D3	0×log(4/1)	0×log(4/1)	1×log(4/3)	0×log(4/1)	0×log(4/1)	1×log(4/2)	1×log(4/1)	1×log(4/1)	0×log(4/1)	0×log(4/1)	0×log(4/1)	0×log(4/1)
D4	0×log(4/1)	0×log(4/1)	0×log(4/3)	0×log(4/1)	0×log(4/1)	0×log(4/2)	0×log(4/1)	0×log(4/1)	1×log(4/1)	1×log(4/1)	1×log(4/1)	3×log(4/1)

Thus, the TF-IDF matrix is computed successfully for the given corpus.

EXAM PATTERN EXERCISE

Including Competency Based Questions

Part I

Multiple Choice Questions

1. Google Translate is Google's free service that instantly translates words, phrases, and web pages between English and over 100 other languages. Google translate uses______.

(a) 4W problem canvas
(b) Neural Networks
(c) KWLH chart
(d) System maps

2. NLP lies in which of the following fields?

(a) Artificial intelligence
(b) Computer science
(c) Both (a) and (b)
(d) None of these

3. Which feature of NLP helps in understanding the emotions of the people mentioned with the feedback? SQP 2023-24

(a) Virtual assistants
(b) Sentiment analysis
(c) Text classification
(d) Automatic summarization

4. Which of the following is used for finding the frequency of words in some given text sample?

(a) Stemming
(b) Lemmatisation
(c) Bag of words
(d) None of these

5. Machine translation feature converts __________.
(a) One language to another
(b) Human language to machine language
(c) Any human language to Programming
(d) Machine language to human language

6. Which of the following comes under NLP?
(a) Chatbots (b) Price comparison websites
(c) Facial recognition (d) All of these

7. __________ is the NLTK tool in Python.
(a) Natural Linguistic Tool (b) Natural Language Toolkit
(c) Neutral Language Kit (d) Neutral Language Toolkit

8. Chatbots are AI systems which
(a) Interact with humans through text or speech
(b) Are able to offer round the clock responses and handle multiple queries simultaneously
(c) Both (a) and (b)
(d) Neither (a) nor (b)

9. What do we call the process of dividing a string into component words?
(a) Regression (b) Word Tokenisation
(c) Classification (d) Clustering

10. Sentence segment is the __________ step for building the NLP model.
(a) First (b) Second
(c) Third (d) Fourth

11. Which of these is not a stopwords?
(a) This (b) Things (c) Is (d) Do

12. What is the stem of the word "Making"?
(a) Mak (b) Make
(c) Making (d) Maker

13. What is the lemma of the word "Making"?
(a) Mak (b) Make (c) Making (d) Maker

14. Which algorithms result in two things, a vocabulary of words and frequency of the words in the corpus? **SQP 2023-24**
(a) Sentence segmentation (b) Tokenisation
(c) Bag of words (d) Text normalisation

15. Which of the following is the type of data used by NLP applications? **SQP 2022-23**
(a) Images (b) Numerical data
(c) Graphical data (d) Text and Speech

16. A corpus contains 12 documents. How many document vectors will be there for that corpus? **SQP 2022-23**
(a) 12 (b) 1
(c) 24 (d) 1/12

17. This real life application of NLP is used to provide an overview of a news item or blog post, while avoiding redundancy from multiple sources and maximising the diversity of content obtained. Which is this application? **Competency Based Ques.**
(a) Chatbot (b) Virtual Assistant
(c) Sentiment Analysis (d) Automatic Summarisation

18. Which of the following words represent an example of a lemma resulting from lemmatisation for "caring" in context to Natural Language Processing (NLP)? **2024**
(a) Care (b) Cared
(c) Cares (d) Car

19. Bag of Words is a.........model which helps in extracting features out of the text which can be helpful in machine learning algorithms. **2024**
(a) Data Science (DS)
(b) Virtual Reality (VR)
(c) Natural Language Processing (NLP)
(d) Computer Vision (CV)

20. Select the correct features of Smart Bot **2023**
(a) Smart-bots are flexible and powerful
(b) Coding is required to take this up on board
(c) Smart bots work on bigger databases and other resources directly
(d) All of the above

21. For .... the whole corpus is divided into sentences. Each sentence is taken as a different data so now the whole corpus gets reduced to sentences. **2023**
(a) Text Regulation (b) Sentence Segmentation
(c) Tokenisation (d) Stemming

22. A corpus contains 4 documents in which the words such as 'an, is, the' were appearing frequently. Identify the term that is used for such words. **2025**
(a) Stop word (b) Rare word
(c) Missing word (d) Removable word

23. Which application of NLP helps to provide an overview of a news item or blog post? It also avoids redundancy from multiple sources and maximises the diversity of content obtained. **2025**
(a) Virtual Assistants (b) Sentiment Analysis
(c) Text Classification (d) Automatic Summarization

24. Which of the following application of NLP (Natural Language Processing) is associated with spam filtering in e-mails? **2025**
(a) Virtual Assistants (b) Sentiment Analysis
(c) Text Classification (d) Automatic Summarization

25. In the context of NLP, which of the following words represents a stem resulting from stemming for "Studies"? **2025**
(a) Study (b) Stud (c) Studi (d) Studied

Answers

1. (b)	2. (c)	3. (b)	4. (c)	5. (a)
6. (a)	7. (b)	8. (c)	9. (b)	10. (a)
11. (b)	12. (a)	13. (b)	14. (c)	15. (d)
16. (a)	17. (d)	18. (a)	19. (c)	20. (d)
21. (b)	22. (a)	23. (d)	24. (c)	25. (c)

Statement Based Questions

1. **Statement 1 Natural language processing (NLP) is a subfield of Artificial Intelligence (AI).**

   Statement 2 This is a widely used technology for personal assistants that are used in various business fields/areas.

   (a) Both Statement 1 and Statement 2 are correct
   (b) Both Statement 1 and Statement 2 are incorrect
   (c) Statement 1 is correct but Statement 2 is incorrect
   (d) Statement 2 is correct but Statement 1 is incorrect

2. **Statement 1 Chatbot is a software application or web interface that is designed to mimic human conversation through text or voice interactions.**

   Statement 2 Modern chatbots are typically online and use generative artificial intelligence systems.

   (a) Both Statement 1 and Statement 2 are correct
   (b) Both Statement 1 and Statement 2 are incorrect
   (c) Statement1 is correct but Statement 2 is incorrect
   (d) Statement 2 is correct but Statement 1 is incorrect

3. **Statement 1 Companies can use tokenisation in a lot of ways such as to find out the emotions of their target audience.**

   Statement 2 Sentiment analysis, however, is able to recognise subtle nuances in emotions and opinions ? and determine how positive or negative they are.

   (a) Both Statement 1 and Statement 2 are correct
   (b) Both Statement 1 and Statement 2 are incorrect
   (c) Statement 1 is correct but Statement 2 is incorrect
   (d) Statement 2 is correct but Statement 1 is incorrect

4. **Statement 1 Text normalisation is a key step in natural language processing (NLP).**

   Statement 2 It involves cleaning and preprocessing text data to make it consistent and usable for different NLP tasks.

   (a) Both Statement 1 and Statement 2 are correct
   (b) Both Statement 1 and Statement 2 are incorrect
   (c) Statement 1 is correct but Statement 2 is incorrect
   (d) Statement 2 is correct but Statement1 is incorrect

Answers

1. (a) **2.** (a) **3.** (d) **4.** (a)

Assertion & Reason Based Questions

1. **Assertion (A) Stemming is a technique used to reduce an inflected word down to its word stem.**

   Reason (R) For example, the words "programming," "programmer," and "programs" can all be reduced down to the common word stem "program".

   (a) Both A and R are correct and R is the correct explanation of A
   (b) Both A and R are correct but R is not the correct explanation of A
   (c) A is correct but R is not correct
   (d) A is not correct but R is correct

2. **Assertion (A) Lemmatisation is the process of grouping together the different inflected forms of a word so they can be analysed as a single item.**

   Reason (R) Lemmatisation is similar to stemming but it brings context to the words.

   (a) Both A and R are correct and R is the correct explanation of A
   (b) Both A and R are correct but R is not the correct explanation of A
   (c) A is correct but R is not correct
   (d) A is not correct but R is correct

3. **Assertion (A) The bag of words model is a simple way to convert words to numerical representation in natural language processing.**

   Reason (R) This model is a simple document embedding technique based on word frequency.

   (a) Both A and R are correct and R is the correct explanation of A
   (b) Both A and R are correct but R is not the correct explanation of A
   (c) A is correct but R is not correct
   (d) A is not correct but R is correct

4. **Assertion (A) TF-IDF is a natural language processing (NLP) technique that's used to evaluate the importance of different words in a sentence.**

   Reason (R) It's useful in text classification and for helping a machine learning model read words.

   (a) Both A and R are correct and R is the correct explanation of A
   (b) Both A and R are correct but R is not the correct explanation of A
   (c) A is correct but R is not correct
   (d) A is not correct but R is correct

Answers

1. (a) **2.** (a) **3.** (a) **4.** (a)

Part II

Very Short Answer Type Questions

1. What is NLP? 2022

Ans. NLP is a field of artificial intelligence focused on the interaction between computers and humans through natural language.

2. Name any two commonly used applications of NLP. 2022

Ans. Sentiment analysis, language translation

3. Name the process of dividing whole corpus into sentences. 2022

Ans. Sentence segmentation

4. Identify the given chat bot type:

It learns from its environment and experience. It also builds on its capabilities based on the knowledge. These can collaborate with humans, working alongside them and learning their behaviour. Competency Based Ques.

Ans. Smart bot

5. What NLP stands for?

Ans. Natural Language Processing

6. What is a chatbot?

Ans. Chatbots are computer programs designed to simulate conversation with human users.

7. Ayushi was learning about NLP. She wanted to know the term used for the whole textual data from all the documents altogether. Help her in identifying the term used for it. Competency Based Ques.

Ans. Corpus

8. What is the full form of TF-IDF? SQP 2022-23

Ans. Term Frequency Inverse Document Frequency

9. Identify the type of chatbot with the information given below Competency Based Ques.

These bots work on pre-programmed instructions inside the application/machine and are generally easy to develop. They are deployed in the customer care section of various companies. Their job is to answer some basic queries that they are coded for and connect them to human executives once they are unable to handle the conversation.

Ans. Script bot

10. What will be the output of the word "studies" if we do the following: SQP 2021-22

(a) Lemmatization

(b) Stemming

Ans. (a) The output of the word after lemmatization will be study.

(b) The output of the word after stemming will be study.

11. How many tokens are there in the sentence given below? Competency Based Ques.

Traffic Jams have become a common part of our lives nowadays. Living in an urban area means you have to face traffic each and every time you get out on the road. Mostly, school students opt for buses to go to school.

Ans. 46 tokens are there in the given sentence.

12. Identify any 2 stopwords in the given sentence:

Pollution is the introduction of contaminants into the natural environment that cause adverse change. The three types of pollution are air pollution, water pollution and land pollution. Competency Based Ques.

Ans. Stopwords in the given sentence are: is, the, of, that, into, are, and

13. Which type of Chabot has a wide functionality, is flexible and powerful, and word on bigger databases directly? 2025

Ans. Smart chatbot

Short Answer Type Questions

1. What is Tokenisation? Count how many tokens are present in the following statement:

I find that the harder I work, the more luck I seem to have. 2022

Ans. Tokenisation is the process of breaking down text into individual words or tokens. In the given statement, there are 14 tokens: "I", "find", "that", "the", "harder", "I", "work", "the", "more", "luck", "I", "seem", "to" "have".

2. Kaira, a beginner in the field of NLP is trying to understand the process of stemming. Help her in filling up the following table by suggesting appropriate affixes and stem of the words mentioned there:

S.No.	Word	Affixes	Stem
1	Tries		
2	Learning		

Competency Based Ques.

Ans.

S.No.	Word	Affixes	Stem
1	Tries	es	Tri
2	Learning	ing	Learn

3. Explain the following picture which depicts one of the processes on NLP. Also mention the purpose which will be achieved by this process. 2022

HELLO	HeLlo	HELLLo	hELLO	hElLO	HellO

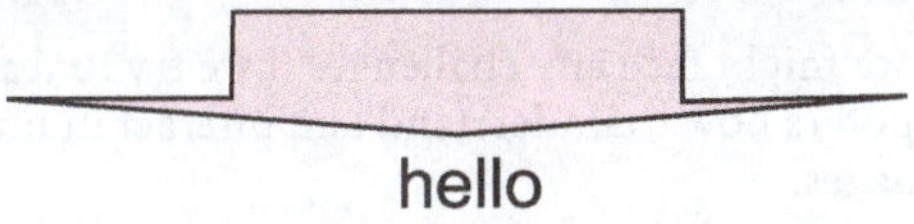

Ans. The process depicted is case normalisation, where all letters are converted to lowercase for consistency. The purpose achieved by this process is to ensure that text processing algorithms treat words with different capitalisations as equivalent, thus improving accuracy in tasks like word frequency counting or search.

4. Identify any two stop words which should not be removed from the given sentence and why?

Get help and support whether you're shopping now or need help with a past purchase.

Contact us at abc@pwershel.com or on our website <u>www.pwershel.com</u> SQP 2023-24

Ans. Two stopwords in the given sentence which should not be removed are:

@ (at), . (fullstop)

In the above sentence, these tokens are part of email id. removing these tokens may lead to invalid website address and email ID. So these words should not be removed from the above sentence.

5. What will be the results of conversion of the term, 'happily' in the process of stemming and lemmatisation? Which process takes longer time for execution? SQP 2022-23

Ans. In stemming, the term "happily" would typically be reduced to its root form, which might result in "happi" or "happi." Stemming operates by removing suffixes or prefixes to reduce a word to its base or root form.

In lemmatisation, however, the term "happily" would be converted to its lemma, which is the base or dictionary form of the word. In this case, "happily" would likely be lemmatised to "happy."

In terms of execution time, lemmatisation generally takes longer than stemming.

6. What do we get from the "bag of words" algorithm? SQP 2022-23

Ans. Bag of words gives us two things

1. A vocabulary of words for the corpus
2. The frequency of these words (number of times it has occurred in the whole corpus)

7. Write any two applications of TF-IDF. SQP 2021-22

Or With reference to data processing, expand the term TF-IDF. Also give any two applications of TF-IDF. 2023

Ans. TF-IDF - Term Frequency - Inverse Document Frequency

1. Document Classification

   Helps in classifying the type and genre of a document.

2. Topic Modelling

   It helps in predicting the topic for a corpus.

8. Write down the steps to implement bag of words algorithm. SQP 2021-22

Ans. The steps to implement bag of words algorithm are as follows

1. **Text Normalisation** Collect data and pre-process it
2. **Create Dictionary** Make a list of all the unique words occurring in the corpus. (Vocabulary)
3. **Create document vectors** For each document in the corpus, find out how many times the word from the unique list of words has occurred.
4. Create document vectors for all the documents.

9. What are the primary differences between Script-bots and Smart-bots? 2024,2022

Ans. Script bots are pre-programmed with a specific use case in mind. They cannot functionally 'learn' or change. Smart bots leverage AI to adapt and perform a wide array of complex stats, but they cannot be programmed to take surveys.

10. Define Chatbot. What are its types? 2023

Ans. Refer to text on page 168 and 169 (Chatbots, Types of Chatbots).

11. What is the primary difference between Human Language and Computer Language? 2025

Ans. Primary difference between Human Language and Computer Language:

Ambiguity: Human language is inherently ambiguous, relying on context and interpretation. Computer languages are designed for precision and lack ambiguity.

Long Answer Type Questions

1. Consider the text of the following documents: 2022

Document 1 Sahil likes to play cricket

Document 2 Sajal likes cricket too

Document 3 Sajal also likes to play basketball

Apply all the four steps of Bag of words model of NLP on the above given documents and generate the output.

Ans. Step 1: Tokenization

Document 1 [Sahil, likes, to, play, cricket]

Document 2 [Sajal, likes, cricket, too]

Document 3 [Sajal, also, likes, to, play, basketball]

Step 2 Vocabulary Creation

Vocabulary: [Sahil, likes, to, play, cricket, Sajal, too, also, basketball]

Step 3 Document-Term Matrix (DTM) Construction

Step 4 Term Frequency-Inverse Document Frequency (TF-IDF) Calculation

	Document 1	Document 2	Document 3
Sahil	1	0	0
likes	1	1	1
to	1	0	1
play	1	0	1
cricket	1	1	0
Sajal	0	1	1
too	0	1	0
also	0	0	1
basketball	0	0	1

TF-IDF values for each term in each document can be calculated using the term frequency and inverse document frequency formulas, which provide a measure of the importance of each term in each document relative to the entire corpus.

2. With reference to NLP, explain the following terms in details with the help of suitable example:
(i) Term Frequency
(ii) Inverse Document Frequency

Ans. (i) **Term Frequency** Term Frequency (TF) is a measure used in natural language processing to quantify the frequency of a term (word) in a document relative to the total number of terms in that document. It indicates how often a particular term appears within a document.

Example Suppose we have a document containing 100 words, and the word "apple" appears 5 times in that document. The term frequency of "apple" in this document would be:

TF("apple", document) = 5/100 = 0.05

(ii) **Inverse Document Frequency** Inverse Document Frequency (IDF) is a measure used to determine the importance of a term in a collection of documents. It quantifies how rare or common a term is across all documents in the corpus. Terms that occur frequently in many documents are considered less important, while terms that occur rarely in few documents are considered more important.

Example: Suppose we have a corpus containing 1,000 documents, and the term "apple" appears in 100 of these documents. The inverse document frequency of "apple" would be:

IDF ("apple") = log (1000/100) = log (10) = 1

3. We, human beings, can read, write and understand many languages. But computers can understand only machine language. Do you think we might face any challenges if we try to teach computers how to understand and interact in human languages? Explain. SQP 2023-24

Ans. Yes, we might face any challenges if we try to teach computers how to understand and interact in human languages.

The possible difficulties are

1. **Arrangement of the words and meaning** the computer has to identify the different parts of a speech. Also, it may be extremely difficult for a computer to understand the meaning behind the language we use.
2. **Multiple Meanings of a word** same word can be used in a number of different ways which according to the context of the statement changes its meaning completely.
3. **Perfect Syntax, no Meaning** Sometimes, a statement can have a perfectly correct syntax but it does not mean anything. For example, take a look at this statement:

   Chickens feed extravagantly while the moon drinks tea.

   This statement is correct grammatically but does this make any sense? In Human language, a perfect balance of syntax and semantics is important for better understanding.

4. Samiksha, a student of class X was exploring the Natural Language Processing domain. She got stuck while performing the text normalisation. Help her to normalise the text on the segmented sentences given below:

Document 1: Akash and Ajay are best friends.

Document 2: Akash likes to play football but Ajay prefers to play online games. Competency Based Ques.

Ans. 1. Tokenisation

Akash, and, Ajay, are, best, friends Akash, likes, to, play, football, but, Ajay, prefers, to, play, online, games

2. Removal of stopwords

Akash, Ajay, best, friends Akash, likes, play, football, Ajay, prefers, play, online, games

3. Converting text to a common case

akash, ajay, best, friends akash, likes, play, football, ajay, prefers, play, online, games

4. Stemming/Lemmatisation

akash, ajay, best, friend akash, like, play, football, ajay, prefer, play, online, game

5. Consider the following two documents:

Document 1 ML and DL are part of AI.

Document 2 DL is a subset of ML.

Implement all four steps of the Bag of Words (BoW) model to create a document vector table. Depict the outcome of each step. 2024

Ans. Four steps of the Bag of Words (BoW) model for the given documents:

Step 1 Tokenization

Tokenization involves breaking the text into individual words or tokens.

For Document 1:

Tokens: ["ML", "and", "DL", "are", "part", "of", "AI"]

For Document 2:

Tokens: ["DL", "is", "a", "subset", "of", "ML"]

Step 2 Lowercasing

Lowercasing converts all words to lowercase to ensure consistency.

For Document 1:

Tokens: ["ml", "and", "dl", "are", "part", "of", "ai"]

For Document 2:

Tokens: ["dl", "is", "a", "subset", "of", "ml"]

Step 3 Removing Stopwords (Optional)

Stopwords are common words like "and", "is", "a", etc., that may not contribute much to the meaning of the text. This step is optional and can be skipped depending on the application.

For Document 1:

Tokens: ["ml", "dl", "part", "ai"]

For Document 2:

Tokens: ["dl", "subset", "ml"]

Step 4 Creating Document Vectors

Document vectors represent the frequency of each word in the document.

For Document 1:

Document Vector: {"ml": 1, "dl": 1, "part": 1, "ai": 1}

For Document 2:

Document Vector: {"dl": 1, "is": 1, "a": 1, "subset": 1, "of": 1, "ml": 1}

Document Vector Table

Word	**Document 1**	**Document 2**
ml	1	1
dl	1	1
part	1	0
ai	1	0
is	0	1
a	0	1
subset	0	1
of	0	1

6. Create a document vector table from the following documents by implementing all the four steps of Bag of words model. Also depict the outcome of each step.

Document 1: Sameera and Sanya are classmates.

Document 2: Sameera likes dancing but Sanya loves to study mathematics.

Will it be valid to say that not all the devices which are termed as "smart" are AI-enabled? Justify this statement. Explain any two examples from the daily life which are commonly misunderstood as AI. **2023**

Ans. Step of the Bag of Words (BoW) model for the given documents:

Step 1 Tokenization

Tokenization involves breaking the text into individual words or tokens.

For Document 1:

Tokens: ["Sameera", "and", "Sanya", "are", "classmates"]

For Document 2:

Tokens: ["Sameera", "likes", "dancing", "but", "Sanya", "loves", "to", "study", "mathematics"]

Step 2 Lowercasing

Lowercasing converts all words to lowercase to ensure consistency.

For Document 1:

Tokens: ["sameera", "and", "sanya", "are", "classmates"]

For Document 2:

Tokens: ["sameera", "likes", "dancing", "but", "sanya", "loves", "to", "study", "mathematics"]

Step 3 Removing Stopwords (Optional)

Stopwords are common words like "and", "are", "to", etc., that may not contribute much to the meaning of the text. This step is optional and can be skipped depending on the application.

For Document 1:

Tokens: ["sameera", "sanya", "classmates"]

For Document 2:

Tokens: ["sameera", "likes", "dancing", "sanya", "loves", "study", "mathematics"]

Step 4 Creating Document Vectors

Document vectors represent the frequency of each word in the document.

For Document 1:

Document Vector: {"sameera": 1, "sanya": 1, "classmates": 1}

For Document 2:

Document Vector: {"sameera": 1, "likes": 1, "dancing": 1, "sanya": 1, "loves": 1, "study": 1, "mathematics": 1}

Document Vector Table

Word	Document 1	Document 2
sameera	1	1
sanya	1	1
classmates	1	0
likes	0	1
dancing	0	1
loves	0	1
study	0	1
mathematics	0	1

This table shows the frequency of each word (token) in each document. The BoW model represents each document as a vector where each element corresponds to the frequency of a word in the document.

7. Consider the following documents: **2025**

Document 1: NLP is a domain of AI

Document 2: NLP stands for Natural Language Processing

Implement all the four steps of Bag of Words (BoW) model to create a document vector table.

Ans. Documents

Document 1: NLP is a domain of AI.

Document 2: NLP stands for Natural Language Processing.

Steps

1. **Tokenization** Break each document into individual words (tokens).

   Doc 1: [NLP, is, a, domain, of, AI]

   Doc 2: [NLP, stands, for, Natural, Language, Processing]

2. **Vocabulary Creation** Create a unique list of all words across all documents.

   Vocabulary [NLP, is, a, domain, of, AI, stands, for, Natural, Language, Processing]

3. **Vectorization** Represent each document as a vector, where each element corresponds to the count of a word from the vocabulary in that document.

   Doc 1 Vector: [1, 1, 1, 1, 1, 1, 0, 0, 0, 0]

   Doc 2 Vector: [1, 0, 0, 0, 0, 0, 1, 1, 1, 1]

4. Document Vector Table:

Word	**Doc 1**	**Doc 2**
NLP	1	1
is	1	0
a	1	0
domain	1	0
of	1	0
AI	1	0
stands	0	1
for	0	1
Natural	0	1
Language	0	1
Processing	0	1

SELF ASSESSMENT

Multiple Choice Questions

1. NLP can be useful in which of the following areas?
   (a) Automatic Text Summarisation (b) Virtual Assistants
   (c) Machine Translations (d) All of the mentioned
2. Simplification of human language in order to be easily understood by computers is called?
   (a) Sentence Planning (b) Text Normalisation
   (c) Text Realisation (d) None of these
3. Given a sound clip of a person or people speaking, determine the textual representation of the speech.
   (a) Text to speech (b) Speech to text
   (c) Both (a) and (b) (d) None of these
4. What is the primary goal of Natural Language Processing (NLP) ?
   (a) To generate random text (b) To understand, interpret and generate human language
   (c) To analyse only written text (d) To automate data visualization
5. Identify the process of stemming and lemmatization
   i. Studi ii. study
   (a) This is tokenisation (b) i-lemmatization ii-stemming
   (c) i-stemming ii-lemmatization (d) None of these
6. Siri and Alexa are examples of ....
   (a) Real time Assistants (b) Neural Networks
   (c) Virtual Assistants (d) Computer Vision

Very Short Answer Type Questions

7. What is the purpose of tokenization in NLP?
8. Give an example of a popular NLP library.

Short Answer Type Questions

9. Differentiate between tokenization and word tokenization.
10. Write any two applications of TF-IDF.

Long Answer Type Questions

11. Explain the Bag of Words model in detail and discuss its advantages and limitations in natural language processing.
12. Discuss the challenges and advancements in sentiment analysis in NLP, including the methods used and their applications in various domains.

CHAPTER 07

Advanced Python

Editors play a crucial role in the process of writing programs by providing a user-friendly interface for developers to write, edit and manage their code. They also provide features like syntax highlighting, code completion, error detection, version control integration, debugging tools, and customization options to enhance productivity and code quality. They facilitate the writing, editing and management of code throughout the software development process.

In class 9th, we have learned to work with Python IDLE. There are many other platforms used these days to write and develop Python programs. In this chapter, we are going to learn about one of the popular platforms - Jupyter Notebooks.

7.1 Jupyter Notebook

A Jupyter Notebook is a powerful tool widely used in the field of data science, research, and education. It provides an interactive computing environment that allows you to create and share documents containing live code, equations, visualisations, and narrative text.

Jupyter Notebooks support various programming languages, but it is most commonly associated with Python.

Working with Jupyter Notebook, virtual environment is one of the most important tools that used by Python developers.

Introduction to Virtual Environment

A virtual environment is a self-contained directory that encapsulates a specific Python interpreter and its associated libraries. It allows you to create an isolated environment for your Python projects, preventing conflicts between dependencies and ensuring that each project has its own set of libraries and packages.

7.2 Installing Jupyter Using Anaconda

By creating separate Python virtual environments for each project

1. To install Python virtual environment – JUPYTER Notebook using ANACONDA, type the link: **https://www.anaconda.com/products/individual**
2. Click on Download
3. Begin the installation process.
4. Getting through the License-Agreement

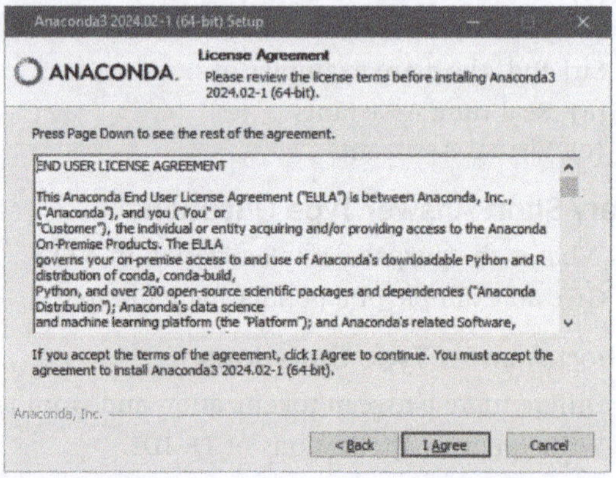

5. Select Installation Type: Select Just Me if you want the software to be used by a single user

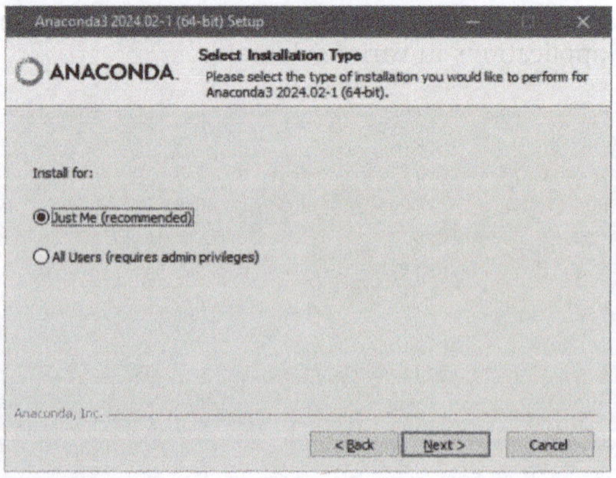

6. Choose Installation Location.
7. Click on 'Install' button.
8. Getting through the Installation Process.

9. Finishing the installation.

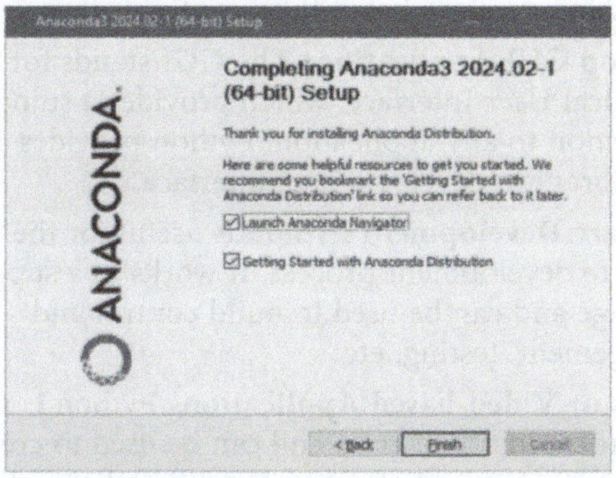

Once the installation is done, you can start using Anaconda.

Open Anaconda from the Start menu or by double click on the Anaconda icon on your desktop (if you have the icon). Anaconda Navigator will open.

From the Anaconda Navigator – click on Launch button JUPYTER Notebook.

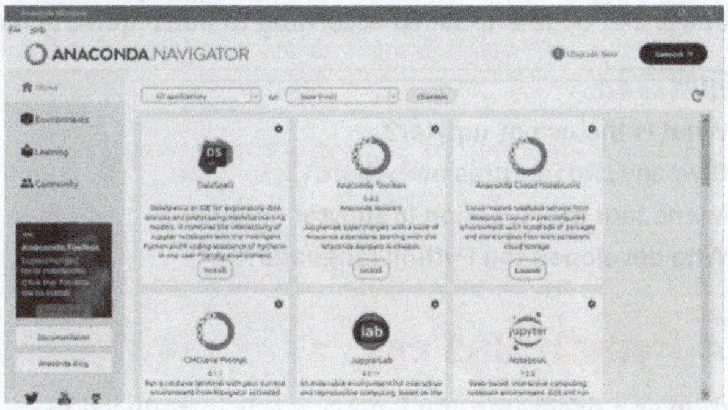

The Jupyter notebook will open in the default browser.

From the New, select Console.

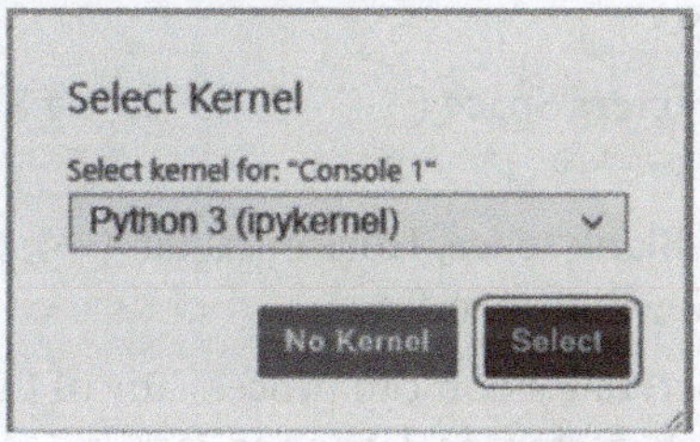

Getting Familiar With Jupyter Notebook

Let's get familiar with the components of Jupyter Notebook

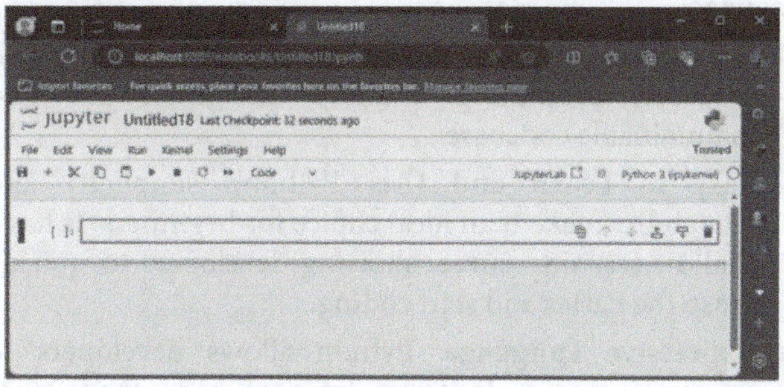

I. **The Notebook Dashboard:** The Notebook dashboard has two tabs.

   (a) **Files** – All the programs that are saved earlier can be visualised under this section. The extension of these files is **.ipynb.**

   (b) **Running** – All notebooks that are opened presently can be seen under this tab.

II. **Notebook Kernel:** The programs that we save on the notebook gets run with the help of an in-built interpreter. Kernel executes the code and shows the result.

The window of the Jupyter notebook has the following parts:

(a) **Title bar** – Name of the program is displayed here.

(b) **Menu bar** – The menu bar has the following tabs:

(c) **Toolbar** – It provides different tools to work with.

(d) **Editor** - Here you can write the code.

7.3 Introduction To Python

Python is a versatile and high-level programming language known for its readability and simplicity. It is created by **Guido van Rossum.**

Python supports multiple programming paradigms, including Procedural, Object-Oriented, and Functional Programming. It has a comprehensive standard library and a vast ecosystem of third-party packages.

Its syntax promotes clean and concise code, contributing to increased productivity.

Features of Python

Here are some key features of the Python programming language:

- **Readability:** Python's syntax is designed to be clear and readable, promoting a more straightforward and maintainable codebase.
- **Easy to Learn and Use:** Python's simplicity and readability make it an ideal choice for beginners. It has a shallow learning curve, allowing developers to quickly grasp the basics and start coding.
- **Expressive Language:** Python allows developers to express concepts in fewer lines of code than other languages like C++ or Java.
- **Interpreted Language:** Python is an interpreted language, which means that code can be executed directly without the need for compilation.
- **Dynamic Typing:** Python uses dynamic typing, allowing developers to create flexible and adaptable code.
- **Large Standard Library:** Python comes with a comprehensive standard library that includes modules and packages for various purposes, such as web development, data manipulation, networking, and more.
- **Community Support:** Python has a large and active community of developers. This results in a wealth of resources, tutorials, and third-party libraries that can be easily accessed, contributing to problem-solving and collaborative development.
- **Cross-Platform Compatibility:** Python is platform-independent, meaning that Python code can run on various operating systems without modification.
- **Object-Oriented Programming** Python supports Object-Oriented programming, allowing developers to create and use classes and objects, promoting modularity and code reuse.
- **Integration Capabilities:** Python can be easily integrated with other languages like C and C++, enabling developers to use existing code and libraries.
- **Databases:** Python provides interfaces to many commercial and open-source databases, making it a suitable choice for database applications.
- **Scalability:** Python is scalable, making it applicable for small scripts as well as large projects.

Python Applications

Here, we are specifying application areas where Python can be applied.

- **Web applications** We can use Python to develop web applications. It provides libraries to handle internet protocols such as HTML and XML, JSON, Email processing, request, beautifulSoup, Feedparser, etc.
- **Desktop GUI Applications** The GUI stands for Graphical User Interface, which provides a smooth interaction to any application. Python provides a Tk GUI library to develop a user interface.
- **Software Development** Python is useful for the software development process. It works as a support language and can be used to build control and management, testing, etc.
- **Audio or Video-based Applications** Python is flexible to perform multiple tasks and can be used to create multimedia applications. Some multimedia applications which are made by using Python are TimPlayer, Cplay, etc.
- **Enterprise Applications** Python can be used to create applications that can be used within an Enterprise or an Organization. Some real-time applications are OpenERP, Tryton, etc.
- **Image Processing Application** Python contains many libraries that are used to work with the image. The image can be manipulated according to our requirements.

Try These 7.1

1. **What is the use of Jupyter?**
2. **Give any two features of Python.**
3. **Name four menu option in Jupyter notebook.**
4. **Who developed the Python language?**

7.4 Python Basics

Python as a programming language was introduced in class 9. Let us now do a quick recap of some important concepts and syntax necessary for writing a program.

Python Character Set

Character set is a set of valid characters that a language can recognise. A character represents any digit, alphabet and special symbol. The character used in a Python source program belongs to unicode standard.

Python supports the following character set.

Alphabets - A to Z (uppercase), a to z (lowercase)

Digits - 0 to 9

Special Characters Space ( ) + – * /\ ^ & % # $ { } [ ] ! _ (underscore) >< ? @ . ; : ' " etc.

White Space Blank space, Horizontal tab (→), Carriage return (↵), Newline, formfeed

Other Characters Python can process any of the ASCII and unicode characters as data or as literals

Identifiers

The identifier is a sequence of characters taken from Python character set.

Identifiers are used to give the name to data items like variables, objects, classes, functions, arrays, etc., to specify their names.

The rules in Python for identifiers are

(i) Only alphabets, digits and underscores are permitted.
(ii) Identifier name cannot start with a digit.
(iii) Keywords cannot be used as identifier.
(iv) Uppercase and lowercase letters are distinct because Python is case sensitive language.
(v) Special characters are not allowed.

e.g. Name, name_1, FirstName etc.

Keywords

Keywords are predefined reserved words by the programming language that have some special or predefined meanings. These are reserved for special purpose and must not be used as identifier names. Some commonly used keywords in Python, which are listed below:

False	assert	del	for	in	or	while
None	break	elif	from	is	pass	with
True	class	else	global	lambda	raise	yield
and	continue	except	if	nonlocal	return	
as	def	finally	import	not	try	

Operators

Operators perform a specific task/computation when applied on variable or some other objects in an expression (known as operands). Operators are used in programs to operate on data and variables.

There are two types of operators as follows:

(i) Unary Operators

Those operators that work on single operand to form an expression are known as unary operators.

Following are some unary operators:

+	unary plus
–	unary minus
~	Bitwise complement
not	logical negation

(ii) Binary Operators

Operators that work upon two operands are known as binary operators.

There are various types of binary operators in Python as follows.

(a) **Arithmetic operators** These operators are used to do arithmetic operations. These operators are

+	Addition
–	Subtraction
*	Multiplication
/	Division
%	Remainder / Modulus
**	Exponent (raise to power)
//	Floor division

(b) **Logical operators** These operators are used to make a decision on two conditions. Logical operators are typically used with boolean values and what they return is also a boolean value. These operators are

and	Logical AND
or	Logical OR

(c) **Relational operators** Relational operators compare two operands to one another. These operators are

<	less than
>	greater than
<=	less than or equal to
>=	greater than or equal to
==	equal to
!=	Not equal to

(d) **Assignment operators** Assignment operators are used to assign the value of an expression to a variable. These operators are

=	assignment
/=	divide and assignment
+=	Add and assignment
*=	Multiply and assignment
%=	Modulus and assignment
–=	Subtract and assignment
**=	Exponent and assignment
//=	Floor division and assignment

(e) **Bitwise operators** Bitwise operators work on bits and perform bit by bit operation. These operators are

&	Bitwise AND
^	Bitwise XOR
|	Bitwise OR

(f) **Shift operators** These operators are used to shift value left or right. These operators are

<<	shift left
>>	shift right

(g) **Identity operators** These operators are

is	is the identity same ?
is not	is the identity not same?

(h) **Membership operators** These operators are

in	whether variable in sequence
not in	whether variable not in sequence

Info Wall

A delimiter is a sequence of one or more characters used to specify the boundary between separate, independent regions in plain text or other data streams. e.g. ( ) { } [ ] , ; :

Expressions

An expression is a combination of operators, constants and variables as per rule of the language. Any part in a program which can have a value, is an expression. It will have operands and operators together to produce a value.

e.g. `4 * i, x + y/10, (a < b) etc.`

Statements

A statement is a logical instruction, which Python interpreter can read and execute. In Python, it could be an expression or assignment statement. The assignment statement is fundamental to Python.

e.g.
```
if x == y:
    print ("x is equal to y")
```

when expression will be evaluated, statement or group of statements executed.

Comments

Comments are non-executable statements that are ignored by the interpreter or compiler and are not executed by the computer.

Comments are written to explain what each block of the program is doing.

There are two types of comments used in programs as follows

(a) **Single line comment** A single line comment starts with # symbol.
e.g. # Here is define the function of addition

(b) **Multi-line comment** A multi-line comment starts with a '''symbol and ends with'''.
e.g. x = 20 '''Here we initialise the value of variable x as 20'''

Indentation

Indentation indicates the relationship between various statements and thus allow us to get a better picture of the overall organisation and structure of the solution given in the program. It improves the readability of the program.

e.g.
```
if (a==b):
    print ("Value of a is equal to b")
    print (" Finished")
```

This is block with all its statements same indentation.

Try These 7.2

1. What are character set?
2. Name any two keywords used in Python.
3. How many operand are used with unary operator?
4. What is the use of comment?

7.5 Variables

Variable is a container object that stores a meaningful value that can be used throughout the program.

Each variable has a specific type, which determines the size and layout of the variable's memory, the range of values that can be stored within that memory and the set of operations that can be applied to the variable.

A variable can be created anywhere in Python program.

e.g.
```
Name = 'Neha'
Subject = 'Computer'
Marks = 80
```

Above is an assignment statements which used to assign values to variables.

7.6 Dynamic Typing

Python is a dynamically type language. It does not know about the type of the variable until the code is run, so declaration is not used. It stores that value at some memory location and then binds that variable name to that memory container. We have assigned a value to variable.

```
>>> a = 10
```

But to find the type of this variable, use the type ( ) module

Syntax

```
type (variable_name)
```

To find the type of above variable, we use

```
>>> a = 10
>>> type (a)
<class 'int'>
```

7.7 Input and Output in Python

Input/Output or I/O is the communication between information processing system (such as a computer) and the outside world, possibly a human or another information processing system.

Inputs are the data received by the user, and outputs are the data sent to user. In almost every computer program, the user has to input some data that will be stored in computer's memory and then subsequently processed.

And finally, there is need to output the results of the computations. The output can be displayed on the computer screen.

Input Statement

Python has an input() function which lets you ask a user for some text input.

input( ) function first takes the input from the user and then evaluates the expression, which means Python automatically identifies whether user entered a string or number or list.

If the input provided is not correct, then either syntax error or exception is raised by Python.

Syntax

```
variable_name = input (< Message to be
displayed >)
```

e.g.
```
>>> a = input ("Enter a number:")
Enter a number : 25
>>> print (a)
25
>>> name = input ("Enter your name:")
Enter your name : Neha
>>> print (name)
Neha
```

Output Statement

To output your data to the screen, use the print ( ) function. print() function gives output an entire (complete) line and then goes to next line for subsequent output. To print more than one item on a single line, comma (,) may be used.

Syntax

```
print (expression / constant / variable)
```

e.g.
```
>>> print ("Arihant")
Arihant
>>> print (5.65)
5.65
>>> print (10 * 3)
30
```

7.8 Data Types

Data types are the classification or categorisation of data items. It represents the kind of value that tells what operations can be performed on a particular data. The following are the standard or built-in data types in Python:

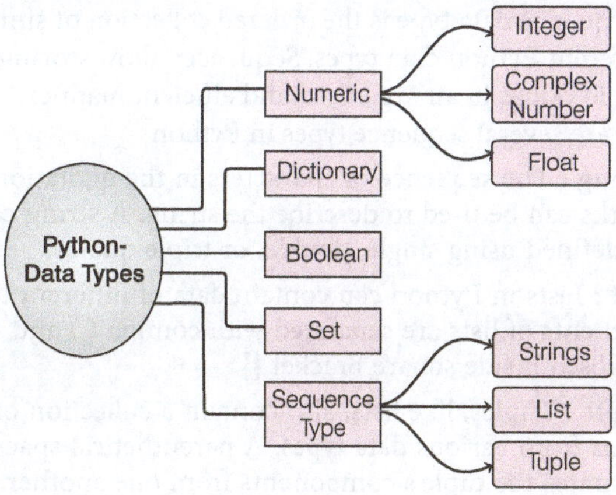

Numeric

The numeric data type in Python represents the data that has a numeric value. A numeric value can be an integer, a floating number, or even a complex number. Numeric data type is further classified into three categories.

- **Integers** This value is represented by int class. It contains positive or negative whole numbers (without fractions or decimals).
- **Float** This value is represented by the float class. It is a real number with a floating-point representation. It is specified by a decimal point. Optionally, the character e or E followed by a positive or negative integer may be appended to specify scientific notation.
- **Complex Numbers** A complex number is represented by a complex class. It is specified as (real part) + (imaginary part)j. For example – 2+3j

Dictionary

A dictionary is a key-value pair set arranged in any order. It stores a specific value for each key, like an associative array or a hash table. Value is any Python object, while the key can hold any primitive data type.

The comma (,) and the curly braces are used to separate the items in the dictionary.

Boolean

Data type with one of the two built-in values, True or False is known as boolean data type. Boolean objects (True or False) are denoted by the class bool.

Set

It is iterable, mutable(can change after creation), and has remarkable components. The elements of a set have no set order.

Sequence

The sequence data type is the ordered collection of similar or different Python data types. Sequences allow storing of multiple values in an organised and efficient manner. There are several sequence types in Python –

- **String :** The sequence of characters in the quotation marks can be used to describe the string. A string can be defined using single, double, or triple quotes.
- **List :** Lists in Python can contain data of different types. Elements of lists are separated with comma (,) and enclosed inside square bracket [].
- **Tuple :** Tuples, like lists, also contain a collection of items from various data types. A parenthetical space () separates the tuple's components from one another.

Try These 7.3

1. **Give one example of variable.**
2. **What is the use of type()?**
3. **Name input function used in Python.**
4. **How many types of sequence data type are there in Python?**

7.9 Control Structure

A control structure is a programming language construct which affects the flow of the execution of program.

Various types of control structure are described below

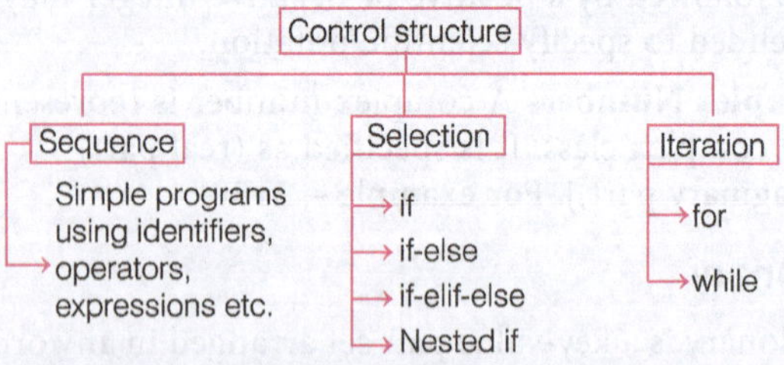

Sequence Statements

Sequence statement refer to the instructions that are executed in the sequence in which they are written in the program. When a program is run, the CPU begins execution, executes some number of statements and then terminates at the end.

For example

```
print("A program which adds two integers\n")
x = int(input("Enter first integer:"))
y = int(input("Enter second integer:"))
sum= x + y
print("Sum is : ", sum)
```

Output

A program which adds two integers
Enter first integer : 5
Enter second integer: 11
Sum is : 16

Selection Statements

These statements allow a program to execute a statement or a set of statements depending upon a given condition. These statements are also called **conditional statements** or **decision statements.**

Python provides three types of selection statements are described below:

1. if statement

The if statement is the most simple decision-making statement. It is used to decide whether a certain statement or block of statements will be executed or not.

Syntax

```
if(conditional expression):
    statement(s)
```

e.g.

```
x = 1
y = 3
x = x + y
if (x > y):
    print ("x is greater")
```

Output x is greater

2. if-else statement

This statement also tests a conditional expression. If the condition is true, the entire block of statements following the if block and it will be executed.

Otherwise, the entire block of statements following the else block and it will be executed.

Syntax

```
if(conditional statement):
    statement(s)
else:
    statement(s)
```

e.g.

```
x = 0
y = 3
x = x + y
if (x > y):
    print("x is greater")
else:
    print("we are in else part because x is
    not greater")
```

Output

we are in else part because x is not greater

3. if-elif-else statement

Sometimes, we need to execute different statement to perform in different conditions. It requires the evaluation of several conditions.

First of all, the first condition is evaluated, if it is true then respective statements are processed. Otherwise, the next condition is evaluated to process another say of statements.

This process is continued for several times.

Syntax

```
if (condition 1):
    statement 1
elif(condition 2):
    statement 2
else:
    statement 3
```

or

```
if(condition 1):
    statement 1
elif(condition 2):
    statement 2
```

Expression is tested from the top towards the downside. As soon as the true condition is found, the associated set of statement is executed.

x = 55

e.g.
```
if((x % 5 = = 0) and (x % 8 = = 0)):
    print("Divisible by both 5 and 8")
elif(x % 8 = = 0):
    print("Divisible by 8")
elif(x % 5 = = 0):
    print("Divisible by 5")
else:
    print("Divisible by none")
```

Output

Divisible by 5

4. Nested if statement

Nested means if statement or if-else statements are placed in the statement block of if statement or else statement.

Syntax

```
if(condition 1):
    if(condition 2):
        statement 1
    else:
        statement 2
else:
    statement 3
```

```
a = 10
b = 15
c = 8
```

e.g.
```
if(a > b):
    if(a > c):
        result = a
    else:
        result = c
else:
    if(b>c):
        result = b
    else:
        result = c
print ("result", result)
```

Output

result = 15

The nested if can have one of the following four forms:

(i) **if nested inside both, if part and else part**

```
if(condition 1):
    if(condition 2):
        statement 1
    else:
        statement 2
else:
    if(condition 3):
        statement 3
    else:
        statement 4
```

(ii) **if nested inside if part**

```
if(condition 1):
    if(condition 2):
        statement 1
    else:
        statement 2
else :
    statement 3
```

(iii) **if nested inside else part**

```
if(condition 1):
    statement 1
else:
    if(condition 2):
        statement 2
    else:
        statement 3
```

(iv) **One if inside another if statements**

```
if(condition 1):
    statement 1
    if (condition 2):
    statement 2
```

range( ) Function

The range( ) function is used to generate a sequence of numbers overtime. At its simplest, it accepts an integer and returns a range object (a type of iterable).

The range ( ) function has two forms as follows:

(i) range (stop)

- **stop** number of integers to generate, starting from zero. e.g. range (5)= = [0,1, 2, 3, 4]

(ii) range ([start,] stop [,step])

- **start** starting number of the sequence.
- **stop** generate numbers upto, but not including this number.
- **step** difference between each number in the sequence.

Iterative Statements

Iterative statements or loops enable a program with a cyclic flow of logic. Each statement which is written under the scope of a looping statement gets executed the number of times the iteration/looping continues for. There are two basic types of looping statements available in Python, they are as follows:

1. while loop

A while loop tests for its ending condition before executing the statements enclosed in the loop body even the first time.

So, if the ending condition is met when the while loop beings, the lines of instructions its contains will never be carried out. This loop is also known as Entry control loop.

Syntax

```
while(loop-condition):
    statement(s)
```

A while loop continues iteration cycle till its loop condition is evaluated as true. If the loop-condition is false for the first time iteration, then loop will not execute even once.

e.g.
```
x = 0
sum = 0
x = int(input("Enter a natural number:"))
while(x > 0):
    sum = sum + x
    x = x - 1
print(" Sum is :" , sum)
```

Output

Enter a natural number : 10

Sum is : 55

2. for loop

The for statement encloses one or more statements that form the body of the loop, the statements in the loop repeat continuously a certain number of times.

This loop is also an entry control loop, as condition is checked before entering into the scope of the loop.

Syntax

```
for variable in <sequence>:
    statement(s)
```

e.g.
```
for i in range (1,5):
    print("A")
    print("B")
```

Output

A
B
A
B
A
B
A
B

7.10 Python Packages

Python has a rich ecosystem of libraries and packages that extend its functionality for various purposes. Here are some widely used Python libraries and packages:

- **NumPy** It provides support for large, multi-dimensional arrays and matrices, along with mathematical functions to operate on these arrays.
  Usage Data science, machine learning, scientific computing.
- **Pandas** It offers data structures like DataFrame for efficient data cleaning, exploration, and analysis.
  Usage Data analysis, data cleaning, data manipulation.
- **Matplotlib** Comprehensive 2D plotting library.
  It allows the creation of static, animated, and interactive visualizations in Python.
  Usage Data visualization, plotting graphs.
- **Scikit-learn** Machine learning library built on NumPy, SciPy, and Matplotlib. It provides simple tools for data mining and data analysis.
  Usage Machine learning, data mining.
- **Beautiful Soup** Library for pulling data out of HTML and XML files. It provides Pythonic idioms for iterating, searching, and modifying the parse tree.
  Usage Web scraping.
- **Django** High-level web framework for building web applications quickly. It follows the model-view-controller (MVC) architectural pattern.
  Usage Web development.
- **Flask** Lightweight web framework. It simplifies web application development by providing tools and libraries needed.

Usage Web development.

NLTK (Natural Language ToolKit) Library for working with human language data. It provides easy-to-use interfaces for tasks such as classification, tokenization, stemming, tagging, parsing, and more.

Usage Natural Language Processing (NLP), text mining.

OpenCV (Open Source Computer Vision) Library for computer vision and machine learning. It provides tools for image and video analysis.

Usage Computer vision, image and video processing.

Try These 7.4

1. **What is control structure?**
2. **Name one entry control loop.**
3. **Give the syntax of range().**
4. **What is the use of Pandas package?**

Glossary

Jupyter Notebook It is a powerful tool widely used in the field of data science, research, and education Jupyter Notebooks support various programming languages, but it is most commonly associated with Python.

Virtual Environment It is a self-contained directory that encapsulates a specific Python interpreter and its associated libraries.

Package It is a collection of Python modules organised in a directory hierarchy.

Keywords They are reserved words that have special meanings and cannot be used as identifiers.

Identifiers They are names used to identify variables, functions, classes, modules, or other objects in the code.

Conditional statement It allows you to control the flow of program based on certain conditions.

Loops They are used to repeatedly execute a block of code until a specified condition is met.

NCERT FOLDER

Complete Explanations of all NCERT's Questions

Subjective Questions

Q.1 What is Jupyter Notebook?

Ans. Jupyter Notebook is an open-source web application that allows users to create and share interactive documents containing live code, equations, visualizations, and text. It's particularly popular in AI-related projects and primarily uses Python, although it supports other programming languages too.

Q.2 How to access Jupyter Notebook?

Ans. To access Jupyter Notebook:

1. Install Anaconda.
2. Open Anaconda Navigator.
3. Launch Jupyter Notebook from the Navigator interface or by using the Anaconda Prompt with the command jupyter notebook.

Q.3 What is Virtual Environment?

Ans. A virtual environment in Python is a self-contained directory that houses a Python interpreter and its own set of libraries and dependencies. It allows developers to work on multiple projects with different dependencies without conflicts.

Q.4 What are the key features of Python? Mention various applications along with it.

Ans. Refer to text on page 188 (Features of Python, Python Applications).

Q.5 What is a Jupyter Notebook ?

Ans. Refer to text on page 186 (Jupyter Notebook).

Q.6 How can install jupyter notebook in anaconda prompt?

Ans. Refer to text on page 186-187 (Installing Jupyter Using Anaconda)

Q.7 Why do we need to install a kernel before running jupyter notebook?

Ans. We need to install a kernel before running Jupyter Notebook because:

1. **Language Execution** It allows Jupyter to execute code in a specific programming language.
2. **Runtime Environment** The kernel provides the necessary environment to run and manage code.
3. **Interactive Computing** It facilitates communication between the notebook interface and the code execution process.
4. **Output Handling** The kernel processes code execution and returns outputs, including results and error messages, to the notebook.

EXAM PATTERN EXERCISE

Including Competency Based Questions

Part I

Multiple Choice Questions

1 Which of the following is a loop statement?

(a) a+ = 1 (b) if a > b;
(c) while a > 7: (d) whilenot a > 7:

2 Which of the following statement(s) is/are incorrect about Python?

i. Python is an Object Oriented language
ii. Python is a machine level language
iii. Python needs high maintenance
iv. Python doesn't focus on readability

(a) (i) and (iii) only
(b) (ii), (iii) and (iv)
(c) (iv) only
(d) (ii) and (iii)

3 Which of the following is not used as a loop in Python?

(a) while (b) for
(c) do while (d) None of these

4 Which symbol is used to represent a comment in Python?

(a) // (b) #
(c) – (d) !

5 What is a variable in Python used for?

(a) To store and manipulate data
(b) To perform calculations
(c) To draw shapes
(d) To display the comments

6 Which function is used to take user input in Python?

(a) get_input() (b) user_input()
(c) inputs() (d) input()

7 What is the purpose of control statements in Python?

(a) To control the flow of program execution
(b) To control the screen brightness
(c) To control the font size
(d) To control the flow of text

8 Which of the following is a valid data type in Python?

(a) character (b) loop
(c) string (d) new character

9 What command is used to display the output in Python?

(a) print() (b) display()
(c) show() (d) None of these

10 Which symbol is used for exponentiation in Python?

(a) ^ (b) ** (c) % (d) $

11 What is the purpose of packages in Python?

(a) To organise code into modules
(b) To wrap gifts
(c) To create graphics
(d) To organise data

12 Which of the following is not a valid data type in Python?

(a) float (b) decimal
(c) complex (d) int

13 What is the purpose of if statement in Python?

(a) To define a function
(b) To create a loop
(c) To make decisions in the code
(d) To swap values

14 Which command is used to install external packages in Python?

(a) import (b) install
(c) pip (d) export

15 Which of the following is a logical operator in Python?

(a) ++ (b) AND (c) // (d) IF

16 Which of the following is a correct match?

1. Keyword	**(i) Integer**
2. Data type	**(ii) #**
3. Comment	**(iii) finally**

(a) 1 → (iii); 2 → (ii); 3 → (i) (b) 1 → (i); 2 → (ii); 3 → (iii)
(c) 1 → (ii); 2 → (i); 3 → (iii) (d) 1 → (iii); 2 → (i); 3 → (ii)

Answers

1. (c)	2. (b)	3. (c)	4. (b)	5. (a)
6. (d)	7. (a)	8. (c)	9. (a)	10. (b)
11. (a)	12. (b)	13. (c)	14. (c)	15. (b)
16. (d)				

Statement Based Questions

1. Statement 1 Jupyter Notebook App is a server-client application that allows editing and running notebook documents via a web browser.

Statement 2 Jupyter Notebook App can be executed on a local desktop requiring no internet access

(a) Both Statement 1 and Statement 2 are correct
(b) Both Statement 1 and Statement 2 are incorrect
(c) Statement 1 is correct but Statement 2 is incorrect
(d) Statement 2 is correct but Statement 1 is incorrect

2. Statement 1 Python is a high-level, general-purpose, and very popular programming language.

Statement 2 It was created by James Gosling, and released in 1991.

(a) Both Statement 1 and Statement 2 are correct
(b) Both Statement 1 and Statement 2 are incorrect
(c) Statement 1 is correct but Statement 2 is incorrect
(d) Statement 2 is correct but Statement 1 is incorrect

3. Statement 1 The process of traversing a sequence is known as iteration.

Statement 2 Loop iterates until the final item of the sequence are reached.

(a) Both Statement 1 and Statement 2 are correct
(b) Both Statement 1 and Statement 2 are incorrect
(c) Statement 1 is correct but Statement 2 is incorrect
(d) Statement 2 is correct but Statement 1 is incorrect

4. Statement 1 Tuples, like lists, also contain a collection of items from various data types.

Statement 2 A parenthetical space [] separates the tuple's components from one another.

(a) Both Statement 1 and Statement 2 are correct
(b) Both Statement 1 and Statement 2 are incorrect
(c) Statement 1 is correct but Statement 2 is incorrect
(d) Statement 2 is correct but Statement 1 is incorrect

Answers

1. (a) 2. (c) 3. (a) 4. (c)

Assertion & Reason Based Questions

1. Assertion (A) A variable in Python can change its value during the execution of the program.

Reason (R) Python is a dynamically typed language.

(a) Both A and R are correct and R is the correct explanation of A
(b) Both A and R are correct but R is not the correct explanation of A
(c) A is correct but R is not correct
(d) A is not correct but R is correct

2. Assertion (A) The if statement is used for conditional execution in Python.

Reason (R) The if statement is followed by a block of code that is executed only if the condition is true.

(a) Both A and R are correct and R is the correct explanation of A
(b) Both A and R are correct but R is not the correct explanation of A
(c) A is correct but R is not correct
(d) A is not correct but R is correct

3. Assertion (A) The % operator is used for modulo arithmetic in Python.

Reason (R) The / operator is used for integer division in Python.

(a) Both A and R are correct and R is the correct explanation of A
(b) Both A and R are correct but R is not the correct explanation of A
(c) A is correct but R is not correct
(d) A is not correct but R is correct

4. Assertion (A) for loop is also called as "Entry controlled loop".

Reason (R) For loop can be written to traverse a sequence.

(a) Both A and R are correct and R is the correct explanation of A
(b) Both A and R are correct but R is not the correct explanation of A
(c) A is correct but R is not correct
(d) A is not correct but R is correct

5. Assertion (A) The while loop in Python is used to repeat a block of code while a condition is true.

Reason (R) The for loop in Python is used to iterate over a sequence of values.

(a) Both A and R are correct and R is the correct explanation of A
(b) Both A and R are correct but R is not the correct explanation of A
(c) A is correct but R is not correct
(d) A is not correct but R is correct

Answers

1. (a) 2. (a) 3. (c) 4. (b) 5. (b)

Part II

Very Short Answer Type Questions

1 What is the output of print(type(25))?

Ans. The output is <class 'int'>.

2 Give one example of variable.

Ans. age = 25, where age is the variable storing the value 25.

3 Define Pandas libraries.

Ans. Pandas is an open-source data manipulation and analysis library for Python. It provides data structures like DataFrame for efficient data handling.

4 Define operator precedence.

Ans. Operator precedence determines the order in which operators are evaluated in an expression. It ensures that certain operators are evaluated before others.

5 Give one example of each of the following:

(a) Unary operator

(b) Comparison operator

Ans. (a) Unary operator: ~ x (negation)

(b) Comparison operator: == (equality)

6 Mention any one feature of List in Python.

Ans. Lists in Python are versatile and can store elements of different data types in an ordered and mutable sequence.

7 What do you understand by iteration in programming?

Ans. Iteration is the process of repeatedly executing a set of statements or a block of code.

8 Give any two features of OpenCV.

Ans. Two features include image recognition and object detection.

9 Name the operator used for the following:

(a) To assign a value to a variable

(b) That returns True or False.

Ans. (a) =

(b) Comparison operators, such as == or !=

10 What is the minimum number of iterations that while loop could make?

Ans. while loop could make minimum 0 iteration.

Short Answer Type Questions

1. Identify and correct the error(s) from the given below variables.

(i) STD - - **(ii) 5STD**

(iii) D$ **(iv) (Marks)**

Ans. (i) **Error STD - -** is not allowed. The correct form is STD.

(ii) **Error 5STD** First character must be alphabet. The correct form is STD5.

(iii) **Error D$** $ is not allowed. The correct form is D.

(iv) **Error (Marks)** Brackets are not allowed. The correct form is Marks.

2. Differentiate between identifier and keyword.

Ans. Differences between identifier and keyword are as follows

Identifier	Keyword
Identifier consists any combination of letters, numbers and underscores.	Keyword must consist only letters.
It allows both uppercase and lowercase.	It allows only lowercase.
e.g. x, sum_5, _mul etc.	e.g. finally, continue, yield etc.

3. What is the difference between statement and expression ?

Ans. Differences between statement and expression are as follows

Statement	Expression
A statement is a complete line of code that performs some action.	An expression is any section of the code that evaluates to a value.
Statements can only be combined vertically by writing one after another or with block constructs.	Expressions can be combined horizontally into larger expressions using operators.

4. Shreya is programming in Python and writing a following code. But she found an error, what is the reason? **Competency Based Ques.**

```
a = 10
b = 20
c = a + b
        print ("The output is :", c)
```

Ans. The above code is identation error and correct code is

```
a = 10
b = 20
c = a + b
print ("The output is :", c)
```

5. Find the syntax error in the following program and underline after correct them.

```
w = 90 ;
while(w > 60)
    print(w)
    w = w - 50
```

Ans. Correct code is

```
w = 90
while(w>60):
    print(w)
    w = w - 50
```

6. Construct logical expressions to represent the following conditions.

(i) Weight is greater than or equal to 115 but less than 125.

(ii) Donation is in the range of 4000-5000 or Guest is 1.

Ans. (i) (weight >=115 and weight < 125)

(ii) ((Donation > = 4000 and Donation <= 5000) or Guest = =1)

7. Write a Python program to calculate simple interest and display it.

Ans.

```
p = int(input("Enter the principal:"))
r = int(input("Enter rate of interest:"))
t = int(input("Enter time:"))
si = (p*r*t)/ 100
print("The simple interest is", si)
```

Output

Enter the principal : 5000

Enter rate of interest : 10

Enter time : 2

The simple interest is 1000.0

8 What is a Python package?

Ans. A Python package is a way of organising related modules into a single directory hierarchy. It helps in structuring Python's module namespace and avoids naming conflicts. Packages are directories containing module files and an __init__.py file. They provide a means of creating a hierarchical structure to organise and distribute Python code.

Long Answer Type Questions

1. What do you understand by string literals? Explain.

Ans. The literal which is stored in a variable within single quotation mark or double quotation marks is called string literal. These represent a sequence of zero or more characters enclosed by double quotes. It can also include blank spaces.

Some valid string constants are

'A'	"Science"	'₹560.50'	'The output is'
"24567"	"0.34"	'MP'	'Delhi'

Some Invalid string constants are

Neha	Not enclosed in double or single quotes
"Hello"	Number of quotes must be even either double or single.

There are two types of strings supported in Python:

(a) **Single Line String** Strings that are terminated within a single line are known as single line strings.

e.g. >>> value = 'Arihant'

(b) **Multiline String** A piece of text that is spread along multiple lines is known as multiple line string.

There are two ways to create multiline strings:

(I) Adding backslash at the end of each line

e.g.
```
>>> value = 'Arihant\
Publication'
>>> value
'ArihantPublication'
```

(II) Using triple quotation marks

e.g.
```
>>> value = '''Welcome
to
Python '''
>>> print (value)
Welcome
to
Python
```

2. Write a Python program with output to convert the centimeter value into meter and kilometer.

Ans.

```
centimeter = float (input ("Enter value
in centimeters: " ))
meter = centimeter / 100.0;
kilometer = centimeter / 100000.0;
# Driver Code
print("Length in meter = ", meter , "m");
print("Length in Kilometer = ",
kilometer , "km");
```

Output

Enter value in centimeters: 5000

Length in meter = 50.0 m

Length in Kilometer = 0.05 km

3. An electricity board charges according to the following rules.

For the first 100 units - 40 P per unit

For the next 200 units - 50 P per unit

Beyond 300 units - 60 P per unit

All users have to pay meter charge also, which is ₹ 50. Write a program to read the number of units consumed and print out the charges.

Ans.

```
charges = 0.0;
units = int (input ("Enter the number of units
consumed:"))
if(units<=100):
    charges = (units * 0.4)+50
elif(units<=300):
```

```
        charges = ((units-100) * 0.5+40)+50
    elif(units>300):
        charges= ((units-300) * 0.6+140)+50
    print("The charges is:", charges)
```

Output

Enter the number of units consumed: 125

The charges is : 102.5

4. Write a program to check whether a number is prime or not.

Ans.

```
n = int (input("Enter the number:"))
print ("n=" , n)
if n>1:
    for i in range (2, n//2):
        if(n%i) = = 0:
            print(n, "is not a prime number")
            break
        else:
            print(n, "is a prime number")
else:
    print(n, " is not a prime number")
```

Output

Enter the number : 67

n = 67

67 is a prime number

5. Write a program in Python to accept monthly salary from the user, find and display income tax with the help of following rules.

Monthly Salary	Income Tax
9000 or more	40% of monthly salary
7500-8999	30% of monthly salary
7499 or less	20% of monthly salary

Ans.

```
itax = 0
sal = int(input("Enter monthly salary:"))
if (sal>=9000):
    itax = sal * 0.40
elif (sal>=7500 and sal <= 8999):
    itax=sal * 0.30
elif (sal<=7499):
    itax = sal * 0.20
print("Income tax is ", itax)
```

Output

Enter monthly salary: 15000

Income tax is 6000.0

6. Write a Python program which enter the cost price and selling price of an item and find profit or loss.

Ans.

```
cost_price = float(input(" Please Enter the Cost Price of an Item: "))
selling_price = float(input(" Please Enter the Selling Price of an Item: "))
if(cost_price > selling_price):
    amount = cost_price - selling_price
    print("Total Loss Amount =", amount)
elif(selling_price > cost_price):
    amount = selling_price - cost_price
    print("Total Profit = ", amount)
else:
    print("No Profit No Loss!!!")
```

Output

Please Enter the Cost Price of an Item: 15000

Please Enter the Selling Price of an Item: 17500

Total Profit = 2500.0

SELF ASSESSMENT

Multiple Choice Questions

1. Which of the following are the most obvious kind of constants?
(a) Keywords (b) Literals (c) Variables (d) Identifiers

2. .... is a logical instructions which Python interpreter can read and execute.
(a) Expression (b) Statement (c) Comment (d) Identation

3. Which function is used to generate a sequence of numbers overtime?
(a) range() (b) len() (c) limit() (d) lim()

4. These statements enable a program with a cyclic flow of logic
(a) sequence (b) compound (c) single (d) iterative

5. The operating system supported by the Anaconda.
(a) Linux (b) MacOS (c) MS Window (d) All of these

6. Which of the following have the same precedence level?
(a) Division, Multiplication, Addition and Subtraction
(b) Division and Multiplication
(c) Subtraction and Division
(d) Power and Division

Very Short Answer Type Questions

7. Give two examples of functions used in Python.

8. Write the use of step value in loop.

Short Answer Type Questions

9. Find the errors in the following program and correct them

```
num1 = 1.2
num2 = 6
sum = int(num1) + float(num2)
print(sum)
```

10. Write the syntax of nested if statement.

11. Give example of single line comment and multiple line comment.

Long Answer Type Questions

12. Describe five features of toolbar in Jupyter notebook with symbols.

13. Explain any five data types used in Python with examples.

Practical Work

1. Write a program to add the elements of the two lists.

```
def add_lists(list1, list2):
    if len(list1) != len(list2):
  print("Error: Lists must be of equal length")
        return None
    sum_list = []
 # Iterate over the lists and add corresponding
elements
    for i in range(len(list1)):
        sum_list.append(list1[i] + list2[i])
        return sum_list
list1 = [1, 2, 3, 4]
list2 = [5, 6, 7, 8]
result = add_lists(list1, list2)
print("Sum of lists:", result)
```

Output

Sum of lists: [6, 8, 10, 12]

2. Write a program to calculate mean, median and mode using Numpy.

```
import numpy as np
def calculate_mean(arr):
    return np.mean(arr)
def calculate_median(arr):
    return np.median(arr)
def calculate_mode(arr):
unique, conts = np.unique (arr,
return_counts=True)
    mode_index = np.argmax(counts)
    return unique[mode_index]
data = np.array([1, 2, 3, 4, 5, 6, 6, 7, 8, 9])
print("Mean:", calculate_mean(data))
print("Median:", calculate_median(data))
print("Mode:",calculate_mode(data))
```

Output

Mean : 5.1

Median : 5.5

Mode : 6

3. Write a program to display line chart from (2,5) and (9,10).

```
# You'll need to have matplotlib installed to
run this code.
import matplotlib.pyplot as plt
x_values = [2, 9]
y_values = [5, 10]
# Plot the line chart
plt.plot(x_values, y_values)
# Add labels and title
plt.xlabel('X-axis')
plt.ylabel('Y-axis')
plt.title('Line Chart')
# Display the chart
plt.show()
```

Output

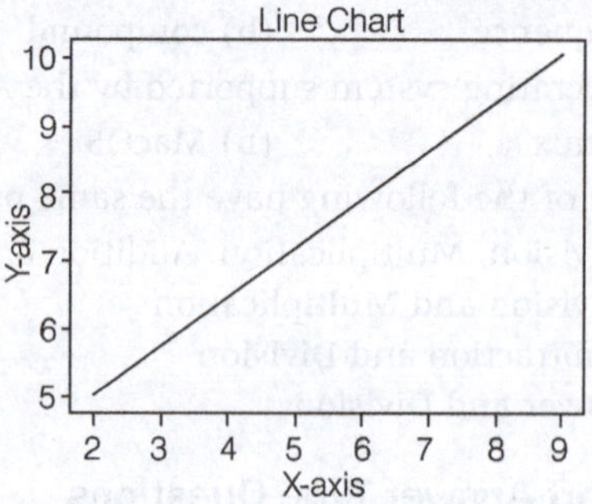

4. Write a program to display a scatter chart for the following points (2,5), (9,10) , (8,3),(5,7),(6,18).

```
import matplotlib.pyplot as plt
# Define the points
points = [(2,5), (9,10), (8,3), (5,7), (6,18)]
x_coords = [point[0] for point in points]
y_coords = [point[1] for point in points]
# Plot the scatter chart
plt.scatter(x_coords, y_coords)
# Add labels and title
plt.xlabel('X-axis')
plt.ylabel('Y-axis')
plt.title('Scatter Chart')
# Display the chart
plt.show()
```

Output

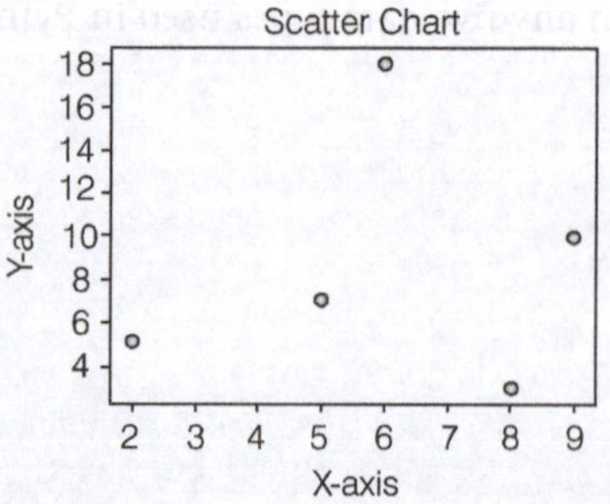

5. Read csv file saved in your system and display 10 rows.

```
import csv
data = [
    "Python",
    "JavaScript",
```

```
        "Java",
        "C++",
        "Ruby",
        "Swift",
        "Rust",
        "Go",
        "PHP",
        "HTML/CSS"
]
file_name = 'comp_languages.csv'
# Writing data to CSV file
with open(file_name, mode='w', newline='') as file:
    writer = csv.writer(file)
    writer.writerow(['Language'])
    for language in data:
        writer.writerow([language])
print(f"CSV file '{file_name}' created
successfully!")
```

Output

CSV file 'comp_languages.csv' created successfully!

 # Read 10 rows from 'comp_languages.csv'

```
import csv
# Specify the CSV file name
file_name = 'comp_languages.csv'
# Reading and displaying 10 rows from the CSV file
with open(file_name, mode='r') as file:
  reader = csv.reader(file)
  for i, row in enumerate(reader):
    if i >= 10:
      break
    print(row)
```

Output

['Language']
['Python']
['JavaScript']
['Java']
['C++']
['Ruby']
['Swift']
['Rust']
['Go']
['PHP']

6. Read csv file saved in your system and display its information.

```
import pandas as pd
# Replace 'data.csv' with the path to your CSV file
file_path = 'comp_languages.csv'
# Read the CSV file into a DataFrame
df = pd.read_csv(file_path)
# Display basic information about the DataFrame
print("Basic Information:")
print(df.info())
# Display the first few rows of the DataFrame
print("\nFirst few rows:")
print(df.head())
# Display summary statistics of the DataFrame
print("\nSummary Statistics:")
print(df.describe())
```

Output

```
Basic Information:
<class 'pandas.core.frame.DataFrame'>
RangeIndex: 10 entries, 0 to 9
Data columns (total 1 columns):
 #  Column    Non-Null Count  Dtype
---  ------   --------------  -----
 0  Language  10 non-null     object
dtypes: object (1)
memory usage: 208.0 + bytes
None
First few rows :
   Language
0 Python
1 JavaScript
2 Java
3 C++
4 Ruby
Summary Statistics:
 Language
count     10
unique  10
top       Python
freq      1
```

7. Write a program to read an image and display using Python.

```
import matplotlib.pyplot as plt
import matplotlib.image as mpimg
def display_image(image_path):
    # Read the image
    img = mpimg.imread(image_path)
    # Display the image
    plt.imshow(img)
    plt.axis('off')  # Hide axis
    plt.show()
# Replace 'image_path' with the path to your image
file
image_path = 'image.jpg'
display_image(image_path)
```

Note Make sure to replace 'image.jpg' with the actual path to your image file.

8. **Write a program to read an image and identify its shape using Python.**

```
import cv2
def detect_shape(image_path):
    # Read the image
    image = cv2.imread(image_path)
    # Check if the image was loaded successfully
    if image is None:
        print("Error: Could not read the image.")
        return
    # Convert the image to grayscale
gray = cv2.cvtColor(image, cv2.COLOR_BGR2GRAY)
    # Detect contours in the image
  contours, _ = cv2.findContours(gray,
cv2.RETR_EXTERNAL, cv2.CHAIN_APPROX_SIMPLE)
    # Iterate through each contour and detect the
shape
    for contour in contours:
        # Approximate the contour to reduce the
number of vertices
        epsilon = 0.04 * cv2.arcLength(contour, True)
        approx = cv2.approxPolyDP(contour, epsilon,
True)
        # Get the number of vertices
        num_vertices = len(approx)
        # Determine the shape based on the number of
vertices
        shape = ""
        if num_vertices == 3:
            shape = "Triangle"
        elif num_vertices == 4:
            shape = "Rectangle"  # Assuming rectangle
for simplicity, could be further refined
        elif num_vertices == 5:
            shape = "Pentagon"
        elif num_vertices == 6:
            shape = "Hexagon"
        else:
            shape = "Circle"  # Assuming circle for
any other shape
        # Display the shape
        cv2.drawContours(image, [contour], 0, (0,
255, 0), 2)
        cv2.putText(image, shape, (approx.ravel()[0],
approx.ravel()[1]), cv2.FONT_HERSHEY_SIMPLEX, 0.5,
(0, 0, 255), 2)
    # Display the result
    cv2.imshow("Shapes Detected", image)
    cv2.waitKey(0)
    cv2.destroyAllWindows()
# Path to the image file
image_path = "path_to_your_image.jpg"  # Replace with
your image path
detect_shape(image_path)
```

Note This code should help you identify basic shapes like triangles, rectangles, pentagons, hexagons, and circles in the image.

CBSE EXAMINATION PAPER 2025
Artificial Intelligence

Time : 2 hrs	M.M. : 50

1. Please read the instructions carefully.
2. This Question Paper consists of **21 questions** in two sections: Section A & Section B.
3. Section A has Objective type questions whereas Section B contains Subjective type questions.
4. **Out of the given (5 + 16 =) 21 questions, a candidate has to answer (5 + 10 =) 15 questions in the allotted (maximum) time of 2 hours.**
5. All questions of a particular section must be attempted in the correct order.
6. **SECTION A - OBJECTIVE TYPE QUESTIONS (24 MARKS):**
   i. This section has 05 questions.
   ii. Marks allotted are mentioned against each question/part.
   iii. There is no negative marking.
   iv. Do as per the instructions given.
7. **SECTION B – SUBJECTIVE TYPE QUESTIONS (26 MARKS):**
   i. This section has 16 questions.
   ii. A candidate has to do 10 questions.
   iii. Do as per the instructions given.
   iv. Marks allotted are mentioned against each question/part.

Section A : Objective Type Questions

1. Answer any 4 out of the given 6 questions on Employability Skills **(4 × 1 = 4)**

(i) Which of the following does not help in stress management?
(a) Healthy food (b) Sound sleep
(c) Yoga asanas (d) Negative thoughts

(ii) Spam refers to
(a) Unnecessary images (b) Temporary files
(c) Junk mails (d) Music files

(iii) Assertion (A) Sustainable agriculture is environment friendly.
Reason (R) It prevents use of chemical fertilizers to protect soil.
(a) Both (A) and (R) are correct and (R) is the correct explanation of (A).
(b) Both (A) and (R) are correct but (R) is not the correct explanation of (A).
(c) (A) is correct but (R) is not correct.
(d) (A) is not correct but (R) is correct.

(iv) Which of the following is not a step to build self-motivation?
(a) Focusing on your goal.
(b) Planning to achieve your goal.
(c) Being indisciplined.
(d) Finding out your strength.

(v) Which of the following types of communication takes place when the number of people is small enough to communicate with each other effectively?
(a) Interpersonal communication
(b) Public communication
(c) Intrapersonal communication
(d) Small group communication

(vi) Reema has started her own restaurant. She keeps on trying new ideas to make different dishes for her customers. As an entrepreneur, Reema is:
(a) Impatient (b) Creative
(c) Under-confident (d) Lazy

2. Answer any 5 out of the given 6 questions **(5 × 1 =5)**

(i) Assertion (A) When a machine is able to mimic human traits, it is said to be artificially intelligent.
Reason (R) A fully automatic washing machine is artificially intelligent.

(a) Both (A) and (R) are correct and (R) is the correct explanation of (A).
(b) Both (A) and (R) are correct and (R) is not the correct explanation of (A).
(c) (A) is correct but (R) is not correct.
(d) (A) is not correct but (R) is correct.

(ii) Platforms such as Spotify, Facebook, Instagram, Amazon, Netflix etc. shows recommendation on the basis of what you like. Which is the technology behind this?
(a) Human Intelligence
(b) Platform Intelligence
(c) Artificial Intelligence
(d) Application Intelligence

(iii) Statement 1 In "When" block of 4Ws canvas we find the stakeholders.

Statement 2 Stakeholders are the people who face a particular problem and would be benefitted with the solution.
(a) Both Statement 1 and Statement 2 are correct.
(b) Both Statement 1 and Statement 2 are incorrect.
(c) Statement 1 is correct but Statement 2 is incorrect.
(d) Statement 2 is correct but Statement 1 is incorrect.

(iv) Whenever we want an AI project to be able to predict an output, we need to ....
(a) first test it using the data.
(b) first train it using the data.
(c) Both (a) and (b)
(d) Neither (a) nor (b)

(v) What does the term "image processing" refer to in Computer Vision?
(a) Editing videos
(b) Extracting meaningful information from images
(c) Playing audio files
(d) Compiling codes

(vi) A corpus contains 4 documents in which the words such as 'an, is, the' were appearing frequently. Identify the term that is used for such words.
(a) Stop word (b) Rare word
(c) Missing word (d) Removable word

3. Answer any 5 out of the given 6 questions **(5 × 1 = 5)**

(i) Identify the logo of an application of AI given below. It helps us to navigate to places.

(ii) Which of the following data science application is not associated with genetics and genomics?
(a) To understand the impact of DNA on health.
(b) To analyze reactions to drugs and disease.
(c) To find individual biological connection.
(d) To search the house address of a relative on the Internet.

(iii) In Computer Vision, which of the following tasks is used for single object?
(a) Object Detection
(b) Classification + Localisation
(c) Instance Segmentation
(d) Non-Localisation

(iv) It Is A Domain-Specific Language That Is Designed For Managing Data Held In Different Kinds Of Dbms (Database Management System). It Is Particularly Useful In Handling Structured Data. Which Computer Language Is This?
(a) SQL (b) CSV
(c) Spreadsheet (d) TXT

(v) Which application of NLP helps to provide an overview of a news item or blog post? It also avoids redundancy from multiple sources and maximises the diversity of content obtained.
(a) Virtual Assistants
(b) Sentiment Analysis
(c) Text Classification
(d) Automatic Summarization

(vi) Which condition of evaluation does the following diagram indicate?

Prediction: No	Reality: Yes

(a) False Positive (b) False Negative
(c) True Positive (d) True Negative

4. Answer any 5 out of the given 6 questions **(5 × 1 = 5)**

(i) Which of the following is the correct expansion of CSV?
(a) Comma and Space Value
(b) Comma Separated Values
(c) Control Separated Values
(d) Character Separated Values

(ii) Statement 1 Overfitting is not recommended for evaluation of a model.

Statement 2 This is because the model will simply remember the whole training set, and will therefore always predict the correct label for any point in the training set.

(a) Both Statement 1 and Statement 2 are correct.
(b) Both Statement 1 and Statement 2 are incorrect.
(c) Statement 1 is correct but Statement 2 is incorrect.
(d) Statement 2 is correct but Statement 1 is incorrect.

(iii) It is one of the parameters for evaluating a model's performance and is defined as the percentage of true positive cases versus all the cases, where the prediction is true.

Which of the following evaluation parameter is this?

(a) Precision (b) Recall
(c) F1 score (d) Accuracy

(iv) Which form of learning-based approach does the following diagram indicate?

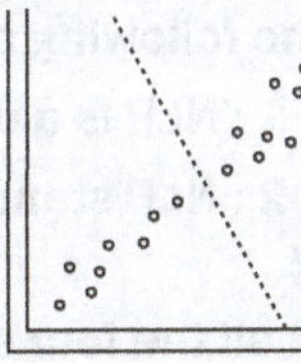

(a) Clustering
(b) Classification
(c) Regression
(d) Dimensionally Reduction

(v) Which of the following applications of NLP (Natural Language Processing) is associated with spam filtering in e-mails?

(a) Virtual Assistants
(b) Sentiment Analysis
(c) Text Classification
(d) Automatic Summarisation

(vi) Raghav can turn on and off any appliance remotely using an internet enabled device. This is an example of ....

(a) Artificial Intelligence (AI)
(b) Internet of Things (IoT)
(c) Computer Vision (CV)
(d) Deep Learning (DL)

5. Answer any 5 out of the given 6 questions (5 × 1 = 5)

(i) Musical intelligence is a concept that

(a) assesses one's ability to regulate, measure and understand numerical symbols, abstraction and logic.
(b) measures the language processing skills both in terms of understanding or implementation in writing or verbally.
(c) evaluates the ability to process information on the environment around us.
(d) describes a person's ability to recognise and create sounds, rhythms and sound patterns.

(ii) With respect to evaluation, for which of the following does the prediction and reality match?

(a) True positive and False positive
(b) True positive and True negative
(c) False positive and False negative
(d) True positive and False negative

(iii) Statement 1 Various search engines and e-commerce portals now have a new feature called image-based search using computer vision.

Statement 2 Image-based search helps in finding items, people and places by giving their sounds to the system.

(a) Both Statement 1 and Statement 2 are correct.
(b) Both Statement 1 and Statement 2 are incorrect.
(c) Statement 1 is correct but Statement 2 is incorrect.
(d) Statement 2 is correct but Statement 1 is incorrect.

(iv) In the context of NLP, which of the following words represents a stem resulting from stemming for "Studies"?

(a) Study (b) Stud
(c) Studi (d) Studied

(v) Which of the following scenarios might have a high False Negative (FN) cost?

(a) Viral Disease Outbreak
(b) Spam
(c) Mining
(d) Image Search

(vi) Which type of chat-bot has a wide functionality, is flexible and powerful, and works on bigger databases directly?

Section B : Subjective Type Questions

Answer any 3 out of the given 5 questions on Employability Skills. Answer each question in 20-30 words. **(3 × 2 = 6)**

6. Explain the importance of following a healthy lifestyle in effectively dealing with stress. Write any one common factor that causes stress among the children nowadays.

7. If you are a team leader of a team of 20 people in an organisation, mention any two methods that you will use for effective communication with your team members. visuals.

8. Write any two tasks that entrepreneurs do when they run their business.

9. Enlist any two measures that an individual should follow to take care of his/her digital devices.

10. Discuss the following problems related to sustainable development:

(i) Water

(ii) Fuel

Answer any 4 out of the given 6 questions in 20-30 words each **(4 × 2 = 8)**

11. Differentiate between Computer Vision (CV) and Natural Language Processing (NLP).

12. Define the following with respect to AI project cycle

(i) Data Exploration

(ii) Data Features

13. One of the applications of Data Science is Airline Route Planning. List any two tasks that airline companies can do using Data Science.

14. Give any two key impacts of Computer Vision on medical imaging.

15. What is the primary difference between Human Language and Computer Language?

16. Suppose you are developing an AI model to detect fraudulent financial transaction risk. Describe False Positives and False Negatives in this context.

Answer any 3 out of the given 5 questions in 50-80 words each **(3 × 4 = 12)**

17. What do you understand by AI Bias and AI Access? Give one example of each to support your answer.

18. What is the use of problem statement template with respect to 4Ws of problem scoping? Draw a problem statement template depicting all key elements.

19. Consider the following diagram. It explains how a system of organized machine learning algorithms perform certain tasks. Identify the concept and explain its working.

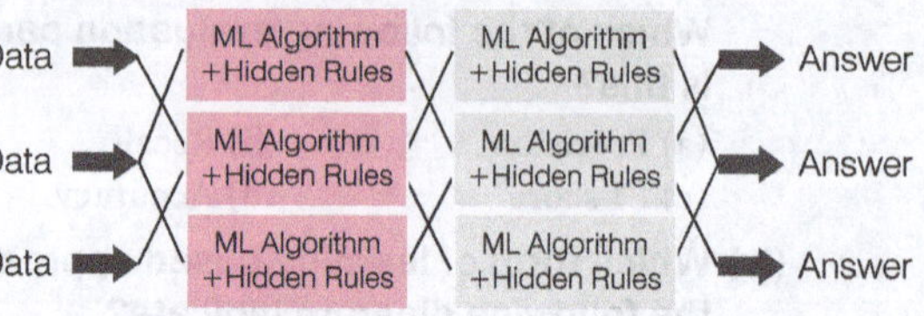

20. Consider the following documents:

Document 1 : NLP is a domain of AI.

Document 2 : NLP stands for Natural Language Processing.

Implement all the four steps of Bag of Words (BoW) model to create a document vector table.

21. An AI model has been developed to test specimens of blood/urine/cough etc. to diagnose ailments (diabetes/liver infection etc.). The model was tested on a data-set of about 630 tests and the resulting confusion matrix is as follows:

Confusion Matrix		Reality	
		Yes	No
Prediction	Yes	110	60
	No	50	140

(A) How many total cases are True Negative in the above scenario?

(B) Calculate Precision, Recall and F1 Score.

Answers

1. (i) (d) (ii) (c) (iii) (a) (iv) (c) (v) (d) (vi) (b)
2. (i) (c) (ii) (c) (iii) (a) (iv) (b) (v) (b) (vi) (a)
3. (i) (maps) (ii) (d) (iii) (b) (iv) (a) (v) (d) (vi) (b)
4. (i) (b) (ii) (a) (iii) (a) (iv) (b) (v) (c) (vi) (b)
5. (i) (d) (ii) (b) (iii) (c) (iv) (c) (v) (a) (vi) (Smart chatbot)
6. **Importance of a Healthy Lifestyle in Dealing with Stress**
   - **Physical Health** Exercise releases endorphins, improving mood and reducing stress hormones.
   - **Mental Clarity** Proper nutrition and sleep enhance cognitive function, making it easier to manage stressors.
   - **Resilience** A healthy lifestyle builds resilience, making you better equipped to handle challenges.

   Common Stress Factor among Children Nowadays
   - **Academic Pressure** High expectations and competition in school create significant stress.
7. **Effective Communication Methods for a Team Leader (20 people)**
   - **Regular Team Meetings** Provide a platform for open discussion, updates, and addressing concerns.
   - **One-on-One Check-ins** Allow for personalised communication, feedback, and addressing individual needs.
8. **Two Tasks Entrepreneurs Do**
   - **Market Research** Understanding customer needs and market trends to inform business decisions.
   - **Financial Management** Handling budgets, investments, and ensuring the business's financial health.
9. **Measures to Take Care of Digital Devices**
   - **Regular Software Updates** Protect against security vulnerabilities and improve performance.
   - **Physical Cleaning** Remove dust and debris to maintain functionality and prevent damage.
10. **Problems Related to Sustainable Development**

    (i) **Water**
    - **Scarcity** Depletion of freshwater resources due to overuse and pollution.
    - **Access** Unequal access to clean water, affecting health and sanitation.

    (ii) **Fuel**
    - **Fossil Fuel Dependence** Leads to greenhouse gas emissions and climate change.
    - Depletion: Finite resources are being consumed at unsustainable rates.
11. **Differentiate between Computer Vision (CV) and Natural Language Processing (NLP)**
    - **Computer Vision (CV)** Focuses on enabling computers to "see" and interpret images or videos, extracting meaningful information.
    - **Natural Language Processing (NLP)** Focuses on enabling computers to understand, interpret, and generate human language (text or speech).
12. (i) **Data Exploration** The initial phase of analysing and understanding the dataset. This involves summarising data, identifying patterns, and visualising relationships to gain insights relevant to the project's goals.

    (ii) **Data Features** The individual measurable properties or characteristics of the data used as input for the AI model.

    They are the variables that the model uses to make predictions or decisions.
13. **Two tasks airlines can do using Data Science in Route Planning**
    - **Predicting Flight Demand** Analyse historical data to forecast passenger numbers for different routes, optimizing flight schedules.
    - **Optimising Fuel Efficiency** Use weather patterns and flight data to determine the most fuel-efficient routes, reducing costs and emissions.
14. **Two key impacts of Computer Vision on medical imaging**
    - **Improved Diagnosis** Automated analysis of scans (X-rays, MRIs) to detect anomalies and assist in early disease detection.
    - **Enhanced Surgical Precision** Real-time image guidance during surgeries for more accurate procedures.

15. Primary difference between Human Language and Computer Language

Ambiguity Human language is inherently ambiguous, relying on context and interpretation. Computer languages are designed for precision and lack ambiguity.

16. False Positives and False Negatives in Fraudulent Financial Transaction Detection

- **False Positive** The AI model flags a legitimate transaction as fraudulent (incorrectly identifying a non-fraudulent transaction as fraudulent).
- **False Negative** The AI model fails to detect a fraudulent transaction (incorrectly identifying a fraudulent transaction as non-fraudulent).

17. AI Bias and AI Access

- **AI Bias** Systematic and repeatable errors in an AI system that create unfair outcomes.
  Example Facial recognition software trained primarily on lighter skin tones may perform poorly on darker skin tones.
- **AI Access** The ability of individuals and groups to use and benefit from AI technologies.
  Example Lack of internet access or digital literacy in rural areas hinders AI adoption.

18. Use of Problem Statement Template with 4Ws

Purpose Provides a structured way to define a problem, ensuring clarity and focus for AI projects.

4Ws (What, Who, Where, Why)

- **What** What is the problem?
- **Who** Who is affected?
- **Where** Where does it occur?
- **Why** Why is it a problem?

Template (Example)

- Problem: [Clearly state the problem]
- Who: [Target audience or affected group]
- Where: [Context or location]
- Why: [Impact and consequences]

19. Concept and Working of the Diagram

Concept Neural Network (specifically a simplified representation of a deep neural network).

Working

1. **Data Input** Data is fed into the network.
2. **Hidden Layers** The data passes through multiple layers of interconnected nodes (machine learning algorithms with hidden rules).
3. **Feature Extraction** Each layer extracts increasingly complex features from the data.
4. **Output** The final layer produces the answer or prediction based on the learned patterns.

20. Documents

- **Document 1** NLP is a domain of AI.
- **Document 2** NLP stands for Natural Language Processing.

Steps

1. **Tokenisation**

- Break each document into individual words (tokens).
- **Doc 1** [NLP, is, a, domain, of, AI]
- **Doc 2** [NLP, stands, for, Natural, Language, Processing]

2. **Vocabulary Creation**

- Create a unique list of all words across all documents.
- **Vocabulary** [NLP, is, a, domain, of, AI, stands, for, Natural, Language, Processing]

3. **Vectorisation**

- Represent each document as a vector, where each element corresponds to the count of a word from the vocabulary in that document.
- **Doc 1 Vector** [1, 1, 1, 1, 1, 1, 0, 0, 0, 0]
- **Doc 2 Vector** [1, 0, 0, 0, 0, 0, 1, 1, 1, 1]

4. **Document Vector Table**

Word	Doc 1	Doc 2
NLP	1	1
is	1	0
a	1	0
domain	1	0
of	1	0
AI	1	0
stands	0	1
for	0	1
Natural	0	1
Language	0	1
Processing	0	1

21. Refer to text on page no. 129 Question no. 7 (Long Answer Type Questions)..

Sample Question Paper 1
Artificial Intelligence

Time : 2 hrs	M.M. : 50

1. Please read the instructions carefully.
2. This Question Paper consists of **21 questions** in two sections: Section A & Section B.
3. Section A has Objective type questions whereas Section B contains Subjective type questions.
4. **Out of the given (5 + 16 =) 21 questions, a candidate has to answer (5 + 10 =) 15 questions in the allotted (maximum) time of 2 hours.**
5. All questions of a particular section must be attempted in the correct order.
6. **SECTION A - OBJECTIVE TYPE QUESTIONS (24 MARKS):**
   i. This section has 05 questions.
   ii. Marks allotted are mentioned against each question/part.
   iii. There is no negative marking.
   iv. Do as per the instructions given.
7. **SECTION B – SUBJECTIVE TYPE QUESTIONS (26 MARKS):**
   i. This section has 16 questions.
   ii. A candidate has to do 10 questions.
   iii. Do as per the instructions given.
   iv. Marks allotted are mentioned against each question/part.

Section A : Objective Type Questions

1. Answer any 4 out of the given 6 questions on Employability Skills **(4 × 1 = 4)**

(i) Physical exercise is used as a stress management technique because

(a) it improves blood circulation
(b) improves self-image
(c) makes us feel better
(d) All of the above

(ii) Self-awareness refers to

(a) our knowledge and understanding of ourselves
(b) systematic efforts to direct thoughts and actions
(c) ability to identify effective methods to move from thought to action.
(d) None of the above

(iii) To find a suitable market an entrepreneur performs the functions of

(a) advertisement and publicity
(b) appointment of selling agents
(c) new organisation structure
(d) Both (a) and (b)

(iv) It provides scheduling to each process to be run on.

(a) Time sharing OS (b) Distributed OS
(c) Real-time OS (d) Single-user OS

(v) Visual communication among the people are dependent on ....

(a) Signs, symbols and pictures
(b) Text messages
(c) Posture
(d) Body language

(vi) Assertion (A): With increasing population and income, the consumption of goods is increasing day by day.
Reason (R): This has led to increase in production and utilisation of natural resources, which are required for producing goods.

(a) Both A and R are true and R is the correct explanation for A.
(b) Both A and R are true and R is not the correct explanation of A.
(c) A is true, but R is false.
(d) A is false, but R is true.

2. Answer any 5 out of the given 6 questions (5 × 1 =5)

(i) Assertion (A): Neural network are the backbone of deep learning algorithms.

Reason (R): Neural networks use vast amounts of data.

(a) Both A and R are true and R is the correct explanation for A.

(b) Both A and R are true and R is not the correct explanation of A.

(c) A is true, but R is false.

(d) A is false, but R is true.

(ii) Recall Evaluation method is

(a) defined as the fraction of positive cases that are correctly identified.

(b) defined as the percentage of true positive cases versus all the cases where the prediction is true.

(c) defined as the percentage of correct predictions out of all the observations.

(d) comparison between the prediction and reality.

(iii) A business problem where in we categorize whether an observation is "Safe," "AtRisk," or "Unsafe" is an example of

(a) Classification (b) Clustering

(c) Regression (d) Dimensionality Reduction

(iv) Statement 1: The output given by the AI model is known as reality.

Statement 2: The real scenario is known as prediction.

(a) Both Statement 1 and Statement 2 are correct

(b) Both Statement 1 and Statement 2 are incorrect

(c) Statement 1 is correct but Statement 2 is incorrect

(d) Statement 2 is correct but Statement 1 is incorrect

(v) Which is the most common pixel format where this number is stored as an 8-bit integer giving a range of possible values from 0 to 255?

(a) Byte image (b) Resolution

(c) Pixel (d) Grayscale

(vi) ________ is the process of finding instances of real-world objects in images or videos.

(a) Instance segmentation (b) Object detection

(c) Classification (d) Image segmentation

3. Answer any 5 out of the given 6 questions (5 × 1 = 5)

(i) Which two evaluation methods are used to calculate the F1 score?

(a) Precision & Accuracy (b) Precision & Recall

(c) Accuracy & Recall (d) Precision & F1

(ii) Which of the following is true about neural networks?

(a) Neural Networks tend to perform better with larger amounts of data.

(b) Neural Networks tend to perform poorer with larger amoun's of data.

(c) Neural Networks tend to perform better with smaller amounts of data.

(d) Neural Networks need no data

(iii) In computer vision which of the following tasks is used for multiple objects?

(a) Classification

(b) Classification + Localisation

(c) Instance Segmentation

(d) Localisation

(iv) Which of the following is an application of data science?

(a) Text summarization

(b) Target Advertisements

(c) Face lock in smartphones

(d) Email filters

(v) Which of the following is valid data type in Python?

(a) character (b) loop

(c) string (d) new character

(vi) In spam email detection, which of the following will be considered as "False Negative"?

(a) When legitimate email is accurately identified as not spam.

(b) when a spam mail is mistakenly identified as legitimate

(c) When an email is accurately recognised as spam

(d) When an email is inaccurately lebelled as important

4. Answer any 5 out of the given 6 questions (5 × 1 = 5)

(i) ________ helps us to summarise all the key points into one single outline so that in future, whenever there is need to look back at the basis of the problem, we can take a look at it and understand the key elements of it.

(a) 4W Problem canvas

(b) Problem Statement Template

(c) Data Acquisition

(d) Algorithm

(ii) **Which of the following is defined as the measure of balance between precision and recall?**

(a) Accuracy (b) F1 Score
(c) Reliability (d) Punctuality

(iii) **Assertion (A) The bag of words model is a simple way to convert words to numerical representation in natural language processing.**

Reason (R) This model is a simple document embedding technique based on word frequency.

(a) Both A and R are correct and R is the correct explanation of A
(b) Both A and R are correct but R is not the correct explanation of A
(c) A is correct but R is not correct
(d) A is not correct but R is correct

(iv) **Which form of learning based approach does the following diagram indicate?**

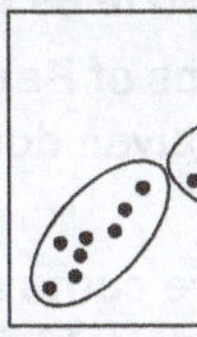

(a) Clustering (b) Classification
(c) Regression (d) Dimensionaly Reduction

(v) **Name the two methods of collection data.**

(a) Surveys and Interviews
(b) Rumors and Myhts
(c) AI models and application
(c) Imagination and thoughts

(vi) **Which of the following is the correct feature of Neural network?**

(a) It can improve the efficiency of two models
(b) It is useful with small dataset.
(c) They are modelled on human brains and nervous system
(d) They need human intervention.

5. Answer any 5 out of the given 6 questions (5 × 1 = 5)

(i) **What is the purpose of defining the problem statement during the Problem Scoping stage in an AI project cycle?**

(a) To collect data
(b) To understand the aim and objective of the project
(c) To train the model
(d) To process data

(ii) **Statement 1 A Convolutional Neural Network (CNN) is a type of deep learning algorithm that is particularly well-suited for image recognition and processing tasks.**

Statement 2 Fully connected layer is the second layer of CNN.

(a) Both Statement 1 and Statement 2 are correct
(b) Both Statement 1 and Statement 2 are incorrect
(c) Statement 1 is correct but Statement 2 is incorrect
(d) Statement 2 is correct but Statement 1 is incorrect

(iii) **Reinforcement learning is particularly useful forscenarios where:**

(a) Large amounts of labeled data are available.
(b) The desired outcome is clear, but the path to achieve it is unknown.
(c) The data is structured and easily categorized.
(d) The task requires reasoning and logical deduction.

(iv) **Which of the following scenario result in a high false positive cost?**

(a) Viral outbreak (b) Forest fire
(c) Flood (d) Spam filter

(v) **Priya was confused with the terms used in the evaluation stage suggest her the term used for the percentage of correct predictions out of all the observations**

(a) Accuracy (b) Precision
(c) Recall (d) F1 score

(vi) **What is the stem of the word "Making"?**

(a) Mak (b) Make (c) Making (d) Maker

Section B : Subjective Type Questions

Answer any 3 out of the given 5 questions on Employability Skills. Answer each question in 20-30 words. (3 × 2 = 6)

6. Why is self-regulation important in life?

7. Explain the short-term solutions related to sustainable development.

8. Which measures must be adopted to overcome the factors causing communication barriers?

9. Describe the advantages of entrepreneurship.

10. What is an operating system?

Answer any 4 out of the given 6 questions in 20-30 words each **(4 × 2 = 8)**

11. Suhana works for a company wherein she was assigned the task of developing a project using AI project cycle.

She knew that the first stage was scoping the problem. Help her list the remaining stages that she must go through to develop the project.

12. What do you mean by Bioethics?

13. What is clustering and how is it different from classification?

14. How Google translate uses computer vision?

15. What will be the results of conversion of the term, 'happily' in the process of stemming and lemmatisation? Which process takes longer time for execution?

16. Give an example of a situation where in false positive would have a high cost associated with it.

Answer any 3 out of the given 5 questions in 50-80 words each **(3 × 4 = 12)**

17. Automated trade industry has developed an AI model which predicts the selling and purchasing of automobiles during testing the AI model game with the following predictions.

To Confusion Matrix		Reality	
		Yes	No
Predicated	Yes	60	25
	No	05	10

(a) How many total tests have been performed in the above scenario?

(b) Calculate precision, recall and F1 score.

18. What is the significance of AI project cycle? Also explain in detail about how Data Acquisition is different from data exploration.

19. Identify and explain the types of the learning-based approaches in the figures given below.

20. Consider the text of the following documents:

Document 1 Sahil likes to play cricket

Document 2 Sajal likes cricket too

Document 3 Sajal also likes to play basketball

Apply all the four steps of Bag of words model of NLP on the above given documents and generate the output.

21. Imagine that you have come up with an AI based prediction model which has been deployed on the roads to check traffic jams. Now, the objective of the model is to predict whether there will be a traffic jam or not. Now, to understand the efficiency of this model, we need to check if the predictions which it makes are correct or not. Thus, there exist two conditions which we need to ponder upon: Prediction and Reality.

Traffic Jams have become a common part of our lives nowadays. Living in an urban area means you have to face traffic each and every time you get out on the road. Mostly, school students opt for buses to go to school. Many times, the bus gets late due to such jams and the students are not able to reach their school on time.

Considering all the possible situations make a Confusion Matrix for the above situation.

Sample Question Paper 2

Artificial Intelligence

Time : 2 hrs	M.M. : 50

1. Please read the instructions carefully.
2. This Question Paper consists of **21 questions** in two sections: Section A & Section B.
3. Section A has Objective type questions whereas Section B contains Subjective type questions.
4. **Out of the given (5 + 16 =) 21 questions, a candidate has to answer (5 + 10 =) 15 questions in the allotted (maximum) time of 2 hours.**
5. All questions of a particular section must be attempted in the correct order.
6. **SECTION A - OBJECTIVE TYPE QUESTIONS (24 MARKS):**
   i. This section has 05 questions.
   ii. Marks allotted are mentioned against each question/part.
   iii. There is no negative marking.
   iv. Do as per the instructions given.
7. **SECTION B – SUBJECTIVE TYPE QUESTIONS (26 MARKS):**
   i. This section has 16 questions.
   ii. A candidate has to do 10 questions.
   iii. Do as per the instructions given.
   iv. Marks allotted are mentioned against each question/part.

Section A : Objective Type Questions

1. Answer any 4 out of the given 6 questions on Employability Skills **(4 × 1 = 4)**

(i) Which one of the following is a symptom of stress?

(a) Increased sweating (b) Dry mouth
(c) Cold hands or feet (d) All of these

(ii) It uses pictures (called icons) and menus displayed on the screen to send commands to the computer system.

(a) Command-based user interface
(b) GUI
(c) System Utility
(d) API

(iii) Which of the following is the process in which the receiver interprets and understands the message?

(a) Decoding (b) Encoding
(c) Feedback (d) None of these

(iv) How can entrepreneur can get the work done from his/her team?

(a) By creating a spirit of teamwork
(b) By motivation
(c) Using harsh words and actions
(d) Both (a) and (b)

(v) We have the ability to work independently, if we ....

(a) need regular feedback to make progress in our work
(b) work best at our own pace
(c) need a structured environment to work efficiently
(d) need to be prodded to work faster

(vi) Assertion (A): Organic farming technique is an example of a green skill that is essential for sustainable agriculture.
Reason (R) Organic farming technique prioritise environment friendly and sustainable practices such as using natural fertilisers, avoiding synthetic pesticides and promoting soil health.

(a) Both (A) and (R) are true and (R) is the correct explanation for (A).
(b) Both (A) and (R) are true and (R) is not the correct explanation of (A).
(c) (A) is true, but (R) is false.
(d) (A) is false, but (R) is true.

2. Answer any 5 out of the given 6 questions **(5 × 1 =5)**

(i) In what ways can AI models be categorized based on the type of data fed into them?

(a) Two domains (b) Four domains

(c) Three domains (d) Five domains

(ii) Assertion: The sum of the values in a confusion matrix's row represents the total number of instances for a given actual class.

Reason: This enables the calculation of class-specific metrics such as precision and recall, which are essential for evaluating a model's performance across different classes.

(a) Both A and R are true and R is the correct explanation for A

(b) Both A and R are true and R is not the correct explanation for A

(c) A is True but R is False

(d) A is false but R is True

(iii) A neural network with multiple layers of interconnected neurons is called a:

(a) Single-layer network (b) Deep Neural Network

(c) Linear network (d) Perceptron

(iv) Prediction and Reality can be easily mapped together with the help of

(a) Prediction (b) Reality

(c) Accuracy (d) confusion matrix

(v) Which technology is Teachable Machine built on?

(a) PyTorch (b) TensorFlow.js

(c) OpenCV (d) Keras

(vi) What is the primary purpose of a Convolutional Neural Network (CNN)?

(a) Object detection (b) Image classification

(c) Text generation (d) Reinforcement learning

3. Answer any 5 out of the given 6 questions **(5 × 1 = 5)**

(i) What computer application is depicted in the given image?

(ii) The process of adjusting the weights in a neural network to improve performance is called:

(a) Activation (b) Learning

(c) Optimization (d) Training

(iii) How is the relationship between model performance and accuracy described?

(a) Inversely proportional

(b) Not related

(c) Directly proportional

(d) Randomly fluctuating

(iv) What type of tool is Orange?

(a) Open-source (b) Closed-source

(c) Paid software (d) Hardware

(v) Artificial neural networks are inspired by the structure and function of:

(a) The human brain

(b) Quantum computers

(c) Complex mathematical models

(d) High-speed processors

(vi) A high F1 score generally suggests:

(a) A significant imbalance between precision and recall

(b) A good balance between precision and recall

(c) A model that only performs well on specific data points

(d) The need for more training data

4. Answer any 5 out of the given 6 questions **(5 × 1 = 5)**

(i) Statement 1: To evaluate a model's performance, we need either precision or recall.

Statement 2: When the value of both Precision and Recall is 1, the F1 score is 0.

(ii) Which of the learning algorithm can bunch the unknown data according to patterns or trends identified out of it ?

(a) Clustering

(b) Dimensionality reduction

(c) Classification

(d) Regression

(iii) Jayashree has completed the first stage of the AI project cycle. Now she is going to begin with the second stage of the AI Project cycle. Select the 2nd stage out of the following:

(a) Problem Scoping (b) Data Acquisition

(c) Data Exploration (d) Modelling

(iv) **Which of the following is not a task of Computer Vision?**
(a) Guest Recognition (b) Air Line route plan
(c) Attendance System (d) Snap Chat Filters

(v) **Which algorithms result in two things, a vocabulary of words and frequency of the words in the corpus?**
(a) Sentence segmentation
(b) Tokenisation
(c) Bag of words
(d) Text normalisation

(vi) **As humans can see things, analyse them, and then take required action based on what they see. Which of the following helps machines to perform similar kinds of tasks?**
(a) Data Science
(b) Natual Language Processing
(c) Computer Vision
(d) Camera Vision

5. Answer any 5 out of the given 6 questions (5 × 1 = 5)

(i) **Which of the following is a subset of Artificial Intelligence?**
(a) Machine Learning
(b) Reinforcement Learning
(c) Artificial Learning
(d) Self Learning

(ii) **In agriculture, problem scoping can be done on**
(a) pest issues (b) yield rates
(c) sowing (d) All of these

(iii) **Statement 1: Developing algorithms to get the intelligence outputs are called machine learning**
Statement 2: Writing codes to make machine intelligence artificially is called deep learning.
(a) Statement 1 is True
(b) Statement 2 is True
(c) Statement 1 and 2 both are True
(d) Statement 1 and 2 both are incorrect

(iv) **_______ is such an application which analyses images through a camera and generates a very accurate estimate of the items available in the store.**
(a) Inventory management
(b) Customer management
(c) ERP Software
(d) Account Management

(v) **_______ is defined as the percentage of correct predictions out of all the observations.**
(a) Predicitons (b) Accuracy
(c) Reality (d) F1 Score

(vi) **Which feature of NLP helps in understanding the emotions of the people mentioned with thefeedback?**
(a) Virtual assistants
(b) Sentiment analysis
(c) Text classification
(d) Automatic summarization

Section B : Subjective Type Questions

Answer any 3 out of the given 5 questions on Employability Skills. Answer each question in 20-30 words. (3 × 2 = 6)

6. **What are the techniques that are used to manage stress?**

7. **"Entrepreneurs are born, not made." Do you agree with this statement? Justify your answer.**

8. **In a communication cycle, explain the term 'medium'. What problems may the medium create and how?**

9. **What general precautions should you take while cleaning the computer/components?**

10. **Why there is a need for sustainable development? Give reasons.**

Answer any 4 out of the given 6 questions in 20-30 words each (3 × 2 = 6)

11. **Why do we need ethical frameworks for AI?**

12. **Mention the factors which knowingly or unknowingly influence our decision-making.**

13. **What is the difference between labeled and unlabeled data in Machine Learning?**

Or **What is the purpose of a training dataset in AI modeling?**

14. **Differentiate between Max pooling and Average pooling.**

15. **Write down the steps to implement bag of wordsalgorithm.**

16. **Define True Positive (TP) and False Positive (FP) with examples.**

Answer any 3 out of the given 5 questions in 50-80 words each **(3 × 4 = 12)**

17. **What is a confusion matrix, and why is it useful in machine learning?**

18. **What are the two main types of ethical frameworks for AI, and how do they differ?**

19. **How does a classification model differ from a regression model? Provide examples.**

20. **Samiksha, a student of class X was exploring the Natural Language Processing domain. She got stuck while performing the text normalisation. Help her to normalise the text on the segmented sentences given below:**

Document 1: Akash and Ajay are best friends.

Document 2: Akash likesto play football but Ajay prefers to play online games.

21. **An AI model made the following sales prediction for a new mobile phone which they have recently launched:**

Confusion Matrix		Reality	
		Yes	No
Prediction	Yes	50	40
	No	12	10

(i) Identify the total number of wrong predictions made by the model.

(ii) Calculate precision, recall and F1 Score.

Sample Question Paper 3
Artificial Intelligence

Time : 2 hrs	M.M. : 50

1. Please read the instructions carefully.
2. This Question Paper consists of **21 questions** in two sections: Section A & Section B.
3. Section A has Objective type questions whereas Section B contains Subjective type questions.
4. **Out of the given (5 + 16 =) 21 questions, a candidate has to answer (5 + 10 =) 15 questions in the allotted (maximum) time of 2 hours.**
5. All questions of a particular section must be attempted in the correct order.
6. **SECTION A - OBJECTIVE TYPE QUESTIONS (24 MARKS):**
   i. This section has 05 questions.
   ii. Marks allotted are mentioned against each question/part.
   iii. There is no negative marking.
   iv. Do as per the instructions given.
7. **SECTION B – SUBJECTIVE TYPE QUESTIONS (26 MARKS):**
   i. This section has 16 questions.
   ii. A candidate has to do 10 questions.
   iii. Do as per the instructions given.
   iv. Marks allotted are mentioned against each question/part.

Section A : Objective Type Questions

1. Answer any 4 out of the given 6 questions on Employability Skills **(4 × 1 = 4)**

(i) Stress management is vital because it leads to following benefits:
(a) Improves mood (b) Promotes longevity
(c) Boosts immune system (d) All of these

(ii) Which of the following is an inner urge to do something, achieve their goals without any external pressure I lure for award or appreciation?
(a) Self-awareness (b) Self-motivation
(c) Self-regulation (d) Self-control

(iii) Which of the following is a function of an entrepreneur?
(a) Following the traditional method of business
(b) Innovation
(c) Keeping all the profit to himself/herself
(d) Avoid taking decisions

(iv) A _____ is a software program that attaches itself to other programs and alters their behavior.
(a) Operating system (b) Firewall
(c) Antivirus (d) Computer Virus

(v) Identify the object, verb and subject in the sentence,
'The car crashed into a tree.'
(a) Object: a tree; Verb: crashed; Subject: the car
(b) Object: The car; Verb: crashed; Subject: a tree
(c) Object: crashed; Verb: the tree; Subject: the car
(d) Object: crashed; Verb: the car; Subject: the tree

(vi) Assertion (A) Organic farming technique is an example of a green skill that is essential for sustainable agriculture.
Reason (R) Organic farming technique prioritise environment friendly and sustainable practices such as using natural fertilisers, avoiding synthetic pesticides and promoting soil health.
(a) Both A and R are true and R is the correct explanation for A.
(b) Both A and R are true and R is not the correct explanation of A.
(c) A is true, but R is false.
(d) A is false, but R is true.

2. Answer any 5 out of the given 6 questions (5 × 1 = 5)

(i) Assertion: Ethics provide guidance in distinguishing right from wrong.

Reason: Ethics consist of a set of values and morals that aid individuals in making moral judgments and decisions.

(a) Both Assertion and Reasoning are true, and Reasoning is the correct explanation of the Assertion.
(b) Assertion is true, but Reasoning is false.
(c) Both Assertion and Reasoning are true, but Reasoning is not the correct explanation of the Assertion.
(d) Assertion is false, but Reasoning is true.

(ii) Statement 1 Unsupervised learning uses labeled datasets to train algorithms to predict outcomes and recognize patterns.

Statement 2 In unsupervised learning, the training data provided to the machines work as the supervisor.

(a) Both Statement 1 and Statement 2 are correct
(b) Both Statement 1 and Statement 2 are incorrect
(c) Statement 1 is correct but Statement 2 is incorrect
(d) Statement 2 is correct but Statement 1 is incorrect

(iii) Raunak was learning the conditions that make up the confusion matrix. He came across a scenario in which the machine that was supposed to predict an animal was always predicting not an animal. What is this condition called?

(a) False Positive (b) True Positive
(c) False Negative (d) True Negative

(iv) Classification and localization are used for

(a) Single Objects (b) Only two objects
(c) Three objects (d) Multiple objects

(v) Which of the following tasks identifies the object present in the image and where it is present in the image?

(a) Classification
(b) Classification and Localization
(c) Object Detection
(d) Instance Segmentation

(vi) What information does the document vector table provide?

(a) The frequency of each word across all documents
(b) The frequency of each word in a single document
(c) The total number of words in the entire corpus
(d) The average word length in the entire corpus

3. Answer any 5 out of the given 6 questions (5 × 1 = 5)

(i) Differentiate between Prediction and Reality.

(a) Prediction is the input given to the machine to receive the expected result of the reality.
(b) Prediction is the output given to match the reality.
(c) The prediction is the output which is given by the machine and the reality is the real scenario in which the prediction has been made.
(d) Prediction and reality both can be used interchangeably.

(ii) The ________ layer of nueral network is known as input later.

(a) first (b) second
(c) third (d) fourth

(iii) The number of pixels in an image is called ________ of image.

(a) Dimension (b) Width
(c) Resolution (d) Height

(iv) Manisha is preparing a model where a customer is given a discount according to the category. The categories are Gold, Silver and Platinum. Which type of model she can use?

(a) learning-based (b) algorithm-based
(c) customized (d) rule-based

(v) Which of the following is/are neural network features?

(a) modelled on the human brain and nervous system
(b) automatically extract features of data without any input
(c) every node is essentially a machine algorithm
(d) All of these

(vi) This real life application of NLP is used to provide an overview of a news item or blog post, which avoiding redundancy from multiple sources and maximising the diversity of content obtained. Which is this application?

(a) Chatbot
(b) Virtual Assistant
(c) Sentiment Analysis
(d) Automatic Summarisation

4. **Answer any 5 out of the given 6 questions** **(5 × 1 = 5)**

(i) Divya is doing problem scoping. She is not familiar with the term used for the people who face the problem and would be benefitted from the solution. Who are they

(a) customers (b) shareholders
(c) houners (d) stakeholders

(ii) The ________ is anamoly in the output of machine learning algorithms which could be due to prejudiced assumptions made during developing algorithm and training data.

(a) AI Access (b) AI Bais
(c) AI Security (d) Data Privacy

(iii) Statement 1: Classification deals with discrete data

Statement 2: Regression deals with continuous data

(a) Statement 1 is correct
(b) Statement 2 is correct
(c) Statement 1 and B both are correct
(d) Statement 2 and B both are incorrect

(iv) Dhilan has downloaded an image with a resolution of 2000 x 1280. However, he is confused about which pixels are considered from one side to another and which ones are from top to bottom. Assist him by selecting an appropriate option out of the following:

(a) 2000, 1280
(b) 1280, 2000
(c) Resolution is not considered as 2000 x 1280 only not one side another or top to bottom
(d) None of these

(v) Which of the following is not an example price comparison website?

(a) PriceGrabber (b) DealTime
(c) ShopZilla (d) Kaggle

(vi) Which of the following is an advantage of the online surveys?

(a) Data can be affected by surveyed research bais
(b) Data can be affected by the validity of the survey responses
(c) Data can be visualized and analyzed easily
(d) Cannot collect a large volume of data

5. **Answer any 5 out of the given 6 questions** **(5 × 1 = 5)**

(i) The aim is to achieve 17 SDGs by the end of

(a) 2025 (b) 2030 (c) 2035 (d) 2040

(ii) In grayscale images, the total presence of color is

(a) The lightest possible shade is white
(b) The darkest possible shade is black
(c) The darkest possible shade is gray
(d) The lightest possible shade is yellow

(iii) The relevant and authentic data only collected through

(a) Any websites (b) Google
(c) Government Websites (d) None of these

(iv) Statement 1: Ethics are concerned with what is good for individuals and societies

Statement 2: Ethics are concerned with what is good for machines and data

(a) Statement 1 is correct
(b) Statement 2 is correct
(c) Both statements are correct
(d) Both statements are incorrect

(v) What will be the outcome, if the Prediction is "Yes" and it matches with the Reality? What will be the outcome, if the Prediction is "Yes" and it does not match with the Reality?

(a) True Positive, True Negative
(b) True Negative, False Negative
(c) True Negative, False Positive
(d) True Positive, False Positive

(vi) Identify the given Chat bot type: It learns from its environment and experience. It also builds on its capabilities based on the knowledge. These can collaborate with humans, working along-side them and learning from their behavior.

Section B : Subjective Type Questions

Answer any 3 out of the given 5 questions on Employability Skills. Answer each question in 20-30 words. **(3 × 2 = 6)**

6. **Why there is a need for sustainable development? Give reasons.**

7. **"Entrepreneurs are born, not made." Do you agree with this statement? Justify your answer.**

8. **Describe the three types of barriers to communication in one sentence each with examples.**

9. **Sameera is always punctual at school. She has a regular schedule that she follows every day. She plans for study and play time in advance.**

Enlist the four steps, Sameera must have followed for effective time management.

10. What general precautions should you take while cleaning the computer/components?

Answer any 4 out of the given 6 questions in 20-30 words each (4 × 2 = 8)

11. For a healthcare organisation's objective of predicting disease outbreaks and efficiently allocating resources through the analysis of medical records, would you recommend using supervised learning or unsupervised learning as the preferred machine learning approach? Explain your choice briefly.

12. Outline the main steps in the AI Project Cycle briefly.

13. What is supervised, unsupervised and reinforcement learning? Explain with examples.

14. Draw the confusion matrix for the following data

- The number of true positive = 100
- The number of true negative 47
- The number of false positive = 62
- The number of false negative = 290

15. Explain the following picture which depicts one of the processes on NLP. Also mention the purpose which will be achieved by this process.

HELLO	HeLlo	HELLLo	hELLO	hElLO	HellO

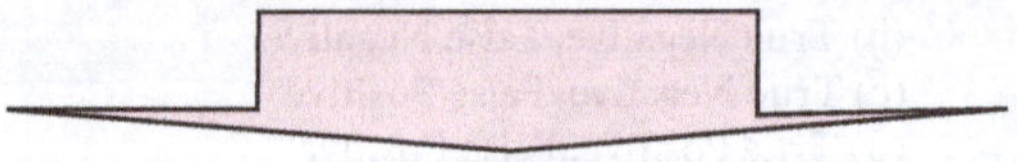

hello

16. Identify which metric (Precision or Recall) is to be used in the following cases and why?

(a) Email Spam Detection
(b) Cancer Diagnosis
(c) Legal Cases(Innocent until proven guilty)
(d) Fraud Detection
(e) Safe Content Filtering (like Kids YouTube)

Answer any 3 out of the given 5 questions in 50-80 words each (3 × 4 = 12)

17. Traffic Jams have become a common part of our lives nowadays. Living in an urban area means you have to face traffic each and every time you get out on the road. Mostly, school students opt for buses to go to school. Many times, the bus gets late due to such jams and the students are not able to reach their school on time. Thus, AI model is created to predict explicitly if there would be traffic jam on their way to school or not. The Confusion Matrix for the same is:

The Confusion Matrix	Actual 1	Actual 0
Predicted 1	50	50
Predicted 0	0	0

Explain the process of evaluating F1 score for the given problem.

18. Give difference between rule based and learning based AI models.

19. What roles does computer vision play in agricultural monitoring systems?

20. Through a step-by-step process, calculate TFIDF for the given corpus
Document 1: Johny Johny Yes Papa,
Document 2: Eating sugar? No Papa
Document 3: Telling lies? No Papa
Document 4: Open your mouth, Ha! Ha! Ha!

21. Calculate Accuracy, Precision, Recall and F1 Score for the following Confusion Matrix on Heart Attack Risk. Also suggest which metric would not be a good evaluation parameter here and why?

The Confusion matrix	Reality : 1	Reality : 0
Prediction : 1	50	20
Prediction : 0	10	20

The Confusion Matrix	Reality : 1	Reality : 0	
Prediction : 1	50	20	70
Prediction : 0	10	20	30
	60	40	100